W9-ADA-442

For Dan Coquillette,

With respect,
gratitude, and
friendship

Deportation Nation

Deportation Nation

Outsiders in American History

Daniel Kanstroom

HARVARD UNIVERSITY PRESS

Cambridge, Massachusetts

London, England

2007

Copyright © 2007 by the President and Fellows of Harvard College
All rights reserved
Printed in the United States of America

ISBN-13: 978-0-674-02472-4
ISBN-10: 0-674-02472-9

The Cataloging-in-Publication Data is available from the Library of Congress.

"Deportee (Plane Wreck at Los Gatos)," words and music by Woody Guthrie
and Martin Hoffman © 1961 (Renewed 1989) Tri-Ludlow Music, Inc./BMI

For my father,
who taught me about justice and how to reason.

For my grandmothers and my mothers,
who taught me to look beyond reason.

And for my daughters, Emily and Hannah,
who taught me the deepest reasons.

Contents

Preface

The history of the United States is often told as a parable about the virtues of open immigration for the individual and for the nation. Few, if any, national myths have ever resonated so strongly and for so long. From Thomas Paine's ringing call in 1776 to "prepare in time an asylum for mankind" to Thomas Jefferson's plaintive question in 1801, "Shall oppressed humanity find no asylum on this globe?," the ideal has endured and thrived. As Ronald Reagan once put it, with echoes of Emma Lazarus's poetics, "Can we doubt that only a Divine Providence placed this land, this island of freedom, here as a refuge for all those people who yearn to breathe free?"[1]

This open immigration ideal has powerful inherent attractions—linked as it is to truths that many consider "self-evident." The classical liberal conception of individual autonomy is nowhere embodied more profoundly than in a nation-state said to have been founded upon principles to which any willing applicant could adhere. Important values of diversity, pluralism, and protection of refugees are also well sustained by the "nation of immigrants" myth and relatively open admission policies.

But we are now immersed in a time to which we may one day look back—as we do to the McCarthy era, the World War II Japanese internments, the Palmer Raids, the late nineteenth-century exclusion and deportation of Chinese laborers, and the Alien and Sedition Acts—and see that the core of our national mythology is being tested. We are in the midst of a large-scale, decade-long deportation experiment. The fact that this episode has received rather little public attention renders it no less significant. Deportation is the ever-present companion to the nation of immigrants. It was always there. Indeed, Paine's plea for asylum was preceded by his assertion that freedom had been "expelled" from Asia and Africa and that "England hath given her warning to depart." Doctrinally grounded in nineteenth-century conceptions of sovereignty, contemporary deportation is a living legacy of historical episodes marked by ideas about race, imperialism, and government power that we have largely rejected in other realms. Implicating much more than border control, deportation is also a fulcrum on which majoritarian power is brought to bear against a discrete, marginalized segment of our society. This book does not describe the development of a melting pot, a mosaic, or, as a more engaging metaphor puts it, a stir-fry. Rather, it is a history of the assertion, development, and refinement of centralized, well-focused, and often quite harsh government power subject to minimal judicial oversight.

I once received a plea for help from a tearful U.S. citizen who was the mother of a young man from Panama. She told me that her son had lived in Boston with his entire family since the age of four. He thought he was a U.S. citizen, like all of his relatives here. But he was mistaken. She said he was beginning his second tortuous week in solitary confinement: twenty-three hours per day in a New Hampshire jail—with no right even to a bail hearing—as he awaited deportation because of a past simple assault incident. On the advice of his lawyer, he had pled guilty and received a mild suspended sentence—in effect, probation. Although it was not a basis for deportation at the time of the plea, assault was retroactively deemed a so-called aggravated felony. The young man now faced deportation and a lifetime ban from this country for what any criminal lawyer or judge would undoubtedly see as a minor offense. "How can this be true in America?" his mother had asked me. This book is my attempt to structure an answer to that simple question.

I am most grateful to Deans Avi Soifer and John Garvey and to my colleagues at Boston College Law School for their support. Special thanks to Alex Aleinikoff, Lenni Benson, David Cole, Larry Cunningham, Nora Demleitner, Kent Greenfield, Steve Legomsky, David Martin, Theresa Miller, Nancy Morawetz, Hiroshi Motomura, Michael Olivas, Gerald Neuman, Sophie Robin-Olivier, Joe Singer, Margaret Taylor, Patricia Zell, and participants at conferences and workshops at Boston College, Boston University, Harvard Law School, Kent Law School, Canterbury,

U.K., Vermont Law School, University of Buffalo, University of Cincinnati Law School, the University of Paris X, Nanterre, and Université Cote d'Opal, Boulogne sur Mer, for most helpful conversation, critique, and advice. Two reviewers for the Harvard University Press offered sharp questions and very useful suggestions.

I have benefited from the assistance of talented editors at Harvard University Press and outstanding research assistants: Eric Averion, Debra Bouffard, James Coburn, Kristen Corman, Diana Cruz, Julie Dahlstrom, Tina Elfenbein, Maria Guerrero, Renee Latour, Karen Mankiewicz, Moira Smith, Sydney Urbach, and Christina Zemina.

Finally, I thank my clients for sharing their lives and their truths with me.

Some of the ideas presented in this book have appeared previously in an earlier form. The Introduction and Chapter 3 borrow from "Deportation, Social Control, and Punishment: Some Thoughts about Why Hard Laws Make Bad Cases," 113 *Harv. L. Rev.* 1890 (2000). Chapter 1 reprises material from "From the Reign of Terror to Reining in the Terrorists: The Still-Undefined Rights of Non-Citizens in the 'Nation of Immigrants,'" 9 *New Eng. Int'l & Comp. L. Ann.* 47 (2003). Chapter 4 derives from "The Long, Complex, and Futile Deportation Saga of Carlos Marcello," in David A. Martin and Peter H. Schuck, eds., *Immigration Stories* (2004). Chapter 5 includes ideas from "St. Cyr or Insincere: The Strange Quality of Supreme Court Victory," 16 *Geo. Imm. L. J.* 413 (2002), and "Surrounding the Hole in the Doughnut: Discretion and Deference in U.S. Immigration Law," 71 *Tul. L. Rev.* 703 (1997).

Good-bye to my Juan, good-bye Rosalita,
Adiós mis amigos, Jesus y Maria,
You won't have a name when you ride the big airplane,
All they will call you will be deportee.

—"Deportee (Plane Wreck at Los Gatos),"
words and music by Woody Guthrie
and Martin Hoffman © 1961

Introduction

We can no longer afford to take that which was good in the past and simply call it our heritage, to discard the bad and simply think of it as a dead load which by itself time will bury in oblivion.

—Hannah Arendt, *The Origins of Totalitarianism* (1966), xxxi

In May 1920, a remarkable pamphlet was circulated by a group called the National Popular Government League. Signed by well-known lawyers and legal academics, including Dean Roscoe Pound and Professors Zechariah Chafee, Jr., Felix Frankfurter, and Ernst Freund, the work was provocatively titled "Report on the Illegal Practices of the United States Department of Justice." A boldface banner caption on its first page addressed it "To the American People."

The pamphlet dealt with the so-called Palmer Raids, led by then-Attorney General Mitchell Palmer against foreign "radicals." Thousands had been arrested for deportation proceedings. The document recounted, in meticulous detail, what it termed a "continued violation" of the Constitution and the laws of the United States by the Department of Justice. It described "wholesale arrests" made without warrants, men and women jailed and held incommunicado without access to friends or counsel, entry into homes without search warrants, illegal seizure and destruction of property, and the abuse and maltreatment of suspects.

The report had a profound impact. It rallied popular support against Palmer, inspiring many to denounce that now-infamous episode. It has also been cited frequently since, a staple component of works chronicling the period. Upon rereading it, however, I was struck by its constitutional and legal indictments of the deportation procedures of that era.

1

The authors challenged the lack of bail, arrests without warrants, unreasonable searches and seizures, selective prosecution, the mistreatment of detainees, and the practice of forcing persons to be witnesses against themselves. Although the legal scholars did not offer a full doctrinal analysis of how these constitutional protections applied in the deportation context, it is clear that they believed that they did apply.

One wonders how those who experienced the Palmer Raids would react if they could have foreseen that, nearly a century later, over 325,000 people would face removal proceedings in a single year, many under mandatory detention, unprotected from unreasonable searches and selective prosecution, only a third represented by counsel, and none with the right to appointed counsel.[1] What would they make of the fact that many types of deportation decisions made by government agents are now precluded from any review by the federal judiciary? Surely they would think that this is a situation in need of some serious thought.

The Deportation System

This book examines the nature and the history of a particular exertion of U.S. government power over noncitizens: its power to detain and to deport. Buried within the proud history of our nation of immigrants, shrouded but always present, there exists a distinct system. From its early, decentralized, and inefficient beginnings, this system has grown steadily.

The United States clearly remains a nation of immigrants, with more than 32.5 million foreign-born people, some 20 million of whom are noncitizens.[2] Over 1 million persons became legal permanent residents in 2005, a rather average year by recent historical standards.[3] Millions more temporary nonimmigrants legally enter the United States each year.[4] But these numbers also mean that the deportation system, which controls all noncitizens within U.S. territory, potentially affects tens of millions of legally resident people. Also, uncounted millions have entered the United States without inspection, mostly across the southern border. For the vast majority, there currently is no available path to legalization. By the best estimates, more than 10 million such people without legal immigration status now live in the United States. Millions more live in a variety of tenuous, quasi-legal statuses. They are all potentially subject to deportation.[5] There is also a critical linkage among deportation, race, and ethnicity. The vast majority of those who face deportation proceedings are young people of color.[6]

Any noncitizen, including permanent-resident "green card" holders, may be deported for a wide variety of reasons, some quite clear, others mind-numbingly technical. The law proscribes arcane status violations and requires all noncitizens to report changes of address within ten days.[7] Conviction of minor crimes such as shoplifting and marijuana possession may suffice, as will drug addiction. Another type of deportation law also aims at "any activity *a purpose* of which is the opposition to, or the control or overthrow of, the Government of the United States by force, violence, or other unlawful means."[8]

Millions of noncitizens have become naturalized U.S. citizens, thereby escaping the potential reach of the deportation system. But naturalization is far from easy or automatic. One must first attain lawful permanent-resident status, which can take many years. Then, there is a second waiting period of five years (in most cases), plus additional processing times. A welter of nontrivial requirements include continuous residence, literacy, English-language ability, knowledge of U.S. history and form of government, "good moral character," and proof that an applicant is "attached to the principles of the Constitution . . . and well disposed to the good order and happiness of the United States."[9] Advocacy of a wide variety of ideas and membership in a long list of groups will result in denial of naturalization.[10] From 1999 to 2004, some 3.6 million naturalization petitions were filed. More than one-third—about 1.3 million—were denied, with many denied applicants immediately placed in deportation proceedings.

The size of the deportation system is impressive, if little known. Since 1925, the number of times an individual noncitizen has been caught somewhere on U.S. soil and determined to be subject to deportation has exceeded 46 million, with more than 44 million people actually ordered to leave. From 2001 through 2004, the total number of formal removals of persons from within the United States was over 720,000, while those expelled pursuant to a grant of "voluntary departure" (an often informal procedure the alternative to which is forced removal) exceeded 4 million.[11]

The number of family members, citizens, and noncitizens who are affected by this system runs into many millions. And the deportation system seems likely only to get bigger. One factor is an increase in detention—a response to well-publicized high rates of no-shows at deportation hearings, especially near the southern border.[12] In 2004, the Department of Homeland Security (DHS) detained over 235,000 people for at least twenty-four hours.[13] Congress has authorized the construction of up to 40,000 additional immigration detention bed spaces over the next five years.[14] A particularly striking new initiative is a "family-focused" detention facility to detain families that "come across [the border] illegally."[15]

Imagine a noncitizen who is arrested as a suspected undocumented alien, a possible visa "overstay," or because of a criminal violation. This may be the result of an anonymous tip, a workplace raid, a call from a probation officer, or even simply because the individual "looks" undocumented.[16] What rights does such a person have? Compared with criminal defendants, the rights of deportees are minimal. Suppression of evidence that may have been seized in violation of the Fourth Amendment will be impossible in most cases.[17] The noncitizen will not be read "Miranda" rights.[18] Indeed, he may not even be advised that he has the right to obtain a lawyer (at his own expense) until after a government agent has interrogated him. He will never have the right to appointed counsel.[19] If he believes he has been singled out due to race, religion, or political opinion, he will generally not be able to raise a "selective prosecution" defense.[20] He will never have the right to a jury trial. If he has a formal hearing before an immigration judge, he will have certain due process rights: to be heard, to examine evidence, and to receive a written decision. He may, however, find that the burden of proof will be shifted to him once the government has made a showing of "alienage."[21] If he wants to appeal the immigration judge's decision, he may face incarceration during the length of that appeal—which could easily be years. He may then receive a summary decision made by a single member of the understaffed and overwhelmed Board of Immigration Appeals produced after a ten-minute review of his case.[22] If he seeks a further appeal to a federal court, he may well find that the court declines review of "discretionary" questions, such as his potential eligibility for "relief" from removal.[23]

Two Deportation Models: Extended Border Control and Post-Entry Social Control

How should we understand this system? Is it simply an instrument of immigration policy?[24] The basic thesis of this book is that deportation is now, and always has been, considerably more than that. To be sure, it is part of our immigration control system, though it has worked remarkably poorly even in that realm. But it is also a powerful tool of discretionary social control, a key feature of the national security state, and a most tangible component of the recurrent episodes of xenophobia that have bedeviled our nation of immigrants. It is a mechanism of scapegoating, ostracism, family and community separation, and, of course, banishment.[25] It lives in a peculiar equipoise with our society's openness to legal immigration, our legal system's general protections for the rights of noncitizens, and our grant of birthright citizenship to virtually all persons born on U.S. soil.[26]

For an appreciation of the complexity of the deportation system, it is useful to note that there are two basic types of deportation laws: *extended border control* and *post-entry social control*. The extended border control model implements basic features of sovereign power: the control of territory by the state and the legal distinction between citizens and noncitizens. Extended border control deportation laws have two variants, each of which has been a part of U.S. law for many years. First, there are laws that mandate the deportation of persons who have evaded border controls, either by surreptitious entry or by fraud or misrepresentation. These laws most directly support the border control regime, and their legitimacy, such as it is, is most closely linked to that of sovereignty itself.

There are also laws that permit the deportation of persons who violate an explicit condition on which they were permitted to enter the country. For example, a person who enters the United States as a student must maintain a full course load, and a person with a work visa must work for a particular employer. The legitimacy of such laws, also derived from border control and sovereignty, is enhanced by the contractual aspect of the deal that permitted entry.

One might well be troubled by various features of the extended border control laws, such as the potential for uneven or discriminatory enforcement and insufficient flexibility for changed circumstances, hardship, strong family claims, or the possibility that a border violation was motivated by fear of persecution. And, of course, if one is uncomfortable with the border regime itself—as many are in the case of Mexico—then extended border control laws are mere adjuncts to an unjust historical structure.

Such concerns may be greater for deportation laws that combine extended border control with a rather different goal: post-entry social control.[27] Deportation laws routinely govern conduct for a specific period following the time of admission.[28] The purest post-entry social control laws, however, proscribe criminal or political conduct within the United States, often without time limit. They are often not directly connected to visa issuance, admission, or immigration processes at all. There is no requirement that a noncitizen be informed of them at entry. Indeed, they may be changed retroactively: a noncitizen may be deported for conduct that was not a deportable offense when it occurred.

Such post-entry social control deportation laws derive from what might be termed an "eternal probation" or an "eternal guest" model. The strongest version of this model would suggest that the millions of noncitizens among us, including long-term lawful permanent residents, are harbored subject to the whim of the government and may be deported for any reason. The earliest federal post-entry social control law, the 1798 Aliens Act, authorized highly discretionary executive deportation power to be used against noncitizen dissidents. A fierce debate arose not only over the politics of the law, but also over its basic legal legitimacy. As James Madison put it, "it can not be a true inference, that because the admission of an alien is a favor, the favor may be revoked at pleasure."[29]

Rethinking Deportation History

The current deportation system is best understood within a long historical frame. It has grown slowly, incrementally, and reactively. Though in many ways "a mess,"[30] it has a rather clear pedigree. Its direct roots lie in the late nineteenth-century exclusion and then removal of Chinese laborers from the United States, the early twentieth-century "war on crime," the Palmer Raids, Prohibition, and the Cold War McCarthy era. Its growth was closely linked to the development of the Federal Bureau of Investigation (FBI) and the careers of J. Edgar Hoover, Frances Perkins, Estes Kefauver, and Robert F. Kennedy, among others. Those who today face deportation for minor crimes would likely be surprised to learn that they bear the burden of decades of government frustration over such well-known criminals as Meyer Lansky, "Lucky" Luciano, and Carlos Marcello. Technical aspects of deportation cases derive from years of politicized deportation proceedings against union leader Harry

Bridges and an experiment in due process presided over by one of the founders of modern administrative law, former Harvard Law School dean James Landis.

To understand our current system fully, we should return to 1919, when Emma Goldman was denaturalized without notice and then deported back to Russia as an "alien radical." The legal doctrines that permitted many of the tactics used against anarchists were crafted in the case of Fong Yue Ting, a Chinese laborer deported some twenty years earlier because of his inability to find the "credible white witness" required by law. The extreme judicial deference to such racist laws was formally grounded in a particularly blunt theory of sovereign authority over immigration-related matters. But the deeper roots of such reasoning long preceded the anti-Chinese hysteria that had swept the country. These ideas extend back to the legitimating theories of the brutal removal of the Cherokee and other American Indians from their lands and to the laws governing thousands of fugitive slaves, captured and forcibly sent back to their masters from the late eighteenth through the mid-nineteenth century. The origins reach to Moreau de St. Méry, who fled the United States, along with many of his French compatriots, in fear of Federalist enforcement of the Alien and Sedition Acts, and to still earlier colonial "warning out" systems. Though clearly different from each other in many ways, especially in their complex use of the citizen/noncitizen construct, these systems also share some striking similarities. They all involved the application of majoritarian power—through legal structures and with the use of force—against a particular group of people, largely identifiable by race or nationality, to compel their removal from one place to another. More specifically, these systems have built one upon the other in important and doctrinally traceable ways to form our current system.

Historical legal discourse about deportation is also fascinating to study. The debates over the 1798 Alien and Sedition laws, in particular, provide a useful framework for current discussions of deportation laws, notwithstanding the many obvious historical differences. Among the more powerful objections to these laws was the assertion that they violated basic principles of separation of powers, constituting "a refinement upon despotism," and that the arguments used by the Federalists to support the bills could equally support similar measures against citizens.[31] In 1798, Thomas Jefferson warned that "the friendless alien has indeed been selected as the safest subject of a first experiment, but the citizen will soon follow."[32] These arguments, grounded in constitutional legal structure and fear of excessive government power, raised concerns that are surely as relevant today as they were more than two centuries ago.[33]

These arguments also help to conceptualize the problems raised by three recent trends in deportation law. First, the post–September 11 period witnessed an increased use of the extended border control regime for social control purposes aimed at certain groups. Second, there has been a dramatic increase in post-entry social control deportations. Third, there has been a recent expansion—deep onto U.S. soil—of informal deportation mechanisms that were originally envisioned as appropriate only at the border and ports of entry.

Deportation Law and the "War on Terrorism"

In 1919, Zechariah Chaffee, Jr., noted how deportation law could operate against "aliens" in ways that would be politically and legally problematic for citizens.[34] A similar phenomenon occurred after September 11, 2001. Thousands of people in the United States were subject to interrogation, intimidation, arrest, and incarceration as the deportation system was used to achieve goals that had little, if anything, to do with immigration policy as such.

Consider the reported case of Tarek Mohamed Fayad, an Egyptian dentist who came to the United States in 1998 to study.[35] On September 13, 2001, he was arrested near his home in California and told that the Immigration and Naturalization Service (INS) thought he was illegal. When friends tried to post bond, they were told his bond had been rescinded. Mr. Fayad was interrogated by FBI agents and then transferred to the high-security Metropolitan Detention Center in New York. Taunted by guards as "a terrorist," he was awakened every half hour during the night. He was held in a cell twenty-three hours a day for three months before anyone could locate him.

Deportation law was a central part of the government's response to the September 11 attacks. In October 2001, Attorney General John Ashcroft referred to an "enemy within our borders." He continued: "Robert Kennedy's Justice Department, it is said, would arrest mobsters for 'spitting on the sidewalk' . . . [We will] use the same aggressive arrest and detention tactics in the war on terror . . . Let the terrorists among us be warned: If you overstay your visa—even by one day—we will arrest you. If you violate a local law, you will be put in jail and kept in custody as long as possible."

The attorney general was as good as his word, but many more people than "the terrorists among us" were affected. Thousands were held in detention, virtually all for technical violations that were clearly pretextual. Aggressive government action swept many innocent people into the enforcement net. Noncitizens encountered at the scene of the arrest of a person "of interest to the September 11 investigation" were detained. A government report describes how a "Muslim man in his 40s" was arrested after an acquaintance wrote a letter to law enforcement officers stating that the man had made general "anti-American statements." He was arrested for overstaying his visa. Though cleared of any terrorist links, he languished in detention for more than four months before being deported.[36]

In November 2001, a program of ostensibly voluntary interviews began for some 5,000 men who had entered the United States since January 2000 from countries where Al Qaeda was said to have a "terrorist presence or activity." No European country was on the list. In June 2002, INS required similarly defined noncitizens to register.[37] Failure to do so, or the discovery of even minor immigration violations during registration, could result in arrest, detention, and/or deportation.[38] Registrants faced interviews with a wide variety of questions. One "Special Registration Worksheet" reportedly prepared by INS for student visa holders included this rather stunning question, to be answered under oath: "Are you associated with anyone who is potentially dangerous to the United States?"

It has been reported that many thousands of the Arab and Muslim men who registered with immigration authorities have faced deportation proceedings, though almost none of them have been linked in any way to terrorism.[39] In 2005, FBI agents, posing as social workers, interrogated a 16-year-old girl about her religious and political beliefs. Arrested later in an early-morning raid of her home, the girl was separated from her frantic parents for more than two weeks. They were told that she had been incarcerated for deportation proceedings due to her "unlawful presence." In fact, she was being interrogated by agents from the FBI's Joint Terrorism Task Force.[40] Soon thereafter, she was deported.

Deportation and the "War on Crime": The Growth of Social Control Deportation

The Bush Administration has said that the "war on terror" should not be a war on immigrants. But hundreds of thousands of noncitizens have faced a dramatic convergence between the deportation system and an earlier declared "war" against crime. Since 1997, more than 300,000 people have been deported from the United States because of post-entry criminal conduct, some serious, some as minor as possession of marijuana or shoplifting.[41] DHS reported that 88,897 "criminal aliens" were removed from the United States in 2004 alone. More than one-third of these removals were for drug-related offenses.[42]

Over the past two decades, the post-entry social control deportation system has become more efficient, less discretionary, and much more rigid. Such deportations (and the post–September 11 detentions) were facilitated by two laws passed in 1996: the Antiterrorism and Effective Death Penalty Act (AEDPA) and the Illegal Immigration Reform and Immigrant Responsibility Act (IIRIRA).[43] Passed in the chaotic aftermath of the Oklahoma City bombing, these laws embodied a prosecutorial wishlist that had awaited the most propitious moment to advance. The laws:

- radically changed many grounds of exclusion and deportation
- retroactively expanded criminal grounds of deportation
- eliminated some and limited other discretionary waivers of deportability
- created mandatory detention for many classes of noncitizens
- expedited deportation procedures for certain types of cases
- eliminated judicial review of certain types of deportation (removal) orders
- authorized increased state and local law enforcement involvement in deportation
- created a new type of streamlined removal proceeding—permitting the use of secret evidence—for noncitizens accused of terrorist activity[44]

The 1996 laws have been severely criticized for the devastation they have wrought on families, for their rigidity, and for their retroactivity.[45] But they endure. A constitutional challenge to mandatory detention was brought by a long-term lawful permanent resident in 2003. The Supreme Court upheld the statute, noting that in the exercise of its "broad power" over immigration, "Congress regularly makes rules that would be unacceptable if applied to citizens."[46] Thus, a noncitizen merely accused of certain violations of deportation law will not be released from custody until proceedings have been concluded, a process that can—and often does—take years.

Consider how the criminal deportation and detention laws work in practice. Twenty-three-year-old Edna Borges had lived in the United States as a lawful permanent resident since she was a toddler.[47] Her entire family—including its most recent addition, her baby daughter, Juliana, born in late July 2003—lived in the United States. As a teenager, Edna had gotten into some trouble and was arrested for shoplifting and possession of pepper spray. As these are among the most minor offenses in the criminal justice system, Edna pled guilty and was, in effect, placed on probation. But someone notified the immigration authorities, and Edna was ordered to check in with them every three months. She did this without major incident until her August 2003 appointment.

Eight days after baby Juliana was born, and while she was still being breast-fed, Edna showed up at the Boston office of U.S. Immigration and Customs Enforcement (ICE) for her appointment. Without warning, she was immediately arrested and sent to a jail in Dartmouth, Massachusetts. She was not permitted contact with Juliana, who, she was informed, was refusing to drink formula. She was told that her next scheduled hearing date before an immigration judge was more than one year in the future and that as a "criminal alien" she would not be released and had no right to bail at all. As a flurry of publicity began to surround her case, and as lawyers, including myself, rallied to her cause, a spokeswoman for the DHS offered a sad refrain: "We have no discretion . . . It's that conviction that does it"[48] Due to the extraordinary efforts of her primary lawyer, Susan Church, Edna was ultimately granted discretionary relief from deportation and was then released from DHS custody.

Edna may not have thought so, but she was lucky. She had more rights than many others. A fast-track deportation system, known as "expedited administrative removal," applies to certain nonresident aliens with criminal convictions.[49] They have no right to in-person hearings—their cases are adjudicated on paper. They are given only ten days to respond, in English, to charges against them. They do not even have the right to be provided with a copy of the evidence against them. If found deportable, they are barred from applying for asylum or other relief, are permanently banned from the United States, and face enhanced criminal sanctions if they reenter without authorization. Even some spouses and children of U.S. citizens may face expedited administrative removal, as do tourists, business visitors, students, temporary workers, exchange program participants, and other nonimmigrants, many of whom have lived in the United States for many years.[50]

The Growth of Extended Border Control and the Internalized Border

According to the best estimates, some 30 percent of the foreign-born population in the United States is Mexican, by far the largest percentage from any single country. However, the undocumented Mexican population in the United States has grown faster than the legal population.[51] Millions of Mexicans now live in the United States without legal status, heirs to more than a century of failed immigration policies. Indeed, some 80 percent of the Mexicans who entered the United States from 1990 to 2002 remain undocumented today. To date, all proposals to regularize their status have met with failure.[52]

The last major legislative effort to address this issue was the 1986 Immigration Reform and Control Act (IRCA), which "legalized" nearly 3 million people within the United States, some 75 percent of whom were from Mexico.[53] The drafters of IRCA also envisioned a kind of future deal. The law created a new mechanism for the recruitment and hiring of agricultural workers and sought to "regain control of [the country's] borders" by requiring employers, for the first time in U.S. history, to verify whether new hires were authorized to work in the United States.[54] Clearly, this plan has not worked. Still, apprehension by the Border Patrol near the Mexican border is by far the most common form of deportation.[55] Hundreds of thousands of people each year are simply rounded up, processed, and returned to Mexico.[56] Many—driven by desperate poverty, the pull of the U.S. labor market, and deeply ingrained historical patterns—risk danger and death to return. The number of those deported as "previously removed—ineligible for re-entry" grew from 1,052 in 1994 to 19,773 in 2004.[57]

The number of extended border control deportations from the interior is also quite large. Of the more than 202,000 people removed from the United States in 2004, some 86,000 were deemed "present without authorization."[58] These deportees have the right to formal removal hearings before immigration judges. Their hearings must comport with basic standards of "fundamental fairness." Still, extended border control enforcement from the interior may have harsh effects. A 2004 immigration raid at a poultry plant in Arkansas netted 119 noncitizens but apparently left some 30 children stranded in day care. As Mayor Charles Hollingshead reported, "they didn't know why Mommy or Daddy didn't come pick them up."[59]

Those who are caught near the border, however, face a regime of law that is in many respects the same as they would encounter were they apprehended outside U.S. territory. In effect, they experience government power largely unmediated by constitutional or significant legal constraint. The power of government agents to detain and question anyone at the border has been extended to the "functional equivalent of the border."[60] Within many miles of the border, vehicles may be stopped and their occupants subjected to warrantless searches and seizures. Private land may be entered by government agents without warrants, to search for illegal aliens.[61] Hundreds of children—many of whose parents live in the United States without documentation—are held in detention centers. When their parents seek to have them released, the parents themselves are frequently placed in deportation proceedings.

Spending on border control increased tremendously through the 1990s. High-profile pilot projects were developed with an increasingly militaristic orientation. In July 1993, President Clinton delivered "a strong and clear message. We will make it tougher for illegal aliens to get into the country." High-tech patrols, new walls, fences, and radar soon followed. The Border Patrol, described by Clinton as "breathtakingly understaffed," was expanded with 600 new agents and a 148 percent increase of its budget.[62] The operations have been effective in some ways—such as decreasing the embarrassing spectacles of "kamikaze runs" across the border in Southern California. And they certainly look effective. Operation Rio Grande in Texas used floodlights, watchtowers, video surveillance, and infrared sights along more than thirty miles of border. But the border control operations have also had tragic, if predictable, consequences.[63] Hundreds of thousands of people continue to cross the border each year, but they do so in ever more dangerous ways and through more inaccessible areas. The Mexican government has estimated that more than 2,100 people have died crossing the border since 1997.[64] The vast border regions have now become, in many places, a kind of de facto killing zone in which the bodies of failed migrants lie in the desert or on the banks of the river, a grim and mute testimony to incomplete and ineffective policies.

Moreover, increased border enforcement has created an ever more professional criminal cadre of border crossers (known as "coyotes").[65] A 1997 study concluded that increasing use of professional smugglers, in response to the U.S. border operations, "helps to explain why most migrants attempting unauthorized entry [still] succeed despite significantly more U.S. Border patrol agents and technology on the border."[66] Also, ironically, border enforcement has disrupted deep, historical return patterns.[67] Many migrants have historically worked in the United States but returned to Mexico to rejoin their families when the work season was over. This has now become virtually impossible for many. Thus, workers who might otherwise be temporarily here are now "locked in."[68]

Deportation has expanded as part of this failed system. Much of the attempt to control the border has moved inward.[69] The norms of the external border control system are being increasingly internalized. A system known as "expedited removal" has, since 1996, targeted arriving noncitizens at U.S. ports of entry. It is a quick and efficient system of exclusion.[70] If a DHS officer determines that a person is "inadmissible" (i.e., that he or she lacks proper entry documents or is attempting entry through fraud or misrepresentation), the officer may forbid admission and order the person to return from wherever he or she came. This determination is made on the basis of an informal interview. The arriving person is not permitted to communicate with family, friends, or counsel. The officer's determination is not subject to administrative review by immigration judges and faces only very limited potential judicial review. An order of this type results in the immediate exclusion or removal of the person from the United States and then a five-year ban.[71] At ports of entry, more than 80 percent of expedited removals are accomplished within two days.[72] As problematic as this can be for entrants, it is worse when applied deep within the United States. The government has expanded expedited removal to certain noncitizens apprehended within the United States.[73] It now applies to noncitizens who have been caught within 100 air miles of the U.S. land borders—north and south—and coastal areas, who have not been legally admitted or paroled, and who cannot prove that they have been physically present in the United States continuously for the previous fourteen-day period.[74] Thus, noncitizens can now be removed, virtually without legal process, from vast areas of U.S. territory as if they were simply standing at the border or arriving at an airport.[75] DHS reported 41,752 expedited removals in 2004.[76]

Rethinking Deportation Law

Few would argue with the proposition that all people, regardless of their legal status or what they may be alleged to have done, have the right not to be subjected to an arbitrary, disproportionately harsh system. Most would also agree that punishment should not be retroactive. Whether the U.S. deportation system violates these basic norms, however, involves more nuanced questions. First, there looms the problem of the ambiguous constitutional status of deportation.[77] As Gerald Neuman has noted, constitutional argument "serves as the nation's preeminent vehicle for asserting constraints of fundamental principle."[78] Noncitizens have participated in this argument in important ways since the founding of the republic. But the outcome in immigration and deportation law has been decidedly different from the norms that have emerged elsewhere.

The text of the Constitution does not specifically confer authority to regulate immigration. It says nothing about deportation. This is not a small problem for a nation of immigrants whose Supreme Court made quite clear early on that the federal government has only enumerated powers and may exercise only those powers it has been granted and those necessary and proper for their execution.[79] Congress was empowered to "establish an uniform rule of Naturalization."[80] But the naturalization clause says nothing explicitly about either the admission or the deportation of noncitizens.[81] Although some have seen the migration clause as applicable to immigration, it has long been interpreted to refer only to the slave trade.[82] Nor have the taxation clause, treaty power, the domestic and foreign commerce clauses, or war powers been viewed as sufficient to confer the necessary authority.[83]

The Constitution is also rather ambiguous about the rights of noncitizens. The Fourteenth Amendment was held, in 1886, to protect noncitizen Chinese laundry owners against discriminatory enforcement of a San Francisco ordinance.[84] The most widely accepted reading of the Constitution envisions due process and equal protection guarantees for "persons"—a category that includes both citizens and noncitizens.[85] Noncitizens in the United States are thus entitled to most of the constitutional protections afforded citizens, and in general, discrimination based on alienage requires substantial justification by the government. Indeed, the Supreme Court, in some contexts, has applied "strict scrutiny" to such state discrimination, and something less to the federal government.[86] But even that lesser scrutiny becomes considerably diminished when one challenges immigration and deportation laws or practices.

In 1982, the Supreme Court held in *Plyler v. Doe* that the undocumented children of undocumented noncitizens in Texas had a right to public school education. The Court rejected the argument that undocumented "aliens" were not "persons within the jurisdiction" of the state of Texas and that they had no right to equal protection under the Fourteenth Amendment. Indeed, wrote the Court, "sheer incapability or lax enforcement of the laws barring entry into this country, coupled with the failure to establish an effective bar to the employment of undocumented aliens," had led to the creation of a substantial "shadow population" within the country's borders. The Court recognized that this situation raised "the specter of a permanent caste of undocumented resident aliens" and that such an "underclass presents most difficult problems for a Nation that prides itself on adherence to principles of equality under law."[87]

Consider this: had the federal government, immediately after *Plyler* was decided, simply arrested and deported all of the affected schoolchildren and their parents, it would likely have raised no cognizable legal claim.[88] The basic reason for this apparent anomaly is the so-called plenary power doctrine. In the 1889 case of *Chae Chan Ping v. United States,* the Court reviewed an exceptionally harsh exclusion law that raised deep problems of basic rights.[89] Could a person who had not violated an entry condition be excluded, following a temporary sojourn abroad, simply because the entry laws had changed after he departed? The Court rejected all arguments asserted by Chae Chan Ping's lawyers: contract, vested rights, constitutional protections, and limited government powers. To do this, the Court defined sovereign, constitutionally unrestrained "plenary power." Soon thereafter, this exceedingly deferential approach to exclusion was applied to extended border control deportation in *Fong Yue Ting v. United States,* a case that has since been cited by the Supreme Court more than eighty times.[90]

The Court has mitigated some of the harshest implications of the plenary power doctrine.[91] Justice Harlan wrote in 1903 that for an "alien who has entered the country and has become subject to its jurisdiction and a part of its population," administrative process must at least comply with certain basic due process norms. It could not be arbitrary and the alien must, at a minimum, be given an opportunity to be heard. Over time, this standard developed into a flexible touchstone of fundamental fairness, which has ameliorated some of the worst procedural problems in deportation cases. Still, the plenary power doctrine has impeded the development of coherent substantive principles of constitutional deportation law.[92]

The modern deportation regime is also based on what has been called "citizenship-as-membership." This is the theory that citizens are full members of the United States' constitutional community, whereas noncitizens are something less. Its strongest version is grounded in a particular conception of popular sovereignty that equates citizenship status with "We, the people."[93] During the Cold War, for example, the Court held that whether a long-term, legal permanent resident could remain in the United States was merely "a matter of permission and tolerance."[94]

Modern constitutional deportation doctrine developed in the late nineteenth century mostly in relation to extended border control laws. Though often quite harsh, these deportation laws were essentially contractual. A condition was imposed at entry. If the condition was violated, the remedy fit the contract model: to return the government and the individual to the status quo ante. Indeed, even an innocent violation of an entry requirement could nullify one's status. In the early twentieth century, however, deportation law expanded from extended border control to increased acceptance of post-entry social control laws. This expansion arose out of a "war on crime" and concerns about political dissidents during a period of mandatory loyalty, rigid conformity, intrusive government, and fear. The Supreme Court's acceptance of such deportation laws was rather incremental and uncritical, standing on the doctrinal shoulders of the earlier Chinese deportation cases. This doctrinal structure has rendered tenuous any claims by noncitizens to concrete, substantive constitutional rights against, for example, retroactive deportation or deportation for espousing unpopular ideas. Reaffirmed in the McCarthy-era deportations of alleged Communists and sympathizers, it has, of course, failed to satisfy some commentators over the years. As one dissenting Supreme Court justice wrote, "Banishment is punishment in the practical sense. It may deprive a man and his family of all that makes life worth while."[95]

Deportation doctrine adopts a remarkably parsimonious reading of the constitutional choice *not* to use the word "citizen" in such significant places as the first, fourth, fifth, sixth, and eighth amendments. It also does not realistically grapple with long-standing demographic realities in the United States. Those whom deportation laws affect live among us and often have formed family and community connections. In an increasingly mobile world, the system seems a rigid, vestigial anachronism. The formalistic exclusion of deportable noncitizens from our rich traditions of constitutional discourse also risks the creation of a caste from a "discrete and insular minority." It facilitates irrational discrimination against the noncitizens who live, work, pay taxes, raise children, and participate in communities alongside citizens every day.[96] And practices that take root against noncitizens may provide models for actions against citizens. It is, for example, quite interesting to view from this perspective the recent Supreme Court opinion in the case of U.S. citizen Yaser Hamdi.[97] Citizens—as Hamdi later was—may be transformed into foreigners in order to be ostracized and banished.[98] Emma Goldman, one of history's most famous deportees, was a U.S. citizen.

We therefore should not view deportation law solely as an adjunct to sovereignty or as merely a part of the immigration border control system. We need an understanding of sovereignty, membership, citizenship, and government power that is "supple and flexible" and more functionally reflective of reality as it is experienced by those who have faced this kind of state power.[99] The rights of noncitizens, in sum, should be clearer and grounded more in mainstream constitutional norms, more in their humanity than in their immigration status.

As Gerald Neuman has noted, "the vast bulk of immigration enforcement involves such routine matters as poverty, crime, regulatory violations, and protection of the domestic labor market."[100] But even deportation practices aimed at foreign relations or national security do not override basic rights claims. Consider how extended border control laws were used in the service of stepped-up post–September 11 "spitting on the sidewalk" enforcement as promised by Attorney General Ashcroft. One might analogize this practice to the use of IRS audits against certain political dissidents, selected by race or ethnicity. The fact that the targets may actually have claimed an improper deduction certainly does not compel the conclusion that the prosecutorial selection process evades scrutiny. There are powerful, legitimate concerns about executive-prosecutorial discretion being exercised in such ways. It is the role of the judicial branch to police the outer boundaries of such hard cases, especially when the executive branch seeks to avoid the rights protections of the criminal justice system.[101]

More specifically, the constitutional norms applicable to criminal cases should inform the approach to deportation for crime. The proponents of these laws often understand them as punishment. As Senator William Roth once put it, in a typical formulation, "the bill broadens the definition of aggravated felon to include more crimes *punishable by deportation*."[102] The concern is not with the quantity of immigrants but with their personal qualities. Criminal deportation laws aim permanently to cleanse our society of certain people, many of whom have lived here legally for years. Locally, and in the short-term, deportation as a crime control strategy may seem efficient.[103] If "criminal aliens" are no longer here, and if they are prevented from returning, they are apparently no longer part of our crime problem. They may, of course, become somebody else's problem, as recent news accounts of increasing gang violence in Central America attest.[104] Nevertheless, " '[o]ut of sight, out of mind' perhaps best describes the traditional U.S. response" to the problems that our deportees may cause in their receiving nations.[105] Indeed, the propriety of our current criminal deportation laws seems so self-evident to some that much of the recent scholarly literature on the subject has focused more on critiques of the government for its alleged failure to deport enough criminal aliens than on why we have such a policy in the first place and what its constitutional and foreign policy implications are.[106] But it does not require much analysis to see that the dramatic increase in deportation of long-term legal residents, who may have lived in the United States since early childhood, for increasingly minor post-entry criminal conduct raises profound humanitarian and constitutional concerns.[107]

Deportation, in sum, is now—and always has been—about much more than border control. It implicates the concepts of belonging, cleansing, and scapegoating, as the very term "illegal alien" demonstrates.[108] It facilitates tighter bonds of solidarity among others who share anger and indignation. Like criminal enforcement, it "brings together upright consciences and concentrates them."[109] It renders the offender not simply a foreigner, but an expelled, banished, criminal foreigner—as complete an outcast as one can imagine. Given its size, its consequences, and its trends, this system deserves considerably more thought than it has received.

2

Antecedents

Laws of exclusion and deportation, paradoxically, may be understood as both the darker sides of and the necessary prerequisites to the ideal of the United States as a nation of immigrants.[1] U.S. political leaders, from the earliest days of the republic, have been acutely aware of this complex dynamic. In a 1783 address to a group of recent Irish immigrants, George Washington expressed the point clearly: "The bosom of America is open to receive not only the Opulent and respectable Stranger, but the oppressed and persecuted of all Nations and Religions; whom we shall welcome to a participation of all our rights and privileges if, by decency and propriety of conduct, they appear to merit the enjoyment."[2]

These underlying concerns of "decency," "propriety of conduct," and the particularly vague, discretionary notion of "merit" have long coursed like a dark underground river beneath the fertile landscape of the nation of immigrants myth. To understand how these concepts have influenced the development of the deportation system, it is necessary to distinguish between two rather distinct pedigrees. The first, of course, is that of the formal, legal concept of citizenship. This aspect, well considered by other writers, is not the major theoretical focus of this work.[3] The second, which is less well studied, is that of various historical forms of exclusion and forced removal, many of which had little to do with citizenship law as such.

In the modern view, it is the lack of citizenship status in a particular nation-state that allows one to be deported from it. This is, of course, the basic legal premise on which the deportation system is based. But to view the history of deportation only through this formal lens would be inadequate. This chapter, therefore, will consider various mechanisms of state power over the free movement of individuals—some citizens, some not—that foreshadowed the federal deportation system that developed in the late nineteenth and early twentieth centuries. It will also examine early colonial, state, and federal systems for the removal of people, including American Indian law, colonization plans, and fugitive slave laws. There are, of course, vast differences among these indefinite antecedents; and the line from them to modern deportation law is not a straight one. However, mid-nineteenth-century laws excluding "coolies" began a rather direct process that ultimately led to the exclusion of all Chinese laborers and then to the development of federal deportation machinery. Such laws illustrated the pervasive legacy of slavery and emancipation as well as the racialized foundation of the U.S. immigration and deportation systems.[4] The debates over these laws were replete with references to the decaying slave system. As a *New York Times* editorial noted in 1852, "the only medium between forced and voluntary labor, is that offered by the introduction of Orientals."[5] Indeed, those who later debated the Chinese deportation laws saw a clear link between earlier removal regimes and the deportation of the Chinese.

More subtly, each of these three regimes served as a conceptual model for the nascent deportation system of the 1890s. They help to explain why the obvious racial aspects of the deportation system seemed both so objectionable and yet so familiar to the dissenting justices of the Supreme Court in the *Fong Yue Ting* case:[6]

- The expulsion of a race may be within the inherent powers of a despotism . . . [A]mong the powers . . . not delegated to the government is that of determining whether whole classes in our midst shall, for no crime but that of their race and birthplace, be driven from our territory.
- [This law] . . . places the liberty of one individual subject to the unrestrained control of another.
- According to [the majority's] theory, Congress might have ordered executive officers to take the Chinese laborers to the ocean and put them into a boat and set them adrift; or to take them to the borders of Mexico and turn them loose there; and in both cases without any means of support; indeed, it might have sanctioned towards these laborers the most shocking brutality conceivable . . .

- [D]eportation from the realm has not been exercised in England since Magna Charta, except in punishment for crime, or as a measure in view of existing or anticipated hostilities. But even if that power were exercised by every government of Europe, it would have no bearing in these cases . . . Indeed, all the instances mentioned have been condemned for their barbarity and cruelty.[7]

Part 1: English Roots, Colonial Controls, and Criminal Transportation

English Roots

> He who disturbs the public tranquility, who does not obey the laws, who violates the conditions on which men mutually support and defend each other, ought to be excluded from society, that is, banished . . . The reasons ought to be stronger for banishing a citizen than a stranger.
>
> —Cesare Beccaria, *Of Crimes and Punishments* (1764)

The modern U.S. concept of citizenship evolved from medieval English roots of personal allegiance to one's birthplace. The United States has maintained a strong version of *jus soli*—the right of citizenship based on place of birth—even as citizenship has grown, over time, into a complex notion of legal status, membership, identity, and loyalty with concomitant powerful rights claims.[8] What is most important for our purposes is the development of one modern attribute of citizenship—the right to remain within the territory of a sovereign—or the right not to be deported.

By the seventeenth century, a relatively clear line in English law had emerged between insiders, or "subjects," and outsiders, or "aliens." Important subcategories existed for each. Contemporary seventeenth-century jurists thus could distinguish among "perpetual aliens, "alien friends," and "alien enemies," each with different legal rights.[9] The rights of aliens in England evolved significantly during the mid-seventeenth century, as did fluidity between subjects and aliens.[10] Sir Edward Coke's famous decision in Calvin's Case in 1608 had described subjectship as a "personal relationship" with the king, based on natural law, which therefore made it eternal and impossible to change. This essentially medieval view conflicted sharply with emerging political ideas of consent and social contract. A more fluid concept of "domicile," linked to one's place of residence rather than personal allegiance, began to emerge and to mitigate some of the rigidity of earlier doctrine.[11] As James Kettner has described, by the mid-eighteenth century, English concepts of subjectship foundered on a central ambiguity: "society and government had come to be seen as resting on individual consent and compact." However, "the legal status and obligations of the individual remained natural, perpetual, and immutable."[12]

In the colonies, such ambiguity hindered the main theoretical task of nascent revolutionary thinkers: to define and legitimate the rights of colonists against English imperial authority. By the time of the Revolution, the idea that the colonists were perpetually bound to the crown as subjects was superseded by the natural rights theory of the Declaration of Independence.[13] But, as Judith Shklar has noted, "natural rights theory makes it very difficult to find good reasons for excluding anyone from full political membership in a modern republic."[14] Slaves, American Indians, women, and an increasing array of aliens thus represented powerful potential dilemmas. The first three of these groups were rather easily dismissed by all but the most radical eighteenth-century American thinkers.[15] But aliens, especially white, male, European aliens, raised both definitional and normative questions: Who was a citizen? Who was an alien? What was the difference in terms of rights? These were far from simple questions in the English colonies. Englishmen who settled in the colonies clearly remained subjects of the monarch.[16] The children of English colonists generally had birthright claims to being English subjects and therefore also to the "rights of Englishmen." Many colonial charters guaranteed these rights explicitly, as did the common law.[17]

The status of non-English immigrants was more complicated. Various legal categories defined their rights.[18] The common law concept of a "denizen" approximated that of a "subject."[19] As Blackstone put it, "A denizen is in a kind of middle state, between an alien and a natural-born subject, and partakes of both of them."[20]

Liberal naturalization policies had been opposed in early eighteenth-century England because of fears about immigration. Granting naturalization to persons going to the colonies was somewhat less controversial. Colonial naturalizations were also common but had only local effect: aliens could be naturalized by colonial authority, but they would be considered Englishmen only within that colony.[21] This system, from the English perspective, had pragmatic virtues.

A grant of English naturalization, legally conferred by English authorities, was used frequently throughout the first three decades of the eighteenth century as an inducement to other Europeans to settle in the colonies. Colonial governments had also accommodated newcomers with denization, a practice that was effectively ended by an order-in-council issued to limit such colonial authority without the express authorization of the governor's commission.[22] Over time, however, grants of English naturalization became more closely linked to colonial residence. The 1740 Plantation Act conferred English naturalization on any non-Catholic who had resided for at least seven years in any American colony, had received the sacrament in a Protestant church, swore allegiance to the king of England, and professed belief in Christianity. Certain special provisions even allowed some Quakers and Jews who satisfied the residence requirement to naturalize.[23] The view of Parliament was that "many Foreigners and Strangers . . . might be induced to come and settle in some of his Majesty's colonies, if they were made Partakers of the Advantages and Privileges which the natural born Subjects of this Realm do enjoy."[24]

Despite having long been sought by such colonial promoters as William Penn, these liberal naturalization policies faced a decidedly mixed reception in the colonies.[25] Though European immigration was, in general, widely supported, there was concern that the full rights of Englishmen would be granted to certain immigrants "before they knew how to use them."[26] Nevertheless, by the mid-eighteenth century, non-English foreigners were entering the colonies in ever-increasing numbers, many with full English naturalization. Colonial governments also continued to pass their own naturalization laws. This practice was outlawed in 1773 by an order-in-council that ultimately gave rise to one of the most specific grievances cited in the Declaration of Independence: of King George III "obstructing the laws for the naturalization of foreigners."[27]

Under eighteenth-century English law, naturalization granted the full political and legal rights of Englishmen, which were clearly superior to those of aliens.[28] In America, however, the political, economic, and legal rights of aliens varied widely. The Massachusetts Bay Colony, in 1641, had granted to "every person within this Jurisdiction, whether Inhabitant or forreiner [*sic*] . . . the same justice and law, that is general for the plantation" while also allowing noncitizens to participate in town meetings.[29] In North Carolina, it was reported in 1706 that "all sorts of people, even servants, Negroes, Aliens, Jews and Common sailors were admitted to vote."[30] In 1761, Georgia granted the right to vote to unnaturalized aliens, following a specified period of residence.[31]

The direct link between citizenship status and the "right to remain" is a modern one. The movement of English subjects had been restricted—with distinctions based on class and social status—by laws stretching back to the fourteenth century and by earlier feudal practices. One's right to enter, to remain within, and even to leave the realm were all controlled.[32]

The earliest American ideas of deportation, with English antecedents, were similarly linked rather loosely to citizenship status. New World colonization itself was facilitated by English removal laws aimed at overpopulation, forced movement of the poor and of laborers, control of political dissidents, and punitive measures aimed at convicted criminals. Legal permission was required for all those who wished to emigrate. Elaborate structures developed for the grant of necessary licenses and, in the case of foreigners, legal status. Sir Walter Raleigh had written passionately of the need for England to "disburden" itself of excessive population "and lay the load upon others."[33] Such arguments, of course, were primarily aimed at the English poor, who were seen not only as an economic and social burden, but as a potentially revolutionary underclass.[34] Political leaders and economic elites vacillated between two approaches: the voluntary encouragement of some to leave and the compulsory removal of others. A variety of measures, some voluntary, others not so, resulted in the movement of hundreds of thousands of people to the New World by 1760.[35]

Rather different mechanisms developed to compel certain people to leave the realm. Queen Elizabeth's policies in Ireland were an early, brutal example of English expulsion practices. Fearing the development of Catholic and Spanish influence, Elizabeth first offered Irish land to loyal fortune-seeking settlers. The idea initially had been to replace rebellious Irish chieftains with pliable English leaders. But Ireland was not so easily ruled. When the replacement of one leadership cadre by another proved unworkable, England embarked on a quite different policy: the forced removal of the Irish population and their replacement with English transplants.[36]

As the New World required cultivation and labor, it is not surprising that large-scale programs of removal and transportation of laborers were seen as an excellent way to accomplish that aim. As Marilyn Baseler has noted, "When the native Irish proved intractable, England embarked on a massive program of removal and replacement . . . When similar problems occurred in America, the same devices of removal and transplantation were adopted."[37] From the English perspective, the nation of immigrants was thus conceived also as a "nation of removal."

The removal of criminals also was integral to the "peopling" of the New World by the English. In 1603, James I ordered the implementation of an earlier act aimed at "Rogues Vagabonds and Sturdy Beggars." The Privy Council designated, among other destinations, "The Newfound Land, [and] the East and West Indies" as places to which "any such incorrigible or dangerous Rogues shall be banished." In 1611, the governor of Virginia proposed that some English convicted felons be sent to the new colony for three years. The practice was begun in 1615 through the formal mechanism of a reprieve and stay from execution and transport to the New World for labor.[38] The popularity of forced transportation waxed and waned during the ensuing 150 years, as concerns mounted in England about the negative effects of population loss. By the eighteenth century, many in the English government had decided that a better long-term strategy would be to populate the colonies "with people not her own."[39] Nevertheless, well into the eighteenth century, the temptation to rid England of "such as will not be reformed of their rogish kinde of lyfe" proved irresistible. Indeed, it was also applied to political and religious dissidents, such as "certain persons called Quakers, and others, refusing to take lawful oaths," who would be punished "by abjuration of the realm or transportation to the plantations."[40]

The system known as indentured servitude, as it developed in seventeenth- and eighteenth-century England, was also a major component of the peopling of the New World with white laborers.[41] Their removal from England and transportation to the New World was accomplished by a variety of mechanisms. The basic model was that people who were unable to pay the cost of passage to the New World were bonded as servants to a colonial master for a fixed period. The active recruitment of such people to Virginia was recorded as early as 1609, when "all workmen of whatever craft they may be . . . men as well as women" were invited to come to Sir Thomas Smith's house in Philpot

Lane, where they would be offered "houses to live in, vegetable gardens and orchards, and also food and clothing at the expense of the Company." After seven years, they were offered a share of lands and profits.[42] The reality that faced those who signed up for this plan was extremely unpleasant: harsh, forced labor under deplorable conditions of heat, humidity, disease, and hunger. In most cases, there were no profits.

Over time, the entrepreneurial, profit-sharing schemes yielded to a system that began to look much more like forced removal. At first, the recruiters sought to maintain some of the incentives of the original system. Tenant farmers would be sent, free of charge, to Virginia and "furnished with provisions of victuall for one whole year . . . Cattle . . . apparell, weapons, tooles and implements." Though still entitled to half the profits from the land, the tenant would also be "tyed by Coveneant, to continue upon that Land for the Terme of seven yeares," after which he could stay or leave "at his own will and pleasure."[43] Gradually, however, the profit-sharing concept diminished, and, for most indentured servants, vanished completely. It was replaced by a relatively standard contract in which the servant agreed to serve the master for a specific length of time in return for transport to the colony and then little more than food, drink, clothing, and shelter. Occasionally, there would also be an agreement for a fixed reward at the successful completion of the term. Similar systems were used to remove children. In 1618, some 200 poor children were removed from the streets of London and sent to the colonies as apprentices. Many women and girls were also sent to the colonies as wives for planters. By the late seventeenth century, "redemptioners"—at first mostly Germans who lacked sufficient funds to pay their passage—would contract with merchants to be transported to the New World. After migrating, they were given a fixed period to repay the cost. If they could not do so, they were sold into indentured servitude. This soon became a common scheme for Irish and English emigrants as well. The redemptioner system more typically applied to whole families, whereas indentured servants were almost always single.

Early Exclusion and Expulsion

It surely cannot be said that the colonies were enthusiastic about the entry of newcomers. Indeed, the feeling of the colonists about immigration has been well described as "welcome tinged with misgiving."[44] The propriety of laws of exclusion of "strangers" was generally recognized from the very beginning of New World colonization. In 1637, the same year in which Anne Hutchinson was banished, the General Court of Massachusetts ordered that no town or person "shall receive any stranger" who intended to reside in "the jurisdiction" without official permission.[45] Legal structures that encouraged immigration were invariably accompanied by laws of regulation and exclusion. Early New England towns routinely provided that no stranger could be accepted as an inhabitant without a vote by the town. Consent of the town was often also required even to sell, let land, or provide housing to strangers.[46]

The history of removal reflects similar ambivalence with the added problem that its subjects were, by definition, already situated in communities. The question of their rights, be it as subjects, denizens, aliens, or simply as people, had to be addressed. International deportation from the New World was virtually unknown. The colonies were places to which people came or were brought or sent, rather than those from which they were removed. The costs and difficulties of Atlantic passage, the vast expanses of land, the insatiable need for labor, and fears of slave revolts and Indian attacks rendered international deportation from America largely unknown for European settlers. Confusion about the respective authority of England and the colonies as to naturalization and denizenship also impeded development of deportation laws until well after the recognition of the United States as a sovereign nation. And yet it would be clearly wrong to say that there was no deportation in the colonies. Indeed, the functional forbears of much of our current system may be easily seen. It was widely assumed that the right to exclude included the right to admit prospective inhabitants on specific conditions, such as establishing a business. More general conditions, such as being of "peaceable conversation" or "inoffensive carriage," were also common.[47] In 1634, John Stone, suspected of adultery, referred to Justice Roger Ludlow as "just ass" and was banned from the colony on pain of death. Such legal proceedings often involved a considerable amount of discretion—later to become a signal feature of deportation laws. John Winthrop was known to have frequently allowed those ordered banished to "linger" in order to reduce their hardship. Rigid "strictness" in the enforcement of such laws, wrote Winthrop, "was offensive to many."[48]

Ideological and Religious Exclusion and Removal

The Declaration of Independence listed as a grievance against George III that he had tried "to prevent the population of these states; for that purpose obstructing the laws for naturalization of foreigners, refusing to pass others to encourage their immigration thither." It is far from clear, however, that the colonists' desire for immigrants derived from an Enlightenment ideal of a right to free movement analogous to other truths held to be "self-evident." The colonists—before, during, and after the Revolutionary War—sought immigrants, but most definitely not of all types.

Exclusion and removal based on religion and political ideology long preceded the Alien and Sedition Acts.[49] Indeed, the deportation provisions of the 1798 laws may be understood as the fruits of a gradual acceptance of the legitimacy of ideological exclusion and removal laws. The ideal of America as an asylum seemed to many to demand the exclusion of those "whose moral or social characteristics would introduce in America the decadence and corruption of Europe."[50] Roger Williams, who had studied under Edward Coke and well understood the tenuous relationship between political and religious freedom, was expelled from the Massachusetts Bay Colony in 1636. Anne Hutchinson was brought to trial before the General Court of Massachusetts the next year. Her last interchange with John Winthrop, following her conviction and sentence of banishment, evokes many modern deportation hearings:

"I desire to know wherefore I am banished."
"Say no more, the Court knows wherefore and is satisfied."[51]

In 1643, a Virginia law ordered Catholic priests to be deported within five days of their arrival.[52] By 1717, Pennsylvania's council, concerned about the entry of "great numbers of Foreigners from Germany, strangers to our Language and Constitutions," ordered shipmasters to provide lists of incoming passengers and required all immigrants to take loyalty oaths upon arrival.[53] A Connecticut exclusion and deportation law in 1743, aimed at Moravian immigrants, was entitled "Act providing Relief against the evil and dangerous Designs of Foreigners and Suspected Persons."[54]

Such laws became more common during the Revolutionary War. A vengeful mood of ideological conformity swept through the colonies, spawning test oaths, treason prosecutions, and legal actions of exclusion, banishment, and internment of those thought to be subversive to the cause.[55] Loyalty concerns were widespread during this period, even for native-born supporters of the king. But foreigners were especially vulnerable. The connections among citizenship status, residence, and loyalty were quite complex. In January 1776, the Continental Congress resolved that those who refused to receive congressional bills of credit or who discouraged their circulation would be deemed enemies of the country "and precluded from all trade or intercourse with the inhabitants of these colonies."[56] In effect, such persons were treated as enemy aliens.

There was, however, considerable confusion during this period about the legitimacy of colonial sanctions for disloyalty against those who were, after all, also British subjects. The Continental Congress disaggregated allegiance from subjectship or citizenship status.[57] Allegiance was demanded of all those who sought residence and legal protection. As important, it was residence and entitlement to legal protection that essentially defined membership in the developing national community. Thus, on June 24, 1776, the following resolution was passed: "That all persons residing within any of the United Colonies, and deriving protection from the laws of the same, owe allegiance to said laws, and are members of such colony; and that all persons passing through, visiting or make [sic] a temporary stay in any of the said colonies, being entitled to the protection of the laws . . . owe, during the same time, allegiance thereto."[58]

This newly formalized loyalty demand was of considerable importance, as a violation of it was deemed by the Congress to be treason. In the revolutionary-era rush of fines, property seizures, banishment, and prosecution against those deemed disloyal to the cause, the criterion of loyalty was more important than that of formal citizenship status.[59]

Three distinct groups were recognized. The first was composed of true British subjects who had never become citizens of a state and who maintained loyalty to the king. From the perspective of the revolutionaries, these people were simply enemy aliens. Thomas Jefferson, writing in 1781, described a Tory as "a traitor in thought, but not in deed." He explained how some had fallen on the wrong side of the citizen-alien divide: "By our separation from Great-Britain, British subjects became aliens, and being at war, they were alien enemies. Their lands were of course forfeited, and their debts irrecoverable."[60]

At the opposite pole were state citizens who supported the Revolution and were entitled to all membership rights. Some loyalists occupied an obscure middle ground. They may have been legal state citizens by birth or naturalization, but they maintained allegiance to Great Britain.[61] Their formal legal status directly conflicted with their loyalty. Those who had voluntarily left America during the war or who had aided Great Britain provoked grave, often violent, controversy as to whether they should be permitted to return.[62]

The latent ambiguity in the American immigration ideal was subjected to severe pressure as a result of the war, especially in the South. A 1782 Georgia law had prohibited the entry of Scottish immigrants because "the People of Scotland have in General Manifested a decided inimicallity [sic] to the Civil Liberties of America and have contributed principally to promote and Continue a Ruinous War." In an early example of an extended border control deportation law, Georgia also ordered that "every such Person, being a Native of Scotland shall within three days after his arrival within this State be apprehended and Committed to Gaol there to remain without bail or mainprize untill an opportunity offers of shipping or Transporting him to some other part of the English Kings Dominions."[63]

As Moses Coit Tyler noted, "the exasperation of public feeling against the tories was, at that time, so universal and so fierce" that no statesman could safely oppose it. However, many recognized that the former loyalists could be highly beneficial to the development of the new states. Patrick Henry told the Virginia House of Delegates: "Your great want . . . is the want of men . . . Do you ask how you are to get them? Open your doors, sir, and they will come in . . . [S]hall we, who have laid the proud British lion at our feet now be afraid of his whelps?"[64] The exact legal status of many of the "whelps," however, remained a hotly contested issue. The British viewed American Tories as British citizens who should not have been subject to treason prosecutions in America. It was thought that they might apply, if they wished, for naturalization after the war."[65]

Gradually, a more lenient attitude took hold for returning loyalists. The Continental Congress in 1787 ultimately urged (lacking the authority to order) the repeal of all state laws that conflicted with the provisions of the Treaty of 1783 regarding the treatment of the persons and property of British subjects.[66] Still, the enormous potential fiscal consequences were not finally resolved until 1802, with the payment of a lump sum to Great Britain and a delegation of authority to British authorities to determine who, at least for these purposes, was a "real British subject."[67]

The animus directed against loyalists reversed some common tendencies among those who strongly differentiated between citizens and aliens: American-born Tories who had supported the British were more commonly seen as traitors, while the British-born supporters of the ancien régime inspired somewhat less antipathy.[68] Over time, however, state laws that had been designed to exclude departed loyalists evolved into restrictions on the rights of certain aliens to naturalize. Citizenship itself became increasingly viewed as both a matter of place of birth and one of consent. The consensual aspect sometime conflicted with demands of loyalty, particularly for women. As one court put it: "A wife who left the country in the company of her husband did not withdraw herself; but was . . . withdrawn by him."[69]

In any case, by the end of the eighteenth century, it was well accepted that naturalization was a prize not to be lightly bestowed on the disloyal. The Naturalization Act of May 16, 1790, made naturalization available to any free white person "of good moral character" who, after two years of residence in the United States, would take an oath to support the Constitution of the United States.[70] These character and loyalty criteria became staples of many later exclusion and deportation laws.

Controlling the Movement of the Poor

A subtle truth is revealed by Emma Lazarus's choice of tense in her great poem "The New Colossus," which is engraved at the base of the Statue of Liberty. On behalf of America, the poem asks the world to

> Give me your tired, your poor,
> Your huddled masses yearning to breathe free.

The poem is written in the present tense and expresses an aspiration for the future. It was not written as a statement of historical fact nor could it have been.[71] Indeed, much of the regime of modern deportation law may be traced to mechanisms for the exclusion and the forced relocation of poor people.[72]

Among the early antecedents were English practices, going back to the sixteenth century, that permitted local officials to remove beggars "to the next constable, and so from constable to constable, till they be brought to the place where they were born or most conversant for the space of three years, there to be nourished of alms."[73] On first blush, such laws may seem unrelated to deportation as they did not explicitly differentiate between citizens and foreigners. The 1662 Law of Settlement and Removal, for example, applied to any person who did not own property and who for any reason whatsoever "came into a parish in which he had not a settlement." If such a person could not prove that he would never become chargeable to the parish, the law authorized him to be "summarily removed in custody, together with his wife and children."[74] The ultimate point of return, however, was the place of one's birth. Thus, in effect, the poor were always subject to removal.

The colonies, and later the new states, adopted similar laws and practices to those of England. There was, of course, no centralized, governmentally run "social safety net" in the New World. Local governments, by necessity, assumed responsibility for the poor. The costs of such relief were supported by local taxes. Large communities constructed group facilities—"almshouses" or "poorhouses"—while smaller ones relied on caretaker systems such as "outdoor relief." The fiscal burdens imposed by this system compelled differentiation of people entitled to local support from those who could be sent elsewhere. The colonies thus developed laws providing that relief would be categorically denied to those who applied in towns that were not their "legal settlement."[75]

New England towns regulated the admission of new members very carefully to protect and maintain social cohesion. Those who could not offer "a good and satisfactory account of their wandering up and down" faced corporal punishment and banishment.[76] As early as 1634, Charlestown, Massachusetts, ordered "that none be permitted to sit down and dwell in this town without the consent of the town first obtained." In 1635, the general town meeting of Boston resolved that "noe further allotments shall be granted unto any new comers, but such as may be likely to be received members of the Congregation." Admission upon conditions—a predecessor of both types of extended border control deportation—were common. A 1640 Boston record stated that "John Palmer, carpenter, now dwelling here, is to be allowed an inhabitant, if he can get a house." In 1648, a stranger was admitted as an inhabitant of Woburn, "provided that he unsettle not any inhabitant and bring testimony of his peaceable behavior which is not the least questioned."[77]

Such laws were aimed largely at the poor. New Plymouth in 1658 commanded the return "whence they came" of any persons who might be "chargeable or burthensome to the plantation." Massachusetts later passed a more comprehensive law in 1700 requiring "sufficient security" to be given for immigrants who were "impotent, lame or otherwise infirm, or likely to be a Charge to the Place."[78] Rhode Island, in 1700, ordered shipmasters bringing in foreigners to post bonds.[79] Similar exclusionary and bonding legal provisions were passed in New Hampshire in 1718, New York in 1721 ("Any persons that cannot give a good Account of themselves to the Mayor or like [sic] to be a Burthen"), New Jersey in 1730 ("Old persons, Infants, Maimed, Lunatic or Vagabond or Vagrant persons."),[80] and, with some local differences, throughout the other colonies.

Over time, a proto-deportation system, known as "warning out," developed in New England.[81] Virtually no colonial restrictions on residence or mobility differentiated explicitly between subjects and aliens. The important question was where a poor person had a "settlement." Legal status was not entirely irrelevant, however. Aliens, as noted, were often restricted in their legal rights to land ownership and their ability to pass title after death. Whether one could be warned out depended to a large degree on one's wealth. Aliens faced impediments in proving sufficient holdings to avoid being considered poor transients.[82]

Legal mechanisms increasingly resembled modern deportation systems. They required "more routinized means for sustaining social order" than had the earlier face-to-face systems.[83] Also, the system demanded that a clear, legal differentiation be made between what in New England were termed "inhabitants" versus transients. The latter term, like the current legal term "alien" in the Immigration and Nationality Act, was defined negatively. An alien is, essentially, not a citizen. A transient was a person who lived in a particular town but was not a legal inhabitant.[84] Transients, though lacking legal status, provided indispensable (generally menial) labor in virtually every New England colonial town. Inhabitant status could be acquired in various ways throughout the colonies, but it most typically involved birth in the town, successful completion of an apprenticeship or servitude in the town, purchase of a freehold, or marriage by a woman to a male inhabitant. Again, the rough similarities to modern immigration laws are apparent. Rhode Island law even provided that formal legal settlement status could be granted to transients after one year of residence. In a practice that is similar to modern U.S. immigration law concepts known as "parole" and "deferred-action status," local officials sometimes circumvented this possible grant of status by issuing yearly citations to keep transients "under warning" without necessarily ordering them out of town. The major purpose of this practice was apparently to prevent long-term residents from achieving the full rights of inhabitants.

The discretionary nature of this social control device led to interesting uses of the warning-out order. Orders were commonly based on poverty, sickness, or even birth of a child. But they might also derive from socially objectionable or minor criminal behavior, such as trespassing or keeping an annoying dog. A 1734 order from Canton described a promising newcomer who owned considerable land in Connecticut, but warned "that a glass of good liquor stands a very narrow chance when it lies in his way."[85] There were also such cases as that of one Mary Worsley, who was reportedly warned out of Gloucester because she had "an unruly tongue," and that of Samuel Eldred, his wife, and four children, who were said to be "unwholesome" and "people of bad morals" and to "make great disturbance in the neighborhood where they live."[86] Women were especially vulnerable. A 1672 Roxbury, Massachusetts, record described a woman named Mercy, who was "neere the time of her [delivery and] not [provided] for by her said husband . . . but continues heer with her father, contrary to good order and to the hazarding of a charge upon the towne." Mercy was ordered to "speedily" leave the town "and betake herself to her said husband."[87]

Those familiar with modern deportation proceedings will be struck by more subtle similarities to warning out—procedurally, functionally, and, for lack of a better term, existentially. In her study of the warning-out system in Rhode Island, Ruth Wallis Herndon describes how, when a poor family came into a town, the head of the household would be summoned to a hearing to determine whether the transients should be sent out and, if so, where. Such hearings had all the elements of deportation, albeit in very close quarters. The hearings took place for the most basic reason: "Warned out people were ordered to appear before town leaders because they had chosen to live where others—property owners—now (suddenly) did not want them." On one side of a council table sat the respectable, full-fledged, propertied members of the established community. On the other side of the table stood people who, however deep their attachment to the community might have seemed to them, did not belong. These were, in general, people who were simply "struggling to maintain a place in the towns where they lived."[88]

One could not better describe the essential feel of many modern deportation hearings, especially those of the post-entry social control type. The similarities continue when one considers enforcement. A family that had been warned out, could be forcibly removed by the town sergeant and constables. Family members would either be brought directly to the appropriate town, or if it was too far away, they would be delivered to an adjoining town where the process would be repeated until they reached their town of legal settlement.[89] As had long been the case in England, if a transient returned to a town from which he had been warned out, he faced punishment that could include whipping.

The application and enforcement of the warning out and similar laws appear to have been highly discretionary and often quite harsh, especially for people of color. The General Court of Massachusetts passed a special act in 1796 to remove vagrants and "strolling poor people" from the District of Marshpee (Cape Cod), as it had reportedly become a place of shelter for the transient poor and was populated largely by Indians and blacks.[90] One study has found that over a fifty-year period, from 1751 to 1800, more than 21 percent of the warned-out transients were people of color. This percentage spiked dramatically from the mid-1780s, exceeding 40 percent during the 1790s, a time when large numbers of African Americans gained manumission only to face unemployment, transience, and poverty. This is especially striking in light of the fact that people of color are estimated to have accounted for only 5 percent of the population of Rhode Island by 1800. Though practices varied widely throughout the colonies, explicitly race-based removals certainly occurred: as an example, in 1780, the East Greenwich, Rhode Island, council ordered the immediate departure of all transient "Indians, mulattoes [and] Negroes."[91] Poor transient families were apt to be separated by government officials with little apparent concern for the effects of such separation on children.

Ruth Wallis Herndon describes the story of "a Negro man" called Titus Guinea, who was born in Africa and had been brought to Newport as a slave around 1751.[92] After having been sold four times to different masters, the last time to Theophilus Pickering of Ipswich, Guinea managed to purchase his freedom through labor. He finally became a free man in 1769. He moved to Providence, where there was an established community of free people of color; found work; and, in 1784, fathered a child, named Susannah, who was born in North Providence. Unfortunately, Titus Guinea was not an inhabitant of Providence, and in 1788, when he was about sixty years old, his daughter was held to "belong" to North Providence. Two weeks later, the four-year-old child was forcibly "delivered" to an overseer for the poor in North Providence. Although Susannah's mother, Binah Pearce, lived in Providence, she was not deemed able to support the child and so, in modern terms, lost custody of her daughter. By 1789, Titus Guinea, apparently also unable to care for himself financially, was removed back to Ipswich, too far away for regular visits with his daughter.

The evolutionary line from colonial practices to modern deportation law is a rather direct one. Controls on transients steadily became more routine and centralized. By 1740, legal residency—previously possible simply by virtue of residence—generally required the formal agreement of the town government. As Douglas Lamar Jones has noted, "The granting of poor relief, the laws of settlement, and the practice of warning transients to leave town were interrelated aspects of the legal structure employed by towns . . . to preserve their social order."[93] Some warning-out laws provided that a person who resided in a town for three months without being warned out became entitled to poor relief.[94] In larger towns, this required government agents. As early as 1670, Salem had hired a man named Thomas Oliver—perhaps the first New World deportation agent—"to go to each house once a month to inquire about the presence of 'strangers.'" Later, with the inception of "entertainment laws" that prevented transients from remaining more than twenty days in a town without special permission, the enforcement burden was shifted to those who provided transients with food and shelter. By 1767, this approach had yielded in Massachusetts to one that resembled modern immigration and deportation laws: all transients were required to notify the selectmen as they entered a town.[95] In 1794, Massachusetts advanced to a still more modern system that replaced the warning-out system with a statewide procedure for the return of transients to their legal residences.[96] Transients now received important procedural protections including the right of an appeal to the court system.

Many post–Revolutionary War state laws that were aimed at poor, foreign-born immigrants reflected—sometimes with identical language—the colonial systems that had authorized the exclusion and removal of poor noninhabitants. During this early state-law period, as before, the status of being poor was as significant as that of alienage.[97]

Following independence, laws of exclusion and registration in the new states led quickly to laws of removal. The first step, illustrated by a 1788 New York law, was an authorization to return an unacceptable immigrant immediately "to the place from whence he or she came."[98] A Connecticut law, passed in 1784, provided that foreigners residing in the state who were "likely to become a public charge" could be sent away.[99] Similarly, Massachusetts enacted a statute in 1788 that required the registration of foreigners and prohibited the landing of aliens who seemed likely to require public relief.[100] The 1794 Massachusetts law also contained provisions that expressly authorized forcible removal of poor people to other states or even "to any place beyond the sea, where he belongs."[101] In this latter aspect, the law stands as one of the earliest examples of a foreign deportation law in the United States.[102] Then as now, it appears that many of these measures were not especially effective and that many "undesirable" immigrants managed to enter the United States without much difficulty.[103]

The Exclusion and Removal of Convicts

By the mid-seventeenth century, the disruption of feudal, agrarian society in England led to the dislocation of large numbers of poor people. With no social safety net and virtually no social or economic mobility, many turned to crime. The legal system responded harshly, designating some 300 crimes—including relatively minor offenses such as theft of property worth more than a shilling—as felonies for which the penalty of death was prescribed.[104] Although the death penalty was prescribed by law, it could be avoided by so-called pleading of clergy and by royal pardon. This elaborate discretionary system sent people to the colonies even though the common law and the Habeas Corpus Act had generally outlawed the punishments of exile and transportation. Thus, a convict would be pardoned on the condition that he be transported out of the country for a fixed period. From about 1655 to 1718, this was the primary mechanism for transportation of convicts to the colonies.[105]

The transportation system initially was privately run and could be quite profitable. Merchants would pay various fees arising out of the criminal process in exchange for the right to transport the convict. In the New World, the merchant could sell the felon into indentured servitude. The system inspired mixed reactions in the colonies, where the pressing need for labor conflicted with persistent worries about the character traits of the new immigrants. Thus, by the end of the seventeenth century, privately run transportation declined in part because of economic problems and increasing resistance to the practice in the colonies. A new system developed, however, which was functionally similar in many respects to future U.S. deportation laws, with the very important caveat that it applied to subjects as well as aliens.[106]

The 1717 Transportation Act converted the English system into a government-subsidized one.[107] The act, seen as both a crime-control and removal measure, was entitled "An act for the further preventing of robbery, burglary, and other felonies, and for the more effectual transportation of felons." It directly allowed courts to order convicts to the colonies for up to fourteen years, "as soon as conveniently may be." The 1717 law further permitted offenders to be ordered "to the use of any person or persons, who shall contract for the performance of such transportation." This was apparently a highly workable system from all perspectives, except, of course, from that of the transportees and their families. It combined criminal punishment with indentured servitude. It is estimated that some 30,000 people were sent from Great Britain to America through this mechanism in the eighteenth century.[108] If they were miserable in the New World (and many were), their options were severely limited. The penalty for a premature return from transportation abroad was death.

Colonial attempts to regulate this trade, especially those that sought to impose duties on the importations, faced often insurmountable legal impediments from Parliament and the Board of Trade.[109] The convict transportation system remained fully in effect until the Revolution, despite powerful arguments against it. Some in Great Britain argued (in the thinking of many colonists, disingenuously) that colonial protectionist measures against the practice were "against Publick Utility," in that they interfered with the "Improvement and Well Peopling of the Colonies."[110] It is also true, however, that there were those in England who saw the Transportation Act policies of deportation and banishment in idealistic terms, as having rehabilitative and humanitarian virtues, especially when compared with the likely alternative available to many convicts: hanging.[111] Sir John Fielding wrote in 1773 that transportation was "the wisest, because most humane and effectual, punishment we have . . . which immediately removes the evil, separates the individual from his abandoned connexions, and gives him a fresh opportunity of being a useful member of society."[112] Many of the convicts apparently disagreed with this assessment, as some reportedly said they would rather be hanged than transported a second time.[113]

The colonists became increasingly fearful of crimes being committed by the new arrivals. The *Virginia Gazette* reported on May 24, 1751: "When we see our Papers fill'd continually with accounts of the most audacious Robberies, the most Cruel Murders, and infinite other Villanies perpetrated by Convicts transported from Europe, what melancholy, what terrible Reflections must it occasion!"[114]

Ben Franklin addressed this argument by noting that rattlesnakes, which were "Felons-convict from the Beginning of the World," were likewise to be put to death "by Virtue of an old Law." Franklin sarcastically suggested, however, that "this is a sanguinary Law, and may seem too cruel," especially as the creatures "may possibly change their Natures, if they were to change the Climate." It was for this reason that he suggested that the rattlesnakes, too, might have their death sentences changed to transportation, in this case to England, and in particular that they be "carefully distributed in St. James's Park, in the Spring—Gardens and other Places of Pleasure about London; in the Gardens of all the Nobility and Gentry throughout the Nation; but particularly in the Gardens of the Prime Ministers, the Lords of Trade and Members of Parliament; for to them we are most particularly obliged."[115]

The policy of shipping convicts to the New World was officially ended by the British government in 1776, which ostensibly found it to have become "attended with various inconveniences, particularly by depriving this kingdom of many subjects whose labour might be useful to this community."[116] The practice resumed after the war, however. A ship with eighty felons landed in Maryland in 1783.[117] Opposition from the receiving states quickly began to mount. In 1788, the Continental Congress was sufficiently aware of the problem that it reported to the British secretary for foreign affairs that "it does not become the court of Great Britain to countenance, nor the United States to tolerate so nefarious a practice."[118] The practice was soon stopped again, and the British began sending convicts to newly established colonies in Australia.

Ideas about international deportation from the United States also began to surface during this period. In 1787, for example, Benjamin Franklin returned to the subject he had made famous with his 1751 rattlesnakes proposal. More than thirty years later, post-independence, Franklin's thoughts had moved from facetiousness to the somewhat more serious (if still sardonic) concept of social control deportation:

> We may all remember the Time when our Mother Country, as a Mark of her parental Tenderness, emptied her Jails into our Habitations, "for the BETTER Peopling," as she express'd it, "of the Colonies." It is certain that no due Returns have yet been made for these valuable Consignments . . . The Felons she planted among us have produc'd such an amazing Increase, that we are now enabled to make ample Remittance in the same Commodity. And since . . . many of our Vessels are idle through her Restraints on our Trade, why should we not employ those Vessels in transporting the Felons to Britain?[119]

Franklin proposed a deportation system in which "every English Ship arriving in our Ports with Goods for sale, should be obliged to give Bond . . . engaging that she will carry back to Britain at least one Felon for every Fifty Tons of her Burthen."

No federal or national policy was developed, however. The Continental Congress likely assumed that laws of exclusion or regulation of entry of convicts were the primary responsibility of the state governments. Thus, on September 16, 1788, the Continental Congress resolved "[t]hat it be and it is hereby recommended to the several states to pass proper laws for preventing the transportation of convicted malefactors from foreign countries into the United States."[120] Most of the states did so. In 1788, Connecticut banned the entry of convicts sentenced to transportation. A 1789 Pennsylvania law not only banned the entry of convicts, but required the persons responsible for bringing the convict into the state to remove the convict from the United States at their own expense.[121]

Many states have historically utilized banishment, transportation, and conditional pardons to remove convicted criminals from their borders.[122] Though such statutes did not generally distinguish aliens from citizens, two caveats should be noted.[123] First, as discussed more fully in

Part 3, both slaves and free people of color were specially targeted by these sanctions. Contemporary legislative and judicial views about their citizenship status (or lack thereof) render comparisons to the later deportation system plausible.[124] Second, by the early nineteenth century, some states did specifically exempt citizens from the punishments of exile and transportation.[125]

The Acadian Deportation: Le Grand Dérangement

> Where is the thatch-roofed village, the home of Acadian farmers—
> . . .
> Waste are those pleasant farms, and the farmers forever departed!
> Scattered like dust and leaves, when the mighty blasts of October
> Seize them, and whirl them aloft, and sprinkle them far o'er the ocean.
>
> —Henry Wadsworth Longfellow, *Evangeline* (1847)

In 1604, settlers from the provinces of northern France, Brittany, Normandy, Picardy, and Poitou established a French colony called Acadie in present-day Nova Scotia, New Brunswick, Prince Edward Island, and part of the state of Maine.[126] These colonists, called Acadians, prospered for some 150 years. In the early eighteenth century, Britain gained control over the area and, in 1713, renamed it Nova Scotia.[127] The Acadians, though now formally British subjects, were permitted the free exercise of their religion and the right to choose whether to remain on their lands, as British subjects, or to leave, taking their movable goods and the proceeds from the sale of their immovable property.[128]

However, British governors, fearing the development of potentially dangerous French communities in their midst, were reluctant to permit Acadian settlements in other parts of Canada and New England.[129] They also began to put increasing pressure on the existing communities. The British ultimately offered the Acadians a stark choice: either take an oath of allegiance to the British crown or leave Acadia. Tensions mounted over the course of the next three decades. At one point, the British agreed to accept a restricted oath of allegiance that exempted the Acadians from having to bear arms on behalf of England.[130] After 1730, when the Acadians pledged allegiance to the British not to take up arms against either France or England, the Acadians were commonly referred to by English authorities and colonists as "French Neutrals."[131] Despite the legal provisions of the treaty of Utrecht, there was uncertainty about the status of the Acadians as either "temporarily conquered people or prospective British subjects." (Interestingly, the "French neutrals" were not counted as "white" people in a provincial census taken in Massachusetts in 1768.)[132] Many undoubtedly expected the Acadians to move to French territory.[133] They did not do so voluntarily, thus sparking the first major deportation of European settlers in the New World.

Fearing Acadian alliances with indigenous peoples and with the French, the British government—which by some accounts also may have coveted the fertile land of the Acadians—declared the compromise oath invalid on the grounds that Parliament had not given its consent. In 1749, the British government demanded that all Acadians take an unqualified oath of allegiance, swearing loyalty forever to England and agreeing to bear arms against her enemies.[134] The great majority of Acadians refused to take such an oath. Then, on September 5, 1755, all males of Grand Pre over ten years of age were summoned to the village church. Colonel John Winslow read aloud what he described as "the King's instructions" that "all French be removed."[135] The Acadians were then driven from their farms, and it was ordered that all their buildings be burned to the ground.[136]

After this, and throughout the period of the Seven Years' War, the British forcibly deported some 8,000 Acadians.[137] Thousands reportedly died during this exile.[138] Some contemporary accounts of the deportation condemned it. Edmund Burke wrote, "We did, in my opinion, most inhumanely and upon pretenses that, in the eye of an honest man are not worth a farthing, root out this poor, innocent, deserving people, whom our utter inability to govern, or to reconcile, gave us no sort of right to extirpate."[139] Reports of the criticism of the deportation by William Pitt (the elder), then the British secretary of state, are repeated to this day.[140]

Many of the Acadian deportees returned to France. Others were shipped to British colonies throughout the New World, particularly New Haven, Boston, New York, Philadelphia, Hampton Roads, Charleston, and Savannah. Apparently, however, the governors of the settlements to which the Acadians fled received no notice of their intended arrival and no support from the British authorities for their resettlement.[141] They were very poorly received. Philadelphia accepted them reluctantly. Georgia refused to admit them at all because of its law against the settling of Catholics.[142] Their forced movement thus gave rise to some of the earliest known examples of detention and deportation proceedings in America. The governor of Virginia, for example, sheltered them through the winter but then expelled them to England.

The story of Jacques Maurice Vigneau and his family, forcibly deported from Acadia to Georgia in the fall of 1755, is not atypical. The governor at first denied them permission to land and held them on board their ship docked at Savannah. When it became known that the Acadians were ill and running out of food, Vigneau and the others were allowed to land. They were immediately asked to leave the colony and were granted "passes" to South Carolina—in effect, deportation orders from Georgia. South Carolina, however, also had frequently detained Acadians on their ships and jailed them on land.[143] The group of Acadians struggled to make their way back north, with the hope of someday returning to Nova Scotia. Vigneau and a group that included nearly 100 people were detained in North Carolina, then New York, and, finally, Massachusetts. They ultimately were permitted to travel to the French island of Miquelon in 1763.[144]

In 1755, following the arrival of some 600 Acadians to Charles Town harbor, Governor James Glen and the assembly determined that they would not be allowed into the colony. A committee of the assembly reported that the Acadians had "borne Arms against his Majesty's Subjects," were devout Catholics, "professed an inviolable attachment to the French Interest," and "obstinately refused to take the Oath of Allegiance." The committee also worried that the Acadians would "have an opportunity of sowing the seeds of discontent and rebellion among our Slaves" and might gather military intelligence for the French.[145] The assembly and governor eventually did allow the Acadians to land, but they were confined to Charles Town under guard.

After the governor of South Carolina was convinced that he lacked legal authority simply to deport the Acadians, he proposed inviting them to resettle on islands off the South Carolina coast.[146] In 1756, a new governor, William Lyttleton, decided with the assembly to indenture some Acadians and release others for resettlement throughout the colony.[147]

Among the many interesting and tragic aspects of the Acadian deportation is the way in which the Acadians were, in effect, transformed into aliens by the British. Those who refused to swear allegiance to the king, it was argued, were aliens. The Acadians were viewed as foreigners throughout the British colonies.[148] As we have seen, under English law aliens had no right to tenure of real property. Thus, in an attempt to attract more acceptable settlers to the vacated Acadian farms, the General Assembly passed a statute in 1759 that explained why the Acadians never had lawful title and then, by law, invalidated any title that they might have had.[149] In June 1760, some 650 families from Boston and Rhode Island arrived in Nova Scotia and occupied the former Acadian lands. By 1763, 12,500 people from New England had taken some of the most fertile land in North America.[150] Many deported Acadians were not allowed to return. Indeed, in March 1764, Lord Halifax wrote: "the safety of this Province depends on the total expulsion of the French Acadians."[151] Those who did manage to return were not allowed to reoccupy their former lands and instead resettled on inferior lands (limited to forty acres per family) in the northern and western extremities of Nova Scotia. It is estimated today that descendants of the Acadians make up approximately 5 percent of the population of Nova Scotia, and others are known as the Cajuns of Louisiana.[152] For our purposes, however, what is equally interesting is how this episode undoubtedly continued to live in the consciousness of Jefferson, Madison, and Longfellow and, later, in that of well-educated easterners such as George Frisbee Hoar. It likely contributed to the emotional core of their eloquent opposition to the deportation laws of their era. Later still, it reemerged in the song writing of Woody Guthrie, as a compassionate paean to deported twentieth-century Mexican workers.

Part 2: The Alien and Sedition Acts: A "First Experiment"

> Nothing is more annoying . . . than this irritable patriotism of the Americans. A foreigner will gladly agree to praise much in their country, but he would like to be allowed to criticize something, and that he is absolutely refused.
>
> —Alexis de Tocqueville, *Democracy in America* (1831)

The Tension between Deportation and the Nation of Immigrants Ideal

For those who seek to understand the history of deportation in the United States, a return to some of the earliest debates in this country over the basic constitutional rights of noncitizens is most instructive. Despite intense concerns raised over immigration in the century before the Revolutionary War, the Constitution, as noted, contained only the most oblique references to immigration control, let alone deportation authority. In the states, the immigration power was considered part of the police power—like the power to protect against criminals or to quarantine.[153]

This was undoubtedly due in part to the preoccupation of the new national government with an infinite array of other more pressing challenges. It was also a consequence of a fundamental contradiction in the attitudes of the new nation toward immigration. The ideological power of the republican vision of an asylum for the oppressed and a nation founded on basic "self-evident" principles of individual liberty conflicted with more pragmatic concerns about the economic consequences of unregulated immigration of the poor, the social consequences of forced transportation of convicts, and the political consequences of allowing monarchists and others to enter. Still, the general tendency, through the 1780s, was for policies that fed a "growing assumption that membership status was and ought to be undifferentiated." As James Kettner has noted, "In America the foreign immigrant's contribution to the welfare of the community—its military security, its economic prosperity, its rapid and sustained growth—was obvious and highly valued. To limit his right seemed senseless on grounds both of self-interest and abstract justice."[154]

There was an important corollary development, however, the importance of which has been less thoroughly considered by historians: the gradual demise, after 1700, of the status of the denizen as a legal membership concept in the colonies. This meant that the array of statuses was rendered less nuanced and the distinction between a citizen and an alien became more of a bright line.[155] By the late 1790s, therefore, the debates over the Alien and Sedition Acts focused on the legal statuses of citizen and alien as such, with less than clear consideration of the possibility of a middle status that might perhaps protect a person from certain forms of deportation.

The idealistic vision of immigration to America was itself problematic. Some viewed continuing population growth as an unalloyed good; others feared that it contributed to societal decay.[156] Differing views of republican ideals and democracy implied differing views of immigration. Those—such as Jefferson—who tended toward a less elitist view were nevertheless concerned about the political inclinations of new immigrants, for it was assumed that they would soon have political power.

Instrumentalist reasons to support immigration were also well entrenched in the soil of the new nation. Competition among the colonies had long been a powerful factor favoring liberal immigration and naturalization laws. The lieutenant governor of New York had noted in 1761 that if New York did not accede to the relatively easy laws of naturalization that were available elsewhere, "it would draw all foreigners, who are willing to settle and improve lands, from this Colony to the others."[157] As before the Revolution, European labor was sought, and white population growth in general was seen to increase the military and economic strength of the new nation.[158] Religion, wealth, health, and morality were the common measures of acceptability. This began to change, however, and as one historian has noted, by the end of the seventeenth century, "in the popular colonial mind the fact that a Huguenot was a Protestant was overshadowed by the more evident fact that he was a Frenchman."[159] And of course, throughout the eighteenth century, the specter of the unresolved problem of slavery also loomed large over immigration policy debates. As Edmund Morgan has noted, "Virginians may have had a special appreciation of the freedom dear to republicans, because they saw every day what life was like without it."[160] By the late 1790s, then, the new United States was a relatively open society—at least for white men—but one in which the seeds of future harsh laws of exclusion and deportation easily took root.

The debates over the Alien and Sedition Acts of the 1790s illustrate a major unresolved tension in U.S. constitutional history: between a robust rule-of-law version of the nation of immigrants ideal (with its attendant general values of openness, diversity, equality, and fundamental rights) and the categorical, status-based distinctions that legitimize government action against noncitizens that would be unacceptable if applied to citizens. One should take care not to overstate the parallels, of course. Many aspects of politico-legal debate in 1798 were obviously different from what we encounter more than 200 years later.[161] Still, there are important similarities. Most generally, it was in this tumultuous, highly charged time that the basic tensions between open immigration and post-entry social control deportation first became a matter of great public concern in America. Although the deportation parts of the Alien Acts were not directly enforced by the Adams administration, the assertion of federal deportation power—particularly highly discretionary executive power—and, as important, the responses to that assertion, have influenced debates over every subsequent U.S. deportation law.

It was a striking aspect of the post–September 11 debate that both the administration and its critics generally supported open immigration admission policies. This, too, was true in the 1790s. Indeed, despite vast differences of time, place, and various background norms, debates over the relationship between noncitizens' rights within the United States and the general ideals of American constitutional democracy have remained surprisingly constant over time. The specific issues are invariably historically contingent, to be sure, but never completely so. However, unlike the free speech restrictions of the Alien and Sedition laws, which have been described as overturned in the "court of history,"[162] the deportation aspects have never been so resolved.

Throughout the 1790s (and ever since), a recurring concern about deportation laws has been that of precedent or the "slippery slope": government actions that are first tolerated against noncitizens, it is argued, may expand to citizens.[163] History generally supports this concern, as the progression of government action in the 1790s, the Palmer Raids, and the McCarthy era shows.[164] Perhaps no single objection to the targeting of noncitizens has been more consistently and eloquently expressed. Thus, Jefferson's concern for the attack on the "friendless alien" was that "the citizen will soon follow."[165] Despite its obvious rhetorical power and historical accuracy, however, this argument is not necessarily a principled statement in support of noncitizens' rights.[166] Indeed, it could well be understood as an argument in favor of a profound differentiation between citizens' and noncitizens' rights. Should one support attacks on the rights of noncitizens to liberty and free speech by a government that guaranteed it would never do the same to citizens? If not, why not? The answer requires a more fundamental theory. Such problems were debated but not resolved during Jefferson and Adams's generation.

The Development of the Alien and Sedition Acts

The 1790s were a time of intense factionalism, great fear, legal uncertainty, and political and journalistic discourse that seems rabid by modern standards.[167] The fundamental political differences between the Federalists and those who later became known as Republicans, apparent from the earliest post–Revolutionary War debates, were central to the debate over the first American deportation laws. The Federalists, holding a position that had been well articulated by Edmund Burke, generally supported an aristocratic, elitist view of government, the main mechanism of which was "virtual representation." They were relatively sympathetic to loyalists, with whom they tended to share much in terms of class and values, and they urged a post–Revolution policy of forgiveness and repatriation. Ironically, in light of events that were to occur in a mere decade, the Federalists of the 1780s generally promoted open immigration and easy naturalization, believing that the beneficiaries of such polices (if the policies were properly undertaken) would be persons of wealth and "quality" who would increase the general prosperity and power of the new United States. This comported with their main goals for government: political stability and the protection of private property.

The Democratic-Republicans, on the other hand, tended more toward the views articulated by Rousseau as to the need for government to reflect the "general will." With greater faith in the common people and stronger egalitarian ideals, the Democratic-Republicans generally supported more direct mechanisms for majority rule—at least among propertied white males. They feared "tyranny" as the Federalists feared rule by what Hamilton had called the "mass of the people."[168] In the years following the Revolutionary War, many Democratic-Republicans disagreed with Federalist policies about immigration, slavery, and the relationship between state and federal governmental power.

Those Democratic-Republicans who opposed immigration were often concerned about the political-economic views of returning loyalists. They saw little contradiction in viewing America as a haven for the oppressed[169] while restricting entry of those who disagreed with their ideas. Their ideal of citizenship, more than that of the Federalists, required a shared, general commitment to certain common values. And the ideal Republican type—the independent farmer—could be threatened by unrestricted immigration, especially of those with monarchist tendencies.[170] Thus, neither group can be said to have been fully pro- or anti-immigration. Both groups shared a general acceptance of the nation of immigrants admissions ideal, while both worried about certain qualities of the immigrants. By the 1790s, however, the Federalists had come to worry much more.

The French Revolution, the Reign of Terror, and the military victories of Napolean had led many Federalists to find their domestic political opponents "doubly offensive."[171] In addition to being political rivals, they were increasingly seen as a "foreign" element. The Republicans' belief in the possibility of government by people who were neither wealthy nor property owners was one concern. Their sympathy for the French revolutionaries' ideals was another. Indeed, some Federalists began to view Republicans as traitors and as "Frenchmen in all their feelings and wishes."[172] Immigration concerns became entangled in domestic political struggles and were ultimately turned into the first national deportation laws. One Federalist newspaper yearned, "Would to God the immigrants could be collected and re-transported to the climes from whence they came."[173]

In its early years, the United States found itself torn between mighty geo-political forces emanating from England and France. Among the most important disputes were American neutrality and different conceptions of "freedom of the seas." The Jay Treaty of 1794 between England and the United States, which sought to resolve a series of long-standing disputes and to avoid a possible second war with England, caused as many problems as it solved.[174] The Republicans campaigned vigorously against the practice of British impressment of U.S. sailors. The *Philadelphia Aurora,* in a typical report, published a story entitled "BRITISH ATROCITY!" that told of an American captain, Blackmore, who had been shot through the face by a British frigate.[175] At the same time, though, French privateers also began to increase predations on American vessels. Thus, Federalists had their own special concerns about foreign interference with American shipping. Moreover, French political involvement in American society was increasing substantially. France's foreign minister, Charles Delacroix, believed that the pro-British Jay Treaty was the equivalent of a declaration of war against France. Realizing that such a war would be foolhardy for France, he carefully became more involved in American politics, hoping to aid a Republican victory in the upcoming elections.[176] During the 1796 campaign, Pierre Adet, the French minister to the United States, boldly wrote in implicitly pro-Republican and anti-Federalist terms, O! Americans covered with noble scars! You who have so often flown to death and to victory with French soldiers! . . . Let your government return to itself, and you will still find in Frenchmen faithful friends and generous allies.[177]

The outrage felt by the Federalists was palpable. Indeed, by March 1797, many Federalists had concluded that war with France was inevitable and perhaps preferable to the alternatives.[178] Though it surely seems to have been exaggerated, the potential threat from France was far from a fantasy. President John Adams and others concluded that the victories of Napoleon Bonaparte throughout Europe created great possible dangers for America. Adams feared that the great powers of Europe, including even Great Britain, would make peace with the Directory.[179] If that were to happen, the aggressive focus of the French might well turn on America.[180] Even those Federalists who did not support a war with France actively supported the anti-French mood that had begun to sweep through the country, believing that this atmosphere would help them gain support in upcoming elections. Not only the substance but the tone of public debate changed dramatically. Alexander Hamilton published an essay, part of a series, entitled "The Stand," in which he railed against "FIVE TYRANTS of France [who] after binding in chains their own countrymen . . . have . . . decreed war against all nations not in league with themselves."[181] He called for the creation of an American army 50,000 strong—more than double the size that anybody had ever called for before—to be led by George Washington.

By January 1798, political fear had reached a crisis. Rumors swirled that envoys sent to France had been unable to reach a settlement. Adams and his cabinet seriously contemplated war with France. In the spring of 1798, the so-called XYZ Affair decisively turned the tide of public opinion against the Republicans. A secret dispatch arrived from envoys, whom Adams had sent to France. It stated that French Foreign Minister Talleyrand had refused even to receive the diplomats. It then asserted that agents, denominated W, X, Y, and Z, had approached them and demanded the payment of bribes, the extension of loans to France, and an apology from President Adams for certain anti-French statements he supposedly had made in 1797. Adams, fearing for the safety of the envoys, did not wish to disclose the contents of the dispatch until the Americans had left France. The president sought to convey to Congress a sense of the situation without releasing the dispatches. Jefferson and other Republicans, however, were distrustful of Adams and successfully pressed for their disclosure.[182] The result of this political miscalculation was a dramatic upsurge of support for the Federalists. A bill was passed to distribute 10,000 copies of the dispatches, leaving the Republicans in complete disarray. As Abigail Adams put it, the "lower class of people" was "now roused."[183] The upper class was certainly in a similar state.

Underlying much of the fearmongering that was so characteristic of the 1790s were powerful cultural and racial currents. Federalist fears of the French and, more particularly, of armed black troops from Santo Domingo were sometimes, to say the least, wild: "Your houses and farms would fire, plunder and pillage! And your wives and sweethearts with ravishment and assassination, by hard outlandish sans-culotte Frenchmen!!"[184] The connection between anti-French sentiment and racial concerns was illustrated by one advertisement in a Federalist newspaper that advised that if appeasement rather than war was the option, Americans should move their wives, "or you may prove witnesses of their violation and expiring agonies, or if reserved for future infamy, may increase your families not only with a spurious, but with a colored breed. Remove your daughters unless you would be silent spectators of their being deflowered by the lusty Othellos."[185] Of course, Republican slaveholders, including Thomas Jefferson, had their own concerns about slave revolts. Theirs, however, were not linked to the French and did not translate into the creation of federal laws during this period.

For many Federalists, the struggle with the Republicans was akin to a biblical conflict between good and evil.[186] Indeed, much of their rhetoric may strike the contemporary observer as familiar in its linkage between a moral-religious discourse and ideological goals.[187] As *Porcupine's Gazette,* on July 19, 1798, put it, "Government should be a terror to evil-doers."[188] These Federalists believed that the Alien and Sedition laws were necessary to suppress a dangerous French faction, "French apostles of sedition,"[189] in the United States who acted at the behest of the Directory. They feared that what they saw happening in other European republics would take place in the United States if dramatic measures were not taken to prevent it. One should not retrospectively trivialize these concerns. As even the most distant observer of the Terror could attest, the dangers were real. What was most problematic for the Republicans, however, was the Federalist idea that the protection against this evil could come only from strong, centralized government power exercised first against noncitizens.

The link between evil and the foreign-born was quite explicitly made by some Federalists. Harrison Gray Otis of Massachusetts said that immigrants would "contaminate the purity and simplicity of the American character." Noah Webster stated that for each "good" European who entered the country, "we receive three or four discontented . . . men . . . the convicts, fugitives of justice, hirelings of France and disaffected off scourings of other nations." The abuse of foreigners "was the road to political favor in Massachusetts; and it was a high road that many Federalists trod."[190] For their part, as noted above, some Republicans also opposed immigration, but for very different political reasons.[191] The Republican newspaper *Aurora* noted in 1798 that immigration would bring "the friends of Order [the Federalists] . . . a numerous cargo of their dearly beloved aristocratical brethren."[192] The crucial difference was that the Federalist anti-immigration position was more directly linked to internal security and to a nascent social-control program. The Federalists were quite concerned about, in addition to the French, Irish and certain English immigrants whom they tended to view as the dregs of society. The Federalists particularly feared that Irish leaders were sympathetic to the ideals of the French Revolution and would pursue such goals in the United States. Harrison Gray Otis summarized this view when he said that he did not "wish to invite hordes of wild Irishmen nor the turbulent and disorderly of all parts of the world to come here with a view to disturb our tranquility, after having succeeded in the overthrow of their own Governments."[193]

The fact that the Irish tended to join the Republican Party also obviously concerned the Federalists greatly. Thus, it is not surprising that the first actions against noncitizens taken by the Federalists were to increase the residence period for naturalization from the two years required by the Act of 1790 to five years in the Act of 1795.[194] The longest naturalization waiting period was created by the Naturalization Act of 1798, which raised the requirement to fourteen years.[195] It appears clear that the aim of this law was to prevent the foreign-born, presumably Republican supporters, from voting for as long as possible.[196]

Though Adams was much more thoughtful and mild-mannered than his secretary of state, the dour Timothy Pickering, the president's public statements became noticeably more belligerent in both content and tone throughout the spring and summer of 1798.[197] Adams affected an increasingly warlike demeanor. He said that it would be cowardly not to fight, that war would be "a lesser evil than national dishonor," and that "neither Justice nor Moderation, can secure Us from a Participation in the War."[198]

The Alien Enemies Act and Alien Friends Act Debates

As we have seen, fundamentally contradictory visions of America as an "asylum for mankind" had long been apparent in various state and local immigration laws. The development of a unified nation required the creation of centralized federal systems of immigration entry controls and naturalization, which, in turn, forced consideration of important questions about the source and extent of government power. The most volatile questions arose when the power of government was sought to deport those already resident here. Such proposals involved not just the rights of immigrants but the nature and limits of federal government power. These problems were among the first to come to a head in the late eighteenth century. Ironically, they were among the last to be addressed by courts.

The least controversial legal manifestation of the warlike attitude developed by the Federalists was a law called the Alien Enemies Act.[199] Though clearly aimed at French aliens, it required as a trigger a declaration of war or imminent invasion. The Alien Enemies Act stated that, in such a case, "all natives, citizens, denizens or subjects of the hostile nation . . . shall be liable to be apprehended, restrained, secured and removed, as alien enemies." Unlike the more troubling Alien Friends Act, which was limited to two years, the Alien Enemies Act was envisioned as a permanent change to U.S. law and had broad bipartisan support. Indeed, it is still a part of the law of the United States.[200]

For some Federalists, the provisions of the Alien Enemies Act were not sufficiently strong to meet the threats they saw. They argued that further measures would be necessary "against the residents of alien enemies existing in the bosom of the country, as the root of all the evil which we are at present experiencing."[201] Harrison Gray Otis asserted that Venice, Switzerland, and Holland had been defeated by France because they had waited for a declaration of war before acting against French agents in their midst.[202] Nathaniel Smith noted that acts equivalent to war might surely be perpetrated by foreign governments and their nationals without a formal declaration of war. Otis proposed a law that would allow the removal of aliens whose government "shall authorize hostilities against the United States." He expressed concern that the United States, with or without a declaration of war, should be able to defend itself against "that crowd of spies and inflammatory agents which overspread the country like the locusts of Egypt, and who were continually attacking our liberties. Others spoke of "the cankerworm which is corroding in the heart of the country." John Allen of Connecticut went considerably further: he argued that the president should simply be granted unlimited discretionary power to deport any alien from the United States at any time for any reason.[203]

The Federalists ultimately prevailed with the passage of the "Act concerning aliens," also known as the Alien Friends Law.[204] Their first proposals, following Allen's lead, illustrate how far they were willing to go in pursuit of their vision of security. The Alien Friends bill, arising from the Federalist-controlled Senate, initially sought to give the president authority to deport any alien whom he judged to be "dangerous to the peace and safety of the United States." It further permitted the president to expel any foreigner whom he had "reasonable grounds to suspect" was "concerned in any treasonable or secret machinations against the government." There was no provision for jury trial, nor for any process other than delivery of a copy of the order "or leaving the same at his usual abode." Indeed, there was not even a requirement that the order of removal specify any particular findings on which it was based. The burden of proof for all issues, including a claim of citizenship, was placed on the alien. The law also envisioned a national registration requirement for aliens and a centralized surveillance system. Aliens could not remain in the country without a special presidential permit. Those who returned after deportation faced criminal prosecution and preclusion from citizenship.[205]

The deeply controversial nature of the bill was immediately apparent, and the debate in Congress—and later throughout the country—was fierce. Edward Livingston from New York called it "a sacrifice of the first-born offspring of freedom." It was expected by many Republicans to be defeated in the House, having been described by Benjamin Bache, publisher of the *Aurora*, as a "statutory monster now squeaking for existence" that "completely unmasked the principles and plans of the federal aristocratical . . . friends of order." Bache continued that "a numerous body of people are to be subjected to ruin at the arbitrary mandate of the President."[206] Jefferson described it as "a most detestable thing."[207] The opponents of the bill thus argued that it was beyond the powers delegated to the federal government by the Constitution, that it violated constitutional requirements of separation of powers, and that it infringed on an array of constitutional rights guaranteed to citizens and noncitizens alike. More general concerns about the rule of law also figured prominently in the public debate. Benjamin Bache sarcastically noted that at least the proposed law would not punish aliens because they were "suspected of being suspicious."[208]

The Federalist supporters of the bill met each of these charges by highlighting the extreme danger facing the country and the need for effective and expeditious government action. Their comments reflected both their trust in government and their deep distrust of foreigners. As to the problem of guilt by suspicion, for example, Gordon argued that "persons who come here with a view of overturning the government will not commit any overt act which shall bring them under the laws of the country."[209]

The constitutional delegation problem was posed most forcefully by Albert Gallatin, himself an immigrant. The question was whether the federal government had the power to deport alien "friends" at all. Gallatin (and others) pointed out that such power was not expressly delegated to the federal government in the Constitution, nor did they think that it was implied by any other power. Indeed, one of their more specific arguments was that the Tenth Amendment meant that the deportation power was reserved for the states or the people. They further argued that the migration clause prevented congressional action of this type before 1808. This argument, in various permutations, was also strongly made in the so-called Virginia and Kentucky Resolutions, in which Jefferson and Madison highlighted their view that the Constitution was primarily a pact among state governments and that the Aliens Act went beyond federal authority.[210] Though powerfully felt at the time, this argument, as we shall see, is the least relevant today.

Other Republican constitutional claims retain more current critical bite. James Madison, for example, suggested an important differentiation between the government's power over "alien enemies" and its power over those who came from friendly nations: "With respect to alien enemies, no doubt has been intimated as to the Federal authority over them . . . With respect to aliens who are not enemies, but members of nations in peace and amity with the United States, the power assumed by the Act of Congress is denied to be constitutional."[211]

It is not entirely clear from this passage whether Madison, like Gallatin, was again denying all federal governmental power to deport friendly aliens or focusing more on the particular type of power asserted by the Federalist legislation. If the latter, his critique of what might be termed the outer limits of discretionary social control deportation authority is not dissimilar to arguments made by some civil libertarians today. That is, one might accept power to deport even "friendly" noncitizens who violate immigration laws or commit crimes while denying government the power to do so solely on the basis of national origin, religion, or political opinion.[212] Republicans also denounced the bill as "an open, wanton, and undisguised attack on the guarantees of Civil Rights in the Constitution." They highlighted contradictions between the bill and the guarantees of the Fifth and Sixth Amendments. Some referred to its deportation aspects as "[the punishment of] transportation without a trial by jury." Others saw the bill as a constitutionally impermissible suspension of the right of habeas corpus.[213] Livingston described the process envisioned as "a secret and worse than inquisitorial tribunal [where] all is darkness, silence, mystery, and suspicion."[214]

The Federalists responded to the Republicans' structural constitutional arguments in a variety of ways, including citing the Preamble to highlight the generally broad power of sovereignty possessed by Congress.[215] Deportation was, however, most forcefully defended as part of the inherent power of the government to protect the country against foreign aggression. Although, as the later Sedition Act shows, the Federalists were equally concerned with aggression perpetrated by citizens, their initial focus on foreigners was quite specific. In Timothy Pickering's words, "he must be ignorant indeed who does not know that the Constitution was established for the protection and security of American citizens, and not of intriguing foreigners."[216]

All of these arguments implicate a fundamental question: does the Constitution protect noncitizens at all? The Republicans of the 1790s made the case for inclusion both textually and normatively. The textual point is basic: the Preamble and the relevant rights provisions of the Constitution, especially the Fifth Amendment, refer to "we the people" and "persons," not citizens. The normative arguments invariably included concerns about the extension of harsh government action from aliens to citizens, as described earlier. More fundamentally, Republicans offered a contractual theory that highlighted a link between allegiance and constitutional protection.[217] Livingston explained that those "alien friends . . . residing among us, are entitled to the protection of our laws, and . . . during their residence they owe a temporary allegiance to our government. If they are accused of violating this allegiance, the same laws which interpose in the case of a citizen must determine the truth of the accusation, and if found guilty they are liable to the same punishment."[218]

Others focused on the violation of what were asserted to be natural rights, such as freedom of speech, as well as common law rights, such as due process and trial by jury.[219] Many Federalists, conversely, relied strongly on the citizen-noncitizen line. They did not deny that the law was harsh and arbitrary. They simply believed that aliens, because they were not part of "We the people," had no relevant constitutional right to remain in the Unites States.

Rule-of-law concerns about the potential arbitrariness of the law and its highly discretionary quality inspired some of the best rhetoric of the day. Livingston warned that "a careless word, perhaps misrepresented, or never spoken, may be sufficient evidence; a look may destroy, an idle gesture may insure punishment; no innocence can protect, no circumspection can avoid the jealousy of suspicion; surrounded by spies, informers, and all that infamous herd which fatten under laws like this, the unfortunate stranger will never know either of the law, or of the accusation, or of the judgment until the moment it is put in execution; he will detest your tyranny, and fly from a land of desolators, inquisitions, and spies."[220]

Such arguments are especially interesting because they focus on the limits of government power against any person. Madison wrote that even if "aliens are not parties to the Constitution, it does not follow that the Constitution has vested in Congress an absolute power over them . . . If aliens had no rights under the Constitution, they might not only be banished, but even capitally punished, without a jury or the other incidents to a fair trial."[221]

The potential for unchecked, discretionary executive power also caused great concern. St. George Tucker put it, if the president "dislikes the face of a man, if he squints, if he be wrynecked . . . if he fails to make his obeisance as he passes or to shout 'long live the President' when he appears in public, all these may be grounds of suspicion for which the President will not be accountable to anyone but himself."[222] Livingston suggested that the combination of legislative, executive, and judicial powers in the same person "is the peculiar characteristic of despotism."[223] Despite such eloquent opposition, the Alien Friends bill passed the Senate on June 8, 1798, and the House on June 21. It was quickly signed by President Adams and went into effect immediately, with a two-year sunset provision.

The Enforcement and Effects of the Alien and Sedition Laws

Though the tone of Federalist discourse hardened in late 1798, the Aliens Friends Act was never specifically utilized by President Adams.[224] Nevertheless, the sense of insecurity among noncitizens was palpable.[225] As early as May 1798, before the law had actually been enacted, Jefferson noted that "the threatening appearances from the Alien Bills have so alarmed the French who are among us, that they are going off. A ship, chartered by themselves for this purpose, will sail within a fortnight for France . . . Among these, I believe, will be Volney who has in truth been the principle object aimed at by the law."[226]

Volney, a well-known French scientist and author who was seen by many Federalists as an especially dangerous disciple of French revolutionary thought, left the United States for France some three weeks before the Alien Friends Law went into effect.[227] With him on that ship was Victor Marie DuPont, the consul general of the French Republic, whose credentials had not been accepted by the United States. Secretary Pickering was so happy to see them go that he requested free passage for the ship and obtained similar guarantees for other ships bearing Frenchmen back to France from the United States.[228]

Unlike Volney, the French general Victor Collot, another major target of Federalist scrutiny, did not leave the country.[229] Shortly after the passage of the law, Pickering's attention thus turned to him. On October 11, 1798, Pickering requested that Adams sign three blank warrants for use against Collot, an associate named Sweitzer, and Pierre Samuel DuPont de Nemours. Adams agreed to this plan and signed the warrants. Rather than execute the warrants immediately, however, Pickering decided to wait in the hope of gaining further information about the activities of Collot in the United States. In late June 1799, word began to spread that

Collot was preparing to leave. At this point, Pickering, still hoping to gain further information, opposed his removal or even allowing him to leave the United States.[230]

A more poignant example of the effects of the Alien Friends law was that of Mederic-Louis-Elie Moreau de St. Mèry, a member of the French Assembly and a respected scholar, who had fled France for Philadelphia in 1794. Though St. Mèry counted among his acquaintances many officials, including John Adams, he found his name on the list of Frenchmen whom the administration sought to deport. Indeed, St. Mèry was reportedly advised by the French counsel in New York that "all those who have no love for Robespierism [sic] had better get out and get out quick."[231] It is reported that St. Mèry then had his friend Senator John Langdon of New Hampshire question John Adams about why he was placed on that list. The president's reply was reportedly, "nothing in particular, but he's too French."[232] The pressure and fear grew so great during this period that some of St. Mèry's friends reportedly gave him keys to shelters where he could take refuge with his family in the event of an attack on their home. Although this did not happen, St. Mèry and his family left the country for France in August 1798, as quickly as they could.

Noncitizens who were critical of the Federalist administration faced both deportation under the Aliens Act and criminal prosecution under the Sedition Act. One of the most well-known examples was John Daly Burk, who had been born in Ireland and expelled from Trinity College in Dublin following charges of Deism and Republicanism. Burk had fled Ireland as a fugitive from prosecution for sedition. As editor of the *New York Time Piece,* Burk had become one of the strongest Republican voices in the country.[233] Although he knew that Pickering was watching his words and writings carefully, Burk was bold. He reportedly had said of the French coming to America that "he wished to God they would, when every scoundrel in favor of this government would be put to the guillotine."[234] Burk later denied these statements. Nevertheless, he was arrested by two U.S. marshals, pursuant to a warrant signed by President Adams, and charged with seditious libel. Pickering, thought hard about how to proceed. "If Burk be an alien," wrote Pickering, "no man is a fitter object for the operation of the Alien Act." To be safe, though, Pickering decided to proceed first with a criminal prosecution for sedition and then to deport Burk.[235] As Pickering put it, "even if Burk should prove to be an alien, it may be expedient to punish him for his libels before he is sent away." Burk's bail was paid by Aaron Burr, as part of what some historians and contemporaries viewed as "a shrewd play for the Irish vote in New York."[236] Burr was also able to convince the president and Pickering to refrain from prosecuting Burk in exchange for Burk's agreement to leave the country immediately. Apparently because of the federal government's unwillingness to pay the cost of returning Burk to Europe, however, he was able to stay in the United States, making his way to Virginia, where he adopted a pseudonym and disappeared. Ironically, he was killed in a duel with a Frenchman in 1808 after having referred to the French as "a pack of rascals."[237]

Timothy Pickering's list of potential candidates for deportation was longer than that of President Adams. Pickering was interested in deporting Dr. Joseph Priestly, who had settled in Pennsylvania in 1794. Priestly had been driven out of England by a mob in Birmingham that had burned his chapel and destroyed his house, ostensibly because of his views on religion and his support for the French. Adams, however, who had corresponded with Priestly in the past, declined to authorize proceedings against him, writing that "he is as weak as water, as unstable as Reuben or the wind. His influence is not an atom in the world."[238]

It remains an interesting question as to why there were no formal deportations pursuant to the Alien Friends Act. Historians generally concur that the reasons include the moderation of John Adams combined with "the mass exodus of frightened foreigners even before the passage of the law."[239] By late 1798, war fever had cooled considerably and the cost of Federalist policies also became more of an issue. As Jefferson, anticipating opposition to federal tax increases, put it, "the doctor is now on his way to cure, in the guise of a tax gatherer."[240] It also became increasingly clear to the Federalists that the Alien Act was falling against the tide of immigration and the increasing acceptance of foreigners.[241] Part of the explanation may also be the vigorous enforcement of the Sedition Act. As an unprecedented extension "of the authority of the federal government into the lives of American citizens," however, the critique of the Sedition Act had powerful contemporaneous support, and ultimately undergirded the progressive expansion of free speech protections by the Supreme Court in the twentieth century.[242] The path of the law regarding noncitizens' rights, notwithstanding similar rhetorical flourishes by the critics of the Alien Friends Act, has been much less clear.

A welter of different concerns, in the crucible of an incendiary time, had been forged into extreme laws that ultimately heralded the end of Federalist power. The historically victorious Republican critique of the Alien and Sedition Acts was itself contradictory, however. It provided an unstable base for future opponents of later-enacted deportation laws. Jeffersonian concerns about highly centralized, discretionary federal power, which may resonate powerfully for contemporary civil libertarians, were linked to states'-rights positions that supported slavery. Assertions of aliens' rights were often motivated more by electoral pragmatism than by human or constitutional rights concerns.

Still, if the powerful rhetoric of the Republican critics of the Federalists' "Aliens laws" resonates today more than that of the laws' supporters, it is for reasons that should be respected: it speaks to our best constitutional traditions, our highest aspirations, our proudest heritage, and the most expansive egalitarian vision of the nation of immigrants ideal. It reminds us of the transitory nature of fear and of the responsibility of a mature constitutional legal system to transcend fear and to balance it against more long-lasting concerns.

Part 3: Indian Removal, Fugitive Slave Laws, and "Colonization"

Indian Removal

> Conquest gives a title which the courts of the conqueror cannot deny.
>
> —*Johnson v. M'Intosh* (1823)

A significant part of the U.S. deportation story is the forced movement of indigenous people, an antecedent to deportation in two ways: formally, as sovereignty-based legal doctrine, and functionally. Blackstone wrote that the colonies had been obtained "either by right of conquest and driving out the natives . . . or by treaties." Within the ellipse, however, he had confessed that such "right of conquest" and treaties were undertaken with "what natural justice I shall not at present enquire."[243] Formulations such as the "right of conquest"—enhanced by ideas of

Anglo-Saxon superiority, dubious theories of "civilization," and sovereign power—were remarkably similar to those used in the late nineteenth-century Chinese cases. Indeed, as T. Alexander Aleinikoff has noted, Indians were, from the earliest days of European settlement, treated like aliens in many respects. Later, in what still stands as one of the most brutal and widespread forced movements of a people in history, "Indians were forced west—promised land west of the Alleghenies, west of the Mississippi, west of wherever whites wanted to settle next."[244]

There are striking similarities between plenary power doctrine in so-called Indian law and that of immigration law.[245] This is especially clear if one compares U.S. government actions to remove Indians from their land—and the legal doctrinal justifications for those actions—with later deportation laws. These similarities help to answer the question of how and why the Congress, and then the Supreme Court, so easily accepted the move from exclusion to removal. By the late nineteenth century, legal Indian removal was a well-accepted and well-understood conceptual model. It involved forced movement, by the federal government, of non-European people.[246] Originally conceived of as a species of foreign-relations law, Indian law essentially conceptualized its subjects as noncitizens within U.S. territory.[247] Their structural constitutional, treaty-based, and individual rights claims all faced insurmountable doctrinal hurdles grounded in a plenary power doctrine that was essentially the same as that imposed on noncitizens in the *Chinese Exclusion Case* and *Fong Yue Ting*.[248] The national government was seen to have "inherent and plenary power" not only over immigrants, but also "over 'foreigners' already in the midst of a colonial country—unassimilated, tribal, noncitizen, indigenous peoples."[249]

Forced removal from U.S. territory was a central feature of Indian law long before it became such for immigrants. As Philip Frickey has noted, federal Indian law was "the product both of the colonization of the western hemisphere by European sovereigns and of the corresponding displacement of indigenous peoples."[250] The first ratified treaty with an Indian tribe, The Treaty of Fort Pitt of 1778, was signed with the Delaware Nation and conceptualized the tribe as a foreign sovereign nation. The treaty allowed Washington's army "free passage through their country."[251] Though this model obviously did not endure, it is ironic that some of the first removal laws in the New World authorized the removal of white settlers from Indian territory. Provisions in virtually every Indian treaty negotiated immediately before and shortly after the adoption of the U.S. Constitution confirmed Indian jurisdiction over non-Indians who entered Indian lands. The following language from a 1795 treaty is typical: "If any citizen of the United States, or any other white person or persons, shall presume to settle upon the lands now relinquished by the United States, such citizen or other person shall be out of the protection of the United States; and the Indian tribe, on whose land the settlement shall be made, may drive off the settler, or punish him in such manner as they shall think fit."[252] An earlier treaty with the Cherokee had granted the Indians the discretion to punish, or not punish, such settlers "as they please."[253]

The tension between a model of formal legal recognition of Indian sovereignty equivalent to that with foreign nations and the realities of European colonialism emerged in 1823 in the first major Supreme Court decision regarding Indian law: *Johnson v. M'Intosh.*[254] The case arose out of a dispute over a land title. One claimant traced his right to a conveyance from a tribe to a non-Indian; the other relied on a later sale by the tribe to the United States, which had "patented the land in fee simple." The defendants denied that Indians had any effective sovereign rights to their land: "Even if it should be admitted that the Indians were originally an independent people," they argued, they had ceased to be such. "A nation that has passed under the dominion of another, is no longer a sovereign state."[255] This argument clearly presaged that of the *Fong Yue Ting* Court, citing the same chapter of Vattel's treatise on which the *Fong Yue Ting* opinion would later rely. Thus, it was argued that the Indians were "subject to the sovereignty of the United States" and therefore "destitute of the most essential rights which belong to [citizens]." They were "perpetual inhabitants with diminutive rights."[256]

The 1823 Court, though not going quite so far, found the U.S. title to prevail. In his opinion, Chief Justice Marshall developed a basic framework for federal Indian law, derived from the justifications for European colonization of the New World. A principle had developed among European sovereigns whereby "discovery gave title to the government by whose subjects, or by whose authority, it was made, against all other European governments, which title might be consummated by possession." Thus, the Indians' lands could be acquired only by the European "discovering sovereign," not by any private party or lesser sovereign. The "discovering sovereign" could extinguish Indian title "either by purchase or by conquest."[257]

But what was the Court's view of the legal status of the indigenous people of this continent? Marshall's opinion is not as clear as the defendants' argument, but it is similar. Discussing the historical relationship between "the discoverer and the natives," Marshall wrote, "In the establishment of these relations, the rights of the original inhabitants were, in no instance, entirely disregarded; but were necessarily, to a considerable extent, impaired. They were admitted to be the rightful occupants of the soil, with a legal as well as just claim to retain possession of it, and to use it according to their own discretion; but their rights to complete sovereignty, as independent nations, were necessarily diminished." This model continued in his view, post-independence, as the United States acceded to "an exclusive right to extinguish the Indian title of occupancy, either by purchase or by conquest; and gave also a right to such a degree of sovereignty, as the circumstances of the people would allow them to exercise."[258] Phillip Frickey has noted that John Marshall did not engage in much normative justification, which is perhaps just as well. Rather, the chief justice felt that the Court should embrace this approach "for institutional reasons." It would be impossible for the Court to undo by law what had already occurred in fact. Thus, in *Johnson,* the Court "did not mediate the tension between colonialism and constitutional government as much as it simply preferred the former."[259]

To be sure, Marshall did offer some sympathetic observations in dicta. But at base, the justice whose historical place was secured by the maxim that "it is emphatically the province and duty of the judicial department to say what the law is" accepted a notably more deferential posture in this realm.[260] The rights of the conquered were not justiciable—indeed, they were not even clearly rights—but depended on "humanity," "public opinion," and "wise policy." Title by conquest, he wrote,

is acquired and maintained by force. The conqueror prescribes its limits. Humanity, however, acting on public opinion, has established, as a general rule, that the conquered shall not be wantonly oppressed, and that their condition shall remain as eligible as is compatible with the objects of the conquest. Most usually, they are incorporated with the victorious nation, and become subjects or citizens of the government with which they are connected . . . Where this incorporation is practicable, humanity demands, and a wise policy requires, that the rights of the conquered to property should remain unimpaired; that the new subjects should be governed as equitably as the old, and that confidence in their security should gradually banish the painful sense of being separated from their ancient connexions, [sic] and united by force to strangers.[261]

This, as we shall see, is essentially the same tack later adopted by the *Fong Yue Ting* Court. Indeed, more than fifty years before the Chinese were deported, this judicial deference also facilitated formal Indian removal systems.

In 1830, the Indian Removal Act was signed into law by President Andrew Jackson, a man who had made his reputation as an "Indian-fighter."[262] As the very name of the law indicated, removal was now clear federal government policy, though it had taken place in various ways for decades before this. Jackson, in 1830, referred to "the benevolent policy of the government, steady pursued for nearly thirty years, in relation with the removal of the Indians beyond the white settlements." He suggested that it was "approaching to a happy consummation."[263]

How does one justify the forced removal of people or, more to the point, of a people? One might, as Justice Field did in the *Chinese Exclusion Case,* describe the threat posed by the group as "a menace to our civilization." One might seek goals of "public peace and stability."[264] And one might also paternalistically describe forced removal as a benefit for the affected group. Jackson said that removal would "separate the Indians from immediate contact with the settlements of whites; enable them to pursue happiness in their own way and under their own rude institutions; . . . retard the progress of decay, which is lessening their numbers, and perhaps cause them gradually, under the protection of the government and through the influences of good counsels, to cast off their savage habits and become an interesting, civilized, and Christian community."[265]

Similarly, Thomas McKenney, federal superintendent of Indian affairs, had written in support of removal that "the paths of the wilderness are pressed by the fallen bodies of starved and expiring Indians." The judgment of many historians has been harsher, however. Patricia Nelson Limerick has written that "Indian removal in the 1830s found its place as one of the greater acts of inhumanity and cruelty in American history."[266]

The new law established a national policy of removal of tribes to land west of the Mississippi River. It expressly required tribal consent through treaty for any removal, reflecting long-simmering legitimacy concerns.[267] Thus, by the mid-nineteenth century, a regime of Indian removal law had developed that was ostensibly based on consent but was also legitimized in large part by "white man's burden" reasoning.[268] It also was seen as analogous to federal power over foreign affairs because it dealt with a "foreign" people within the United States. This was a trope that appeared elsewhere. Indeed, Justice Taney would allude to the foreign status of Indians in dicta in the *Dred Scott* case: "These Indian Governments were regarded and treated as foreign Governments, as much so as if an ocean had separated the red man from the white . . . and the people who compose these Indian political communities have always been treated as foreigners not living under our Government."[269]

Thirty years later, in *Elk v. Wilkins*, the Court held that an Indian born in the United States and living apart from his tribe was not a citizen under the Fourteenth Amendment and that Congress must confer such citizenship by treaty or statute. The Court reasoned that Indians were "no more 'born in the United States and subject to the jurisdiction thereof'" than children of foreigners born abroad or the U.S.-born children "of ambassadors or other public ministers of foreign nations."[270]

Before this *denouement*, however, the Court vacillated on how "foreign" Indians born in the United States were. The issue arose in the context of questions about federal versus state power. The 1831 case *Cherokee Nation v. Georgia* was a challenge brought by the tribe against a series of harsh Georgia laws. The basic issue was whether the Georgia legislature had acted outside of its authority under the U.S. constitution. Chief Justice Marshall dismissed the case, holding that the Supreme Court lacked original jurisdiction, because the Cherokee Nation was not a "foreign state." Marshall accepted that a tribe is "a distinct political society, separated from others, capable of managing its own affairs and governing itself." He then, however, determined that the tribes were not equivalent to foreign sovereigns but rather were "domestic dependent nations" that "occupy a territory to which we assert a title independent of their will, which must take effect in point of possession when their right of possession ceases." They were so far from equivalent that Marshall used a starkly paternalistic metaphor. The Indians were, he said, "in a state of pupilage. Their relation to the United States resembles that of a ward to his guardian."[271]

Marshall, as he had done in *M'Intosh,* offered some thoughts about the underlying justice of the Cherokees' claim that, though of no help to the Cherokee at the time, are worth recalling:

> If courts were permitted to indulge their sympathies, a case better cal-culated to excite them can scarcely be imagined. A people once nu-merous, powerful, and truly independent, found by our ancestors in the quiet and uncontrolled possession of an ample domain, gradually sinking beneath our superior policy, our arts and our arms, have yielded their lands by successive treaties, each of which contains a solemn guarantee of the residue, until they retain no more of their formerly ex-tensive territory than is deemed necessary to their comfortable subsis-tence. To preserve this remnant, the present application is made.[272]

Though surely moving, such words resonate more for the implicit help-lessness Marshall seems to have assumed as a judge in the face of such history and such policies.

The next year, however, the Marshall Court returned to Indian law in *Worcester v. Georgia,* a case that arose when the state imprisoned two white missionaries for refusing to obtain state permission to be on the reservation and to swear a loyalty oath to the state. The issue was whether Georgia law applied on the Cherokee reservation. The Court held that Georgia law was preempted by the special type of sovereign re-lationship that existed between the tribe and the federal government. But what was the nature of this sovereignty? The brutal history of the re-lationship between white colonizers and the Indians was again to be nei-ther fully ignored nor fully redressed. As Marshall deftly and tragically put it: "power, war, conquest, give rights, which, after possession, are conceded by the world; and which can never be controverted by those on whom they descend."[273]

Marshall limned a version of depreciated sovereignty—effective as against the states and sufficient to control entry and permit the forced removal of whites, even if ultimately subsidiary to federal government power: "The Cherokee nation . . . is a distinct community occupying its own territory, with boundaries accurately described, in which the laws of Georgia can have no force, and which the citizens of Georgia have no right to enter, but with the assent of the Cherokees themselves, or in conformity with treaties, and with the acts of congress."[274] He concluded that "the whole intercourse" was vested in the United States government.[275]

Worcester was an important conceptual victory for the tribes in its recognition of some rights and of some sovereign power as against the states. It did, however, leave open an important question that was to become crucial to deportation law: would the exercise of federal government power face any meaningful judicial review?[276] Indeed, even "depreciated" sovereignty was questioned by Andrew Jackson, who reportedly said in reference to *Worcester,* "John Marshall has made his decision: now let him enforce it!"[277]

From the perspective of the Cherokee, the recognition of their sovereignty was a rather Pyrrhic success because the federal government removed them from Georgia soon thereafter.[278] A similar pattern developed between whites and other so-called civilized tribes: the Seminole in Florida, the Creek in Alabama and Georgia, and the Chickisaw and Choctaw in Mississippi. Like the Cherokee, they were forced to move from the lands on which they had lived for generations and to settle in Oklahoma. By 1840, more than 70,000 Indians had been forced west across the Mississippi. This forced march of removal has become known as the "Trails of Tears," during which thousands died as a result of famine, disease, harsh conditions, and exhaustion.[279]

Federal government actions to remove Indians from their lands continued vigorously and systematically through the Civil War.[280] One of the most tragic episodes took place in 1863–1864, when Kit Carson forcibly gathered some 8,000 Navajos and forced them on the "Long Walk," which took them more than 300 miles from their homes to Bosque Redondo, a desolate area of land in eastern New Mexico.[281] Many died on the arduous journey, and four years of horrible conditions followed before undrinkable water, disease, insect infestation, and lack of wood compelled the government, following a congressional investigation, to return the Navajo to their ancestral homes.[282]

The Rise of Plenary Power

Over time, increased white settlement in the west rendered the removal approach increasingly unworkable. Following the Civil War, the policy of dealing with Indians as separate—albeit dependent—nations gave way to a new model.[283] The view of Indian sovereignty in the "Era of Allotment and Assimilation" was marked by a House rider to the Appropriations Act of 1871 that said, "[n]o Indian nation or tribe within the territory of the United States shall be acknowledged or recognized as an independent nation, tribe, or power with whom the United States may contract by treaty."[284]

Assimilation was, of course, not a new idea. Indeed, John Marshall had written most optimistically about it in *M'Intosh*, when he envisioned how, after conquest, "The new and old members of the society mingle with each other; the distinction between them is gradually lost, and they make one people."[285] In the postbellum environment, whites supported this new approach for a wide variety of reasons, ranging from a desire to "civilize" the Indians to the coveting of their land. "Friends of the Indians" also saw a grim reality: Indians would be able to protect themselves from the settlers and the federal government's pattern of breaching treaties only if they could become citizens, voters, and individual landowners.[286]

Still, Indians were deprived of more than two-thirds of their land base as a result of the so-called allotment system.[287] Allotment has been described as "arguably the most disastrous policy in Indian affairs next to the outright massacre or forced removal of Indians from their homelands."[288]

As Nell Jessup Newton has noted, with the end of the treaty-making era, "Indian law became more a matter of domestic law, with Indians regarded as subjects to be governed, rather than foreign nationals." Indeed, as a mark of the new internalized view of Indian law, supervision and appellate control over the Commissioner of Indian Affairs were removed from the secretary of war and given to the secretary of the interior.[289] This was also the period of the romanticized "classic western Indian battles," recreated in innumerable Hollywood films and television shows. Such "wars" were largely a vestigial remnant of conflicting sovereign nations; military resistance was the exception, not the rule.[290] But the violent reality was terrible. Following the Civil War, the U.S. Army, together with civilian contractors, caused deliberate starvation by destroying such Indian food sources as the buffalo.[291] They also engaged in a series of brutal massacres, including the murder of hundreds, if not thousands, of Indian men, women, and children.[292] The last Indian tribe to surrender, 300 survivors of the Chiricahua Apache, did so in 1886.[293] They were then incarcerated in military camps for a generation until 1913, when they were divided into two groups and moved to reservations far from ancestral lands, surrounded by traditional rivals.[294]

During this period, the legal system had to reconcile powerful underlying contradictions between assimilationist statutes and existing treaty obligations. The Supreme Court thus developed a new rationale to justify federal authority over Indians. Building on the federal supremacy aspects and the ward-guardianship metaphor of *Johnson v. M'Intosh* and *Cherokee Nation v. Georgia,* the Court developed a solution to the Indian question that was essentially the same as that used by Justice Field in the *Chinese Exclusion Case:* extra-constitutional "plenary" power. In response to an 1883 Supreme Court decision overturning the conviction of a Sioux for the murder of another tribe member on the Sioux reservation, Congress, in 1885, had passed the Major Crimes Act, which made certain crimes federal offenses if committed by Indians against each other in Indian country, whether or not within the boundaries of any state.[295] In 1886, the Major Crimes Act was challenged in *United States v. Kagama.*[296] The case involved fundamental questions of federal power: Did Congress have the power to criminalize such acts? Did the law infringe on state sovereignty? In an opinion that has been well described as "an embarrassment of constitutional theory," the Supreme Court began to develop the idea that Congress had "plenary power" over Indian affairs.[297] The Court noted that Indian tribes had long been seen as "semi-independent," with limited authority over "internal and social relations."[298] But it confirmed that they were not nations. Indian sovereignty, said the Court, was not recognized by the Constitution, which only recognized two sovereigns—the states and the federal government. The Court thus said that Indians "within the geographical limits" of the United States had to submit to one U.S. sovereign or the other. The Court then held that federal sovereignty controlled. But this conclusion raised a dilemma. What was the source of such federal authority? The Court could not rely on federal power to legislate within the territories, as the land in question was in California.[299] The constitutional power to regulate Indian commerce was also not viewed as a possible basis for decision at that time, due to the lack of a direct nexus between commerce and a federal criminal code applicable within the states.[300] Nor was a treaty involved.[301] The solution in *Kagama,* like that in the later *Chinese*

Exclusion Case, was "inherent" power.[302] The Court saw analogues to early decisions regarding the power to legislate within the territories. The *Doctrine of Discovery,* said the Court, gave the United States "ultimate title" over Indian land wherever it was located. This ownership interest gave the federal government the right to govern Indians on such land. The Court also noted the history of federal supremacy over the states in Indian affairs, describing the tribes as "the wards of the nation." Moreover, as it was soon to note about the Chinese, "[b]ecause of the local ill feeling, the people of the States where they are found are often their deadliest enemies."[303]

Ironically, the *Kagama* decision appeared on the same day as *Yick Wo v. Hopkins,* in which the Court invalidated San Francisco ordinances designed to drive Chinese laundries out of business on the equal protection ground that "no reason for [the laws] . . . exists except hostility to the race and nationality to which the petitioners belong."[304] Chinese residents of California who surely celebrated *Yick Wo* likely did not pay as much attention to *Kagama.* But perhaps they should have. Because three years later, the Supreme Court's model of inherent power would turn to immigration law and, soon after that, to deportation.

This apotheosis of federal power coincided with the near-complete destruction of the Indian population in North America. The 1890 census reported that an estimated population of 10 to 18 million Indian inhabitants of North America had been reduced since contact with the Europeans to approximately a quarter million in the United States.[305] The full story of this destruction is almost too horrible to comprehend. Disease, much of it deliberately induced, was a major factor, as were centuries of aggressive wars, slavery, and forced removal.[306]

Then came the 1903 decision in *Lone Wolf v. Hitchcock,* which has been called "the Indians' *Dred Scott* decision."[307] The Court, sustaining an Allotment Act against challenges based on alleged treaty violations and on due process grounds, easily dismissed the tribe's treaty claim. It ruled that congressional statutory abrogation of treaties was simply not subject to judicial review.[308] A due process claim also failed, this time through dramatic expansion of the reasoning in *Kagama.* In sum, said the Court, "Plenary authority over the tribal relations of the Indians has been exercised by Congress from the beginning, and the power has always been deemed a political one, not subject to be controlled by the judicial department of the government."[309] If there were any doubt about the link in the Court's mind between immigration law and Indian law, the next sentence would assuage it: "But, as with treaties made with foreign nations . . . the legislative power might pass laws in conflict with treaties made with the Indians." Though this doctrine had other antecedents, the case specifically cited in support of it was the *Chinese Exclusion Case.*

Following *Lone Wolf,* the Indian plenary power doctrine was as complete as that of deportation law in *Fong Yue Ting:* congressional power over Indians now apparently faced no constitutional limitations and no judicial oversight at all.

Slave Laws, Racial Exclusion, and Removal

It is impossible for us to remain happy if, after manumission, they remain among us.

—James Galloway of North Carolina, quoted in Henry N. Sherwood, "Early Negro Deportation Projects," *Mississippi Valley Historical Review* (March 1916)

SLAVERY

Once deportation law is conceived, even in part, as a system of social control largely deployed against people of color, then its relationship to slavery law becomes easier to see.[310] Beyond functional similarities, there are specific historical links. Slavery and special restrictions on the entry, movement, and residence of people of African ancestry were fundamentally related to the development of the post–Civil War deportation system.[311] Such laws offered well-developed, well-known conceptual models for future deportation laws. They rendered the late-nineteenth-century deportation system used against the Chinese less strange to the American palate than it might have been otherwise. In particular, the Fugitive Slave Law of 1850 broke important ground as a large, federal, bureaucratized system for the forced movement of people.

Slavery and nascent ideas of race had inspired laws of exclusion and removal from the earliest period of national legal development. Many whites clearly dreaded the thought that African Americans would ever demand full political and social equality.[312] Some state laws restricted the entry of free black people, while others required the posting of sureties.[313] Slaveholding states in particular found the very presence of free African Americans dangerous to the maintenance of the slave system, as it was feared that they would inspire and support slave escapes and revolts.[314] West Indian immigrants, seen as potential black revolutionaries, created particular anxiety. Free states also enacted such race-based exclusion laws, often motivated in large part by fears that slave owners would free slaves who could no longer work and that these people would be long-term financial and social burdens.[315]

Race-based removal laws were also common. Slave states had long used transportation abroad as a specific punishment against slaves—in effect, the first systematic international deportation regime in the United States.[316] As a precursor to later post-entry social control deportation laws, many Southern states added transportation and banishment as a punishment for criminal acts by free African Americans. Such banishment was frequently imposed after the convicted person had served a prison sentence.[317] There was no question that banishment was considered punishment. Virginia's 1823 law provided that "when any free negro or mulatto shall be convicted of an offence, now by Law punishable by imprisonment in the Jail and Penitentiary-house for more than two years, such person, instead of the confinement now prescribed by Law, shall be punished with stripes, at the discretion of the jury, shall moreover be adjudged to be sold as a slave, and transported and banished beyond the limits of the United States."[318]

Some of the cases construing such laws bear interesting similarities to modern criminal deportation cases that turn on the potential length of a criminal sentence.[319] One 1824 Virginia case, involving "a free man of color," considered at some length whether a criminal sentence for larceny of "not less than one, nor more than three years" satisfied the statutory requirement for banishment and transportation that the crime be punishable "for a period exceeding two years." The Virginia Supreme Court held that it did, and the convicted man was thus sentenced to receive "thirty-nine stripes on his bare back . . . [and to be] sold as a slave, and transported and banished beyond the limits of the United States."[320]

The most extreme example of a bridge between slavery and deportation law was an attempt by Arkansas to deport all free African Americans from the state just before the Civil War.[321] These laws had deep roots. In 1783, James Madison wrote of his slave Billy, who, due to his love of liberty, was not "fit as a companion" for other slaves but for whom the harsh punishment of transportation would be unjust.[322] Earlier still, a 1705 Pennsylvania law authorized transportation of any "Negro," whether slave or free, who was convicted of attempted rape or serious theft.[323] South Carolina and Virginia had similar laws. Indeed, Virginia, in 1691, had also mandated the banishment of any white who married "a negro, mulatto, or an Indian."[324]

These laws were, of course, also integral to the developing understanding of the meaning of U.S. citizenship. In 1820, debate over the proposed Missouri constitution—which barred the entry of free "blacks and mulattoes"—sparked vigorous debate in Congress over whether free, native-born African Americans were citizens and therefore protected by the privileges and immunities clause of the Constitution.[325] The Missouri Compromise resulted in two radically different citizenship regimes.[326] In the north, free, native-born African Americans were, for the most part, accepted as legal citizens, albeit with significant restrictions on their rights. In the South, however, they were generally seen as, at most, aliens. They were referred to variously as "subjects," "denizens," and "quasi-citizens."[327] In the minds of many Southerners, such second-class categories were fundamentally insurmountable. In an 1822 case, a Kentucky court noted that the law "indisputably requires something more to make a citizen, than it does to make a subject."[328]

Indeed, slave states treated free African Americans like aliens in many respects: for example, by requiring them to register and to prove their status. North Carolina required all "urban free Negroes" to register and to wear a shoulder patch with the word "FREE" on it.[329] Virginia maintained an official "Register of Free Negroes." Some governments enacted restrictions on the trips free African Americans could take outside of the state by sometimes blocking their return—a regime analogous to that later faced by Chae Chan Ping.[330]

Foreign entrants, particularly free black entrants from Saint Domingue, were sometimes barred by states on racial grounds.[331] Such laws clearly provided models for federal legislation. The very first federal immigration law after the Alien and Sedition Acts was an 1803 statute, inspired by the arrival of immigrants from Guadeloupe, that banned the entry of foreign blacks into states that had enacted laws forbidding their entry.[332] The statute prohibited the entry of "any negro, mulatto, or other person of color, not being a native, a citizen, or registered seaman of the United States."[333]

Litigation over state laws that excluded free people of color was an important part of the development of Supremacy Clause jurisprudence in the nineteenth century and thus an important building block in federal control of immigration.[334] The 1823 case of *Elkison v. Deliesseline* involved the Negro Seaman's Act of 1822 which had been adopted by South Carolina in the aftermath of the crushing of the so-called Denmark Vesey conspiracy.[335] That law barred the entry of any "free negroes or persons of color." In fact, it specifically required that such persons be "seized and confined in gaol until such vessel shall clear out and depart from this state." The law was challenged in federal court by Henry Elkison, a Jamaican sailor. It was struck down by Justice William Johnson, on circuit, as an unconstitutional regulation of commerce by a state.[336] The same view was soon adopted by the Supreme Court in 1824.[337]

THE FUGITIVE SLAVE LAWS

Fugitive slave laws, with roots that extended back to the most fundamental constitutional compromises, contained many elements in common with later deportation laws. A 1902 editorial in the *Nation*, criticizing a proposed extension of the 1892 deportation law that had been aimed at the Chinese, saw this clearly. The writer first remarked on the "incredible" fact that the Senate would even consider a bill that "would make every honest student and teacher from a friendly nation liable to . . . deportation, or to branding as a criminal." The editorial then noted that certain requirements of "the bill [bring] to mind the conditions in the country at the time of the Fugitive Slave Law."[338]

The 1850 Fugitive Slave Act was a federal law that forced movement of people on the basis of their legal status and their race. It involved administrative proceedings, with only minimal judicial review by Article III judges (though it did envision a judicial process for jurisdictional questions). The involuntary movement of an affected person was not considered punishment or criminal process. The law did not generally permit a jury trial. It provided only the most minimal constitutional protections for the alleged runaway slave, and it applied to people who were generally (and by 1857, conclusively) regarded as lacking the rights of citizens. To be sure, there were important differences between the antebellum Fugitive Slave Act and the postwar deportation laws. The former laws involved proceedings instituted by private parties, not the government, for the return of what they deemed to be property to a state in which such property rights in human beings were recognized.[339] To weigh the strength of the case for fugitive slave laws as model and precedent for federal deportation laws, this section examines how they actually operated, the legal questions they raised, the systems they created, and how they were viewed by legal actors and the general population.

Fugitive slave laws derived from the Constitution itself, which provides that "no person held to service or labor in one State . . . escaping into another, shall . . . be discharged from such service or labor; but shall be delivered up on claim of the party, to whom such service or labor may be due."[340] Although this provision also applied to indentured servants, its primary applicability to runaway slaves was certainly clear to the drafters. The first federal Fugitive Slave Law was passed by the Congress in 1793 following a Pennsylvania case in which a free black man had been seized and taken to Virginia. The white men who captured him were charged with kidnapping, and the governor of Pennsylvania sought their extradition. Virginia refused to comply with that request.[341] The 1793 statute authorized a slave owner to apply to a U.S. judge for a certificate of return for the slave to the state from which the slave had fled.[342] As federal judges were rather scarce at the time, the implementation of this law was often quite inefficient, inconvenient, and dangerous. The law did not authorize the issuance of warrants, nor did it allow federal marshals to aid in the pursuit and capture of fugitives.[343] In the later view of the Virginia Assembly, it required "the master . . . a stranger [to] go into a free state, seize his slave without form or process of law, and unaccompanied by a single civil officer . . . carry that slave, in the face of a fanatical and infuriated population . . . a distance of two or three hundred miles to the place where the judge may happen to reside [with] no provision in that law by which the judgment can be enforced, or the power of the national government be invoked, through its marshals and officers, to sustain the rights of property thus adjudicated in his favor."[344]

The 1793 law also became increasingly controversial in the North for very different reasons. Apart from general antislavery sentiment, Northerners feared the intrusion of Southern "slave catchers" into their communities. A particular concern was the kidnapping of free people by those who were motivated by the offer of large rewards by Southern states for the return of fugitive slaves.[345] As a result, some free states passed personal liberty laws designed to protect free black residents.

A key test for such laws was the 1842 case of *Prigg v. Pennsylvania.*[346] A Pennsylvania personal liberty law provided for sanctions against anyone "who should take or carry away from the State any negro with the intention of selling him, as a slave, or of detaining or causing to be detained such negro as a slave for life."[347] Though primarily designed to protect free people from kidnapping, the state law also could be construed to apply to fugitive slaves who had sought refuge in Pennsylvania.[348]

Edward Prigg, an agent for a slave owner, arrested Margarette Morgan as a fugitive slave in 1837. He removed her by force, along with her children, to Maryland. Prigg was later arrested, tried, and convicted pursuant to the Pennsylvania statute. He challenged the constitutionality of the law before the U.S Supreme Court. The issue was not slavery itself. Indeed, the lawyers for Pennsylvania conceded that slaves were neither parties to the Constitution nor embraced by the phrase "we, the people."[349]

What Pennsylvania did claim, however, was "the right of legislating upon this subject so as to bring [slave catchers] under legal restraint" to prevent them from "taking a free man." Their main concerns were for the state's right to protect its free inhabitants by prescribing a regime of "due process of law." The risks to free black people were, however, quite clear: "Now, in a slaveholding state colour always raises a presumption of slavery, which is directly contrary to the presumption in a free or non-slaveholding state; for in the latter, prima facie, every man is a free man. If, then, under this most monstrous assumption of power, a free man may be seized, where is our boasted freedom?"[350]

The opinion of the Court was written by Joseph Story.[351] First, he wrote, the power to legislate on matters involving fugitive slaves was "exclusive in the national government." Although states were not bound to enforce the law through their own judicial systems, the national government was so bound, due to the constitutional Fugitive Slave Law cited earlier.[352] There was no doubt, said the Court, that slave owners had the right to enter any state and to seize and recapture slaves so long as they could do it without "any breach of the peace, or any illegal violence." The Pennsylvania law was therefore deemed unconstitutional.[353]

Prigg is not generally thought of as a specific antecedent to federal deportation laws. Indeed, the Court explicitly stressed the police power of the states to regulate and remove fugitive slaves from their borders.[354]

Nevertheless, when one traces the pedigree of late-nineteenth-century deportation, the determination of exclusive national government authority over fugitive slaves was an important milestone.[355]

By January 1850, Southern demands for a more effective fugitive slave law culminated in specific proposals by Senator James Mason of Virginia.[356] As reported out of the Judiciary Committee, the new bill made several important changes to the 1793 law: it allowed the owner or agent, after arresting a fugitive slave, to take his captive before an array of federal officials, from judges to commissioners, clerks, marshals, postmasters, and customs collectors. Upon sufficient proof of the validity of the case, the officer would then issue a certificate authorizing the removal of the fugitive to the state or territory from which he or she had fled. The new law, like later deportation laws, also provided for a $1,000 fine for anyone who attempted to harbor, conceal, or rescue a fugitive slave. A warrant could be issued to a federal marshal for the arrest of an alleged fugitive slave. In sum, the proposed law dramatically increased the role of the federal government in the capture, processing, and removal of fugitive slaves.

Some Southerners opposed the proposal, thinking it not strong enough. Beyond the fundamental opposition of the abolitionists, Northerners were concerned about the lack of adequate protections for free people who might be kidnapped.[357] Senator William H. Seward offered an amendment to require a trial by jury, but it was tabled.[358] Following a powerful speech by Daniel Webster in which he accepted the Southern position on the basic propriety of fugitive slave laws, however, a mood of compromise developed.[359]

Debate over jury trials and the role of judges continued through the spring of 1850. These debates, as we shall see, were similar to those, thirty years later, over the first national deportation laws. Consider the statement of Roger Sherman Baldwin of Connecticut in favor of jury trials and against the vesting of judicial authority in the hands of "petty commissioners." This was a question "affecting the liberty of an individual who has a right to remain where he is, and to assert his freedom in the State where he happens to be, until his right is disproved by evidence."[360]

A congressional committee, chaired by Henry Clay, offered two amendments to the proposed bill. The first, designed to protect free people, required the alleged owner of a fugitive slave to present an official record from a competent tribunal, "adjudicating the facts of elopement and slavery, with a general description of the fugitive." The second would have allowed a jury trial in the state from which the fugitive had fled, but only in cases in which the fugitive would declare "that he has a right to his freedom." This provision is strikingly analogous to the later distinction developed in deportation cases in which a claim to citizenship was raised. Debate—much of it quite fierce—on these and many other points continued throughout the summer of 1850. On September 18 of that year, however, President Fillmore signed the Fugitive Slave Act of 1850.[361]

Opponents of the law, including most prominently Charles Sumner and Horace Mann, challenged it on a wide variety of constitutional grounds. Most interesting for our purposes are the challenges that were redolent of the Republican critique of the deportation parts of the Alien and Sedition Acts. In particular, the authority of Congress to legislate in this arena was challenged, as were the summary nature of the proceedings, the nonjudicial status of the commissioners who had authority to decide cases, the denial of jury trial, the lack of confrontation rights, and the potential reliance on ex parte testimony.[362]

The nature of the proceedings under the Fugitive Slave Law also raised questions that are similar to some that have reemerged in contemporary debates over the removal of those convicted of crimes. Fugitive slave cases were often analogized to interstate rendition proceedings for criminals.[363] Indeed, Justice Story had held in *Prigg* that fugitive slave cases were like cases of those suspected of crimes in another state. All that was required in the sending state was prima facie proof—in criminal cases, of guilt, and in slave cases, of ownership.[364] The alleged fugitive would then have to rely on the legal processes of slaveholding states, a prospect that did not fill Northerners with great confidence, to say the least.[365] Nevertheless, the fact that a possible trial was available in the slave state permitted the legal conclusion that the summary ministerial proceedings of the federal law were sufficient.[366]

In short, many procedural aspects of the Fugitive Slave Law were later to be adopted by the Congress and accepted by the Supreme Court as legitimate components of the deportation regime. Of course, the repugnant but consistent classification of fugitive slave cases as matters of property renders comparison with the deportation system difficult.[367] Still, in hindsight, it appears that the resolution of problems of judicial authority raised by the fugitive slave laws at least contributed to and probably facilitated the development of an administrative deportation system a generation later. There can certainly be no doubt of an institutional memory of the fugitive slave laws on the Court. Salmon P. Chase of Ohio, appointed by President Lincoln as chief justice in 1862, became known in some quarters as the "Attorney General for Runaway Slaves" due to his legal defense of such cases in the 1840s.[368]

The acceptance of authority of this magnitude by nonjudicial commissioners was also no small matter. Functionally understood, the U.S. legal system had accepted, for the first time, a large-scale, relatively efficient federal system for the forced removal of people from one place to another on the basis of rather scanty proof, with minimal or no judicial oversight, and with only the most flimsy constitutional protections. More abstractly, the implicit exclusion of African Americans from citizenship led to a stark removal discourse.[369] An 1850 editorial in the *Indiana State Sentinel* referred to an anti-Fugitive Slave Law meeting of African Americans as "aliens and enemies." The editors suggested that "some mode should be adopted to rid the country of their presence."[370]

Though northeastern opposition to the fugitive slave laws was fierce and well organized, the compromise of 1850 led the majority of Americans to accept the regime.[371] In his second annual message to Congress in 1851, President Fillmore affirmed that his administration would enforce the laws in spite of episodic and sometimes violent opposition.[372] Three successive administrations—those of Fillmore, Pierce, and Buchanan—enforced the laws vigorously.[373] A well-entrenched, sufficiently funded, and well-accepted federal bureaucracy thus developed over a period of years. Local opposition, such as the highly publicized case of Anthony Burns in Boston, in which a federal agent was killed during an attempt to rescue Burns from his captivity, seemed only to sustain the federal will. As President Pierce reportedly said in a wire to the marshal in Boston, "The law must be enforced."[374]

The Southern view, that the law was not effectively enforced, has prompted substantial debate among historians.[375] For our purposes, however, there can be no doubt whatsoever about the most important points: by 1860 the federal administrative mechanisms for the enforcement of the law were well established and well-known in every part of the country.[376]

Moreover, for those who experienced involuntary return to slave states, the Fugitive Slave Law was analogous to a modern deportation law, with no discretionary or mercy component. People with families, jobs, and various types of roots in new communities to which they had fled faced forced legal removal back to places where they feared the most inhuman treatment.[377] The law operated as a deportation system in another, more traditional, sense as well: it caused many to flee the country for Canada and others for Mexico.[378] Indeed, one scholar has estimated that the law caused as many as 20,000 people of color to flee to Canada.[379] Immediately after the signing of the act, the *Liberator* reported that, fearing the new law, "the fugitives from slavery [were] pressing northward. Many have been obliged to flee precipitously."[380] Many free African Americans fled as well, due to fears of kidnapping by slave catchers.[381] African American Baptist churches in Buffalo and Rochester, New York, reportedly lost hundreds of members, fearing kidnapping and enforcement of the new law.[382] A few months after the passage of the 1850 law, the Anti-Slavery Society of Canada estimated that 4,000–5,000 people had fled the United States.[383]

The Civil War transformed the fugitive question into something more analogous to an international immigration matter in still another sense.[384] Many thousands of newly free African Americans moved to Union territory, inspiring largely negative responses from Northern officials. The mayor and common council of Chicago, for example, "heartily" rejected a proposal to send "negro servants" to the city, allegedly on the grounds that it would be "in violation of the laws of this State and a great injustice to the laboring population."[385] Governor John Albion Andrew of Massachusetts refused to permit the entry of some 500 "contraband negroes." An editorial in the *National Intelligencer* noted wryly that it seemed that "the introduction of members of this oppressed race into a State where they are supposed to have so many sympathizing friends is not regarded with favor by the people of Massachusetts . . . The 'African' is a 'brother,' but South Carolina, not Massachusetts, is left to be the 'brother's keeper.'"[386]

"COLONIZATION" AND DEPORTATION PLANS FOR AFRICAN AMERICANS

The forced movement of African Americans across international borders caused by the Fugitive Slave Law was completely foreseeable. Indeed, it had long been envisioned and even desired by many whites. The prospect of abolition was deeply frightening for whites, Northern and

Southern, as they contemplated the entry into society of such a large population of people widely regarded to be "alien to the body politic."[387] Albert Gallatin had mused that the brutal fate of white Haitian planters was the inevitable consequence of abolition.[388] Even those who supported abolition, such as Ben Franklin, worried about how "such an atrocious abasement of human nature" would affect people long accustomed to being "chiefly governed by the passion of fear."[389] St. George Tucker of Virginia advocated deportation of African Americans on the basis of what he perceived as their "marked physical and intellectual inferiority."[390] This position was also advocated by Thomas Jefferson: "[Slaves] should continue with their parents to a certain age, then be brought up, at public expense, to tillage, arts, or sciences, according to their geniuses, till the females should be eighteen, and the males twenty-one years of age, when they should be colonized to such place as the circumstances of the time should render most proper."[391]

St. George Tucker thought that, with such an approach, "we might reasonably hope, that time would remove from us a race of men, whom we wish not to incorporate with us, which now form an obstacle to such incorporation."[392] Such fears had long led many whites to contemplate deportation. As one Frenchman had observed in Maryland and Virginia in the late 1780s, many feared "that if the Blacks become free they would cause trouble . . . [T]hey know not what rank to assign them in society; whether they shall establish them in separate districts or send them out of the country."[393]

From the beginning, most such plans were a bizarre mix of faux voluntarism and compulsion. For example, an "emancipation plan" that was circulated in 1714 advocated the deportation of all African Americans who did not wish to remain slaves.[394] Similar suggestions were made by many others of that generation. Patrick Henry had once lamented, "To re-export them is impracticable and sorry I am for it."[395] Noah Webster developed a more humane removal plan in 1793 in which freed slaves would be given the status of free tenants and moved to available land in the United States.[396] St. George Tucker reportedly advocated a less-enlightened, though still formally voluntarist, approach: "laws so harsh that freed Negroes would remove themselves rather than suffer under them."[397]

Similar deportation schemes abounded throughout the nineteenth century.[398] Indeed, deportation, also known as "colonization," was a crucial component of the strategy of many Southern emancipationists. It was thought that deportation would make whites more likely to free slaves, as free African Americans were their greatest fear. Moreover— and of great interest as a matter of immigration history—it was envisioned that as slavery was eliminated, immigrant white workers would provide more efficient labor.[399]

Many colonization proponents were naively optimistic about the prospects for freed slaves abroad, believing that they would enjoy "a bright prospect of usefulness and happiness, and freedom."[400] In 1813, a bill supporting a proposal to bring a group of free African Americans to Sierrra Leone passed the Senate, before losing steam in the House.[401] The American Colonization Society (ACS), established in 1816–17, received financial support from state governments throughout the Upper South and ultimately sponsored hundreds of African Americans to self-deport to Africa. Prominent supporters and members of the ACS included Henry Clay, Francis Scott Key, Thomas Jefferson, James Madison, James Monroe, Millard Fillmore, John Marshall, Roger B. Taney, Andrew Jackson, Daniel Webster, Stephen A. Douglas, and Abraham Lincoln.[402] In March 1819, Congress passed the Anti-Slave Trading Act, which appropriated $100,000 to transport African Americans to Africa. President James Monroe, fearing that people who were simply returned to the coast of Africa would likely be reenslaved, acquired territory by treaty on Africa's west coast, which led to the creation of the country of Liberia in 1848.[403]

Following the Nat Turner rebellion, Maryland appropriated funds to send emancipated slaves and freemen to Africa. This was a government-sponsored, well-organized deportation plan. Maryland actually created a state deportation agency: the "Board of Managers for the Removal of Colored People." This agency worked with another, the Maryland State Colonization Society, to remove emancipated slaves to Africa and elsewhere. Freed slaves who wished to remain in the state had to appeal to "orphan's court." Those who were not successful in court could be forcibly deported.[404] Virginia and Tennessee developed similar systems.[405] Over time, these schemes waned because of lack of funding, as fear of slave revolts subsided, but reemerged in the 1850s, along with the Fugitive Slave Act, as most Upper South states reinstituted deportation plans. Virginia appropriated $30,000 per year for its system, funding it in part by taxing free African Americans. Debate over these schemes became quite fierce during this period: a battle between racist fears and an emerging sense of human rights. As one Virginian put it, "every man must have a country, and if this is not the free Negro's country, where is it?"[406] The 1857 *Dred Scott* decision, by confirming the noncitizen status of African Americans, energized proponents of deportation. In 1860, Arkansas, as noted earlier, ordered all free African Americans to leave the state or be sold into slavery.[407]

Abraham Lincoln had supported deportation plans from his earliest public speeches. In an 1854 speech in Peoria, Illinois, Lincoln linked emancipation with removal: "I should not know what to do, as to the existing institution [of slavery]. My first impulse would be to free all the slaves, and send them to Liberia, to their own native land."[408] Explaining his opposition to the Kansas-Nebraska Act in 1857, Lincoln asserted that "there is a natural disgust in the minds of nearly all white people to the idea of indiscriminate amalgamation of the white and black races."[409] For this reason, he supported "a separation of the races" as "the only perfect preventive of amalgamation." The best method to achieve such separation, he suggested, was "colonization," though he conceded that "the enterprise is a difficult one." He saw it potentially as "morally right, and, at the same time, favorable to, or, at least, not against, our interest, to transfer the African to his native clime." And he promised that "we shall find a way to do it, however great the task may be."[410] Many shared this view. Indeed, by 1860, even Frederick Douglas, who had long opposed deportation and emigration schemes of all kinds, wrote that he would "raise no objection to the present movement toward Hayti."[411]

In 1861, as president, Lincoln supported an idea to obtain land in Central America for the resettlement of freed slaves.[412] Philadelphia businessman Ambrose W. Thompson owned several hundred thousand acres in the Chiriqui region of what is now Panama. He offered to transport freed slaves to Central America, where they would mine coal, which Thompson asserted was plentiful there. This coal would then be sold to the U.S. Navy, and the profits would sustain the new black colony.[413] Lincoln eventually sent an emissary from Venezuela to Chiriqui to investigate.[414]

In his first annual message to Congress on December 3, 1861, President Lincoln suggested "that . . . steps be taken for colonizing [freed slaves] . . . at some place, or places, in a climate congenial to them." He went even further than this, however, by asking "whether the free colored people already in the United States could not, so far as individuals may desire, be included in such colonization." Such resettlement, in one form or another, Lincoln believed, was an "absolute necessity."[415]

In April 1862, Lincoln supported a bill to compensate District of Columbia slaveholders some $300 for each freed slave. The bill also appropriated an additional $100,000 "to be expended under the direction of the President of the United States, to aid in the colonization and settlement of such free persons of African descent now residing in said District, including those to be liberated by this act, as may desire to emigrate to the Republic of Haiti or Liberia, or such other country beyond the limits of the United States as the President may determine."[416] Lincoln signed the bill, noting that he was "gratified that the two principles of compensation, and colonization, are both recognized, and practically applied in the act."[417]

One of the saddest documents imaginable is a petition sent to Congress by a group of African American men in April 1862, in which they ask to be sent to Central America.[418] The men state that they believe that "freedom will result injuriously, unless there shall be opened to colored people a region, to which they may immigrate—a country which is suited to their organization . . . which will allow them an honorable position in the families of God's great world."

The petitioners feared return to Liberia, Haiti, or "Africo-West India Islands, where vice reigns supreme where our very blood would be required if we opposed its indulgence." In a particularly poignant passage, the petitioners wrote, "Though colored, and debarred from rights of citizenship, our hearts, none the less, cling to the land of our birth." Thus, they asked to be sent to "a land—part of this your own continent" where they would not be "regarded as an evil . . . [because of competition] with your white labor . . . for the necessities of existence . . . [S]end us . . . that we may not be wholly excluded from you, that we may aid in bringing to you that great commerce of the Pacific, which will still further increase the wealth and power of your country."[419]

In mid-May 1862, Lincoln received a paper from Reverend James Mitchell that argued in favor of removal of African Americans from the United States. Among its normative positions was that the "republican system was meant for a homogeneous people." It further asserted that "as long as blacks continue to live with the whites they constitute a threat to the national life. Family life may also collapse and the increase of mixed breed bastards may some day challenge the supremacy of the white man."[420] Mitchell supported a gradual plan of deportation to Central America and Mexico. President Lincoln, soon after reading this memorandum, appointed Mitchell to the new post of commissioner of emigration.[421]

In July 1862, the second Confiscation Act appropriated an additional $500,000 for executive resettlement of freed slaves who fell under Union military control. A joint congressional resolution made clear that voluntary colonization was deemed an appropriate executive action for such people:[422] "the President is hereby authorized to make provision for the transportation, colonization and settlement in some tropical country beyond the limits of the United States, of such persons of African race made free by the provisions of this act, as may be willing to emigrate."[423]

In August 1862, President Lincoln invited a group of free black men to the White House to ask them to set a positive example and leave the country voluntarily. "You and we are different races," said Lincoln, "It is better for us both, therefore, to be separated . . . The colony of Liberia has been in existence a long time. In a certain sense it is a success." Lincoln conceded, however, that "[m]any of the original settlers have died, yet, like people elsewhere, their offspring outnumber those deceased." Then, in a truly remarkable passage, Lincoln appealed to the consciences of the free black men before him: "But you ought to do something to help those who are not so fortunate as yourselves. . . . It is exceedingly important that we have men at the beginning capable of thinking as white men, and not those who have been systematically oppressed."[424]

Finally, conceding the difficulties of moving to Liberia, Lincoln, now sounding more like a Florida land speculator than a president, proposed a Central American removal plan:

> It is nearer to us than Liberia—not much more than one-fourth as far as Liberia, and within seven days'—run by steamers. . . . The country is a very excellent one for any people, and with great natural resources and advantages, and especially because of the similarity of climate with your native land—thus being suited to your physical condition . . . On both sides there are harbors among the finest in the world. Again, there is evidence of very rich coal mines . . . [I]t will afford an opportunity to the inhabitants for immediate employment till they get ready to settle permanently in their homes.[425]

Reverend Mitchell immediately placed a newspaper advertisement: "Correspondence is desired with colored men favorable to Central America, Liberian or Haitian emigration, especially the first named."[426] Mitchell also sent a memorandum to black ministers urging them to use their influence to encourage emigration.[427] Among other arguments, Mitchell asserted, "This is a nation of equal white laborers, and as you cannot be accepted on equal terms, there is no place here for you. You cannot go into the North or the West without arousing the growing feeling of hostility toward you. The south must also have a homogeneous population, and any attempt to give the freedmen equal status in the South will bring disaster to both races."[428] Administration plans to develop the Chiriqui colony continued through the fall of 1862. In September, Lincoln drafted a preliminary Emancipation Proclamation, which included a statement of purpose, "that the effort to colonize persons of African descent, with their consent, upon this continent, or elsewhere . . . will be continued."[429]

The Chiriqui plan eventually collapsed after Lincoln received a report that Chiriqui coal was "worthless." Also, abolitionists opposed his deportation plans, as did some Republican leaders, anticipating black political support in the South. Senator Charles Sumner argued that black laborers were an important part of the national economy and that removing them "would be fatal to the prosperity of the country."[430] Finally, the nations that would have been most directly affected by resettlement also opposed the plan. In Nicaragua and Honduras, the American consul reported panic over the prospect of "a dreadful deluge of negro emigration . . . from the United States." The governments of Honduras, Nicaragua, and Costa Rica officially protested.[431]

Lincoln was undaunted. In his second annual message to Congress on December 1, 1862, he said, "I cannot make it better known than it already is, that I strongly favor colonization." He even proposed a rather odd constitutional amendment to facilitate such schemes, which he saw as an integral part of emancipation. His proposed wording was as follows: "'Congress may appropriate money, and otherwise provide, for colonizing free colored persons, with their consent, at any place or places without the United States.'"[432]

In early 1863, Lincoln reportedly seriously discussed an incredible plan to "remove the whole colored race of the slave states into Texas." Apparently, no action was taken in support of this idea.[433] The president also considered Florida and then a small island called Ile ä Vache, off the coast of Haiti.[434] He signed a contract with a man by the name of Bernard Kock to settle 5,000 African Americans on the island and to provide them with housing, food, medicine, churches, schools, and employment. Some 450 people were actually transported to the island at the federal government's expense, but the project soon failed miserably, with nearly 100 dead of disease, thirst, and starvation. In February--March 1864, a ship brought the survivors back to the United States at the government's expense. This marked the end of all congressional spending in support of deportation plans until attention turned to the Chinese two decades later.[435] Finally, it seemed, Lincoln also faced reality and gave up on the deportation plans.[436] On July 1, 1864, presidential secretary John Hay wrote in his diary: "I am happy that the President has sloughed off that idea of colonization."[437] On July 2, 1864, Congress repealed the appropriation for colonization.[438]

Allan Nevins has noted that Lincoln envisioned "a far-reaching alteration of American society, industry, and government." This vision involved not only gradual emancipation but also the "transportation of hundreds of thousands and perhaps even millions of people overseas," which, in turn, required enhanced federal government power and would require—as Lincoln knew—more immigrant labor.[439] But as thousands of laborers arrived from China, the conceptual matrices of the Fugitive Slave Laws and colonization plans awaited them.

3

From Chinese Exclusion to Post-Entry Social Control: The Early Formation of the Modern Deportation System

I think this is a good bill . . . my doubts are all removed. As a Southern man I could see why they did not want these Chinese. We have had troubles with a foreign race in my own state, God knows.

—Senator Morgan of Alabama in support of
Geary deportation law (May 3, 1892)

The transcontinental railroad and the U.S. deportation system have much in common. Both started at the coasts and now span the country. Both implicate our grandest national aspirations and hide some of our most shameful historical truths. Both have been episodically updated but retain many essential features of their nineteenth-century origins. Both are in dramatic need of repair. And both were in large measure built on the backs of Chinese immigrant workers who suffered immense hardships in the process of their creation.

The early American state often seemed scattered and ephemeral—Tocqueville's famous invisible social machine.[1] As we have seen, various forms of border control and removal had long existed as part of "an integrated organization of institutions, procedures, and human talents whose specific purpose was to control the use of coercion within the national territory."[2] However, the development of a coherent federal deportation system—especially post-entry social control deportation—required special thought.

It is easy to overlook how significant the creation of the modern de-portation system was. Formal deportation mechanisms had been rather minimal and rare since the debacle of 1798. Indeed, Jefferson's charac-terization of deportation of "friendly" aliens as a radical experiment re-mained apt until well into the twentieth century. The creation of this system involved three distinct steps: the federalization of immigration control; the legitimation of federal deportation laws; and, finally, the ad-dition of post-entry social control deportation laws to extended border control laws. All of these took place in a rather short period of time, roughly from 1862 to 1903.

This chapter considers how and why the first national deportation laws emerged during this era. It also examines how the Supreme Court skirted the deep legal issues raised by these laws, first through the de-velopment of plenary power legitimating doctrine and then through a facile analogy between extended border control and post-entry social control deportation.

Federalization of Immigration Control

Until the mid-nineteenth century, the control of immigration was gener-ally seen as a matter of state police power. As we have seen, each state had its own system of exclusion laws and practices to protect its popula-tion from unwanted immigrants—the poor, criminals, the sick, and var-ious types of "immoral" people. The Supreme Court accepted the pro-priety of such state control in 1837 in *The City of New York v. Miln,* a case that involved a state law requiring masters of ships to provide detailed reports on passengers about to land.[3] Twelve years later, however, in the 1849 *Passenger Cases,* the Court invalidated certain state "head taxes" on immigrants.[4] The dominant rationale of a divided Court seemed to be that the laws violated Congress's constitutional authority to regulate interstate and foreign commerce.[5] This was in part a manifestation of the needs of the expanding national economy. The era of state control was clearly ending. But the commerce clause rationale for federal authority over the movement of people had long been controversial, due in large part to slavery.[6] The House Committee on Commerce had, for example, asserted in 1843 that state legislation restricting African and African American seamen from entry into Southern ports was a violation of the commerce clause.[7] Thus, although the movement toward federal control was fairly clear, its path of legitimation was not.[8]

From the mid-nineteenth century onward, immigration control remained a rather complicated joint state-federal enterprise. The federal government entered the field gingerly, with federal laws aimed first at the most egregious labor practices and then at the exclusion of certain undesirable immigrants.[9] An 1862 law prohibited Americans from participating in the slave trade between Cuba and China. It was designed to eliminate so-called coolie labor.[10] But the dominant trend of the 1860s and 1870s was toward the encouragement of immigration. The Civil War and emancipation created tremendous labor demands. Some twenty-five states took independent, official steps to promote immigration.[11] As for the federal government, President Lincoln's message to the Congress in December 1863 made his administration's views quite clear: "I again submit to your consideration the expediency of establishing a system for the encouragement of immigration . . . [T]here is still a great deficiency of laborers in every field of industry . . . [T]ens of thousands of persons, destitute of remunerative occupation, are thronging our foreign consulates, and offering to emigrate to the United States."[12]

The Immigration Act of 1864 permitted Chinese immigration under the "credit ticket" system and generally allowed certain types of immigrant labor contracts.[13] The act also created the position of commissioner of immigration under the authority of the secretary of state. The commissioner's primary duties were to collect information on the climate and resources of the United States and to disseminate that information throughout Europe.[14] President Lincoln told the Thirty-eighth Congress at the opening of its second session that he regarded "our emigrants as one of the principal replenishing streams which are appointed by Providence to repair the ravages of internal war, and its waste of national strength and wealth."[15]

By the mid-1870s, the national mood had changed. Federal exclusion power was exercised in the Page Act of 1875, which forbade the entry of certain Asian laborers brought to the United States involuntarily and also excluded certain convicts and prostitutes.[16] The relative constitutional authority of states and the federal government to control immigration was still unresolved, however. In two 1876 cases, *Henderson, et al. v. Mayor of New York, et al.*, and *Chy Lung v. Freeman*, the Court invalidated three state bond systems for alien passengers.[17] New York and Louisiana laws required shipmasters to present a list of foreign passengers to state authorities and to post bonds. California authorized its immigration commissioner to require bonds for certain "lewd and debauched women" from China. The Court was especially troubled by the California system, noting, "It is hardly possible to conceive a statute more skillfully framed, to place in the hands of a single man the power to prevent entirely vessels engaged in a foreign trade, say with China, from carrying passengers, or to compel them to submit to systematic extortion of the grossest kind." The Court used these cases to effectively mark the death knell for most state immigration control. The *Chy Lung* Court held that

> [t]he passage of laws which concern the admission of citizens and subjects of foreign nations to our shores belongs to Congress, and not to the States. It has the power to regulate commerce with foreign nations: the responsibility for the character of those regulations, and for the manner of their execution, belongs solely to the national government. If it be otherwise, a single State can, at her pleasure, embroil us in disastrous quarrels with other nations.[18]

As the *Henderson* opinion put it, the regulation of the "great system," "of vast interest to this country, as well as to the immigrants who come among us to find a welcome and home within our borders," was obviously a "regulation of commerce."[19] Still, the Court did not invalidate all state exclusion laws. The *Chy Lung* opinion noted that the Court was "not called upon by this statute to decide for or against the right of a State, in the absence of legislation by Congress, to protect herself by necessary and proper laws against paupers and convicted criminals from abroad."[20]

As state agencies still administered immigration enforcement, some states lobbied Congress vigorously for assistance and for federal exclusion of criminals, "lunatics," and paupers.[21] These efforts, led by New York, succeeded with the passage of the first comprehensive federal immigration law: the Immigration Act of 1882.[22] This law mandated the exclusion and the return "to the nations to which they belong and from whence they came" of a variety of persons, including convicts, "idiots," "lunatics," and persons unable to care for themselves.[23] Although it established ultimate federal control over immigration, the 1882 act used state agents. Inspectors and commissioners of immigration were state officials, under federal authority. A federal head tax of fifty cents per person was implemented to fund the system. The question thus arose of whether Congress had the authority to enact such a law.

The federal government made its first appearance as a party to an immigration case in the 1884 *Head Money Cases*.[24] It is clear that some in the federal government had already formulated the arguments that would later carry the day in the *Chinese Exclusion Case* and *Fong Yue Ting*. The solicitor general's brief relied not as it might have on the foreign commerce clause, but solely on inherent sovereign powers. Congress's power to regulate immigration was said to be "implied in [the] very existence of independent government anterior to the adoption of a constitution." Any constitutional provisions possibly relevant to the power were seen as "merely in recognition, and not in creation thereof." Interestingly, the solicitor general cited Thomas Cooley to argue the rather startling proposition that "as to foreign Governments and nonresident foreigners the United States is not of merely enumerated powers." As to such parties, the government argued that it had "all the powers which according to international law any sovereign society possesses."[25] In a formulation that implies differentiation between exclusion and removal from the United States, the government also argued that "the Constitution is merely a domestic thing, whilst the nation itself has foreign relations, powers and duties, as well as domestic."[26] The 1884 Court was not yet ready to follow this line, however, and grounded its decision in the commerce clause. The Court concluded that "Congress [has] the power to pass a law regulating immigration as a part of the commerce of this country with foreign nations."[27] Major federal immigration control laws soon followed this authorization. But so did a doctrinal shift that has left its mark on deportation law ever since.

On the Backs of the Chinese: The Early Roots of the Plenary Power Doctrine

Had the commerce clause rationale endured, the evolution of U.S. deportation law would have been quite different. But a powerful convergence of racial, ideological, cultural, and doctrinal factors soon led the late-nineteenth-century Supreme Court to make sweeping statements in support of the immigration control power of the federal government and against the rights claims of noncitizens. Treatises on international law, as noted, had long confirmed the basic authority of a sovereign nation-state to exclude aliens. For example, in 1856, *Wheaton's Interna-*

tional Law Digest stated, "Every society possesses the undoubted right to determine who shall compose its members, and it is exercised by all nations, both in peace and war."[28] The existence of such power was not a serious question. But what were its limits? This question was to lead to the broadest imaginable formulation by Justice Stephen Field for the U.S. Supreme Court in the seminal case of U.S. immigration law, *Chae Chan Ping. v. United States,* also known as the *Chinese Exclusion Case:* "The power of exclusion of foreigners being an incident of sovereignty belonging to the government of the United States . . . the right to its exercise at any time when, in the judgment of the government, the interests of the country require it, cannot be granted away or restrained on behalf of any one . . . [T]he political department of our government . . . is alone competent to act upon the subject."[29] This dramatic overstatement of legislative and executive power—with its related deprecation of the rights claims of noncitizens—has been subject to severe criticism over the years.[30] Nevertheless, it remains the law, and it serves to this day as the doctrinal substratum for deportation law.

By the late nineteenth century, many international law scholars had differentiated the power to exclude from the power to expel.[31] A strong line, with powerful rule of law and human rights undertones, had developed at least against the arbitrary assertion of sovereign power against admitted aliens. Pufendorf, long before, had written, "to expel without probable cause guests and strangers, once admitted, surely savours of inhumanity and disdain."[32] Madison had argued that "friendly" aliens, once admitted, had a right not to have their status revoked without good reason. The rights of denizens (long-term lawful resident aliens) had also long been recognized as greater than those of initial entrants or temporary visitors. Vattel distinguished between "alien inhabitants" and "perpetual inhabitants." The former were "bound to the society by their residence," but were entitled to "only the advantages which the law or custom gives them." The latter, however, were "a kind of citizens of an inferior order."[33] Phillimore described permanent residents as "*de facto* though not *de jure* citizens of the country of their [domicile]."[34]

Many nineteenth-century scholars continued in this vein, focusing on hardship, arbitrariness, and expectation. Edward S. Creasy, writing in 1876, suggested that it was "a heinous wrong to withdraw suddenly privileges . . . and to practice spoliation, imprisonment, or ruinous expulsion upon those foreigners who have been exercising them, in all cases where long usage has nurtured a well-founded expectation on the part of the foreigners that such privileges would continue to be respected."[35] David Dudley Field, the brother of Justice Stephen Field, wrote in his 1876 *Outlines of an International Code* that "no nation can expel the members of another nation without special cause."[36]

As the debates of 1798 had shown, however, there was a strong countertradition. Theodore Ortolan wrote in 1845 that even a resident alien was accepted "by simple tolerance, and in no way by obligation."[37] Robert Phillimore, in 1854, simply accepted that the nation-state could "regulate the conditions under which [foreigners] shall be allowed to remain" and could "compel their departure."[38] But the trend through the late nineteenth century was toward more subtlety about the rights of resident aliens. Lawfully admitted aliens were generally seen as "entitled to the ordinary protection of person and property."[39]

The legal doctrine of deportation developed in a much harsher direction, however. The federal power that developed from the late nineteenth century onward was not simply an adaptation to changing conditions. It was a central feature of Progressive state building: "an exercise in reconstructing an already established organization of state power." Federal immigration control during this era may thus be well characterized as a "recasting" of official power relationships within governmental institutions."[40] Woodrow Wilson wrote in 1887: "With a new country . . . we were long exempted from the need of being anxiously careful about plans and methods of administration." But now, "like a lusty child," government was expanding and growing "great in stature."[41] As the earlier diffusion of power yielded to the new federal administrative state, the Court was called on to rationalize and legitimate that trend. Conflicting doctrines of nationalism, constitutionalism, laissez-faire, and substantive due process characterized this era. The Court, on the one hand, adapted to the new continental scale and the new economy and recognized the propriety of increasing government regulation. But it also sought to protect private property and asserted its own ultimate authority to do so.[42] This was a precarious balance, to say the least. But immigration law was different. Indeed, one almost discerns a sigh of relief in the *Chinese Exclusion Case* with its breathless, unequivocal invocation of federal sovereign power, as compared with the complex discussions about the limits of federal government power in many other cases of this period.

Race, of course, was another factor—perhaps the critical factor—in the development of the modern deportation system. In the nineteenth century, as John Higham has noted, "the pattern of nativist thought . . . veered toward racism." Two general types of race thinking were common in the nineteenth century. One may be characterized as romantic or proto-nationalistic. This variant lacked a physiological or biological basis. It was essentially a cultural idea. Another variant, however, was increasingly rooted in the natural sciences. This school associated cultural characteristics with physiological attributes, such as skin color, height, and head shape or size. Throughout the late nineteenth and early twentieth centuries the distinctions between these two schools of thought became less and less clear. In the United States, this convergence resulted in the conversion of what Higham has called the "vague Anglo-Saxon tradition" into a "sharp-cutting nativist weapon and, ultimately, into a completely racist philosophy."[43]

The racial version of nativism that ascended in the late nineteenth century was a national phenomenon. But it developed especially virulently in the West.[44] Part of the reason for this was the greater diversity of the immigrant groups there and, in hard economic times, the concomitant greater availability of scapegoats.[45] As Ronald Takaki has noted, "Chinese migrants found that racial qualities previously assigned to blacks quickly became 'Chinese' characteristics.' "[46] It was in cases infected by such complicated anti-Chinese racism that the Supreme Court developed the doctrinal foundations of modern immigration and deportation law.[47]

Chinese laborers were first drawn to California, like tens of thousands of others, by the gold rush of 1849. Their numbers quickly increased, from 325 in 1849 to 2,176 in 1851 to over 20,000 by 1852.[48] The Chinese, initially welcomed, soon faced hostility, violence, and ostracism. They were subjected to a variety of discriminatory taxes and other local and state legal acts restricting their ownership of property and businesses, choice of schools, and even the right to testify in court. One of the lesser-known facts of the Chinese experience in the United States, however, is the extent to which—and the sophistication with which—they appealed to the judicial system to protect their rights. The results achieved in state courts were decidedly mixed. In 1854, for example, the California Supreme Court considered a challenge to a statute that read, "No black or mulatto person, or Indian, shall be permitted to give evidence in favor of, or against, any white person."[49] The case, *People v.*

Hall, involved the alleged murder of a Chinese man named Ling Sing by a white man named George W. Hall and two others.[50] Following a trial at which three Chinese and one Caucasian witness testified for the prosecution, Hall was sentenced to be hanged. The verdict was challenged on the grounds that Chinese witnesses should not have been allowed to testify against a white defendant. The California Supreme Court reversed the conviction. In a truly remarkable display of ignorance and racism, Chief Justice Hugh Murray asserted that from the time when Columbus thought he had landed on "an island in the China sea . . . the American Indians and the Mongolian, or Asiatic, were regarded as the same type of human species."[51] Justice Murray construed the term "black" to be a generic word that excluded all but Caucasians. This crude racial theorizing was easily combined with public policy concerns: if the Chinese could testify, they would soon appear "at the polls, in the jury box, upon the bench, in our legislative halls." This was unthinkable, wrote Murray, as the Chinese were a race "whose mendacity is proverbial . . . whom nature has marked as inferior and who are incapable of progress or development beyond a certain point."[52]

Such attitudes were widespread among whites throughout the American West. Testimony taken from Judge Hastings, "a well known citizen of San Francisco and an old Californian," before a congressional committee reveals much about the views many whites held of the Chinese: "My opinion is, and I speak from the highest authority, that the Chinese are almost another species of the *genus homo* . . . They vary from the Aryan, or European race; their divergence is very wide. I think they vary so much that the offspring of the Chinaman, united with the American race would be unfertile, or would be imperfectly fertile . . . if not mules."[53]

The Chinese soon began to see that their best hope for relief from oppressive state and local actions was in the federal, not the state, courts. This understanding, though tactically correct, was part of a general pattern of transfer of the conflict from the state to the national level. As local restrictions were overturned by federal courts, violence increased, and pressures developed for federal laws to restrict Chinese immigration. The first such federal law, as noted, was the 1862 law aimed at "coolie" labor.[54] Following the Civil War, the legal and political climate became much more complex. The federal government played an ambivalent role in the conflicts that ensued. Foreign workers were used repeatedly during the mid-1860s to break strikes and undercut union organizing efforts. The 1864 Immigration Act had expressly authorized the government to support imported contract labor. Indeed, in 1866, the U.S. commissioner of immigration specifically approved the use of imported labor to counter increasingly successful strikes.[55] Then, owing in large part to organized labor opposition, the 1864 law was repealed in 1868, removing the federal imprimatur from the use of foreign strikebreakers but still allowing the practice of contract labor importation to continue.[56] The practice itself would not be outlawed until 1885.

The Chinese were prodigious workers. As David Montgomery recounts, "No other railroad builders ever accomplished feats of labor as spectacular as those of the Chinese . . . Chinese workers drove a rail bed from San Francisco to Promontory Point in Utah. They carved a path out of the perpendicular cliffs above the American River by lowering one another in wicker baskets to drill holes, set powder, and fire it off . . . even drilling a tunnel through the Donner Summit while their camps were buried in snow."[57]

However, "[w]hite workers and farmers, who flocked to the Pacific Coast in search of high wages and fertile valleys quickly . . . virtually unanimously came to look on the Chinese (and later the Japanese and others) as the carriers of poverty and social decay."[58] Thus, beginning in the mid-1870s, "a profound racial and nativist strain" began to infect "the political core of trade unionism."[59]

Much, though far from all, of the nationwide antipathy that developed toward the Chinese came from Irish workers, themselves mostly immigrants. Mary Roberts Coolidge noted in 1909 that the Irish constituted as much as one-fourth of the foreign-born population of California from 1870 to 1890 and "a far larger proportion in the active business of politics." Many of the strongest anti-Chinese voices were those of Irish immigrants, the rapidity of whose assimilation, opined Coolidge, was "a great misfortune to the Chinaman."[60] The Irish were motivated to a very large degree by their own deep race and status concerns.[61] Though they had long been the recipients of ugly prejudice and scorn by the English, in the New World—in stark contrast to slaves, Chinese immigrants, and even many free African Americans—the Irish could vote and had much easier access to urban political power. Among all of the immigrant groups that flooded America in the nineteenth century, the Irish were perhaps the most impoverished and the least equipped with marketable skills, as the vast majority had been agricultural laborers.[62] They were, however, well organized in church groups, immigrant aid societies, and nationalist clubs.[63] To obtain the social, political, and economic status of American white men—the highest category of prestige and power— nineteenth-century Irish workers had strongly differentiated themselves from blacks as early as the 1850s.[64] As John Kuo Wei Tchen has noted, labor competition between the Irish and the Chinese in New York City was "not a sufficient explanation for Irish . . . anti-Chinese feelings and actions." There were also deep-seated fears of "amalgamation" and a tendency to achieve "whiteness" and Americanization by participation in ugly racial stereotyping. One purpose of this was to defuse hatred of the Irish by Anglo-Americans and others through the construction of new " 'heathens' to displace their longstanding negative image."[65] The Chinese soon became what Alexander Saxton has aptly termed the "indispensable enemy."[66] They were purposefully excluded from much (though not all) of the labor movement, from much of civil society, and, ultimately, from the country.

By the late 1860s, the government of China also began to play a major role. Eager to develop better relations with the United States, China retained Anson Burlingame, former American minister to China, to negotiate treaties with a number of major world powers. The preamble to the resulting Burlingame Treaty with the United States contained powerful rights provisions, including "the inherent and inalienable right of man to change his home and allegiance" and "the mutual advantages of the free migration and emigration of their citizens and subjects." Soon after the treaty's ratification, however, a violent and extensive anti-Chinese movement took hold. Newton Booth, the governor of California, in his inaugural address of 1871–1872, stated, "[When] banded ruffianism selects for its victims a race notoriously defenseless, when pillage are its exploits, the race from which such wretches are recruited, the community which suffers such deeds to be enacted, the officials who stand supinely by without an effort to prevent the crime, are sharers in a common disgrace."[67]

A Chinese man offered a poignant description of the situation: "[W]hy is it that when our people come to your country, instead of being welcomed with respect and kindness, they are, on the contrary, treated with contempt and evil? It happens even that many lose their lives at the hand of lawless wretches. Yet, although there are Chinese witnesses of the crime, their testimony is rejected. The result is our abandonment to be murdered and our business to be ruined. How hard is it for the spirit to bear such trials?"[68]

In another passage, the same man described in terrible detail what life was like for many Chinese laborers in the United States:

> We go on board the ships. There we find ourselves unaccustomed to winds and waves, and to the extremes of heat and cold. We eat little, we grieve much. Our appearance is plain, and our clothing poor. At once when we leave the vessel the boatmen extort heavy prices; all kinds of conveyances require from us more than the usual charges; as we go on our way we are pushed, and kicked, and struck by the drunken and the brutal; but we cannot speak your language, we bear our injuries and pass on. Even when within doors, rude boys throw stones . . . Passers by, instead of preventing these provocations, add to them by their laughter. We go up to the mines; there the collectors of license make unlawful exactions, and robbers strip, plunder, wound, and even murder some of us . . . [W]hat injury have we Chinese done to your honorable people that they should thus turn upon us and make us drink the cup of wrong even to its last poisonous dregs.[69]

Still, the Chinese population of the United States increased from around 7,500 persons in 1850 to more than 105,000 in 1880.[70] Some 25 percent of the entire California labor force in the 1870s was estimated to be Chinese.[71] These workers generally arrived in groups and were tightly controlled and organized before and after their arrival. The so-called Six Companies not only managed the recruitment of workers from China, but oversaw virtually all aspects of their lives after arrival, including enforcement of their own rules, adjudication of disputes, punishment of transgressors, and apprehension of runaways. They even had an unwritten protocol with shipping companies that prevented the booking of passage for a Chinese worker out of California without a special clearance.[72] As Alexander Saxton has noted, "[i]t was a tight system."[73]

The tightness of this system was matched by a virtually perfect system that excluded most Chinese women from immigrating to the United States.[74] Much of the impetus for this was racist and rigidly moralistic. Anti-Chinese activists, concerned about the development of Chinese families and culture, saw the migration of Chinese women as a distinct threat. One strategy, begun in California, was the passage of antiprostitution laws that were often overenforced.[75] Representative Higby, in a list of anti-Chinese grievances, included the complaint that among Chinese women, "virtue is an exception to the general rule." Chinese men, he said, "buy and sell their women like cattle. That is their character. You cannot make citizens of them."[76] Concerns about social norms, miscegenation, and disease animated politicians to focus on Chinese women.[77] In 1870, Senator Cornelius Cole described Chinese women as "the most undesirable of population, who spread disease and moral death among our white population." He said, moreover, that they inspired him to ask himself, "whether or not there is a limit to this class of immigrants?"[78] California, increasingly blocked by courts in attempts to regulate Chinese immigration used its police power to target Chinese women with an 1870 law entitled "An Act to prevent the kidnapping and importation of Mongolian, Chinese and Japanese females, for criminal or demoralizing purposes."[79] By 1874, California's immigration law required a $500 bond for a wide variety of undesirables, including "lewd or debauched women."[80] This law, struck down by Justice Stephen Field on circuit, was, as noted, later struck down by the U.S. Supreme Court in the *Chy Lung* case. Field, it is interesting to note, had distinguished state exclusion laws from state criminal laws: "[I]f lewd women, or lewd men . . . land on our shores, the remedy against any subsequent lewd conduct on their part must be found in good laws or good municipal regulations and a vigorous police."[81] He did not envision post-entry social control deportation as a viable solution.

Although primarily at first a West Coast problem, the issue of Chinese immigration gradually assumed national proportions. The drafters of the 1875 Page Act were, as noted, clearly concerned about Chinese prostitutes.[82] The bill's sponsor said its purpose was "to send the brazen harlot . . . back to her native country."[83] The law, combined with other measures, seems to have been rather effective in preventing the immigration of any Chinese women to the United States.[84] The relative numbers of Chinese female versus male immigrants decreased from 1876 to 1882, when, of 39,579 Chinese immigrants to the United States, only 136 were women.[85]

As early as 1865, an editorial in the *New York Times* had well illustrated the nexus among race, morality, labor concerns, and Reconstruction politics that began to sweep the country: "we have four million of degraded negroes in the South . . . and if there were to be a floodtide of Chinese population—a population befouled with all the social vices, with no knowledge or appreciation of free institutions or constitutional liberty, with heathenish souls and heathenish propensities . . . we should be prepared to bid farewell to republicanism and democracy."[86] By the 1870s, such fears about Chinese labor were becoming national concerns. Certain national industries, most particularly cigar making, were dominated for a time by Chinese labor. Indeed, the so-called white label developed during this era as a way to signal to consumers which cigars had been made by white workers.[87] As more Chinese workers migrated to the South and East, organized labor became increasingly involved in national movements to control Chinese immigration.[88] In a widely publicized event that occurred in 1870, Asian workers were brought to North Adams, Massachusetts, to break a strike there. The *Springfield Republican* reported that the "Chinese question" was being forced on the country "with a rapidity that no one could have anticipated."[89] Samuel Gompers later wrote in his autobiography, "[W]e were contending against a menace to our trade [that] federal legislation alone could remedy."[90]

Labor struggles became especially desperate in 1877, "a year of violence and crises."[91] Many believed there to the link between foreigners with socialist ideologies and American labor unrest, exemplified by the violent strikes led by the so-called Molly Maguires in the coal fields of Pennsylvania.[92] In July, a series of relatively spontaneous strikes swept the country. Masses of unemployed workers stormed railroad yards and fought violent, highly publicized battles with the police and the military.[93] The *New York Herald*, hearkening back to the 1871 Paris Commune uprising, reported that "foreign demagogues" were responsible and that they had "imported ideas . . . which have repeatedly deluged France in blood." Moreover, in a portentous hint of things to come, the editors asserted that the strikes were "instigated by men incapable of understanding our ideas and principles."[94]

The role of organized labor in the development of deportation laws was much more complex than simply to be a victim of nascent Red-baiting. The year 1877 also saw the birth of the California Workingmen's Party. The progeny of an eastern party of the same name, the California version soon became identified with a radical anti-Chinese agenda. Its leader was Dennis Kearney, a man whose name would become synonymous with a violent anti-Chinese movement. Ironically, Kearney himself was not a workingman but a small business man. Even more ironically, he was not even a U.S. citizen until 1876, having been born in Ireland and arriving in San Francisco on a clipper ship in 1868. An "orator of the sandlots" and a charismatic demagogue, Kearney declared war both against the Chinese and against the two-party system itself, which he argued was infested with monopolism and corruption. Class warfare was fought in California in large part over the bodies of the Chinese. As Kearney reportedly shouted, "I will give the Central Pacific just three months to discharge their Chinamen, and if that is not done, Stanford and his crowd will have to take the consequences."[95]

The culmination of power for the Workingmen's Party was the California Constitutional Convention of 1878, which produced a document described by Henry George as "a mixture of constitution, code, stump speech, and mandamus."[96] It contained virulent anti-Chinese provisions. One provided that "no native of China, no idiot, no insane person, or person convicted of any infamous crime . . . shall ever exercise the privileges of an elector of this State." Another prohibited the employment of "any Chinese or Mongolian" on state or local public works or by any corporation, except in punishment for crime.[97] Many of the proposals violated the Burlingame Treaty and the federal Constitution.[98] Henry George described them as "not worth the paper they were printed on. Why, then, were they passed? Alexander Saxton has suggested that, first, they were "a stage performance for the edification of constituents." Second, they were valuable precisely because they would be invalidated. They amounted to "a plea for private violence with the implication that the authorities, being themselves hampered, would condone and welcome such assistance." This was a program that was distinguished for its "viciousness and irresponsibility."[99] It was also a model that would be repeated for more than two decades, culminating in the passage of national deportation laws.

Historians have vigorously debated the deep motivations behind labor's concern over Chinese immigration.[100] It is clear that many in the labor movement were truly worried about the expansion of the coolie system, in which laborers were imported—involuntarily or as a result of fraud—and then forced to work in deplorable conditions.[101] The most common form of Chinese immigration to the United States, however, was the credit-ticket system. This system involved the advance of passage money to the emigrant who would then repay the debt after his arrival in America.[102] Emigrants, called "contract workers," also signed binding contracts for terms of service in return for the cost of passage. Of the two systems, the credit-ticket system more closely approximated free and voluntary migration. Indeed, Liping Zhu has asserted that, "[f]rom the beginning, the majority of Chinese pioneers to the American West were free."[103] This may be a bit optimistic, but they were certainly not slaves. Perception at the time, however, differed. Indeed, Mary Roberts Coolidge, in one of the first histories of the era, referred to "the coolie fiction" and, later, "the coolie superstition." She concluded, with characteristic class bias, that the "vitality" of this fiction was in part due to "the prejudices of an unintelligent class who wished to believe it and partly, no doubt, to the behavior of the Chinese immigrants, which seemed to make it plausible."[104] Still, fictional superstition or not, concerns about the coolie trade were undoubtedly part of the motivation for laws of exclusion.

A less noble process also took hold in the American psyche. What had previously been anti-black and anti-Indian racism became increasingly focused on the Chinese. There was a terrible lack of communication between Chinese and white workers, because of linguistic and cultural barriers. There seemed also to be "a psychological barrier which foreclosed any exchange of experience."[105] This barrier routinely manifested itself in nasty statements by white labor leaders, such as Samuel Gompers: "the Caucasians . . . are not going to let their standard of living be destroyed by negroes, Chinamen, Japs, or any others."[106] The attitudes of white workers toward the Chinese in the West were clearly shaped by their experiences with Indians and with African Americans, both as slaves and as free men. Indeed, expulsions of the Chinese from mining camps and various anti-Chinese ordinances followed patterns that had previously been used against blacks. The so-called black codes of the midwestern states had been widely discussed in California from as early as 1849.[107] By the 1870s, it was clear in the West that anti-Chinese political organizing was a successful strategy. One underlying reason for this may have been the increasing illegitimacy of anti-black discourse, which, for a time, had acquired an association with secession and the Confederacy. The racism of the anti-Chinese groups, however, "remained untainted . . . and could be woven into a pattern of economic rationalization." The anti-Chinese argument, on the national level, also offered a politically profitable path to the repudiation of abolitionism. The defeat of Charles Sumner's attempt to permit naturalization for the

Chinese was a subtle predictor of the future abandonment of Reconstruction, which occurred simultaneously with the exclusion and then the expulsion of the Chinese.[108]

Of course, the use of immigrant laborers as strikebreakers was not an uncommon phenomenon in late-nineteenth-century America.[109] Jay Gould was reported to have quipped in 1896, "I can hire one half of the working class to kill the other half." Italian immigrants were brought in to destroy nascent union organizing efforts in Pennsylvania in 1874.[110] Mine owners used one immigrant group after another to break strikes and defeat union organizing efforts. As the *Allegheny Mail* noted, "If the Italians are not found to answer the purpose Swedes will be tried and if they fail colored men will be set to work."[111] But the Chinese provoked especially visceral reactions.

In the South, the racial climate was particularly complex. The hiring of Chinese workers was seen for a time as a necessary alternative to the hiring of freed black slaves. Apart from their reputed virtues as prodigious workers, the Chinese were viewed as having a disciplinary effect on the newly free black population. The governor of Arkansas noted that "the underlying motive for this effort . . . was to punish the Negro for having abandoned control of his old master, and to regulate the conditions of his employment and the scale of wages to be paid him."[112] One Kentucky observer offered the opinion that the Chinese would change "the tune" from "forty acres and a mule" to "work nigger or starve."[113]

There was, to be sure, a strong counterdiscourse, as illustrated by the passage of the Civil Rights Act of 1870, which ensured basic civil rights, including the right "to sue, be parties, [and] give evidence" to "all persons within the jurisdiction of the United States," a category that clearly included the Chinese.[114] Jacob Riis, in this spirit, had specifically suggested a very different approach to the Chinese question: "Rather than banish the Chinaman, I would have the door opened wider for his wife; make it a condition of his coming or staying that he bring his wife with him. Then, at least, he might not be what he now is and remains, a homeless stranger among us."[115]

Exclusion and Expulsion

The humanitarian approach of Riis and others sadly faded into obscure irrelevance by the turn of the twentieth century. Calls for exclusion merged into the harsh discourse of expulsion.[116] Dennis Kearney, while calling for laws to prevent further immigration of Chinese laborers, adopted the portentous slogan "The Chinese must go!" Amidst a swirl of rabble-rousing around the country, Kearney made it quite clear that his "chief mission" was "to secure the expulsion of Chinese labor from California."[117] Similarly, among its welter of anti-Chinese provisions, the 1879 California Constitution authorized the state and localities to confine the Chinese to ghettoized communities and also to forcibly remove them.[118]

The West Coast violence, combined with the eastward movement of the Chinese labor issue and the precarious national balance of power between the two major political parties, meant that by 1878 the "banquet table had been perfectly set for exclusion, if not yet expulsion."[119] A bill was passed in the House, virtually without opposition, to limit any vessel from carrying more than fifteen "Mongolian" passengers to the United States on any single voyage. One of its prominent champions was then-Supreme Court Justice Stephen J. Field, who told a newspaper: "We are alarmed upon this coast at the incursion of the Chinese . . . It is to us a question of property, civilization, and existence."[120]

A minority of Senate Republicans, led by George Frisbee Hoar of Massachusetts, opposed the bill, sparking a national debate in which William Lloyd Garrsion and Henry Ward Beecher and others adopted the Chinese cause, as they had previously supported that of slaves. Indeed, the bill was also eloquently opposed by Senator Blanch K. Bruce of Mississippi, a former slave. Upon hearing Senator Beck of Nevada claim that the western states were threatened by "a mongrel race," Senator Hoar invoked "eternal and practical verities," including "the equality of every human."[121] To Stephen Field's assertion that the Chinese would not assimilate, Hoar responded with a bon mot for the ages: "It takes two to assimilate."[122]

The editors of *Harper's Weekly* expressed alarm at the apparent breach of the treaty with China, calling it "a flagrant breach of public faith which sullies the good name of the country." They also expressed considerable skepticism about the alleged Chinese threat to the West: "to argue that the presence of a hundred and ten or twenty thousand Chinese upon the Pacific coast is such an imminent peril to American society and civilization as to justify the peremptory abrogation of a treaty . . . is insulting to common sense."[123]

The political tide was against these opponents, though, as were powerful class currents. Perceived by the western exclusionists as an elitist, hypocritical, aristocratic Brahmin, Beecher, notes Alexander Saxton, "wrapped into one package all those resentments that had been carried to California by displaced workingmen, disappointed farmers, and immigrants, especially the Irish."[124] The Senate easily approved the Fifteen Passenger Bill, and the California Constitutional Convention immediately took time off to thank Congress for its passage, by a resolution vote of 109 to 8. Nevertheless, President Hayes vetoed the bill. The anger that might have been generated by this action was tempered somewhat by the plausible assertion for it: that the statute violated the Burlingame Treaty.[125] A turning point had clearly been reached, however, and the American minister to China, George Seward, was instructed to negotiate a revised treaty.[126] By 1880, the question of Chinese immigration had assumed national proportions. Actions taken in California, such as resolutions to demolish San Francisco's Chinatown, caused an exodus of Chinese workers from the West. The *New York Star* reported that some 600 Chinese were crossing the country. The *New York Times* said the Chinese were coming east "en masse."[127]

The fact that the two major political parties were split evenly enabled California to assume swing vote power to push the issue.[128] Senator Sherman of Ohio observed during the later debate over the deportation law aimed at the Chinese: "I believe the Scott law was one of the most vicious laws that have been passed in my time in Congress . . . [I]t was a mere political race between the two Houses, then opposed to each other in politics, in the face of a presidential election . . . between two political parties to try and influence the vote of the Pacific coast."[129] One should pause at this point to recall that throughout this period the Chinese were categorically precluded from naturalization and therefore from political power by the racial limitations of the 1790 Naturalization Act to free white men.

In 1880, a new treaty with China was concluded, which gave the United States the right to "regulate limit or suspend" the entry of Chinese laborers but not the right to "absolutely prohibit it." The Congress, again responding to pressure from California, passed a law in 1882 that excluded the entry of Chinese laborers for twenty years. Aylet Buckner of Missouri reportedly said of this law, "It consigns to the grave all sublimated sentiment as to the equality of the races of men."[130] The bill was vetoed by President Arthur on the grounds that it violated the 1880 treaty. A second bill reduced the ban to ten years. This, too, provoked eloquent opposition from certain senators, most from the East. Joseph Hawley of Connecticut said that the whole issue looked to him "like the old fugitive slave law." Hawley went on to predict that if this statute were unearthed 100 years hence, "dug out of the dust of ages and forgotten as it will be except for a line of sneer by some historian," one would not be able to find in law the reason for "excluding these men."[131] But the ten-year ban was signed by the president.[132]

The law also provided that "any Chinese person found unlawfully within the United States shall be caused to be removed to the country from whence he came, by direction of the president of the United States, and at the cost of the United States, after being brought before some justice, judge, or commissioner of a court of the United States, and found to be one not lawfully entitled to be or remain within the United States."[133] The mechanisms of such extended border control removals were unclear, however, and interior enforcement was not effective.[134]

The law allowed Chinese laborers to leave the United States temporarily and to return if they wished. To do so, they had to obtain proof of lawful residence. Predictably, there soon developed widespread allegations of fraudulent reentries. Overgeneralizations about the character of the Chinese were common. A congressional committee report referred to "the notorious capabilities of the lower classes of Chinese for perjury."[135] In 1884, Congress strengthened the documentary requirements and provided that a specialized certificate would be "the sole evidence permissible" to establish a right of reentry into the United States.[136]

The problems for the Chinese went far beyond the law, however. Legal exclusion begat violent expulsion. In 1885, in Eureka, California, two rival groups of Chinese workers got into a fight. As white spectators gathered, some Chinese reportedly opened fire. A white boy was wounded and a Eureka city councilman was killed. A thousand men soon gathered and notified the Chinese that they had twenty-four hours to get out of town. A gallows was quickly built at the main entrance of the Chinese quarter to reinforce the point. This racial vigilantism presaged a series of similar incidents throughout the West. As the *San Francisco Call* put it, "The ball that was set in motion in Eureka, seems to be moving with accelerated speed . . . [T]he people of almost every city and town on the Pacific coast have simultaneously resolved to expel the Chinese laborers."[137] Violent anti-Chinese riots resulted in the murder and expulsion of the Chinese from many communities.[138] A massacre of Chinese workers at Rock Creek Wyoming became something of a cause célèbre.[139] An editorial in the *Nation* expressed the hope that indemnities would be demanded by the government of China and that "all the damning facts connected with the massacre may be lodged with the State Department and given to the world." "It is time," wrote the *Nation* editors, "for our Government to bring down the heavy hand on the murderers and brigands of the West, who have so long rioted in the blood of an inoffensive and peaceful class, whose right to be here . . . is as incontestable as that of any human being, native or foreign-born." Indeed, the editors argued that the "spirit of brutality" was actually encouraged by the recent anti-Chinese legislation and by the weakness of the authorities in dealing with "a plain question of human rights."[140]

Still, white juries often would not convict anti-Chinese vigilantes, which resulted in a lawless reign of terror that alarmed U.S. attorneys and prompted calls for federal assistance, as expulsions continued in Tacoma, Seattle, and throughout the Northwest.[141] In February 1886, a particularly brutal episode of vigilantism took place in Seattle. A group of white citizens, led by the police chief, entered "Chinatown," supposedly to investigate health code violations. As the police chief questioned Chinese residents about sanitation, a mob broke into their houses and loaded their furnishings onto wagons. All the Chinese were then forcibly taken to the docks, where they were compelled to wait, in the rain, while the *Queen of the Pacific* prepared to sail for San Francisco. The captain demanded full fares from the Chinese, which few of them had. Some citizens of Seattle actually then attempted to raise money for the fares from local merchants and bankers. When the governor learned what was happening, he ordered the state militia to intervene. The whole group went to the federal court, pursuant to a habeas corpus writ, where they were told by the judge that, although they were under no legal obligation to leave, the "means for their protection if they stayed were at best dubious." Some 200 Chinese residents then immediately decided to board the ship, leaving behind an equal number who wanted to board. The captain reported hearing gunfire as he departed. Two Chinese men were killed and several more were wounded before the governor invoked martial law. The next day, President Cleveland ordered federal troops to Seattle.[142]

The violence in the West in 1885–1886 was clearly part of long-simmering national labor and class struggles. The class divisions of American society, represented by wretched, sprawling urban slums, deep rural poverty, and the rising power of monopoly capitalism, spawned powerful reactions. By the mid-1880s, "poverty stared with fiercer eyes on wealth unshaken and untamed." Many urban reformers, traditionally of a supportive bent toward immigration, began to veer in a different direction. Those who believed in the ideal of an open, welcoming nation of immigrants saw that vision challenged by squalid urban concentrations of newcomers who seemed linked "to every festering problem." Anti-immigrant sentiment began to assume a cast of intellectual respectability as it was severed from its earlier nativist moorings.[143] Concern about the importation of cheap foreign labor swept the country. In 1884, Terence Powderly's Knights of Labor focused tremendous energy against contract immigrant labor. In Congress, legislators spoke of how U.S. monopolists had shipped from Hungary and Italy, "as so many cattle, large numbers of degraded, ignorant, brutal . . . foreign serfs" to compete with U.S. citizen workers.[144] Such concerns culminated in the contract labor laws of 1885 and 1887.[145] These laws forbade the importation of labor under contract, empowered the secretary of the treasury to enforce the law, and, most important, authorized the immediate return of persons who had landed in violation of the exclusion provisions. Although not quite yet an extended border control deportation law, this provision was a clear harbinger of things to come.

Fears about radicalism among immigrants were greatly inflamed by the Haymarket Affair in 1886.[146] On May 3, 1886, Chicago police fired into a crowd of striking workers at the McCormick Reaper Works, killing and wounding several men. The following evening, anarchist and socialist labor leaders organized a meeting near Haymarket Square. As the meeting ended, the Chicago police suddenly arrived on the scene to disperse the crowd. Someone threw a dynamite bomb toward the police, killing one police officer and injuring several others. Shots were then fired, and eight police officers were killed.[147] The police arrested eight Chicago anarchists and charged them with conspiracy to murder. They were quickly found guilty, and seven were sentenced to death by hanging.[148] The Haymarket Affair spawned a powerful national reaction. Editorials railed against "enemy forces [who] are not American . . . but the very scum and offal of Europe." Others saw a purely foreign, ideological danger because, they argued, "there is no such thing as an American anarchist." Some feared "the destruction of our national edifice by the erosion of its moral foundations." As John Higham has noted, "the stain of foreign turbulence tainted the entire labor movement."[149]

In the West, such anger and frustration devolved into "the cheaper currency of anticooleeism," sometimes combined with charges of foreign radicalism.[150] The 1888 California Republican convention expressed alarm over the influx of foreign "radicals." At the same time, a violent, racist expulsion movement spread throughout the West—sometimes as pure vigilantism, sometimes with the imprimatur of local authorities. At least thirty-five separate communities participated in what amounted to a regional deportation drive.[151] The "driving out" problem soon developed national and international ramifications. A Chinese envoy protested to Secretary of State Bayard that "a concerted movement [was] in progress to drive out the Chinese from all the cities and towns of California except San Francisco," and that state and local authorities were either unwilling or unable to protect them.[152]

Calls for more federal restriction of Chinese immigration became stronger and more effective. In 1888, a new treaty was negotiated with China to suspend the entry of laborers for another twenty years. China refused to ratify it. Congress then passed the Scott Act, which simply prohibited the entry of all Chinese laborers, forbade the issuance of return certificates for those who were here and wished to travel, and cancelled all currently outstanding certificates. The law seemed a fulfillment of Aylett Buckner's earlier observation that such exclusion laws "[perform] the last funeral rite over the dead body of the false and nonsensical dogma of government policy that 'all men are created equal.'"[153]

The new law meant that a large number of Chinese residents who had left the United States temporarily, relying on the law as it existed when they departed, were suddenly barred from returning. An estimated 20,000 Chinese laborers, many of whom had families and owned property in the United States, were affected.[154] Moreover, some 600 persons, in possession of what they undoubtedly thought were valid return certificates, were on the high seas at the time the law was passed.

Chae Chan Ping was one of them. He had lived and worked in San Francisco for twelve years. He left the United States in 1887 on a temporary visit to China and was undoubtedly aware of the legal requirements to return. He had a valid return certificate, but while he was away, Congress passed the Scott Act. When he arrived in San Francisco Bay in 1888, he was therefore detained on the ship. Benefiting from a top-notch legal team, he was ultimately able to present to the Supreme Court virtually every conceivable argument one might make against this law, ranging from the most obvious due process and ex post facto clause constitutional challenges, to contractual claims that he had a "vested right" to return under statutes and treaties, and many more. Indeed, his lawyers even argued that the Scott Act violated "natural law." And in one of the boldest (and most futile and poignant) moments of Supreme Court practice, they argued that this was an argument for which they "disdain[ed] to cite authority."[155]

Unfortunately, all of these powerful rights arguments were rejected by the Court. Indeed, with the possible exception of Dred Scott, one could fairly say that Chae Chan Ping lost his case more conclusively, and with more long-term consequences, than any other person in the entire history of American law. This was especially noteworthy in that the author of the Court's opinion, Stephen J. Field, a Democrat who had been appointed by President Lincoln, supported an expansive view of the Fourteenth Amendment (he had dissented in the *Slaughterhouse Cases*) and was known in general as a strong supporter of substantive due process.[156] None of this helped the Chinese.

There were two basic holdings of the case. The first was that the passage of the Scott Act overrode any prior treaty-based rights of travel. In other words, the Court held that the United States could legally abrogate a treaty simply by passing a contrary statute.[157] As to the constitutionality of the statute itself, the Court first considered the source of the exclusion power. The power to regulate immigration, as noted above, was held to be extraconstitutional, plenary, and "inherent in sovereignty." What this meant was that, unlike other actions of the government, which must be justified by reference to a specific source of constitutional authority and then must comply with constitutional standards, such as those of due process, immigration laws would receive only the most minimal sort of judicial review, if any. As Louis Henkin has noted, the case still stands as a "fossil," an example of "pre-rights jurisprudence" that has been rejected virtually everywhere else in the American legal system.[158] Nevertheless, it stands. More than that, it has migrated.

The exclusion of the Chinese was part of an increasingly centralized and restrictive regime of federal immigration control. Throughout the country, allegations of inefficiency and corruption in the state enforcement systems raised great public outcry, as Henry Cabot Lodge and others also railed about the inferior qualities of the "new" immigrants from southern Europe. In 1890, the secretary of the treasury revoked the federal government's contract with New York following investigations of lax and corrupt practices at Castle Garden, the New York immigration control station. Joint congressional hearings recommended new immigration laws to "separate the desirable from the undesirable immigrants, and to permit only those to land on our shores who have certain physical and moral qualities."[159] The federal exclusion bandwagon developed unstoppable momentum.

The 1891 Immigration Act, which applied to all immigrants except for Chinese laborers (who were covered by their own special system and were not subject to general immigration law until 1903), embodied two major attributes: systematization of the previously rather ad hoc "sifting" function and increasingly bureaucratized, centralized federal control.[160] The list of those to be excluded now included polygamists, people with contagious diseases, and those "likely to become a public charge." Most important for our purposes, it also included the first general deportation law since the Alien and Sedition Acts. This law was of the extended border control variant—providing for the deportation, within one year, of those who were later discovered to have been subject to exclusion at entry. Thus, a sort of catch basin was added to the sieve mechanism.[161]

Exclusion had always been pregnant with deportation. In 1882, Alabama Senator John T. Morgan had analogized the Chinese situation to the impossibility of removing African Americans from the United States: "After you have got the Chinese here, and they become incorporated in one way or another with your social, industrial, and political institutions, the power will be found wanting to expel them."[162]

The correct legal approach to take to deportation, as opposed to exclusion at the border, was still an unresolved question, however. In the 1892 case of *Nishimura Ekiu v. United States*, the Court considered a case arising under the "public charge provision" of the 1891 act. Justice Gray, in dicta, expanded the "inherent in sovereignty" formulation to include the power not just to forbid the entrance of foreigners, but also "to admit them only in such cases and on such conditions as [the sovereign nation] may see fit to prescribe."[163] This statement hinted that the power to expel might be inferred from the plenary power to exclude, at least in situations involving the violation of a condition imposed at entry.[164]

At the same time, Congress returned to the Chinese question. The move now was against Chinese laborers still within the United States. A law sponsored by Representative Geary in 1892 sought to extend the exclusion of Chinese laborers. It also required all such Chinese in the United States to register and to bear the burden of proving their legality. The law, an assertion of racially targeted federal power, was in fact doubly racist. Those Chinese who were found without a certificate of residence could avoid deportation only if they could prove two things to a judicial officer:

1. that the failure to obtain the certificate was reasonable, and
2. that they were legally resident in the United States.

This latter fact, however, could be proved only by the testimony of at least one credible white witness.[165]

The Senate debates over the Geary bill offer a fascinating glimpse into the late-nineteenth-century mind-set. The problem of inadequate enforcement of existing border control laws was pointedly raised by Senator Squire of Washington: "[I]t seems to be demagogy of the most arrant kind for the representatives of the United States in Congress assembled to inveigh against the Chinese, and to pass act after act for the alleged purpose of their exclusion from this country [while failing] to provide a reasonable sum of money to enable the law to be efficiently executed."[166]

Senator Felton of California proposed an amendment to require all Chinese in the United States (except for diplomatic personnel and their servants) to apply for certificates of residence and that a person found without such certificates after one year would be "subject to the same fines and penalties as if he had unlawfully come to the U.S. in the first instance." In support of this amendment, Senator Felton asserted, "[T]he Chinese come to the countries adjoining us, pass over the border, and the instant that they are here it is very difficult, almost impossible, to distinguish one from another."[167]

Similar attitudes toward the Chinese were amply evident throughout the debates:

Mr. SQUIRE.(. . .) [T]here should be ingrafted provisions for the registration of Chinese and for the issuance of a certificate containing a true photograph of the applicant, to each Chinese now in this country or who may hereafter come . . .

Mr. KENNA. Can one distinguish between the Chinese so as to identify them?

Mr. SQUIRE. Oh, certainly, one can learn to distinguish between Chinese just the same as between Africans.[168]

It was not merely the alleged Caucasian inability to distinguish one Chinese person from another that concerned the senators, however. Senator Felton continued: "[T]he Chinese have no morals, no regard whatever for the sanctity of an oath. With them the end justifies the means, and the end is to come in here and possess themselves of what we have and return to their own country with it, and let another herd come and take their place."[169]

The statements of Senator Stewart of Nevada, formerly from California, illustrate the lessons he had learned from the *People v. Hall* case:

I have had some experience in relation to Chinese testimony. About forty years ago, I was the district attorney [who] tried the first murder case in which Chinese testimony was used. I labored very hard to ascertain what regard Chinamen had for an oath . . . The question was how an oath could be administered. Some stated it was the habit to administer it by cutting off a chicken's head, others that it was by burning papers . . . We tried them all . . . We thought we would get the truth out of the Chinese witnesses by separating them, and so we hired rooms in different parts of the town, kept them separately . . . but when they came in each one of them told precisely the same story in exactly the same language. [Laughter]

I convicted my man and went to the Supreme Court with great confidence . . . [T]o my astonishment the Supreme Court held that a Chinaman was an Indian, and could not testify against a white man in the state of California. [Laughter][170]

Senator Stewart went on, amidst the laughter of his Senate colleagues, to describe the implications of this problem for a deportation regime:

Because you have got a law if you think it is practicable that you can remove a Chinaman who is improperly here, if you think you can get one out of one hundred thousand of them in twenty years and make a case to extradite him, then I shall be disappointed. I do not believe it can be done. A white man . . . cannot tell Chinamen apart. They will substitute one for another right before your eyes and then go right on with the case. [Laughter][171]

Toward the end of the debate, Senator Morgan offered a chilling assessment of the potential power of government over the Chinese. The government had, he said, not only the power to regulate their entry and residence in the United States, but also "the right . . . to set apart for them, as we have for the Indians, a territory or reservation, where they should not break out to contaminate our people."[172]

The Geary law was passed in 1892, nearly a quarter century after the ratification of the Fourteenth Amendment and the enactment of the post–Civil War Civil Rights Acts. It is thus hardly surprising that many in the legal community thought it was patently unconstitutional. Test cases were quickly organized, and the enforcement of the law was stayed pending a decision by the Supreme Court.

In their Supreme Court brief in *Fong Yue Ting*, Joseph Choate, J. Hubley Ashton, and Maxwell Evarts meticulously argued how the procedures of the Geary law violated the Fourth, Fifth, Sixth, and Eighth Amendments. They focused on the "absolute and arbitrary power" granted to the administrative officials enforcing the act and the lack of full judicial process available to the accused because of the white witness requirement. They argued that this provision was apparently based on a conclusion by the Congress that judges were unable to decide for themselves "whether a witness is to be believed or not." Thus, it was argued that the act was repugnant to the "body and spirit, the very soul of the Constitution."[173] The government position was about as completely to the contrary as one could imagine. Indeed, the government lawyers argued in their brief that Congress could have chosen "to expel these alien residents without process, hearing or evidence of any kind."[174]

The decision from the Supreme Court was, by any measure, a bombshell. Its repercussions are felt to this day.[175] The Court's reasoning derived from the exceptionally broad proposition that "the right of a nation to expel or deport foreigners . . . rests upon the same grounds and is as absolute and unqualified as the right to prohibit and prevent their entrance into the country." Justice Gray wrote that "the power to exclude aliens and the power to expel them rest upon one foundation, are derived from one source, are supported by the same reasons, and are in truth but parts of one and the same power." Noncitizens, the Court determined, "remain subject to the power of Congress to expel them . . . whenever in [Congress's] judgment their removal is necessary or expedient for the public interest."[176] The white witness provision was upheld as within the scope of this extraordinarily broad power and was also said to be simply an evidentiary issue with no constitutional import.[177] The Court also concluded that a deportation proceeding was "in no proper sense a trial and sentence for a crime or offense." Rather, the proceeding was characterized as "simply the ascertainment, by appropriate and lawful means, of the fact whether the conditions exist upon which Congress has enacted that an alien of this class may remain within the country." Moreover, the Court determined that "the order of deportation is not a punishment for crime . . . but [is] a method of enforcing the return to his own country of an alien who has not complied with . . . conditions" for his continuing residence in the United States.[178]

The language of the *Fong Yue Ting* majority—that the power to deport was as "absolute and unqualified" as the power to exclude—was dramatic. Taken literally, it could mean that aliens, legally resident or not, have no constitutional rights at all in deportation proceedings. It is not completely clear, however, that the majority actually meant to go quite so far. The Court specifically addressed how Congress might require proof of lawful status.[179] The case did not squarely present the question of the outer substantive or procedural limits of the power to deport legally admitted residents. It certainly did not involve post-entry conduct or social control deportation at all. Indeed, Justice Gray's formulation, that deportation is appropriate for an alien "who has not complied with . . . conditions," implies that he was considering only the power to expel on the basis of conditions imposed at entry, which, in fact, was the aim of the Geary Act.[180]

Passages in the majority opinion also suggest that the Court thought it important that the case did not involve deportation based on post-entry wrongful conduct. For example, the Court expressly distinguished the expulsion power at issue from what some commentators had referred to as "transportation."[181] This analysis, striking for its recognition that transportation is punishment (apparently even if applied to aliens) but deportation is not, immediately precedes the Court's conclusion that the powers to exclude and to expel are essentially the same. If the latter proposition were completely true, the distinctions between deportation and transportation would be irrelevant.[182]

In any event, the consequences of the *Fong Yue Ting* decision were staggering. Tens of thousands of Chinese workers were now subject to deportation for failure to register. The secretary of the treasury, with a budget of $25,000, faced a task that was estimated to cost $7,310,000.[183] As a result, the secretary chose not to enforce the law immediately, leading to what one newspaper described as "open war" between Californians and the administration.[184] Threats of violence continued as did unusual legal tactics, including the reported swearing out of federal court complaints for deportation against Chinese people by private individuals.[185] The Geary Act had been accompanied by an authorization of a mere $60,000, a clearly inadequate sum. It created no specific deportation machinery nor did it even name the persons who were supposed to deport the thousands of Chinese potentially affected. One newspaper sarcastically noted, "there is no money to deport and we can't drown them."[186] In a New York case, a Chinese laborer was released from custody because there was neither money nor a mechanism to enforce the Geary Act.[187]

The depression years of 1893–1897 were the dreary end of a national period of "recurring calamities and almost unrelieved discontent."[188] A generalized fear of the "stranger" and increasing concerns about the characteristics of the new immigrants from southern and eastern Europe took hold throughout the country. Though, in general, the still rather buoyant American heritage was able to resist these dark streams, this did not help the Chinese. There was a strong revival of violent anti-Chinese expulsions in the West. According to one contemporary report, the pattern was fairly typical: a group of rioters would go to a Chinese camp at night, rout the inhabitants, force them to the railroad, and put them on the first train that arrived. Questions were raised about the character of these rioters (the *Pacific Rural* press—organ of the Granger movement—referred to them as "low tramps and bummers".) And some doubted their ostensible justifications—the failure of the federal government to enforce the exclusion laws.[189] Nevertheless, anti-Chinese demonstrations, clearly motivated in part by frustration over the lack of federal immigration control, were reported in cities throughout the region. Hundreds of Chinese were driven from their jobs; many thousands lived in constant fear.

The depression spawned more general anti-immigrant sentiments as well. The *Los Angeles Times* reported that hundreds of thousands of men were out of work. The editors' proposed solutions illustrate the volatile politics of the time. Huge federal irrigation projects were sought to provide jobs. But the writers also urged the exclusion of "the lower classes of Poles, Hungarians, Italians and some other European nations, which people possess most of the vices of the Chinese and few of their good qualities, besides having a leaning towards bloodshed and anarchy which is peculiarly their own."[190]

There was no shortage of specifically anti-Chinese attitudes among the first federal immigration enforcement personnel, however. Terence Powderly, for example, who served for five years as U.S. Commissioner-General of Immigration from 1897 to 1902, had, only five years earlier, said of the Chinese, "They do not assimilate with our people, do not wear our clothing, do not adopt our customs, language, religion or sentiments. It is said that the Chinese, if given an opportunity, will become Americanized. The Chinese coolie will no more become Americanized than an American can take on the habits, customs, garb and religion of the Mongolian . . . American and Chinese civilizations are antagonistic; they cannot live and thrive and both survive on the same soil." His final words demonstrate the depth of his feeling about his later mission: "One or the other must perish."[191]

Early enforcement of the Geary law was aimed to a considerable degree at a specific subgroup that found virtually no defenders: convicted Chinese felons. An amendment proposed by Representative Caminetti of California provided for the deportation of every Chinese convicted of a felony. It passed by a vote of 178 to 1.[192] As Lucy Salyer has noted, these people were, for white Americans and indeed for many Chinese, "the ideal scapegoat." Among the most inflammatory aspects of the racialized discourse that had festered during the late nineteenth century were lurid descriptions of the Chinese American underworld of gamblers—opium dens and prostitution. An enforcement focus on Chinese criminals was about as politically safe a strategy as one could imagine. Indeed, the Chinese Six Companies, which had vigorously opposed the exclusion and deportation laws, cooperated in the apprehension of prostitutes and convicted felons. These arrests deflected attention from other Chinese and supported the Chinese business community in power struggles with secret societies, known as "tongs."[193] A bridge from Chinese exclusion to the Geary Act's policy of extended border control deportation and then to post-entry social control deportation was thus being built. But was it constitutional?

The Court began to consider this issue in the 1896 case of *Wong Wing v. United States*.[194] The 1892 act contained a section that provided for the sentence of up to a year of hard labor for any Chinese citizen judged to be in the United States illegally.[195] The statute provided no right to trial by jury. The Court held this provision unconstitutional. Detention or temporary confinement was permissible "as part of the means necessary to give effect to the provisions for the exclusion or expulsion of aliens." However, the Court ruled, when Congress pursues deportation policy by subjecting noncitizens to "infamous punishment at hard labor, or by confiscating their property," then "such legislation, to be valid, must provide for a judicial trial to establish the guilt of the accused."[196]

The bright-line distinction drawn by the *Wong Wing* Court between detention "as part of the means necessary" and as "infamous punishment" masks some complex issues that remain unresolved today. The tactics of Wong Wing's lawyers may have contributed to this. They apparently did not argue, as they might have, that the proceedings themselves were quasi-criminal.[197] Instead, the appellants contended that the potential punishment was purely a criminal one and therefore required all relevant constitutional protections.[198] The Court was presented with a binary problem: either the imprisonment at hard labor was a criminal sanction, or it was civil. Major constitutional consequences would flow from that initial categorization.

The *Wong Wing* Court reaffirmed the plenary power holding of *Fong Yue Ting*, though still with a clear extended border-control phrasing: "No limits can be put by the courts upon the power of Congress to protect, by summary methods, the country from the advent of aliens whose race or habits render them undesirable as citizens, or to expel such if they have already found their way into our land and unlawfully remain therein."[199]

As important, the *Wong Wing* Court seems to have viewed the constitutional civil-criminal line as more important than the plenary power doctrine that *Fong Yue Ting* had applied to deportation. This is no small point. The *Wong Wing* Court sought a consistent "theory of our government" with which to distinguish deportation from punishment. Wrapping punishment within the deportation system did not override specific constitutional protections. The Court did not rely on a transcendent sovereignty model or on the status of the accused as "deportable aliens" to avoid the dilemma presented by the 1892 law: "But to declare unlawful residence within the country to be an infamous crime, punishable by deprivation of liberty and property, would be to pass out of the sphere of constitutional legislation, unless provision were made that the fact of guilt should first be established by a judicial trial."[200]

The *Wong Wing* Court also made it very clear that the implications of the equal protection case of *Yick Wo v. Hopkins* were powerful, even in the deportation context.[201] All persons in the United States are entitled to the protections of the Fifth and Sixth Amendments.[202] *Wong Wing* thus raised an important question that has yet to be fully resolved: how should courts draw the line between what might be termed regulatory deportation procedures and those punitive deportation procedures that require constitutional protections analogous—if not identical—to those afforded criminal defendants? The case provides little clear guidance. The fact that the deportation process may involve incarceration does not render the proceedings criminal or punitive. Deprivation of liberty, absent more, is not necessarily punishment.[203] However, incarceration and other possibly punitive aspects of deportation laws must be analyzed to determine whether they warrant special constitutional protections derived from the criminal system.[204]

Consider the problems raised by a deportation regime that involves inevitable long delays and mandatory incarceration during the entire process. Is this not punishment in effect, if not in name? Is it only the intent of the government that matters? If so, whose intent counts? That of Congress? The executive branch? And how is intent to be gauged? What of a system that deports long-term legal residents for minor violations, retroactively defined, and separates them from their U.S. citizen families? These questions, of course, do not arise if we simply accept the plenary power doctrine of *Fong Yue Ting*. *Wong Wing*, however, implies that specific substantive constitutional protections are required for certain types of deportation laws. The key concept is punishment. As we shall see, the Supreme Court has never seriously reconsidered the basic analytical question of how this analysis ought to be made in the deportation context.[205] Why did this happen?

Scholars have offered a number of explanations, both doctrinal and external, for the ease with which the Court dismissed most claims of substantive rights by noncitizens facing deportation in the late nineteenth century.[206] One obvious factor, as discussed above, was the rather nasty attitude about race that was pervasive at this time. The view of immigration as an ideal shifted dramatically in this country as the immigrant population changed from primarily northern and western Europeans to southern and eastern Europeans and Asians.[207] The justices of the Supreme Court, particularly Stephen Field, who had worked hard to restrict Chinese immigration before his appointment to the Court, were far from immune to these attitudes.[208] The closing of the frontier was undoubtedly another important factor, as the earlier limitless vision of continental expansion and demographic need began to fade.[209] Moreover, the development of a muscular type of American nationalism and imperialism fed an assertive sense of sovereign power and border control.[210] In addition, various aspects of contemporary legal doctrine were rather too easily imported into immigration and deportation law. As Peter Schuck has noted, a broad conception of individual "sovereignty" over property, an underlying "consent" principle defining the relationship between individuals and government, and the "right/privilege" distinction all influenced the Court's approach to the rights claims of noncitizens.[211] One sees these themes in various ways. For example, the recurrence of a "guest" metaphor applied to even long-term legal resident aliens shows how the Court saw analogies to the common law of property in deportation cases.[212]

Additional doctrinal analysis should be added to this mix. First, the fact that the Geary law was an extended border-control deportation law may well have facilitated the Court's extension of the plenary power doctrine in *Fong Yue Ting*. The link to the border and to sovereignty was a direct one. Once the legitimacy of extended border-control deportation of alien "friends" became entrenched in the legal firmament, its extension to post-entry social control laws cases was easier than it would have been as a matter of first impression. The new doctrinal structure (plenary power qualified only by flexible procedural due process) derived from those cases has withstood virtually all attempts at reformulation.

Let us consider, then, exactly how extended border-control laws begat post-entry social control deportation. The first general federal immigration statute, the Act of March 3, 1875, excluded convicts and prostitutes.[213] But it did not provide for their deportation except as an immediate part of the exclusion process (i.e., if they evaded border controls and were caught, they could be deported immediately). The post-entry deportation dam was first clearly breached—outside of the Chinese context—by the Contract Labor Laws and then by the Act of March 3, 1891, which provided that "any alien who shall come into the United States in violation of law may be returned . . . at any time within one year thereafter."[214] This one-year limitation was expanded to three years in 1903. Still, the model was one of extended border control. Only those who had entered "in violation of law" were subject to later deportation. The so-called public charge provision of the 1891 act began to bridge the conceptual gap between extended border control and post-entry social control deportation. Deportation was still somewhat tied to entry because one could be deported as a public charge only if the status arose "from causes existing prior to . . . landing."[215]

Proof of post-entry facts was thus linked to pre-entry conditions.[216] Gradually, with virtually no judicial analysis, the legal system moved from this evidentiary linkage to acceptance of pure post-entry social control deportation. Of course, many of the first such cases, in the early 1900s, involved highly charged ideological and criminal deportations. The disinclination of the Supreme Court to rethink subtle underlying doctrinal premises is thus at least understandable, if not necessarily a source of pride. The structure, as we shall see, withstood a second attack in the wake of a similar set of ideological deportation laws upheld in the late 1940s and early 1950s.

Modern post-entry social control deportation laws were, in part, a consequence of an early federal "war on crime." A House report had concluded as early as 1891 that "at least 50 per cent of the criminals, insane and paupers of our largest cities . . . are of foreign birth."[217] At first, deportation law addressed immigrant crime through extended border control laws. People were excluded for pre-entry crime, not generally deported for post-entry crime. Then, a 1907 deportation statute provided that "any alien woman or girl [found to be a prostitute] . . . within three years after she shall have entered the United States, shall be deemed to be unlawfully within the United States and shall be deported."[218] On its face, this language could be read to authorize deportation solely for post-entry conduct, but the law actually related to the long-standing attempt to prevent the entry of prostitutes into the United States. However, the three-year limit caused problems, as it was "often

extremely difficult to prove the illegal entrance of either women or procurers."[219] Noncitizens could avoid expulsion simply by lying about the
critical entry date.[220] Thus, a 1910 refinement eliminated the three-year
period and created what amounted to the first true U.S. post-entry social
control deportation law since the 1798 Alien Friends Act.[221]

The application of this law was challenged in the 1913 Supreme
Court case of *Bugajewitz v. Adams*.[222] Justice Oliver Wendell Holmes, Jr.,
writing for the Court, stated that the facts showed that Ms. Bugajewitz
was a prostitute when she was arrested in 1910. But he also concluded
that "she was a prostitute at the time of entry and entered the United
States for the purpose of prostitution or for an immoral purpose."[223] The
Court, unfortunately, never clearly determined whether her deportation
was based on a presumption of unlawful entry arising from post-entry
conduct or on the post-entry conduct itself. This is the essential difference between an extended border control and a post-entry social control
law. In light of *Wong Wing*, it might well have mattered. Deportation for
post-entry conduct is more readily analogized to punishment for crime
than is an evidentiary presumption.[224] Counsel for Ms. Bugajewitz had
in fact argued that if she was being deported for a crime, she had a right
to a trial.[225] This was an apparent attempt to apply the *Wong Wing* reasoning, with a crucial difference: instead of focusing on the punishment
attached to her deportation, the attorneys asked the Court to note that
her deportation was based on criminal conduct. It was, they argued, a
part of the criminal process. However, what might have been a definitive
turning point in U.S. deportation law was ambiguously analyzed by Justice Holmes simply as, "we must take it, at least, that she is a prostitute
now." Because the act did not actually require a criminal conviction, Justice Holmes reasoned that the coincidence that the predicate facts for
deportation and for a possible criminal conviction were the same did
not necessarily render the deportation proceeding criminal.[226] Again,
this conclusion skirted the most interesting questions. It apparently left
open the question of the constitutional status of deportation cases based
directly on criminal convictions.

The terseness of Holmes's *Bugajewitz* opinion has been noted over the
years.[227] It likely, however, accurately reflected Holmes's opinion that
deportation was not punishment. Indeed, in the same session as *Bugajewitz*, Holmes had considered deportation law in the case of *Tiaco v.
Forbes*.[228] *Tiaco* involved a suit for money damages against the governor

general of the Philippines by Chinese aliens whom he had deported on pure social control grounds: that they were "dangerous to public tranquility." The position of the governor general, who was represented by the young Felix Frankfurter, seems to have been, per *Fong Yue Ting*, that there were simply no substantive constitutional limits to the deportation power. Justice Holmes apparently endorsed this broad proposition: "As Congress is not prevented by the Constitution, the Philippine Government cannot be prevented by the Philippine Bill of Rights alone. Deporting the plaintiffs was not depriving them of liberty without due process of law."[229]

These two cases, one summarily analyzed, the other an imperialist exercise, in effect extended the Court's deference to the political branches to deport any noncitizen who, after admission, engaged in any kind of proscribed conduct.

Challenges to congressional power and claims of substantive rights were not, however, the only arguments made about deportation laws during this period. Two other related issues, the requirements of procedural due process and the role of courts, assumed greater importance as the more substantive constitutional challenges lost force. There was much to be concerned about. Deportation hearings at this time were characterized by a maximum amount of administrative power, with only minimal safeguards against "error and prejudice." As William Van Vleck noted, "certainty, care, and due deliberation [were] sacrificed to the desire for speed."[230]

In 1903, in *Yamataya v. Fisher*, Justice Harlan had made clear that for an "alien who has entered the country and has become subject to its jurisdiction and a part of its population," administrative process must at least comply with due process norms. It could not be "arbitrary," and the "alien" must, at a minimum, be given an opportunity to be heard.[231] Over time, this standard developed into a flexible touchstone of "fundamental fairness."[232] There developed two distinct approaches. On the one hand, some judges were strongly protective of noncitizens' procedural rights. As one court put it, "A full and fair hearing on the charges which threaten his deportation, and an absence of all abuse of discretion and arbitrary action . . . are indispensable to the lawful deportation of an alien."[233]

But for many other courts, such questions were seen as inappropriate for consideration, except, perhaps, in the most extreme situations. Restriction of federal court jurisdiction over administrative deportation cases was concomitant with the rise of the twentieth-century administrative state.[234] Rights claims in many arenas transformed into disputes over the outer limits of the exercise of administrative discretion—an approach that persists in deportation law today.[235] The most basic issue, then as now, was whether federal courts would play any significant role in overseeing the administrative deportation system.

The Supreme Court considered this question of administrative finality in the 1895 case of Lem Moon Sing, a Chinese merchant who challenged an administrative decision to exclude him from the United States. Justice Harlan wrote a majority opinion that concluded that the government agent had been given "exclusive authority to determine whether a particular alien seeking admission into the country belongs to . . . a class forbidden to enter the United States." Any other approach would defeat Congress's apparent intention to strip the federal courts of authority "to review the decisions of executive officers."[236]

But such administrative finality raises deep legal dilemmas, such as how to treat claims of citizenship at the border. The sweeping language of the *Chinese Exclusion Case* and *Fong Yue Ting* created a real conundrum. It was one thing to accept a system with virtually no judicial review of exclusion cases affecting aliens. It was quite another to imagine the exclusion, arrest, or deportation of citizens mistakenly thought to be aliens. But if every alien could obtain a full judicial hearing merely by claiming to have been born in San Francisco, then the judicial role and costs would increase dramatically and many cases would be considerably delayed.

Following the *Lem Moon Sing* decision, many felt that Congress could not constitutionally eliminate judicial review of a citizenship claim.[237] Then, in 1898, the Supreme Court upheld birthright citizenship for Chinese who were born in the United States.[238] There was now a clear tension between the plenary power doctrine and finality versus the rights of U.S. citizens. So-called native son petitions increased dramatically in the California courts.[239] The Court first considered the problem in the New York case *In re Sing Tuck*. The government sought to distinguish "routine" challenges of agency fact determinations—which it argued were precluded from judicial review—from questions of law or situations where "a manifest wrong has been done." The attorneys for the Chinese petitioners countered that citizenship was not simply a fact, but a "jurisdictional" fact, requiring judicial consideration. Justice Holmes, writing for the Court, effectively skirted the issue on technical grounds while noting the tension. "The whole scheme," he opined, "is intended to give as fair a chance to prove the right to enter the country as the necessarily summary character of the proceedings will permit."[240]

The inevitable next test case, *Ju Toy,* arose in California.[241] The Supreme Court decision that emerged was a deep disappointment, not only to the Chinese petitioners, but to many legal scholars as well. Indeed, Felix Frankfurter later called it one of Justice Holmes's "cavalier opinions."[242] The same Court that had dealt a death blow to state regulatory efforts that allegedly interfered with contractual liberty rights in *Lochner v. New York* deferred almost completely to administrative authority when the question was the citizenship of a Chinese person seeking entry into the United States.[243] Although the Court assumed for purposes of argument that the Fifth Amendment applied to a citizen denied entry, due process did not require a jury trial, as the lawyers in *Ju Toy* had argued. Indeed, the Court analogized the situation to that of a person whose property was taken for a tax arrearage. In such cases, due process had long been held not to require judicial process.[244]

In dissent, Justice Brewer, who had also vigorously dissented in *Fong Yue Ting,* called the decision "appalling." He argued that life and liberty interests required greater protection than property and that he could not believe that Congress intended to deprive a citizen of constitutional protection "simply because he belongs to an obnoxious race," and even if it did so intend, he did not "believe that it has the power to do so."[245]

The *Ju Toy* decision, upholding the basic plenary power model, illustrated the need for subconstitutional fail-safe mechanisms at least to protect the rights of citizens. In deportation cases, those mechanisms were judicial review of procedure and methods of statutory interpretation. Advocates for immigrants also used the judicial review mandate of the Geary Act to build on the procedural due process victory in *Yamataya v. Fisher.*[246] This strategy achieved some early success even in deportation cases that involved an alleged denial of a "right to land." Justice Holmes, writing for the Court, held that the administrative finality he had supported depended on "the presupposition that the decision was after a hearing in good faith, however summary in form."[247] "[T]he semblance of a hearing" without a "fair opportunity to present the evidence" would permit the intervention of a federal judge. Indeed, Justice

Holmes now even allowed that if the court determined that a fair hearing had not been provided, it could rehear the case on the merits itself. This was a major breach in the deference granted by courts to the government, providing an important new toehold for attorneys seeking to hold the Bureau of Immigration to due process norms.[248]

But cases involving crime and morality substantially limited the value of that toehold. In a 1912 case involving allegations of improprieties during the deportation of alleged prostitutes in California, the Court held that absent proof that proceedings were "manifestly unfair" or a "manifest abuse of discretion," courts should not intervene.[249] The Court did make clear, though, that the bureau had to follow its own rules. And it restrained agency power to develop substantive law on its own.[250]

Conclusion

Many years before he achieved lasting jurisprudential infamy by authoring *Chae Chan Ping v. United States,* Justice Stephen Field had considered the question of what government action can be legally understood as punishment in *Cummings v. Missouri.*[251] His approach was functional, humanitarian, and generous to the affected individual because he well understood what was at stake, both as a matter of constitutional law and as a matter of discursive symbolism: "The deprivation of any rights, civil or political, previously enjoyed, may be punishment, the circumstances attending and the causes of the deprivation determining this fact."[252]

Justice Field later dissented in *Fong Yue Ting* in part, one assumes, because of the dissonance between his approach to punishment in *Cummings* and the insulation of deportation from meaningful judicial review that was imposed by the majority's extension of plenary power internally to long-term legal residents. The fact that only two other justices agreed with him in *Fong Yue Ting* left deportation law in the harsh, anomalous state in which we still find it today.

4

The Second Wave:
Expansion and Refinement
of Modern Deportation Law

The unnaturalized alien in America has been made a man without a country. He is outside the protection of the commonest safeguards which we throw about a criminal. He has no claims on the Bill of Rights; he is not protected by the Constitution.

—Frederic C. Howe, "Lynch Law and the Immigrant Alien,"
The Nation (February 14, 1920)

Huge social and economic changes gripped American society at the turn of the twentieth century as a nation-state grounded in classical liberalism, a weak central state, and rather fixed social categories gave way to something quite different. Ever stricter exclusion and deportation laws developed during this period, both as powerful tools of centralized, professional, federal extended border authority and of post-entry social control. In this legal arena, as in others, social cohesion, order, and organization were key desiderata as a path was sought between what many viewed as the excesses of individualism and collective ideologies. Indeed, the term "social control" itself derives from this era, as thinkers like Edward A. Ross, Henry Maine, Ferdinand Tönnies, and Emile Durkheim sought systematic accounts of a modern society with conscious organizing principles.[1] The stunning breadth of characteristics for which exclusion and deportation control were deemed necessary emerged in President Theodore Roosevelt's 1905 annual message to Congress, in which he sought "an increase in the stringency of laws to keep out insane, idiotic, epileptic and pauper immigrants. But this is by no means enough. Not merely the anarchist, but every man of anarchistic tendencies, all violent and disorderly people, all people of bad character, the incompetent, the lazy, the vicious, and physically unfit, defective, or degenerate should be kept out."[2]

A signal feature of the Progressive movement that animated much of the politics of this period was the belief in what Morton Keller has termed "regulating a new society." This impulse had important consequences for the increasingly large and assertive immigrant working class. It was completely logical—indeed, almost inevitable—that such ideas led to strict, bureaucratic federal deportation laws in the nation of immigrants. For if the United States was to rely, as it had to, on the labor and revitalizing energy of millions of newcomers, some system was thought necessary to control certain qualities within that group.

As before, one of the main concerns was poverty. Frederic C. Howe wrote that by 1920, "The great majority of aliens are deported because they have broken down in the industrial machine; they have become a public charge. They have been discarded by the mine, by the mill, by the factory, by the packing plant."[3] The 1891 act had mandated deportation of "any alien who becomes a public charge within one year after his arrival . . . from causes existing prior to his landing." In 1917, the period was increased to five years, and the burden was placed on the noncitizen to prove that the cause of becoming a "public charge" arose "subsequent to landing."[4]

A general regulatory ethos over immigrants and concerns about the realities of admitting "poor, tired, huddled masses" cannot, however, explain the turn to post-entry social control deportation laws that marked this era. Of equal importance were the increasing federal attention paid to crime, federal intervention in labor struggles, federal action related to vigilantism, continuous ideological turmoil, and the development and expansion of the border patrol. And, as always, there was the problem of race. In 1917, a "barred Asiatic zone" appeared in U.S. law, expanding the Chinese laws to most Asians.[5] By the early 1920s, such laws had developed into broader immigration quotas based on national origin and more systematized exclusion lists.[6] The Immigration Act of 1924 refined the quota system to reduce the number of new immigrants from eastern and southern Europe.[7] It also excluded all persons "ineligible to citizenship," a euphemism that barred virtually all Asian immigration, including the Japanese.[8] Thus, these laws both instantiated a uniquely American idea of an "Asian" racial category and made racial exclusion a central component of twentieth-century immigration, naturalization, and deportation law.[9]

Deportation for Crime

> A systematic deportation not only eugenically cleanses America of a vicious element but the moral effect upon their native countries makes deportation . . . doubly worth while.
>
> —Edwin E. Grant, "Scum from the Melting-Pot,"
> *American Journal of Sociology* May 1925

By December 1910, the deportation of prostitutes and procurers was well accepted—even, in effect, for post-entry conduct, as exemplified by the *Bugajewitz* case. The effects of these laws could be quite harsh.[10] Still, the idea of deportation for more types of post-entry crime easily garnered public support. Although scholars now question whether there really was any sort of major crime wave in the early twentieth century, there was clearly a general perception at the time of widespread and increasing crime. Indeed, more than fifty major crime surveys were undertaken by various committees and commissions to gather facts, educate the public, and make recommendations for criminal legislation to state and local governments.[11] The summary report of the Dillingham Commission, which had been created to study immigration policy, recommended "a five-year period of deportability of aliens convicted of serious crimes after entry."[12] Although momentum for such new criminal deportation provisions slowed somewhat as the national attention turned toward war, it never completely stopped.[13]

The essential pieces of the modern regime of deportation for post-entry criminal conduct were contained in the 1917 Immigration Act. Unlike any prior law, the 1917 act included a list of otherwise legal resident aliens who were to be "taken into custody and deported."[14] It also radically changed prior law by requiring deportation after entry for a wide variety of reasons and in permitting deportation without time limitation for certain types of cases.[15] The act used three mechanisms to link the criminal justice system to deportation: the seriousness of a deportable crime was determined by the length of sentence and by multiple offenses; the nature of a deportable crime was determined by a rather vague standard, "a crime involving moral turpitude"; and a time limit of commission of the crime "within five years after entry" was included in the interest of fairness, in the case of a single offense. Those sentenced more than once, however, now faced deportation "at any time after entry."[16] The 1917 law did have some important ameliorative features. It recognized pardons as defenses to deportation and permitted a sentencing judge to override its provisions with a binding "recommendation" against deportation.[17]

The 1920 "Act to deport certain undesirable aliens and to deny readmission to those deported" added a number of new bases for criminal deportation, mostly related to espionage, explosives, and wartime offenses.[18] It also made clear, however, that deportation decisions of the secretary of labor "shall be final" and that "all persons who shall be expelled under . . . this Act shall also be excluded from readmission." A number of deportation bills aimed at narcotics violators appeared in 1919–1920, ultimately leading to the passage in 1922 of a law that mandated the deportation of any alien convicted of offenses related to the importation of opium, cocaine, or derivative substances.[19]

As one writer noted, "In the decade from 1920 to 1930 a nostrum often advocated for the ills of the United States was the removal of aliens from the country."[20] Many of those who had advocated for the Quota laws of 1921 and 1924 increasingly turned their attention to the need for more vigorous deportation. For example, Edwin E. Grant, former California state senator and president of the California State Law Enforcement League, wrote a 1925 article entitled "Scum from the Melting Pot." He bemoaned that "the prosperity made possible by our forefathers has lured the parasites of Europe—the scum that could have so well been eliminated from the melting pot." He suggested that for thousands of immigrants "pouring onto American soil," who, "no sooner do they sail past the Statue of Liberty than they mistake liberty for license—and embark on their lives of crime," the best solution would be to "eliminate at all costs" the "scum from the melting pot."[21]

The government was given a rather free hand during this era. The Supreme Court, relying on the "civil" nature of deportation, per *Fong Yue Ting,* accepted the propriety of silence as sufficient proof of deportability. Unlike in criminal matters, "no rule of law . . . prohibits . . . drawing an inference from the silence of one who is called upon to speak."[22] There would be no presumption of innocence and no "right to remain silent" in deportation cases, even in post-entry cases based on crime. The Court also confirmed the permissibility of retroactive deportation. Responding to the claim that such practices violated the ex post facto clause, the Court breezily stated, "Congress . . . was not increasing the punishment for the crimes . . . It was . . . only seeking to rid the country of persons who had shown by their career that their continued presence here would not make for the safety or welfare of society."[23]

Deportation law also developed into a bastion of rather unpredictable moralist discourse, as the vague statutory term "crime involving moral turpitude" inspired widely varying interpretations.[24] Cases were replete with such observations as the following: "[a] thief is a debased man; he has no moral character."[25] Even misdemeanor shoplifting could now result in deportation in some circuits. However, the harshness of these laws did not go unnoticed. Some courts, particularly the Second Circuit Court of Appeals, were willing to parse the language of deportation laws quite closely in order to avoid unjust results. The Second Circuit, for example, made clear in 1929 that it did "not regard every violation of a prohibition law as a crime involving moral turpitude." It also rejected the government's contention that imprisonment for a nondeportable offense would render a noncitizen deportable because he or she was "likely to become a public charge."[26] Commentators began to call for greater uniformity. A 1929 student note in the *Harvard Law Review* advocated for the enumeration of proscribed offenses or reliance on the penalty imposed, instead of "the apocalyptic criteria of individual judges."[27] Such standardization began to occur in controlled substance cases, with proposals to deport narcotics traffickers[28] leading to a 1922 Narcotics Deportation Law.[29] And reliance on the penalty imposed has become a feature of many aspects of criminal deportation laws. But the "moral turpitude" language remains to this day, having withstood a "void for vagueness" Supreme Court challenge in 1951.[30]

Deportation in the early twentieth century was also connected to federal anticrime initiatives under the Eighteenth Amendment and the 1919 National Prohibition Enforcement Act (the Volstead act).[31] The Volstead act created a large, new federal agency: the Bureau of Prohibition within the Bureau of Internal Revenue, with some 1,550 new federal enforcement agents.[32] The federal government soon faced a unique array of new problems that led to a perceived need for effective exclusion and deportation laws.[33] "Rum-runners" at the borders and coast-lines were pervasive and frustrating phenomena. The federal government also soon realized that the use of revenue and customs laws provided a sound basis for illegal liquor trafficking prosecutions, as these laws were well accepted and "carried adequate penalties which courts had grown accustomed to impose upon offenders."[34] This use of one sort of regulatory law to achieve goals for which it was not originally intended soon became a distinctive attribute of the modern deportation system.

Loyalty, Federal Power, and Deportation

It is war that exposes the relative vulnerability of the alien's status . . . While his lot is far more humane and endurable than the experience of our citizens in some enemy lands, it is still not a happy one.

—*Johnson v. Eisentrager* (1950)

In the first two decades of the twentieth century, vast concentrations of wealth and power inspired Progressive reformers and spurred increasingly vigorous and politically radical labor unions.[35] In addition, more than 12 million immigrants dramatically changed urban demographics and transformed political power structures, spawning nativist reactions.[36] Following the assassination of President McKinley by Leon Czolgosz, a native-born American citizen with a foreign-sounding name, the federal government responded quickly with a stream of powerful, ideological exclusion and deportation laws.[37]

In 1903, a new law prohibited the entry of "any person who is opposed to all organized governments, or who is a member of or affiliated with any organization entertaining or teaching such disbelief in or opposition to all governments."[38] The first target of this law in the United States was John Turner, a British union leader and anarchist. In a classic example of an extended border control deportation law used for ideological social control, Turner was arrested during a lecture tour of the United States and was charged with illegal entry. The warrant issued by the secretary of commerce and labor claimed that Turner, "an alien anarchist," had come into the United States contrary to the 1903 law and commanded that he be taken into custody and returned "to the country from whence he came."[39]

Turner's hearing before a board of inquiry at Ellis Island illustrates the legal transition from exclusion to deportation that took place during this era. Turner testified that he was an Englishman and that he had been in the United States ten days. He "would not undertake to deny that he had . . . declared himself to be an anarchist" in a lecture delivered in New York; he admitted that the statement of the inspectors to that effect "was about correct." Thus, post-entry speech was used to prove pre-entry anarchist leanings in order to deport John Turner.[40]

Turner was detained at Ellis Island for several months, as his lawyers fought on his behalf. The case became a cause célèbre, in large part because many saw the statute as a direct assault on the First Amendment. A newly formed group, the Free Speech League, raised funds to retain Clarence Darrow and Edgar Lee Masters to argue Turner's case before the U.S. Supreme Court. They focused their appeal on the free speech aspect of the law as well as a due process claim.[41] They argued, "The law provides for the trial of an alien by a Board of Special Inquiry, secret and apart from the public; without indictment; without confrontation of witnesses; without the privilege to the accused of obtaining witnesses; without the right of counsel. It transfers to the Federal inspectors engaged in executing the orders of the executive department of the government, that judicial power which belongs only to the judiciary under the Constitution of the United States."[42]

As we shall see, these sorts of challenges to the deportation system continued well into the late twentieth century, with very limited success. Turner, in any event, gave up, leaving the United States before a final decision was rendered in his case. His action turned out to be prescient: the Court upheld the law.

One of the most interesting things about the *Turner* case is the blurring—on the part of both counsel and the Court—of the line between exclusion and deportation. Darrow and Masters, for example, sought to revisit the still recent case of *Fong Yue Ting*, arguing that the deportation power was grounded in the commerce clause and therefore constitutionally limited.[43] The Court, however, implicitly focusing on the extended border control aspect of Turner's case, simply recited that, "[r]epeated decisions of this court have determined that Congress has the power to exclude aliens from the United States; to prescribe the terms and conditions on which they may come in; to establish regulations for sending out of the country such aliens as have entered in violation of law, and to commit the enforcement of such conditions and regulations to executive officers."[44]

During the next two decades, such acceptance of a strong power of exclusion would gradually evolve into the modern U.S. system of ideological post-entry social control deportation. By 1920, one could accurately write that "[a] Tolstoy would be deported. So would Bernard Shaw. There is scarcely a critical political philosopher in Europe who would not be deportable under our laws."[45]

As war raged in Europe, the search for a unifying theme for the multiglot United States led Theodore Roosevelt, Woodrow Wilson, and many others to the motifs of "loyalty" and "Americanism."[46] Citizenship status naturally became implicated in this politico-legal discourse. Indeed, in his message to the Sixty-fourth Congress in late 1915, Wilson had focused on the problem of disloyalty among naturalized citizens.[47] To eliminate any doubt as to what this might mean for the "disloyal," Wilson, in 1917, ominously intoned that "if there should be disloyalty, it will be dealt with with a firm hand of stern repression."[48] A huge "preparedness" parade wound its way down New York's Fifth Avenue under a large electric sign that offered a motto for the era: "Absolute and Unqualified Loyalty to Our Country."[49]

As the country succumbed to war fever, it also acquiesced to tremendous executive branch power.[50] Among other initiatives, the president called for a compulsory draft. Despite the powerful drumbeats of loyalty and Americanism, however, many resisted. By the end of the war, an estimated 337,000 men had dodged conscription. The government made effective use of highly publicized "slacker raids," which presaged the later Palmer Raids against aliens. The last slacker raids, which included Chicago, New York, and Boston, netted more than 50,000 draft-age men, taken at the point of a bayonet from ballparks, restaurants, and street corners.[51]

Draft enforcement often led to negative attitudes toward noncitizens. The conscription law exempted alien men who had not filed preliminary citizenship papers—so-called nondeclared aliens. This caused considerable tension in part because the system worked on a national quota model—draft calls were taken proportionately from the states according to the total population. In New York, for example, where there was a high percentage of nondeclared men, this meant that a higher percentage of the remaining population would have to fulfill the New York quota.[52] A House report asserted, "From all over the country comes the cry of the rank injustice of forcing American citizens into war, while alien slackers are here in vast numbers enjoying the peaceful privileges of our country and immunity for fighting for the very integrity of their own countries."[53]

Universal compulsory military service and training held some benefits for noncitizens subject to it. It was seen by many as "an effective homogenizing agent" for a "dangerously diverse society."[54] As one commentator aptly explained, military service could "yank the hyphen" out of Italian-Americans or Polish-Americans.[55] Indeed, one member of the House referred to compulsory military training, in one of the earliest references to what would soon become a ubiquitous metaphor, as "a melting pot which will . . . mold us into a new nation and bring forth the new Americans."[56] But now, noncitizens who opposed the new ideological conformity could be ostracized for a variety of reasons: they were still aliens, but now they were disloyal, and "slackers," too. As John Higham has noted, never before had "the urge for conformity blended so neatly with the spirit of nationalism."[57] This dynamic helps to explain why some of the strongest support for the censorship laws that soon followed came from the foreign-language press, whose publishers desperately felt the need to establish their own loyalty and support for the new conformity. There was, as David M. Kennedy has put it, "something inexorable in the air" as the United States found itself drawn into the unimaginable horrors of the European war. Those who tried to resist the macabre pull of war faced the "noxious odors of repression and hysteria" that would soon dominate the domestic landscape.[58]

The role to be played by post-entry social control deportation laws was evident from the very start. In his 1915 message to Congress, Woodrow Wilson had spoken of people, "born under other flags but welcomed under our generous naturalization laws to the full freedom and opportunity of America, who have poured the poison of disloyalty into the very arteries of our national life." He warned that "[s]uch creatures of passion, disloyalty, and anarchy must be crushed out . . . [T]he hand of our power should close over them at once."[59] It is unsurprising, then, that one of the most significant aspects of the 1917–1918 immigration laws was the expansion of the class of deportable noncitizens from prostitutes and procurers to political dissidents, especially anarchists, without time limit.[60] The 1917 Espionage Act used criminal penalties to suppress opponents of the war and empowered the post-master general to police the mail for material advocating "treason, insurrection, or forcible resistance to any law of the United States."[61] The Sedition Act of 1918 made it a crime for any person to "utter, print, write or publish any disloyal, profane, scurrilous, or abusive language about the form of government of the United States . . . any language intended to . . . encourage resistance to the United States, or to promote the cause of its enemies."[62]

As great an expansion of federal power as these laws were, they were also supplemented by the creation of private organizations to investigate and report to the government any "disloyal" acts or statements.[63] The American Protective League, with at least 250,000 members, worked together with the Department of Justice to investigate "subversion."[64] It has been observed that "[n]o other one cause contributed so much to the oppression of innocent men as the systematic and indiscriminate agitation against what was claimed to be an all-pervasive system of German espionage."[65] The government received as many as 1,000 claims of alleged sedition each day, of which at least 95 percent were worthless. These agents, described by David M. Kennedy as "a rambunctious, unruly *posse comitatus* on an unprecedented national scale," engaged in all sorts of unlawful intrusions into the lives of others, burglary, slander, and illegal arrests.[66] A vigorous organized response also developed, including the formation of the American Civil Liberties Union, for which the new deportation laws were a central focus of its early work.[67]

As in 1798, the government first focused its energies on "enemy aliens," interning those who were deemed guilty of "disloyal conduct." But more than that soon followed. The country witnessed "a frontal assault on foreign influence in American life."[68] As Edward S. Corwin had rather indelicately put it, there were seen to be "irreconcilables in our midst."[69] The 1917 census revealed a frightening statistic: more than 4.6 million people residing in the United States had been born in one of the countries in the Central Powers.[70] In 1919, the educational director of the National Security League declared that "the melting pot has not melted."[71] State laws forbade the teaching of the German language. Hamburgers were renamed "liberty sandwiches" and sauerkraut was "liberty cabbage." A federal law required all German males over the age of fourteen to register, a program that ultimately catalogued some

480,000 persons.[72] Even naturalized U.S. citizens faced severe sanctions. Many legal actions were undertaken by the government to cancel certificates of naturalization, using wartime misconduct as evidence that prior statements of loyalty to the United States had been fraudulent. As Homer Cummings later reported, "The successful outcome of early cases had a marked effect in restraining overt disloyalty on the part of other persons in the same class."[73]

Labor Deportations

The focus on enemy aliens was clearly a harbinger of the Palmer Raids and of modern post-entry social control deportation. Before we consider that episode, however, we should revisit a more amorphous but no less important antecedent: "labor deportations," or the forced removal of striking workers by the combined forces of employers, vigilantes, and local government. The most famous such incident, the Bisbee deportation, took place in Arizona. It is worth considering in some detail not only because it was called a deportation, but because it undoubtedly influenced the federal government action against radical labor leaders that soon followed.

In the 1890s, Arizona's mining district in the town of Globe was "as rough and tough as Billy-be-Damned—a hundred miles off the railroad."[74] Struggles between large copper companies, the railroads, and various—mostly immigrant—labor groups were as violent as any in history.[75] Bisbee, Arizona, sustained some 5,000 miners by 1914. Many were skilled Cornishmen or "Cousin Jacks" who, though often defiant toward governmental authority, were generally seen as loyal to their employers. As mining technology reduced demand for skilled labor, so-called Bohunks or Bear Dancers from Bohemia, Serbia, Austria, Montenegro, Czech areas, and Italy arrived. These newcomers often faced a hostile reaction, but others were treated worse. Bisbee was known as a "white man's camp." Mexicans were not allowed to work for the higher paying underground jobs.[76] There was also "an unwritten law . . . that Chinamen should not remain overnight in Bisbee."[77]

Bisbee was essentially a company town, controlled by a few very powerful mining companies. The local newspaper was owned by one of the biggest mining companies, Phelps Dodge. The area retained a "clannish, self-reliant bent" that, together with company policies, rebuffed union organizers and effectively suppressed union activities for years.[78] For a time, wages were relatively good, though working conditions were hard. During the war years, however, inflation effectively cut the miners' salaries, as it did for millions of other workers.[79] Unions soon began to achieve greater success.[80]

Although never one of the largest unions, the Industrial Workers of the World (IWW) created the greatest anxiety. Founded in 1905, the IWW was a robust, high-spirited, ideological organization of leftist-anarchist bent. It was not averse to violent tactics, including sabotage, and unlike many other unions, it energetically recruited minority workers. In Arizona, the IWW effectively organized Mexican and southern European immigrant workers. On June 24, 1917, the IWW presented demands to the Bisbee companies that included improvements to safety and working conditions and an end to discrimination against foreign and minority workers.[81] All the demands were rejected and a strike ensued. Within three days, nearly half of the workers in Bisbee were on strike. Rumors spread quickly that the unions were infiltrated by pro-Germans, and that weapons and dynamite had been brought to Bisbee for sabotage.

An anti-union group called the Citizen's Protective League was created by businessmen and then placed under the authority of Sheriff Harry Wheeler. One prominent contemporary observer has noted: "At the forefront of the 'patriots' who had engineered the deportation were the executives of the greatest mining-metal corporation in America."[82] Within two weeks, some 2,000 so-called deputies were appointed. The strike was seen as more than a labor matter. Sheriff Wheeler summarized the sentiment thus: "At a time when our country needs her every resource, these strangers persist in keeping from her the precious metal production of an entire district . . . We cannot longer [sic] stand or tolerate such conditions! This is no labor trouble—we are sure of that—but a direct attempt to embarrass and injure the government of the United States."[83] The Phelps Dodge president, Walter Douglas, said, "you cannot compromise with a rattlesnake" and that the IWW showed "a German influence."[84] A *New York Times* headline reported, "Big Copper Strike Blamed on Germans."[85]

The sheriff quickly ordered his men to action. Telegraph lines were cut, and then, without warning, more than 1,000 men were rounded up, including many who had no involvement in the strike or the mines.

They were forced to walk two miles to a ballpark, where they were surrounded by armed men and given a choice to abandon the strike or face drastic consequences. Shortly after that, 1,186 men who refused to join the vigilantes were loaded onto boxcars, accompanied by 186 armed guards. The *Bisbee Daily Review* offered the company perspective:

> Never, since the mountains raised their heads to look down in this pleasant valley, have they seen such a display of patriotism and high-minded public spirit . . . these citizens arose in their just wrath and their righteous might and, at one stroke, in one hour, broke the power of the I.W.W. . . . the agitators, the idlers, the wreckers and the open sympathizers and abettors of this scum in the Warren District forever . . . IT WAS A QUESTION OF BEATING THESE FOREIGN TERRORISTS AND PROFESSIONAL AGITATORS AND STRIKERS TO IT . . . The Mexicans were beginning to parade by the hundred."[86]

The train proceeded to Columbus, New Mexico, where the men were to be turned over to the federal army commandant "for detention as enemies of the country."[87] At Columbus, however, the officer in command refused to detain the men without specific orders from Washington. The train then went to Hermanas, New Mexico, leaving the men in the desert. Some water and food was sent to the deportees, but they had no shelter. Three days later, federal authorities took the men back to Columbus, where some were detained for months. Guards appeared on all the roads into Bisbee to prevent the deportees or other "troublemakers" from entering. An ad hoc "deportation court" was set up for others thought to be opposed to the companies.[88]

A federal "Mediation Commission" was established to investigate the Bisbee deportation. The commission, on which Felix Frankfurter served, noted serious management problems in the mines that had led to the strikes. It also concluded that "a large migratory working force is . . . a disintegrating element . . . men without responsibility of home . . . serving as inflammable material for beguiling agitators to work on." The commission highlighted the "polyglot character of the workers," with as many as thirty-two nationalities in one camp, and opined that "[t]he industry contains within itself the Balkan problem on a small scale." More specifically, "[t]he movement toward Americanization . . . has hardly penetrated into these outposts of industry." Isolation was also seen as a factor: "there was not the cooling atmosphere of outsiders to the conflict." And, finally: "Doctrines of internationalism, the conviction that all wars are capitalistic . . . refusal to display the flag at union headquarters . . . provoked accusations of disloyalty [by] the company and its sympathizers."[89]

What the President's Commission did not focus on was the fact that, by 1917, vigilante "deportation" was "a relatively conventional and well-practiced method of getting rid of undesirables," especially foreigners.[90] Although many considered the Bisbee and other deportations to be spontaneous uprisings, these extralegal actions were in fact often quite well planned and well coordinated. The *El Paso Times* later wrote that "[o]nly in its magnitude was the [Bisbee deportation] very different from the practice common enough all over the country of running undesirables out of town."[91] Indeed, similar deportations soon followed the Bisbee model across the country.[92] On July 14, 1917, a mob of "native Americans" drove hundreds of noncitizen workers (Italians, Russians, and Poles) from the lead-mining areas near Flat River, Missouri. Similar actions took place in Bemidji, Minnesota; Gallup, New Mexico; and Fairbury, Nebraska. In 1919, vigilantes actually cited Bisbee as precedent while undertaking a deportation of orange grove workers from Pomona Valley, California.[93] Well-publicized lynchings of German Americans also took place during this era. The *New York Times,* while duly deploring the lawlessness of lynching, mused that IWW "agitators" were agents of Germany and urged the federal government to "make short work of these treasonable conspirators."[94]

Much of the press across the country supported the deportations. The language of that support illustrates how deeply intertwined in the public mind were the early labor deportations and the later federal deportation raids led by Palmer. Boston's *Transcript* dubbed the Bisbee deportation the "Bisbee Tea Party," suggesting that "[a]s the crow flies, Bisbee is a long way from Boston, but as Americanism goes, Arizona and Massachusetts are next door neighbors." Sheriff Wheeler's proclamation would, it was said, go down in history as a "great document" that "rings with the determination of the people to steady the palsied hand of the Government from the mines of Arizona to the trenches in France."[95]

As with earlier anti-Chinese vigilantism, the lesson often drawn from these incidents was not simply that federal government action was needed to protect targeted workers, but, apparently, that such deportations should be taken over by the government itself. The federal government, said the Boston *Transcript,* had failed to protect Americans from a "foreign foe." The *Phoenix Gazette* attributed the strikes to, among others, "Haywood, Mother Jones, [and] Emma Goldman."[96] The commissioner of the Bureau of Immigration, Anthony Caminetti, later said that there may have been reason to believe the IWW was connected to German funding and that "a successfully conducted campaign against the foreign leaders among these people would produce valuable and far-reaching salutary effects."[97]

In July 1917, Attorney General Gregory responded to all this by ordering the internment of all German aliens who were IWW members. In September, federal agents raided every IWW hall in the United States and arrested more than 300 leaders for prosecution under the Espionage Act. Many others were held for deportation.[98] Robert Bruere, a member of the President's Mediation Commission, wrote in the *Nation* that the Department of Justice had, in fact, "thrown a dragnet around the leaders of the I.W.W. around the country."[99] As John Higham notes, "in deportation the nation grasped its absolute weapon against the foreign-born radical."[100]

Meanwhile, hundreds of deportees brought civil suits against the vigilantes, the railroad, and the copper companies. No case was ever tried, though some settlements were reached. The Cochise County Attorney also eventually charged 210 people with kidnapping.[101] The defense argued a "necessity defense" based on the alleged rights of a community threatened by an "overwhelming peril" to defend itself. The jury agreed, and the defendants were acquitted in 1920. The jury foreman stated that "the verdict of the jury is a vindication of the deportation, if not in the legal sense, at least in the moral sense."[102] As the *Nation* saw it, "Under the Arizona law . . . if two parties fear attacks from each other, the one who attacks first is protected by the State."[103] The government never pursued any further criminal trials.[104]

Postwar Political Deportations

> In the absence of a new Sedition Law against radical citizens, the government has seized upon the new Alien Law and used it with relentless vigor.
>
> —Zechariah Chafee, Jr., *Freedom of Speech* (1920)

I feel so cast out, pursued by the furies, and nowhere at home.

—Emma Goldman, quoted in *Nowhere at Home: Letters from
the Exile of Emma Goldman and Alexander Berkman* (1975)

In the aftermath of the "War to End All Wars," the United States faced the bitter residue of war fever. There was a deep—if unfocused—desire for a return to something called "normalcy." But there were also terrible economic disruptions, including widespread unemployment, strikes, demoralizing inflation, social pressures caused by large immigrant communities, an increasingly radicalized labor movement, and an international millieu traumatized by the success of the Bolshevik Revolution in Russia.[105] In this era, deportation completed its transformation from a primarily instrumentalist tool of extended border control into "a major public policy in its own right."[106]

By late 1919, virtually the entire U.S. wartime military force—some 4 million men—had been demobilized. This rather poorly planned move had massive disruptive effects on the domestic labor market. Organized labor had made impressive gains during the Progressive Era but had generally maintained a truce with management throughout the war. This began to change quickly after the Armistice. Increasingly assertive unions demanded higher wages and better working conditions around the country. Some gains were made, but the "line in the sand" for many employers was the principle of collective bargaining itself. Indeed, as the historian Robert Murray has observed, in 1919 the prototypical American industrialist was "spoiling for a fight." The much ballyhooed "return to normalcy" meant for many employers a return to pre-Progressive Era laissez-faire capitalism. The collision of these powerful social forces caused a wave of labor unrest the likes of which the country had never before seen. In 1919, there were some 3,600 hundred strikes, involving more than 4 million workers.[107] Stories of these strikes, especially a general strike in Seattle, a police strike in Boston, and national steel and mine strikes, gripped the nation.[108]

The epithetic use of the term "Bolshevik" increased as the concept of Americanism ossified and a rigid ideological conformity still dominated the country. Suspicion of the disloyal shifted from Germans to a broader class of potential subversives. The *New York World* offered a "conservative estimate" in late 1919 that there were some 5 million "parlor Reds"—persons with responsible positions who had great influence on others—active in the United States.[109] William Howard Taft referred to the supporters of the closed shop as "embracing Soviet methods."[110] Satirical responses abounded:

> I mustn't call you "Miky" and you
>   mustn't call me "wop,"
> For Uncle Sammy says it's wrong
>   And hints we ought to stop;
> But don't you fret, there's still
>   One name that I'm allowed to speak,
> So when I disagree with you I'll call
>   You Bol-she-vik! Veek! Veek!
> It's a scream and it's a shriek;
>   It's a rapid-fire response to any
> Heresy you squeak . . . [111]

But such humor faded as bombs ushered in a national Red Scare and precipitated a "deportation delirium." A new government agency, the General Intelligence Division of the Bureau of Investigation, was created to investigate "radical" activities. At its head was J. Edgar Hoover, then a special assistant to the attorney general in charge of "counter-radical activities." In its first 100 days of existence, it gathered evidence on more than 60,000 people in the United States. Soon, this number had grown to 200,000, with a detailed, cross-referenced index card system monitoring all known "radical" organizations.[112]

In April and May of 1919, the newspapers were filled with terrifying reports of bombs that had been sent through the mail to various well-known public figures, including the commissioner of immigration, Supreme Court Justice Oliver W. Holmes, Jr., Attorney General Mitchell Palmer, John D. Rockefeller, and J. P. Morgan.[113] On June 3, 1919, a bomb exploded on the front steps of the home of Attorney General Palmer. The home was damaged slightly. The man who carried it, presumed to be an anarchist, was completely torn apart. Pieces of his body were scattered throughout the neighborhood and on the doorstep of Palmer's neighbor, then-assistant secretary of the navy Franklin D. Roosevelt, who had entered his own home some three minutes earlier.[114]

Palmer immediately responded with powerful invocations of legal authority.[115] He stated that such attacks would only "increase and extend the activities of our crime-detecting forces."[116] He later reported that he felt compelled to act strongly and quickly: "I was shouted at from every editorial sanctum in America from sea to sea; I was preached upon from every pulpit . . . to do something and do it now, and do it quick, and do it in a way that would bring results to stop this sort of thing in the United States."[117]

There was truth to this, and deportation was by now sufficiently well accepted to be an effective government tool. During the summer of 1919, the Bureau of Investigation scoured the country for "radicals" who might be subject to deportation.[118] The General Intelligence Division estimated that some 90 percent of domestic radicals were "aliens." Orders were therefore sent out to agents that their major efforts "should be particularly directed to persons, not citizens of the United States, with a view of obtaining deportation cases."[119] While testifying before the Senate, radical attorney Jacob Margolis was asked a question that was clearly on the minds of many: "Don't you think it would be a good thing for the United States to find an island somewhere and put all the people on it that think as you do?"[120]

On October 19, 1919, the Senate unanimously adopted a resolution asking the attorney general "to advise and inform the Senate whether or not the Department of Justice has taken legal proceedings, and if not, why not, and if so, to what extent, for the arrest and punishment [or deportation] . . . of the various persons within the United States who . . . have attempted to bring about the forcible overthrow of the Government."[121]

The country was awash in fear, not only because of widespread labor unrest and the summer bombs, but also because of terrible racial violence. In October 1919, the *New York Times* reported a briefing from a federal official, describing "efforts of the I.W.W., Bolshevist, and radical Socialist groups to stir up discontent among the negroes."[122] A report to the Senate presented by J. Edgar Hoover stated, "the radical organizations in this country have looked upon the Negroes as particularly fertile ground . . . [T]he Negro is 'seeing red.'"[123] The report, a model of Red Scare thinking, powerfully linked race and ideology and led to deportation. African American demands for equality and protection from lynching and other widespread white-perpetrated terror and violence were viewed as the fruits of Bolshevist propaganda. As Hoover wrote, Communism was "the cause of much of the racial trouble in the United States at [this] time."[124] Indeed, during the summer of 1919, the Bureau also focused particular attention on Marcus Garvey, a powerful black nationalist leader and a subject of the British West Indies. Garvey was deemed by Hoover to be "aggressive," corrupt, and a fit prospect for deportation. Despite an intensive investigation, however, Hoover concluded in October 1919 that "[Garvey] has not *yet* violated any federal law whereby he could be proceeded against [for] deportation."[125] Garvey was later successfully prosecuted by Hoover for mail fraud in 1925 and deported to Jamaica in 1927.[126]

Informal, local deportations were also sometimes used for racial cleansing in this period. In 1923, following the murder of three policemen and two detectives by a "drink-crazed Negro," the mayor of Johnstown, Pennsylvania, Joseph Cauffiel, reportedly ordered all black and Mexican people who had not been resident in the city for seven years to leave the city.[127] Cauffiel later denied that he had issued a formal order of deportation. He did note, with apparent pride, that "about 2,000 Negroes have gone within the last three weeks" and that "newly arrived Negro citizens" were still being ordered to leave Johnstown.[128]

The Palmer Raids of 1919 were timed to coincide with the second anniversary of the Bolshevik Revolution. They were, by all accounts, brutal and efficient. The *New York Times* published the following report: "the People's House had been completely surrounded . . . [T]he [people inside] had not the slightest idea of what was coming . . . [O]n one of the top floors a class was in progress . . . At first there were [indications] that the presence of the policemen would be [challenged by] some of the women . . . [T]he harsh command to 'shut up there, you, if you know what's good for you!' brought silence."[129]

Assistant Secretary of Labor Louis Post reported that several of the "victims of this ruffianly raid suffered physical injury without having furnished any excuse for it." One "mild-mannered schoolteacher" had his "legitimate inquiry" answered with "blows that smashed his spectacles and wounded his face severely."[130] Raids of similar focus, scope, and brutality took place simultaneously around the country. The exact figures are not known, but best estimates are that some 6,000 warrants of arrest were issued for alien "reds," and some 4,000 arrests were made.[131] Blanket arrest warrants were issued, reminiscent of the tactics of Timothy Pickering. Although administrative interpretation generally did not support deportation of workers for mere membership in the IWW, thousands of arrests were made pursuant to defective warrants "with a manifest purpose on the part of the . . . Department of Justice to hold the arrested aliens in confinement indefinitely."[132] In Boston, the prisoners were conspicuously marched through the streets in chains. As one investigator mused, "nothing was lacking in the way of display but a brass band."[133]

On Sunday, December 21, 1919, at 3:30 AM, 249 people were loaded onto a ferry in New York, ironically named *Immigrant,* and transported to the *U.S.S. Buford,* for deportation to Finland and then to Soviet Russia.[134] The *Buford,* known popularly as the "Soviet Ark" or the "Red Ark," was a nineteenth-century army transport vessel with the reputation of being a "sea-roller."[135] The deportees were visited at 4:00 AM by J. Edgar Hoover, for whose career this was an early highlight.

A pamphlet written by two of the most well-known of the deportees, Emma Goldman and Alexander Berkman, described the *Buford's* tawdry departure:

> The "Red Ark" is gone. In the darkness of early morning it slipped away, leaving behind many wives and children destitute of support. They were denied even the knowledge of the sailing of the ship, denied the right of farewell to the husbands and fathers they may never see again. After the boat was gone, women and children came to the dock to visit the prisoners, bringing such little comforts as are known to the working class, seedy overcoats for the Russian winter, cheap gloves and odds and ends of food. They were told that the ship was gone. The refined cruelty of the thing was too much for them; they stormed the ferry-house, broke a window, screamed and cried, and were driven away by soldiers.[136]

The government had sought to deport Emma Goldman for many years, as she was a charismatic, energetic, and famous feminist and anarchist leader. These efforts faced what might have seemed an insurmountable problem, however: Goldman was a naturalized U.S. citizen. But she ultimately fell victim to the derivative status accorded wives of U.S. citizens during this era.[137] When her husband was denaturalized—in 1909, after he himself had been a citizen for some twenty-five years—she immediately and automatically lost her own citizenship. She did not participate in her husband's denaturalization and in fact seems to have been unaware of it at the time, even though it was likely aimed at her. In her memoirs, Goldman wrote that her husband was actually dead at the time of his denaturalization.[138]

Louis Post later noted that Goldman had argued to him that she was still a U.S. citizen. If accepted, that would, of course, have been a conclusive defense. Post held, however, that revocation of her husband's citizenship operated as automatic revocation of hers and therefore "operated automatically to subject her to the disabilities of an alien."[139] Goldman ultimately decided not to pursue the matter in court.

Goldman's deportation was based on her political speeches and politically based criminal convictions. She had been convicted in 1893 for inciting to riot and unlawful assembly as a result of a speech she had made to striking New York City garment workers. She had also been convicted in 1917 for violating the selective-draft law. The government, however, argued that Goldman was subject to deportation under the Act of October 16, 1918, simply for being an anarchist.

Goldman fully appreciated the implications of this type of deportation. She offered a statement during her deportation hearing that referred to the process as "star chamber proceedings." She went on to assert that the "very spirit" of her deportation was "nothing less than a revival of the ancient days of the Spanish Inquisition or the more recently defunct Third Degree system of Czarist Russia." She objected both to the grounds on which she was charged and the nature of the process itself, arguing that her deportation was "a denial of the insistent claim on the part of the Government that in this country we have free speech and a free press, and that every offender against the law—even the lowliest of men—is entitled to his day in open court, and to be heard and judged by a jury of his peers."[140]

Because she saw the deportation proceedings as "purely an inquiry into [her] social and political opinions," she believed that the process was "utterly tyrannical and diametrically opposed to the fundamental guarantees of a true democracy." Indeed, Goldman articulated a view of the importance of free speech in the United States that was to be later championed—at least for citizens—by Louis Brandeis and Oliver Wendell Holmes, Jr.: "the people can only profit by a free discussion of the new ideas now germinating in the minds of thinking men and women in society. The free expression of the hopes and aspirations of a people is the greatest and only safety in a sane society." But the object of deportations, she wrote, "is the very opposite. It is to stifle the voice of the people, to muzzle every aspiration of labor."[141]

Louis Post well understood both the political delicacy and the technical complexity of his task. Goldman had argued to him that "[t]he Anti-Anarchist law confuses the most varied social philosophies and isms in order to cover with the same blanket, so to speak, every element of social protest . . . in order to serve the interests of our industrial kings."[142] Post, of course, knew that anarchists were of various kinds, ranging, in his view, from "malignant conspirators and destructive revolutionists" to "apostles of peace, preachers of the principle of non-resistance, of 'turning the other cheek.'" Such persons he characterized as "supremely harmless except to those perverted imaginations which anticipate violent revolutions as consequences of non-resistant propaganda."[143] Though conceding that he was hardly an expert on her work and life, Post saw Goldman as somewhere between these two extremes. Nevertheless, at that time, the official administrative view of the issue was uncomplicated. The 1903 anarchist exclusion law had been ambiguous in its lack of definition of the term "anarchist."[144] By 1919, however, deportation law was broader. The "sole question," as Post saw it, was "whether or not [Goldman] believed that no government would be better for human society than any kind of government." If she did, then she was an anarchist, and "her deportation . . . was mandatorily required by law."[145] Post felt that his duty was clear: he ordered Emma Goldman deported as an anarchist.

The analysis of the state of the law offered by Louis Post bears repeating today: "Whereas a citizen cannot be punished without substantial cause and after conviction at a judicial trial, an alien may be banished for frivolous causes and by autocratic 'administrative process.'"[146] Put simply, deportation was rather easy. Indeed, deportation procedures during this era were rife with practices that might well make the modern lawyer shudder. Separation of prosecutorial from adjudicative functions, the right to be heard, the right to counsel, the right to bail, the right to confront an accuser, and much more were routinely disregarded. The typical process was well described in a 1911 case:

> Complaint that an alien is in this country in violation of law is usually made by . . . [immigration] inspectors . . . Frequently such information is furnished by the city police, or by enemies of the person charged, acting through malice or revenge. Affidavits are obtained and are sent by the inspector to the Secretary at Washington, who, if he thinks a proper case is made out, issues a warrant for the arrest of the persons charged. . . . After the aliens have been taken to Ellis Island,

they are held in seclusion and not permitted to consult counsel until they are first examined by the inspector, under oath, and their answers taken by a stenographer. After this preliminary inquisition has proceeded as far as the inspector wishes, the aliens are then informed that they are entitled to have counsel, and to give any evidence they wish in respect to the charge. Thereafter a further hearing is had before the inspector, at which further evidence may be given by him, and the aliens may appear by counsel and offer evidence in their own behalf.[147]

The judge in this case made no secret of his opinion of such a process, noting that "such a method of procedure disregards almost every fundamental principle established in England and this country for the protection of persons charged with an offense."[148] This was, however, the law.

And it got worse. In January 1920, an important change in administrative practice took place. For many years, the rules had granted considerable discretion to the "immigrant inspectors" as to whether the arrested noncitizens would be able to have a lawyer participate in the hearing. The lack of counsel had often resulted in abandonment of important legal protections, such as cross-examination of adverse witnesses. Secretary of Labor, William B. Wilson had changed this rule and allowed the benefit of counsel from the moment of arrest. However, just before the January 1920 raids, the old approach was reinstated. In a peculiarly Kafkaesque turn, detainees were permitted to inspect the warrant and be advised of a right to retain counsel only after the hearing had proceeded sufficiently "in the development of facts to protect the government's interests."[149] The predictable result was to give "inspectors a discretion so wide that most of them, affected by the delirium of the period and cowed by the dictation of the Department of Justice detectives, completely ignored the legal rights of aliens thus put at their mercy." By the time the more protective rule was restored, it was "too late to conserve the rights of many a victim of the reckless 'red' crusade."[150] Today's regulation is similar to the less protective 1920 rule.[151]

Another important legal issue during the early 1920s was the availability and scope of judicial review of deportation orders. The law provided: "In every case where any person is ordered deported from the United States . . . the decision of the Secretary of Labor shall be final."[152] This provision meant that in many cases no federal court would ever review the deportation order except pursuant to a writ of habeas corpus—which had various specific requirements and restrictions.[153] Zechariah

Chafee, Jr., observed, "The matter at stake here is not a gift from the government, or the payment of a tax . . . Liberty itself, long-established associations, the home, are at the mercy of a bureaucracy."[154] Neverthe-less, as Louis Post reported, "if there is the slightest evidence in the record to justify [the] administrative decision, whatever the counter-proof may be, a writ of *habeas corpus* must be dismissed by the court and the alien turned back for deportation."[155]

All of this was, of course, terrible for noncitizens, but some citizens were also illegally arrested during the Palmer Raids. The case of Peter Frank, reported by Chafee, is illustrative. An issued warrant, which Frank never saw, described "the alien, Peter Frank, who landed at an un-known port." It then recited boilerplate language to the effect that Frank was a member of unnamed violent organizations that violated the Immi-gration Act. At one o'clock in the morning, immigration officers burst into Frank's home, arrested him, and searched his house. He was held for five days, and not allowed to receive visits from friends or counsel, before he was finally released by a federal judge. As it turned out, he was actually born in Ohio, but because the immigration authorities took the position that the burden of proof was his on that point, it required a fed-eral habeas corpus petition to free him.[156]

Nevertheless, Palmer's raids enjoyed widespread support in 1919–1920. When bomb-making material was allegedly found in a second raid of the Russian People's House in New York, a series of new deporta-tion plans soon followed. Bills proposed stripping the Labor Department of ultimate responsibility over deportation and transferring it to the at-torney general. As we shall see, this move was accomplished two decades later. Other legislators advocated denaturalization of radical cit-izens and even their expulsion to a special penal colony in Guam.[157] At-torney General Palmer gleefully joined in the inflammatory discourse of the day: "Out of the sly and crafty eyes of many of [the deportees] leap cupidity, cruelty, insanity, and crime; from their lopsided faces, sloping brows, and misshapen features may be recognized the unmistakable criminal type."[158]

Officials of a more sympathetic bent—or simply a more professional one—felt besieged.[159] Frederic C. Howe, who was in charge of Ellis Is-land from 1914 to 1919, later wrote: "in this struggle there was no one to lean on; there was no support from Washington, no interest on the part of the press. The whole country was swept by emotional excess."[160]

Eventually, opposition to the government's heavy-handed tactics also began to cross ideological lines. Even Samuel Gompers, a strong anti-Leftist, later called for the freedom of those jailed because of the Espionage Act. A rule-of-law mood emerged, as exemplified by one prominent editorial: "We detest the anti-American theories of these radicals, and the more we detest them the more earnestly we hope that they will be combated by American methods."[161] In 1920, Howe, analogizing the deportation system to that of slavery, wrote, "Our experience has shown that even a free people can lose their freedom by denying it to others."[162] Federal Judge George W. Anderson of Boston pointedly noted that "a mob is a mob," even if it was comprised of "government officials, following instructions from the Justice Department."[163] By 1921, the anti-radical hysteria had cooled, and the day before he left office, Woodrow Wilson signed into law a bill that repealed many of the wartime security laws. But the deportation laws and regulations that had facilitated the Palmer Raids remained in force.

The New Mexican "Illegal Aliens"

> My father's own father, he waded that river,
> They took all the money he made in his life;
> My brothers and sisters come working the fruit trees,
> And they rode the truck till they took down and died.
>
> —Woody Guthrie, "Deportees" (1961)

Most Mexicans who entered the United States in the years after the 1848 Treaty of Guadalupe Hidalgo, if aware they were crossing an international border, undoubtedly did not view their passage as international migration in an emotional or psychological sense. They likely saw themselves simply as moving "from one area of Mexican culture to another." And they did this in great numbers. At least 100,000 Mexican nationals had entered the United States by 1914. By 1930, that number is estimated to have been some 1 million.[164] Demand for Mexican workers, who had long provided an alternative source of cheap labor for U.S. employers, increased dramatically in large part due to the improved enforcement of the Chinese Exclusion Act, the 1907 "Gentlemen's Agreement" with Japan, and the Quota Laws of the 1920s.[165] The largest draw came from the massive agricultural expansion that took place in the southwestern United States in the early twentieth century. Mexicans were often seen as less threatening than Chinese and other foreign workers.[166] As Lawrence Cardoso has noted, "the social distance between white culture in the Southwest and brown civilization in Mexico was short compared to the yawning chasm between the worlds of white and yellow."[167]

Largely because of wartime labor needs in 1917, the U.S. government first became systematically involved in the recruitment of Mexican workers, as the Department of Labor suspended the generally applicable "head tax" on immigrants. It also eased exclusion bars against "contract" workers and illiteracy for Mexican workers coming to work for U.S. farmers for up to one year. From 1917 through 1921, an estimated 50,000–80,000 Mexican farm workers entered the United States under this program, establishing a legal model and cultural mindset that endured for many decades.[168]

The Mexicans met a mixed reception. They were considered by some to be "the preferred of all the cheap labor available to the Southwest." But others began to wonder out loud whether the exclusion of the Chinese had been such a good policy after all. Indeed, a 1918 survey of farm labor problems had concluded that, in general, Chinese or "Orientals" were preferred to Mexicans.[169] The editors of the *Los Angles Times* ironically asked in 1920, "who would be injured if 1,000,000 Chinamen were brought to this country to work on the farms . . . ?"[170] Dr. George P. Clements, of the Los Angeles Chamber of Commerce, wrote in 1929 that agricultural work was of a type "to which the oriental and Mexican due to their crouching and bending habits are fully adapted."[171] In any case, it was absolutely clear that for the dominant white culture, the desire was for laborers, not immigrants. Deep patterns of historical conflict and ideas of racial supremacy fed an instrumentalist view of Mexican immigrants that was quite different from the nation of immigrants ethos that welcomed some other groups.

White workers often reacted to their displacement by Mexicans as they had to Chinese immigrants. As Wayne Cornelius has described, labor troubles involving Mexicans were rather common early-twentieth-century phenomena: "mobs of native-born Americans in Texas, Oklahoma, and other states launched attacks on Mexicans in their work places; vigilante groups terrorized them in their homes and destroyed their property."[172] This anti-Mexican campaign resulted in almost

100,000 Mexicans returning to Mexico between 1920 and 1921.[173] Concerns about Mexican immigrants merged with those about national security. On March 1, 1917, one month before the United States entered World War I, a telegram sent by German Foreign Secretary Arthur Zimmerman to his ambassador to Mexico was intercepted and widely published in U.S. newspapers. It suggested to Mexico that if it were to join Germany in a war against the United States, its reward would be the return of its "lost territory" in New Mexico, Texas, and Arizona.[174] Still, throughout the 1920s, as quotas dramatically restricted most other streams of non-European immigration, a "back door" to relatively unrestricted Mexican immigration was kept open.[175] There was no numerical quota for Mexicans or other Western Hemisphere immigrants. The exclusion and deportation systems thus evolved to become primary legal means to regulate this movement of people.

Mae Ngai has argued persuasively that the numerical restrictions of the 1920s Quota Laws in effect created a large, new category of people known as "illegal aliens." During this period, among other problems, "the notion of border control obscured the policy's unavoidable slippage into the interior." This has been a recurrent trend in deportation history and is a major problem today, as expedited removal encroaches along a 100-mile-deep swath of U.S. territory. Ngai has also argued that deportation policy during the 1920s gave rise to an "oppositional political and legal discourse, which imagined deserving and undeserving illegal immigrants, and . . . just and unjust deportations."[176] As we have seen, the idea of just versus unjust deportation may be traced back at least as far as the debates over the Alien and Sedition Acts. It long embodied, implicitly at least, two distinctions. First, there was the difference between extended border control and post-entry social control deportation. Post-entry deportation laws often constitute direct government action against individuals who have asserted rights of free expression and organization. Second, there was the sense that factors such as legal status, length of residence, and family ties should count somehow. Criticism over deportations for minor crimes and sexual offenses in the 1920s and 1930s implicated both concerns: there was arguably excessive government power and there was hardship. The movement of plenary power reasoning from exclusion to deportation had led to a constitutionally unrestrained legislative and executive posture. That free rein facilitated the passage of remarkably harsh laws. With virtually no substantive constitutional restraint, the counterimpulse to recognize hardship in "extraordinary" cases fell to the emerging concept of administrative discretion. But that flexible realm, shadowed from full judicial scrutiny, had major problems. First, it tended to mask various biases that often favored European immigrants over Mexicans.[177] Moreover, it was a fragile reed on which to rest humanitarian impulses—subject to attack from all sides.

The rise of administrative discretion was impelled by a major 1924 change to deportation law that had particular impact on some Mexicans who desired to remain in the United States.[178] The law hardened extended border control laws by eliminating statutes of limitations for certain "over-stays" and for illegal entrants.[179] Deportation of "aliens" without proper documents became a major component of an increasingly large, bureaucratized deportation system. The total number of deportees rose from 2,762 in 1920 to 38,796 in 1929.[180] From 1921 to 1930, of the more than 92,000 people deported, more than 36,000 were found to have entered without proper documents, without inspection, or by fraud.[181]

Mexicans, as noted, were not subjected to numerical quota restrictions during this period.[182] They did, however, face procedural hurdles, and the exclusion grounds of U.S. immigration law applied to them. The Immigration Act of 1917 had applied a head tax and a literacy test to Mexican immigrants.[183] By 1919, it was a clear rule that Mexicans were required by law to apply for admission.[184] In the 1920s, consular officers began to enforce admission laws against Mexicans with increasing vigor. Illiteracy became a common basis for denial of visas, as did strict interpretation of the "liable to become a public charge" (LPC) ground. Mexican visa applicants who had prearranged jobs soon faced an odd catch-22: if they revealed the fact, they could be barred for violation of the still-extant "contract labor" grounds; if they denied it, they would be excludable under the LPC provision. This policy was quite effective in reducing Mexican legal admissions. From an annual average of 62,000 Mexican legal entrants in 1923–1929, the number dropped to less than 2,500 in 1930–1931. By March 1930, as the Great Depression began, no visas were issued to any Mexican laborers, unless they had previously lived in the United States.[185] A deep dissonance thus developed between the formal structure of U.S. immigration law and long-standing cultural and economic realities.

Moreover, for many Mexicans, all of these restrictions were offensive and odd, given the history of the region.[186] Crossing the border, and subjecting oneself to U.S. inspectors, was "a painful and abrupt event permeated by racism and control."[187] The experience included delousing, physical inspection while naked, medical examinations, and questioning by Border Patrol agents.[188] For workers who crossed the border frequently, these requirements were particularly degrading. Indeed, commuting Mexican workers were required to report to an immigration office once a week for mandatory bathing.[189] Apparently, many entered the United States in violation of these requirements. The deportation and criminal systems thus assumed more of the regulatory role.[190] Deportations of Mexicans increased to more than 15,000 by 1929, many conducted by a "rough and ready" Border Patrol that was plagued by violence and that lacked professionalism.[191]

Those Mexican immigrants who managed to stay in the United States faced hard conditions as well. As one contemporary writer put it, "The Mexican is the first to suffer from depression in industrial and agricultural enterprises . . . [C]ompetition has brought home to the Mexican time and again his absolute weakness as a bargainer for employment . . . [B]y dint of necessity he shuffles along with a standard of living which the American worker regards with contempt and alarm."[192] As we shall see in the next chapter, Mexican workers eventually became the prototypical illegal aliens against whom much of the machinery of the deportation system has been directed.[193] This system is often trumpeted as a bastion of the rule of law, a necessary component of legitimate border control policies. But its roots lie in massive labor recruitment by U.S. employers, the contested history of the border regions, the lack of quota restrictions until the 1960s, and the complex and offensive entry requirements that rendered many thousands of people almost inevitably "illegal."

Conclusion

> If this be not a star chamber proceeding of the most stringent sort, what more is necessary to make it one?
>
> —*U.S. v. Ju Toy*, 198 U.S. 253, 268 (1905) (Brewer, J. dissenting)

The government's use of its deportation power has rarely inspired as much passion as it did in the aftermath of the Palmer Raids. A contemporary observer described the involvement of Louis Post in poetically memorable terms: "As [Post] stood there, unbowed, ungrayed by his seventy-three years, there seemed to pass forms, shadowy, real. They were the figures of the ignorant, the hampered, the misunderstood, the Aliens. Back of them were the terrified upholders of our Government. And back of them there seemed, shadowily, to be the Committee of Americanizers that sit in high places. But in the foreground, unterrified . . . stood a little man, cool but fiery, who set his belief in the Constitution of the country above all fears."[194]

The belief in the Constitution that motivated Post and others to resist Palmer and his men illustrates the power of law to concretize principle. The *New York Evening Post* captured much of the legal spirit of the contemporary reaction to the Palmer Raids when it opined, "Louis F. Post deserves the gratitude of every American for his courageous and determined stand in behalf of our fundamental rights. It is too bad that in making this stand he found himself at cross-purposes with the Attorney General, but Mr. Palmer's complaint lies against the Constitution and not against Mr. Post."[195]

This, however, was not quite true of the Constitution as it was interpreted by the Supreme Court. Post's view, though certainly commendable, was an aspiration. The constitutional understanding of deportation in the real legal system was more favorable to Palmer than to Post. The Supreme Court had not held that any of the actions of the Justice Department, let alone the laws passed by the Congress, were unconstitutional. The system, growing exponentially as it focused on the new "illegal aliens" in addition to its focus on morals, crime, and ideology, remained well insulated from penetration by evolving civil liberties norms. Subconstitutional methods of reasoning, flexible procedural due process, and administrative discretion emerged to fill the constitutional vacuum. But the dominant deportation reality by 1930 remained a harsh, bureaucratic one.

5

The Third Wave: 1930–1964

In March 1931, Gardner Jackson wrote in the *Nation* that the U.S. government was "midway in a drive to clear the land of everyone who cannot prove he is lawfully resident here." "Never has Congressional support for our deportation activities been so strong," he said. Although Secretary of Labor William N. Doak reported that "the Civil Liberties crowd always objects," he had opined that "the worse the aliens are the louder the crowd objects."[1]

No historical evidence indicates that the conduct of "aliens" was significantly worse than it had ever been. Indeed, a large number of deportations during the Depression were based on the "likely to become a public charge" provision of law, which had become "so elastic of character that it has terrorized that part of the immigrant population which has been unable to stand the strain of the breakdown of prosperity."[2] What is clear, however, is that the United States experienced a major third wave of systematic deportation development. This third wave was, in many respects, the definitive moment of creation of the current system. Its major elements included a highly technical, bureaucratic system; harsh post-entry social control crackdowns on "criminal aliens" and ideological dissidents; episodic, massive attempts to use deportation to "control the southern border"; restrictions on judicial review; and reaffirmations of the depreciated constitutional rights of noncitizens facing deportation. All of these elements characterize deportation law to this day.

The "War on Crime"

Phase 1

> People no longer respect respectability . . . You must be either with or against the government. There is no middle ground . . . Citizens of this country must become enemies of crime.
>
> —J. Edgar Hoover, "The National Police Officer" (July 1931)

In the 1920s, many people felt besieged by a rising crime wave, trumpeted by newspapers, magazines, and opportunistic politicians. Law enforcement attention increasingly turned to public corruption, "gangsterism," street crime, and morals offenses. A widely shared perception developed that efficient, noncorrupt policing was crucially important to the modern state.[3] As debates raged over the possible causes of crime and corruption—which included Prohibition, the return of young men from World War I, and declining public morality—crime was increasingly viewed as an urban, largely immigrant problem, a visceral expression of what was wrong with American civilization.[4] Some argued that "inferior germ plasm" among immigrant children made them more likely to become criminals than their parents. A famous example of this genre was suggestively entitled *Crime, Degeneracy, and Immigration*.[5]

Ever stricter criminal deportation laws were the almost inevitable outgrowth of such attitudes. Even local politicians felt the temptation to remove criminals somewhere. The liberal New York City mayor, Fiorello LaGuardia, suggested a comically revealing deportation model of law enforcement: "What I'm going to do is, I'm going to grab every tinhorn gambler in the city of New York by the scruff of the neck and throw him over into New Jersey."[6]

It was said in 1929 that "crime is the nation's biggest business," and estimates of the number of criminals at liberty went as high as 1 million, the vast majority thought to be Italian, Irish, and Jewish.[7] David Orebaugh, author of *Crime, Degeneracy, and Immigration*, bemoaned "a mass psychology . . . favorable to the spread of crime" that had become "more atrocious in character, more brutal, less justified, less intelligent." It all indicated to him "a loss of those moral and spiritual qualities which constitute a people's surest safeguards."[8]

In 1930, President Hoover asked Congress to authorize the creation of a national commission to undertake "a searching investigation of the whole structure of our Federal system of jurisprudence."[9] The Wickersham Commission, chaired by the former attorney general, reported that the Bureau of Prohibition had failed as a viable police force and that federal policing had engendered deep resentment owing to "crude methods of enforcement."[10] It also issued a report on "Enforcement of Deportation Laws" that criticized arbitrary and harsh enforcement practices that had caused hardship to individuals and the separation of families.[11] It noted problems of lack of judicial review and administrative disregard of well-established norms of due process.

Two streams began to converge: an anticrime and often rather nativist and xenophobic flow met a centralizing, anticorruption, "good government" administrative ethos. Federal crime control measures became associated with idealized good government. The highly publicized failures of Prohibition enforcement served as powerful stimuli for the development of a "scientific," professionalized federal police force.[12] Leading this movement was the still-young J. Edgar Hoover, who, as we have seen, had begun his career as an enforcer of deportation laws against alien radicals.[13] Hoover thought of crime much as he had of anarchist philosophy: as "a dread disease, like cancer or tuberculosis, or bubonic plague." He would protect the innocent by creating "necessary antiseptic conditions."[14] The Bureau of Investigation under his leadership represented a clean and "positive, masculinized, 'federal' approach to crime" that was widely seen as modern, legitimate, and just.[15] It was also growing fast. The number of federal criminal prosecutions rose from 55,587 in 1920 to 87,305 in 1930.[16]

The evolution of the modern crime-control deportation system paralleled that of the federal criminal justice regime.[17] Deportation, like criminal enforcement, became more centralized, more bureaucratic, harsher, and less forgiving.[18] The proper role of the federal government in criminal law enforcement became a central concern. The Wickersham Commission noted that the liquor problem transcended state lines and thus required a well-organized federal response. Attorney General Mitchell, however, doubted that the American people would tolerate a federal police force. "Dealing with organized crime," he said, "is largely a local problem."[19] But the model of professional, centralized federal enforcement was given a major boost by the Lindbergh kidnapping. Federal criminal jurisdiction was soon dramatically expanded with the creation of a new federal kidnapping statute that severely punished anyone who trans-ported a kidnapped person across state lines or the national border.[20]

The metaphor of a "war on crime" resonated as a powerful call for un-precedented federal power during the first Roosevelt administration. In 1933, Homer Cummings told the Daughters of the American Revolu-tion, "We are now engaged in a war that threatens the safety of our country—a war with the organized forces of crime."[21] Louis M. Howe, a strong supporter of the federal anticrime effort, told Eleanor Roosevelt in July 1933, "This fall we are planning a crusade against crime." He wrote in the *Saturday Evening Post* that the coming "war on crime" would necessitate "a national body of trained crime detectives . . . and fearless government policemen . . . to identify and then pursue the criminal to the ends of the earth if necessary."[22]

By 1934, support for a federal war on crime was sufficiently strong that Attorney General Homer Cummings organized a conference of some 600 representatives of states, localities, and professional organizations to develop better cooperation. He envisioned the Department of Justice as "a nerve center of helpful impulses and a clearing house of useful in-formation." The key was to develop "a more intimate cooperation" among all the arms of government. He supported the development and expansion of federal fingerprint facilities, a model crime laboratory, monthly bulletins of wanted fugitives, and federal collection of crime statistics.[23] In his 1934 State of the Union address, Franklin Roosevelt proposed the first national omnibus crime bill to address, among other things, "organized banditry, cold-blooded shooting, lynching, and kid-napping."[24] Roosevelt signed the first six parts of his proposed bill on May 5, 1934.

The creative use of federal law as a crime-fighting tool also developed in this era, as exemplified by the successful use of tax laws against Al Capone.[25] A leading proponent of such tactics was the U.S. attorney for the Southern District of New York, George Medalie, a Republican child of immigrants and a mentor of Thomas Dewey. Medalie believed that "the armory of the law [has] many powerful weapons that [have] not been used." He noted that "from the point of view of the community it makes no difference what statute you use" so long as a criminal was properly convicted.[26]

The use of criminal deportation laws during this period, however, was blunted by occasional judicial criticism of the laws' harshness. Judge Learned Hand had written in 1926 of deportation as "deplorable" for a deportee who was "as much our product as though his mother had borne him on American soil. He knows no other language, no other people, no other habits, than ours; he will be as much a stranger in Poland as any one born of ancestors who immigrated in the seventeenth century. However heinous his crimes, deportation is to him exile, a dreadful punishment, abandoned by the common consent of all civilized peoples."[27]

Some discretionary relief was available. But it was mostly limited to noncriminal extended border control deportation cases. In 1929, a discretionary mechanism called "registry" allowed certain noncitizens (only those "not ineligible to citizenship"—a euphemism that barred Asian immigrants) to regularize their status if they could "make a satisfactory showing to the Commissioner General of Immigration" that they had resided in the country continuously since 1921, were not otherwise subject to deportation, and were of "good moral character."[28]

The structure and character of the deportation system also generated controversy. With 1,700 employees, the Department of Immigration was the largest single entity within the Labor Department.[29] The department's agents were, by all accounts, rather unmoved by the hardship that might be caused by deportation. Its 1931 annual report compared the "*alleged* hardship to the alien . . . or to his family" to "the hardships inflicted upon the American citizen and lawfully resident and law-abiding aliens in their exposure to the competition in employment of opportunities of bootlegged aliens."[30] Deportation was one of the main goals of the work of the immigration agency in the early 1930s, the numbers rising from 2,762 in 1920 to 19,426 in 1932.[31] In his annual report of 1932, William N. Doak reported, "The past year has been one of unremitting and devoted work in the deportation of aliens."[32] A secret raiding squad of the Immigration Bureau employed twenty-one detectives just for this purpose. The bureau, however, was widely seen as corrupt, rather brutal, and inefficient.[33] Indeed, it was described by one observer in 1934 as "an open sewer . . . and a disgrace to civilization."[34]

Frances Perkins, appointed by President Roosevelt to be secretary of labor, was determined to change all this. Recommended by such contemporary luminaries as the Massachusetts Progressives for Roosevelt League, headed by Felix Frankfurter, Perkins was a child of privilege who had long demonstrated a deep empathy for the poor.[35] She had worked for a time at the famous Henry Street Settlement House, along with Lillian Wald. The Department of Labor she inherited was described as "that most masculine of departments . . . redolent of big men with cigars in their mouths and feet on the desk."[36] As a contemporary observer put it, the department "was a happy hunting ground for superannuated labor union officials and the headquarters of some of the dirtiest deals in the history of the United States."[37]

Perkins's very first official act as the new head of immigration administration in the United States was to eliminate "case fixing and terrorization of aliens," one infamous component of which had been the extortion of money from legal immigrants on threat of deportation. The *New Yorker* magazine observed that Perkins's action was reminiscent of a speech give by her famous forebear, James Otis, in 1761 in which he had decried English search practices as "the worst instrument of arbitrary power [because they placed] the liberty of every man in the hands of every petty officer."[38] Perkins optimistically wrote that "[h]ereafter the deportation laws will be enforced with due regard to human values, international amenities, and economic conditions within our own and other countries."[39] She organized an extraordinary conference on conditions at Ellis Island, which during this era was ironically used as a receiving station for deportees from all over the United States. As we shall see, these well-meaning reforms had some durability, but ultimately meant little in light of the harshness of ideological and criminal deportation law to come.[40]

Phase 2

The criminal deportation law of the postwar era was deeply influenced by the assertion of a "monolithic alien conspiracy"—eventually to be known as the Mafia—largely controlled by Sicilians.[41] This view was pushed vigorously by Harry J. Anslinger, who had headed the Federal Bureau of Narcotics since 1930.[42] The press picked up on the idea energetically. Drew Pearson wrote that fifty men, all members of the "mysterious Mafia," controlled major rackets in the United States and that all but one were either Italian born or of Italian descent.[43] Deportation thus seemed an obvious solution, though its value was brought into some question by testimony that "Lucky" Luciano had continued his narcotics trafficking in the United States even after he was deported to Italy.[44] Others were more cautious about the idea of the Mafia. Indeed, in November 1950, Senator Estes Kefauver stated that his committee had not found evidence of such a national crime syndicate.[45] Later, however, the committee concluded that there was a "nation-wide crime syndicate known as Mafia," an "elusive, shadowy, and sinister organization" that exercised "centralized direction and control over various rackets from coast to coast."[46]

As a result of such conclusions, the postwar federal government enforced criminal deportation laws vigorously, targeting those whom they deemed the leaders of organized crime. The era was marked by a series of high-profile prosecutions. Undoubtedly envisioned by the federal government in large part as public statements, their ultimate effects turned out to be much more ambiguous. One of the most interesting cases was that of Carlos Marcello.

Marcello's deportation saga evokes a famous suggestion made by Oliver Wendell Holmes, Jr., that the law be viewed from the perspective of "a bad man."[47] Indeed, the tale involves many bad men. Dark reminiscences of the Sicilian "Black Hand," the Mafia, public corruption, murder, robbery, and drug dealing abound. Around the edges of this story, however, also lurk tales of quasi-legal skullduggery by Attorney General Robert Kennedy and shadowy government activities from Italy to Guatemala, from Dallas to Formosa. Following one of the longest, costliest, and ultimately most futile deportation cases in U.S. history, there even may be found possible links to the assassination of President Kennedy.

In October 1910, a baby named Calogero Minacore, born in Tunisia, traveled to New Orleans with his mother on the Italian steamship *Liguria*. His father, Giuseppe, who had arrived earlier to work on a sugar plantation, adopted a new name for the new world: Marcello, a less Sicilian, more typically north Italian name. He anglicized his first name to Joseph. His wife, Luigia, became Louise and young Calogero became Carlos Marcello.[48] The family, which was eventually to include eight more children born in the United States, grew fruits and vegetables, which they sold in the so-called French Market, near the *Vieux Carre,* the famous French Quarter of New Orleans. For reasons that remain unclear to this day, both of Carlos's parents eventually naturalized as U.S. citizens but he did not.

Marcello was, by all accounts, a tough kid. Short and muscular, he was not an academically gifted student, and he dropped out of school at the age of fourteen. But he was apparently quite clever and seems to have shown initiative and sought power at an early age. It was in this millieu that he likely encountered a well-established Sicilian criminal network, which had long provoked hyperbolic overgeneralizations about Italian immigrants. Indeed, New Orleans had witnessed one of the uglier incidents of anti-immigrant mob violence in late-nineteenth-century U.S. history. The police chief, David Peter Hennessey, who had begun to crack down on Italian expatriate gangs, was allegedly ambushed while walking home from a police board meeting. According to apocryphal history, Hennessey's final words to Captain Billy O'Conner were "Oh Billy, Billy they have given it to me . . . The Dagos did it."[49] Anti-Italian hysteria emerged in New Orleans and quickly spread around the nation. The police soon rounded up more than 100 Italian suspects. When the jury returned verdicts of not guilty against some defendants, an armed mob stormed the prison, hunted down the terrified Italians, and killed several, hanging one from a lamppost as the crowd took shots at him.

Carlos Marcello began his criminal career rather young—leaving home at eighteen to embark on a string of petty burglaries. In 1929, he successfully led a bank robbery with a group of teenage boys. Apparently, they went to Carlos's father's house with the loot, where the elder Marcello offered to hide it for a $400 payoff. Unfortunately, Carlos's brother Peter went to the police and reported the entire incident to them. All three Marcellos, including Peter, were arrested, and Carlos achieved some fame when the *New Orleans Times-Picayune* published his photograph along with a story describing him as the mastermind of the operation. When all charges were ultimately dropped, Carlos was inspired to continue in this line of work. He reportedly organized a gang of teenage accomplices to plan more bank robberies. But one thirteen-year-old, caught by the police, turned on Carlos. The newspapers described Marcello as a "Fagin" criminal mastermind, and he was convicted and sentenced to nine to twelve years in the state penitentiary.[50] Upon his early release from prison, Marcello was poised to begin what ultimately became one of the most successful criminal careers in U.S. history. He accomplished this by shrewd tactical and strategic sense, a deep appreciation for secrecy, ruthlessness, a deceptive demeanor, good luck, and—perhaps most important—the wisdom to hire a brilliant and energetic immigration lawyer named Jack Wasserman.

Marcello purchased a rundown "colored" bar in the famously corrupt town of Gretna, which he renamed The Brown Bomber after heavyweight champion Joe Louis.[51] Marcello, reportedly a major drug dealer during this period, become close to the Louisiana Mafia, led by Sam "Silver Dollar" Carolla. For a few years, he prospered. But his stewardship of one of the major marijuana-selling operations in the region brought federal attention. In March 1938, Marcello allegedly sold some twenty-three pounds of marijuana to an undercover FBI agent. He pled guilty and was sentenced to a year and a day. This drug conviction later formed the basis for deportation proceedings against him.

By the early 1940s, Marcello was involved in the large-scale, war-related black-market activities for which New Orleans was infamous. His reputation as a ruthlessly efficient operator solidified. As John H. Davis has put it, "Carlos always brought back the bacon. He could be relied on . . . The police . . . were taken care of . . . Carlos could always be counted on to bring back the money."[52] Indeed, Marcello's reputation was sufficiently solid by 1944 to inspire Frank Costello and Meyer Lansky to accept him as a partner.

The government's use of criminal deportation at first worked to Marcello's advantage when Sam Carolla was deported in May 1947.[53] Marcello was positioned to take over his role. In 1950, Washington columnist Drew Pearson referred to him as "the crime czar of New Orleans."[54] Marcello's rise to national prominence was enhanced by a virtuoso performance before the Kefauver Committee. Senator Kefauver, naming Marcello as "the evil genius of organized crime in Louisiana," alleged that his empire rivaled that of the Capone gang.[55] This characterization might have seemed a bit overblown to those who encountered Marcello's drawl and rough manners in the Senate's New Orleans hearings. But he was well advised by counsel and was as shrewd and tight-lipped as any witness who has ever appeared before any government body. Invoking the Fifth Amendment 152 times, he seemed true to the motto posted over his headquarters in the Town and Country Motel in New Orleans Parish: "Three can keep a secret if two are dead."

Kefauver saw deportation as a key tool in the fight against Marcello: "[W]e wanted to find out among other things what was the trouble with naturalization and immigration laws that a man who is apparently having such a detrimental effect on law enforcement and to decency in the community, how can he continue to stay here."[56] He recommended that deportation proceedings be initiated as soon as possible. Those proceedings, which began in 1952, would last more than thirty years, without government success.

Marcello was arrested on December 30, 1952, as a result of his 1938 marijuana convictions.[57] The charge was a violation of Section 241(a)(11) of the Immigration and Nationality Act of 1952 (INA), which mandated deportation for drug offenses. Marcello had a full hearing before a "special inquiry officer," who on February 20, 1953 found him to be deportable. Marcello was advised of his right to apply for the discretionary relief of suspension of deportation, then available if he could prove ten years of continuous physical presence in the United States with "good moral character" and "exceptional and extremely unusual hardship."[58] At first he declined to do so, but later his attorney moved to reopen the hearing for that purpose. The special inquiry officer denied the motion. The Board of Immigration Appeals affirmed speedily, ruling on June 1, 1953. Marcello was rearrested the next day.[59] Marcello appealed the board's decision through a habeas corpus petition. At the time, this was the accepted method for federal court challenges to administrative orders of the board. His attorneys argued that the deportation procedures of the INA conflicted with the Administrative Procedure Act and violated his right to due process and to a fair and impartial hearing.

Administrative law had become increasingly important from the New Deal through the end of World War II. Federal government intervention had gradually gained acceptance as essential protection against inevitable market failures, but controversy continued over how agencies did their work and whether their actions undermined the "rule of law." In 1933, the American Bar Association (ABA) had created a Special Committee on Administrative Law, which expressed great concern about the "judicial function" being exercised by administrative agencies.[60] It is difficult, more than half a century later, to appreciate the passion aroused by these issues at the time. But passion is undoubtedly the right word.[61] Indeed, the president-elect of the ABA once called on lawyers to join the "titanic struggle" against those " 'progressives,' 'liberals,' or 'radicals' who desire to invest the national Government with totalitarian powers in the teeth of Constitutional democracy."[62] In early

1939, President Roosevelt had instructed Attorney General Murphy to appoint a new committee to investigate "the need for procedural reform" in the administrative realm and to make a "thorough and comprehensive study."[63] The committee's final report paved the way for the federal Administrative Procedure Act of 1946 (APA), which easily passed both the House and the Senate.[64] Thus, for the first time in U.S. history, the huge and multifaceted federal administrative process was to be subject to one procedural law with important constraints, such as relative independence for hearing officers and judicial oversight.[65]

By 1950, the APA had been mentioned in twelve Supreme Court cases.[66] But it was the deportation case of *Wong Yang Sung v. McGrath* that offered the Court its first real opportunity to construe the deep implications of the 1946 statute.[67] Wong Yang Sung, a citizen of China, was arrested for having overstayed his admission period. An immigration inspector, after a hearing, recommended deportation. Per standard procedures, the acting commissioner approved this recommendation, and the Board of Immigration Appeals later affirmed it. Wong then filed a habeas corpus petition in which he argued that his deportation hearing was "not conducted in conformity with [sections] of the Administrative Procedure Act," which contained strict requirements for the independence of hearing examiners.[68]

Immigration inquiry officers performed various tasks: interviewing people seeking to enter the country, investigating noncitizens for possible deportation, and, as in this case, actually presiding in a relatively formal judicial capacity over the deportation proceedings. Regulations prohibited an inspector from combining these functions in any particular case. But all inspectors worked out of a common office under common supervision. An inspector would sit in judgment on a case that his colleague had investigated, and vice versa. The conflict between the immigration hearing system and the APA was clear. Hearing examiners were required by the APA to be systematically separated from colleagues involved with inspection and prosecution.

Another issue was that the proceedings themselves were inquisitorial in character. Although in some cases an immigration "prosecutor" would be involved, in many cases—as in this one—the special inquiry officer would conduct the proceedings on his own. Thus, the agent would present the government's case, cross-examine the respondent, interrogate other witnesses, if any, and then rule on evidentiary matters and certify the record with a recommendation to the commissioner.[69]

The government admitted that the deportation system deviated from the APA but argued that the APA did not govern it. The Court thus had to grapple with two threshold questions. First, the relevant APA provisions applied only to those hearings that were "required by statute to be determined on the record after an opportunity for an agency hearing." Strange though it may seem, at that time no statute required deportation hearings. The Supreme Court had, however, long required hearings as a matter of due process.[70] The second question involved APA §7(a), which provided that "nothing in this Act shall be deemed to supersede the conduct of specified classes of proceedings . . . specially provided for by or designated pursuant to statute."[71]

The dominant truth about deportation law had long been one of exceptionalism. It was a field where many constitutional and administrative rules did not hold, because of deference to the plenary power of the political branches. In that light, the fact that the *Wong Yang Sung* Court began by emphasizing the importance of uniformity in administrative proceedings is striking.[72] This was likely due more to the Court's desire to say something important about the APA than about deportation, and the nature of the case permitted the Court considerable leeway.[73] Still, the Court cited a 1940 government report about the INS: "A genuinely impartial hearing . . . is psychologically improbable if not impossible, when the presiding officer has at once the responsibility of appraising the strength of the case and of seeking to make it as strong as possible."[74]

The Court found that the immigration system was "a perfect exemplification of the practices so unanimously condemned." Moreover, in what by current standards seems a remarkably warm appreciation of the harshness of deportation, the Court noted that "this commingling, if objectionable anywhere, would seem to be particularly so in the deportation proceeding, where we frequently meet with a voteless class of litigants who not only lack the influence of citizens, but who are strangers to the laws and customs in which they find themselves involved and who often do not even understand the tongue in which they are accused."[75]

But did the APA apply? The government had argued that because there was no express requirement for any hearing or adjudication in the statute authorizing deportation, these proceedings were not covered. But the

Court concluded that deportation without a hearing would be unconstitutional. Moreover, "[w]hen the Constitution requires a hearing, it requires a fair one, one before a tribunal which meets at least currently prevailing standards of impartiality. A deportation hearing involves issues basic to human liberty and happiness . . . perhaps to life itself."[76] Finally, the Court concluded that nothing in the immigration statute "specifically provides that immigrant inspectors shall conduct deportation hearings or be designated to do so."[77] Thus, the APA governed deportation.

Wong Yang Sung affirmed three basic, intertwined propositions of immense importance:

- The new APA applied to deportation proceedings;
- The constitutional protections of procedural due process applied to deportation proceedings; but
- The Court would save for another day the question of exactly what due process would require if Congress were to exempt deportation cases from the APA.

There were then two major legal developments following the decision in *Wong Yang Sung* and before the commencement of deportation proceedings against Carlos Marcello. Congress adopted a rider to the Justice Department's supplemental appropriation in 1950 that specifically exempted exclusion and deportation proceedings from APA requirements.[78] If matters had stayed there, the Court might have had to confront directly the due process question it had avoided in *Wong Yang Sung*. But there was more to come.

In 1952, Congress enacted a new and comprehensive immigration statute: the INA. A report, covering the full range of immigration, naturalization, and deportation issues, was submitted, along with a comprehensive bill, in April 1950 by Senator Patrick McCarran.[79] Congress had passed McCarran's Internal Security Act, which required the registration of the Communist Party and its members.[80] It also contained provisions that authorized the exclusion and even the retroactive deportation of Communists and members of other organizations considered to be dangerous to public safety and forbade naturalization by a court if deportation proceedings were pending.[81] Testimony in the House gives a good sense of the fearful, pro-deportation tenor of the times: "the Communist network in the United States is inspired and controlled in large part by foreign agents . . . There are, under our present immigration laws, numerous aliens who have been found to be deportable, many of whom are free to roam the country at will . . . One device for infiltration by Communists is by procuring naturalization for disloyal aliens who use their citizenship as a badge for admission into the fabric of our society."[82] Representative Francis E. Walter, coauthor of the act, had reportedly once called critics of the act "professional Jews" who shed "crocodile tears for no reason whatsoever."[83] He also stated that "thousands of criminals and subversive aliens are roaming our streets, a continuing threat to the safety of our people."[84]

As debate over the immigration bill in the Senate commenced in 1951, McCarran said that if the "stream of humanity" that flowed into the "fabric of our society" were "healthy," then the impact would be "salutary."[85] However, "if that stream is polluted our institutions and our way of life become infected."[86] Thus, much of the bill sought to strengthen exclusion laws, especially ideological types. It maintained much of the national-origins quota system of the 1920s. The bill also contained a number of rather harsh deportation provisions. It eliminated statutes of limitation for many types of deportation, reinforced retroactive ideological deportation, limited judicial review, and raised the standard for suspension of deportation. Many criticized McCarran's approach vigorously, and indeed, a major counterproposal was developed by Senators Humphrey and Lehman.[87] The liberals pulled no punches, arguing that the McCarran bill "adopts the arbitrary processes of the police state."[88] Still, Senator Humphrey confirmed that his group was "thoroughly in favor of deporting and excluding undesirable aliens." The difference, he said, was that McCarran's bill was "slipshod" and would "unnecessarily [hurt] the innocent at the same time as it affects the guilty."[89] The main differences between the two groups concerned the procedural relationship between the APA and deportation, the standards and procedures for discretionary suspension, and retroactivity.[90] Humphrey said that to permit deportation "without hearings or findings, and without the possibility of judicial review, would be the beginning of a police state."[91]

Debate in the House over Representative Walter's companion bill was more one-sided in favor of the harsh provisions. Representative Rankin stated, "We have had too many questionable characters swarming into the country already bringing . . . communism, atheism, anarchy, infidelity." He suggested that, rather than admitting more "of that ilk," the

United States should "begin to deport some who have already arrived . . . to save the country from destruction at the hands of the enemies within our gates."[92]

The McCarran-Walter bill ultimately passed by large margins in both the House and the Senate. It was strongly criticized in some quarters, however. A *New York Times* editorial called it "monstrous."[93] President Truman vetoed it, focusing in large part on its maintenance of national-origins quotas, which he termed "utterly unworthy of our traditions and ideals." He also saw the new deportation provisions as "unnecessarily severe" and supported greater humanitarian discretion to be given the attorney general to suspend deportation.[94] Senator McCarran called the president's veto message "one of the most un-American acts" he had witnessed.[95] The veto was overridden.

Carlos Marcello soon faced deportation proceedings under the new INA, with hearing provisions much less procedurally protective than required by the APA. The INA prohibited a hearing officer from presiding only over a particular case in which he or she had performed either investigative or prosecuting functions.[96] It permitted a hearing officer to "present and receive evidence, interrogate, examine, and cross-examine the alien or witnesses." Hearing officers were subject to supervision by the attorney general. In practice, this meant supervision by INS district directors and other officials with enforcement responsibilities. Finally, in a direct swipe at the *Wong Yang Sung* decision, the INA was to be "the sole and exclusive" deportation procedure.[97]

Marcello lost quickly in the Eastern District of Louisiana.[98] The court decision was dated June 8, 1953, a mere six days after his rearrest. The Fifth Circuit affirmed, holding that Congress had now provided a "sole and exclusive" procedure for determining "the deportability of an alien."[99] Although the court conceded that, theoretically, deportation could not proceed in violation of procedural due process, it held that the APA was not synonymous with due process.[100] It also rejected Marcello's due process claims, including his allegation that his case had been prejudged by the board.[101] Marcello alleged that the attorney general had made a public statement announcing his arrest as "the first major deportation move undertaken since the new Immigration and Nationality Act became effective." He also argued that the attorney general had said that he "was an undesirable citizen [*sic*] and had been guilty of many crimes, and that the proceedings were specially designed to deport [him] and that such publicity was bound to have great effect upon the special inquiry officer."[102] No matter, said the court. Even if the attorney general had made such a statement, it could not have prejudiced Marcello or influenced the special inquiry officer because his was not a case with closely contested factual issues.[103] This was a somewhat puzzling conclusion, as Marcello had applied for discretionary suspension of deportation.[104] The board had denied this application, on the basis of multiple factors, including his prior convictions and arrests, newspaper clippings naming him the "number one mobster in Louisiana," and his refusal to testify before the Kefauver committee.[105] For the Fifth Circuit, this calculus was sufficient.[106]

Marcello's ex post facto clause argument was also rejected easily. In as clear, but as frightening, a statement of post-entry social control as one could ask for, the court simply said, "Congress has plenary power over aliens and may deport them from this country at any time for any reason, even on grounds nonexistent at the time of their entry."[107]

The Supreme Court rejected Marcello's appeal. Justice Clark wrote for the majority. The Court concluded that it was "clear that Congress was setting up a specialized administrative procedure applicable to deportation hearings, drawing liberally on the analogous provisions of the Administrative Procedure Act and adapting them to the particular needs of the deportation process."[108] Eschewing the requirement of "magical passwords" to effectuate an exemption from the APA, the Court thus held that the INA expressly superseded its hearing provisions. This was an immensely important conclusion for the functioning of the deportation system. Had the Court held otherwise, virtually every deportation hearing that had been conducted in the preceding couple of years would have been subject to collateral attack.

Beyond such pragmatic concerns, the logic of the majority opinion seems convincing until one reads the dissent authored by Justice Black and joined by Justice Frankfurter, arguably the leading expert on administrative law on the Court at that time and generally a supporter of the plenary power doctrine. The dissent began its analysis from a starkly different basic principle: "A fair hearing necessarily includes an impartial tribunal." The dissenters noted that the officer who had conducted Marcello's hearings, decided his case, and made recommendations for his deportation was inextricably connected to the INS. He was subject to the supervision, direction, and control of the attorney general and the attorney general's subordinates in the Immigration Service who performed investigative and prosecutorial functions. Thus, the hearing officer adjudicated a case against Marcello that his own superiors had initiated and prosecuted. The dissenters found it unnecessary to resolve the profound due process questions this system posed. It was, in their view, a patent violation of the APA. "Human nature," wrote the dissenters, "has not put an impassable barrier between subjection and subserviency, particularly when job security is at stake."[109] They also highlighted the harshness of deporting a long-term lawful permanent resident for post-entry conduct, even one such as Carlos Marcello: "Petitioner was lawfully brought to this country forty-four years ago when he was eight months old and has resided here ever since. He is married and has four children. His wife and children are American citizens."

Still, Marcello's constitutional claims likewise fell easily. The lack of separation of functions did not offend the Court's sense of due process, despite earlier intimations to the contrary in *Wong Yang Sung*. The Court noted that Marcello had not alleged that either the inquiry officer or the Board of Immigration Appeals had seen the attorney general's alleged list, known of its existence, or been influenced by the inclusion of his name on it.[110] The ex post facto argument had been recently rejected by the Court and was not revisited for Marcello.[111] Justice Douglas, however, vigorously confronted the retroactivity problem in his dissent: "The Constitution places a ban on all *ex post facto* laws. There are no qualifications or exceptions."[112] Rejecting formalist descriptions of deportation as a merely civil proceeding, Douglas reiterated that deportation may be as severe a punishment as loss of livelihood.[113] Quoting Justice Brandeis, he stated that deportation may result "in loss of both property and life; or of all that makes life worth living."[114] According to Douglas, "[i]n the absence of a rational connection between the imposition of the penalty of deportation and the *present* desirability of the alien as a resident in this country, the conclusion is inescapable that the Act merely adds a new punishment for a past offense."[115]

In the end, Marcello lost on every theory, and his case had two important doctrinal consequences. First, it largely put to rest the broader due process implications of *Wong Yang Sung* by essentially ignoring the argument that there was any constitutional problem with the deportation system of the 1952 act. Indeed, the Marcello Court did not even mention *Wong Yang Sung* in its breathtakingly short analysis of the normative and constitutional questions that had loomed so large a mere four years earlier: "The contention is without substance when considered against the long-standing practice in deportation proceedings . . . and against the special considerations applicable to deportation which the Congress may take into account in exercising its particularly broad discretion in immigration matters."[116]

Second, the 1954 Court reinforced the exceptionalism of deportation law, reconfirming that it was outside some of the most important procedural protections contained in the APA and required in other arenas by due process. It seems that the Court, at the height of the Cold War, had simply lost the strong "rule of law" spirit that had been engendered by the 1946 APA. Deportation law was again largely relegated, as it had been in the 1890s and again after the Palmer Raids, to extraconstitutional status.

But judicial abdication was not the final word on this subject. There was widespread criticism of the harsh deportation laws and of the INS throughout the mid-1950s. A vigorous academic critique emerged, including important work by Louis Boudin, Will Maslow, and Siegfried Hesse that is well worth rereading today.[117] This critique eventually had some effect, as the Cold War eased. In late 1954, Attorney General Brownell liberalized detention practices. The problem of the quality and mixed functions of special inquiry officers also continued to receive attention as part of systematic reviews of administrative law.[118] After the 1955 Hoover Commission Task Force reported that "[t]hese officers for the most part are unqualified to perform legal or judicial functions," the INS promulgated regulations in 1955 and 1956 requiring the use of a special prosecuting officer in cases involving disputed factual issues.[119] In later years, INS required all special inquiry officers to have law degrees, assigned INS trial attorneys to represent the government in all deportation cases, and redesignated hearing officers as immigration judges. In 1983, the new Executive Office for Immigration Review separated immigration judges entirely from the INS and placed them in a special adjudication unit of the Department of Justice. Deportation hearings now generally conform to the procedural requirements of the APA, although that is not required by statute.[120]

Despite his loss at the Supreme Court, Carlos Marcello was a long way from being deported. The INS moved quickly against him. But now it encountered a new problem. Where exactly could he be sent? The INA listed many countries to which a noncitizen could be deported and accorded considerable leeway to the government.[121] It provided, first, that deportation should be to a country designated by the noncitizen, if that country was willing to accept him into its territory, unless the attorney general concluded that deportation to that country would be prejudicial to the interests of the United States. On June 29, 1955, Marcello designated France. This was not a frivolous choice on his part, as Tunisia had been under French control at the time of his birth there. The government of France, however, was apparently not anxious to welcome Marcello to its bosom. On July 21, 1955, the INS received a formal refusal to accept him from the government of France.

The law also provided that deportation might be directed to any country of which the deportee was "a subject, national, or citizen, if that country is willing to accept him into its territory." Failing that, the attorney general, in his discretion, was authorized to designate certain other countries, including the country from which "the alien last entered the United States" and the country in which he was born. The statute offered a total of seven different choices, the last of which—a poignantly ironic combination of hospitality and rejection—was to any country willing to accept the person into its territory.

After France demurred, the government turned to Italy. But the Italian government suddenly withdrew permission that it had previously granted to Marcello to enter its territory. Exactly why this was so remains mysterious. It appears that Marcello undertook legal proceedings in the courts of Italy to secure a cancellation of his own permission to enter. In light of his record, one can appreciate the reticence of his parents' homeland to welcome him back, but whether that concern, corruption, or something else led to Italy's refusal to accept him remains uncertain.[122]

This left the U.S. government in a bit of a bind. And there matters stewed for some six years, as Marcello became a poster child for "dilatory legal tactics" and an inspiration for further attempts to limit judicial involvement with the deportation system. In 1959, Attorney General Rogers wrote a letter to Senator Sam Ervin, who had already expressed considerable concern about Marcello. The letter recounted how Marcello's attorneys had instituted lawsuits on at least six different occasions, challenging various aspects of his deportation proceedings and leading to several trips to the court of appeals and three to the U.S.

Supreme Court.[123] According to Attorney General Rogers, these suits, though mostly resolved in favor of the government, resulted in "court-imposed restraint from deporting Marcello during most of this time." At the end of the letter, Rogers opined that "[o]n the basis of past experience it is expected that Marcello will attempt other delaying tactics in the courts."

Now begins the strangest part of Marcello's story. In March 1959, Marcello was called as a witness before the McClellan committee, formed to investigate labor and corruption. Then-Senator John F. Kennedy was a member of the committee; its chief counsel was the young Robert F. Kennedy. Before Marcello took the stand, former FBI agent Aaron Kohn provided the committee with extensive historical testimony about the history of the Mafia in New Orleans and the rise of Marcello to his current position of power. No fan of understatement, Kohn asserted that the Marcello organization was poised to achieve virtually complete control of the political and law enforcement machinery of the state of Louisiana.[124] When Robert Kennedy interrogated Marcello, however, he obtained some seventy recitations of refusal to testify on grounds that "it may intend [sic] to incriminate me." By all accounts, the committee members, and especially Robert Kennedy, were exasperated by Marcello's arrogance and his repeated reliance on the Fifth Amendment.

When Robert Kennedy became attorney general, he undoubtedly remembered this interchange and was determined to act decisively against Marcello. Indeed, the New Orleans States-Item reported on December 28, 1960, a promise by Attorney General-designate Kennedy to expedite Marcello's deportation.[125] This fit perfectly with one of his main priorities: to wage all-out war on organized crime. Indeed, he had written in his book, The Enemy Within, "If we do not attack organized criminals with weapons and techniques as effective as their own, they will destroy us."[126] Deportation was clearly such a weapon.[127] One idea, incredible though it may seem in retrospect, was to deport Marcello to Formosa (now known as Taiwan). But what happened next was still more incredible.

Marcello had obtained a false birth certificate from Guatemala in 1956, reportedly by paying a large bribe to the law partner of the Guatemalan president.[128] It is not entirely clear why he did this, but perhaps it was a kind of deportation insurance policy. He was well connected in Guatemala, seems to have traveled there with some regularity, and probably thought he could live there—a mere four-hour flight from New Orleans—if worse came to worst. His misfortune was that the birth certificate fell into the hands of the INS. Officials of the United States quickly asked Guatemala to accept Marcello if he were deported there. Such permission was granted by the Guatemalan government (which, one should note, had been put into power less than a decade earlier through a Central Intelligence Agency-supported coup d'état).

On April 4, 1961, Marcello made his way to the INS office in New Orleans for a regular check-in, as required by the terms of his supervised release. He was accompanied by a lawyer, Phillip Smith, who waited outside while Marcello went in. All seemed normal until the INS agent suddenly began reading to him from a statement that said he was a citizen of Guatemala and would be immediately deported there. Marcello has described what happened next: "I said what for. He say well you been overdue on your visa. I couldn't understand it myself. I just, I just couldn't believe it. So by that time two immigration officers that I have never seen before, they came up and they put the handcuffs on me. Two of them, about six foot something. So I say, could I use the telephone. I say I'd like to call to talk to my attorney. They say no. I say, can I call my wife to get a toothbrush and some money. They said no, let's go."[129]

Marcello was handcuffed and taken quickly out of the building to a waiting car. By all accounts, he did not go easily. He demanded to call Jack Wasserman. His request was denied. He asked to be allowed to get some clothes and some money. Again he was denied. He claimed he was being kidnapped. He said that the deportation was a violation of an order issued by Justice Hugo Black that he be given seventy-two hours notice before being deported.[130] Less than one hour later, however, Marcello found himself the only passenger, along with two immigration agents, a pilot, and co-pilot, on a seventy-eight-passenger plane bound for Guatemala. As he described the scene, "You would have thought it was the President going in instead of me going out."[131]

There is little doubt that the Justice Department knew that the Guatemalan birth certificate was fraudulent. Indeed, on April 6, 1961, two days after Marcello's deportation, Herbert J. Miller, Jr., assistant attorney general in the criminal division, received a communiqué from Edward Silberling, chief of the organized crime and racketeering section, that expressed the worry that "the United States Government may be placed in the embarrassing legal position of having made certain representations . . . about Marcello's birth record while it was in possession of information indicating that the birth record was a forgery." Marcello's later description of the incident thus seems disturbingly accurate: "They just snatched me, and that is it, actually kidnapped me . . . and dumped me in Guatemala."[132]

Marcello's attorneys quickly filed an action in federal court for a declaratory judgment that the Guatemala deportation was invalid.[133] The court was told that the Guatemalan government had cancelled its prior permission to enter and was now seeking to expel him. The judge, however, professed no power to "intrude into any negotiations between the Government of the United States and the government of a foreign country." His reason? "The conduct of foreign relations is left solely to the President and his subordinates." The validity of the birth certificate was "not material" because "[t]he Government of Guatemala has accepted the plaintiff, and once the acceptance was acted on and the plaintiff was brought by our Government to Guatemala and landed there, the transaction is at an end."[134]

After he was in fact expelled from Guatemala, Marcello's lawyers tried again, with a motion to vacate the summary judgment. Again, however, the court declined to intervene, holding that because Guatemala had initially accepted Marcello, "the matter is at an end so far as this country is concerned."[135]

So we know that Marcello lost in court. But what actually happened on the ground? One version of the story is told by Frank Ragano (an attorney for Santo Trafficante, Jr., and Jimmy Hoffa)[136] and also by Robert Blakey: Marcello was deported from Guatemala to El Salvador, where he was held in a military barracks in the jungle for four or five days before being put on a bus, together with Michael Maroun, a visiting lawyer from Shreveport, Louisiana (one cannot help but wonder how this lawyer billed for his time). When the bus stopped at the Honduran border, the two were forced to cross on foot and were abandoned there in a remote area. Marcello, at that time fifty-one years old, "paunchy," and dressed in a business suit and tie, had to trek some seventeen miles in the hot sun before reaching "a peasant village" from which he and his attorney were able to get a ride to Tegucigalpa. Somehow from there, they managed to get a flight and reentered the United States through Miami, "illegally but unhindered."[137] Others tell a less exciting but still interesting tale. Ed Reid, the Pulitzer-prize winning author of one of the first Mafia exposés, reports that Marcello was actually wined and dined by the upper crust of Guatemalan society. He was then flown to a resort area in a private plane belonging to the president of Guatemala, where he was photographed at a racetrack with an old friend who owned the largest shrimp boat fleet in the Gulf of Mexico. According to this version, Marcello made his way to Honduras in comfort and was then escorted home on one of his friend's boats.[138]

In any case, Marcello's story at this point becomes both more astounding and still murkier.[139] Edward Becker, who testified before the House Select Committee on Assassinations,[140] reported that during a September 1962 Mafia business meeting in a country barn in the Louisiana marshes, Marcello cried out, "Livarsi na petra di la scarpa!," a Mafia cry of revenge that translates to "Take the stone out of my shoe!" "Don't worry about that little Bobby son of a bitch," he then reportedly shouted, "He's going to be taken care of!"[141] According to Ed Reid, Marcello knew that to rid himself of Robert Kennedy, he would first have to deal with his brother, the president. As Marcello put it, "The dog will keep biting you if you only cut off its tail."[142] Becker testified that Marcello had explained that he would likely use someone not affiliated with his organization to do the job. Reportedly, the use of "a nut," as John H. Davis later phrased it, was a venerable Mafia tradition.[143]

Frank Ragano reports a conversation with Marcello that he had in March 1962. Ragano claims that Marcello said to him, "You, Jimmy, and me are in for hard times as long as Bobby Kennedy is in office. Someone ought to kill that son-of-a-bitch . . . Someone ought to kill all those goddamn Kennedys."[144] In September 1962, Santo Trafficante reportedly told Jose Aleman, a leader of the Cuban expatriate community in Miami, that John F. Kennedy was "going to be hit."[145] Soon thereafter, in July 1963, Ragano claims that he had lunch with Jimmy Hoffa to prepare for a meeting that he was going to have later with Carlos Marcello and Santo Trafficante. Ragano says that Hoffa told him, "Something has to be done. The time has come for your friend [Trafficante] and Carlos to get rid of him, kill that son-of-a-bitch John Kennedy . . . We're running out of time—something has got to be done."[146] Ragano asserts that he communicated this instruction to Trafficante and Marcello, thinking it was "a joke." Ragano says that he waited for the laughter but there was only silence, and "[t]heir facial expressions were icy." Then, when the news came from Dallas on November 22, 1963, Ragano says that Hoffa called him and said, "Did you hear the good news? They killed the son-of-a-bitch bastard. Yeah, he's dead . . . Lyndon Johnson is going to be sworn in as president. You know he'll get rid of Booby [sic]."[147]

Later, according to Ragano, Marcello told him to tell Hoffa that "he owes me and he owes me big." Ragano also asserts that Hoffa said to him, with a grin, "I told you they could do it. I'll never forget what Carlos and Santo did for me."[148] Thirty years after that, according to Ragano, Santo Trafficante, on his deathbed, told his lawyer, "Carlos fucked up. We shouldn't have killed Giovanni. We should have killed Bobby."[149]

The assertion that Carlos Marcello was a leader of a successful Mafia conspiracy to assassinate President Kennedy is far from universally accepted.[150] However, the House Assassinations Committee Report did state that the most likely organized crime figures to have participated in a unilateral assassination plan were Carlos Marcello and Santo Trafficante. Marcello, according to the committee, had the motive, means, and opportunity to have President Kennedy assassinated.[151] The committee stated that "Marcello exhibited an intense dislike for Robert Kennedy . . . claiming that he had been illegally 'kidnapped' by Government agents during the deportation." Marcello was also found to have had "credible associations" with both Lee Harvey Oswald and Jack Ruby as well as with one David W. Ferrie, a shadowy figure with links to Oswald, who was also reportedly a pilot for Marcello.[152]

Marcello denied any involvement in organized crime or the assassination of President Kennedy. The committee had noted that his "uniquely successful career in organized crime" was based to a large extent on "a policy of prudence." He was not reckless. On the basis of the available evidence, the committee opined that it was "unlikely that Marcello was in fact involved in the assassination of the President." On the other hand, "the evidence that he had the motive and the evidence of links through associates to both Oswald and Ruby, coupled with the failure of the 1963–64 investigation to explore adequately possible conspiratorial activity in the assassination, precluded a judgment by the committee that Marcello and his associates were not involved."[153]

In one of the many ironies of his story, just as Marcello was experiencing an illegal deportation, he was inspiring the creation of new laws to make legal deportation much easier for the government.[154] In 1961, Congress added a new section to the INA that dramatically changed judicial review procedures.[155] Among its major provisions, the new law channeled most deportation orders away from district courts. Review generally now would take place through a petition for review filed in courts of appeals, though persons in custody and those seeking entry into the United States could still file district court habeas corpus petitions. The system required exhaustion of administrative remedies, restricted repetitive filings, and eliminated an entire layer of court review. Congress undoubtedly thought it would expedite cases such as Marcello's in the future by preventing declaratory judgment actions such as those utilized by Jack Wasserman. As it turned out, the success of this endeavor has been rather mixed.[156]

Though Marcello faced sustained federal law enforcement attention for some thirty years, the INS never could legally deport him, in part because of complications caused by the illegal 1961 deportation, in part perhaps because of behind-the-scenes influence, but mostly because of the sustained efforts of Jack Wasserman—who received an estimated $2 million in legal fees for his work.[157] Criminal prosecutors, however, eventually had better success. Although acquitted by a jury of perjury and conspiracy charges on the very day of John Kennedy's assassination, Marcello was again indicted in 1964 for "conspiring to obstruct justice" by "fixing a juror" and seeking the murder of a government witness.[158] The case was tried in 1965, and Marcello was represented, again, by Jack Wasserman. The verdict was not guilty. He was tried in 1968 for assaulting a federal agent (the background story seems to be that the agent was having an affair with Marcello's daughter). He was convicted on this charge but served less than six months in a federal prison medical center.[159]

By the 1970s, the understanding of the Mafia was compared to that of God in the late Middle Ages: "all that there is to know about the Mafia is known by now except whether it actually exists."[160] This was less true of Carlos Marcello: he was famous. LIFE magazine, in 1970, described him as "the second most powerful Mafia leader in the United States . . . after Carlo Gambino of New York."[161] The House Select Committee on Crime determined in 1972 that Marcello "has become a formidable menace to the institutions of government and the people of the United States."[162] Marcello was again indicted in New Orleans on racketeering charges under the Racketeer Influenced and Corrupt Organizations Act and on mail and wire fraud and conspiracy charges in 1980 following an elaborate FBI sting operation.[163] Before a packed courtroom, he was convicted in 1981. He was indicted the next day in Los Angeles for conspiring to bribe a U.S. district court judge. On January 25, 1982, the seventy-two-year-old Marcello was sentenced to seven years. He was, however, released on $300,000 bond, having described himself to the sentencing judge as "a salesman for the Pelican Tomato Company." In April 1982, he was sentenced in Los Angeles to ten years. The Los Angeles judge, echoing the earlier statement by Holmes, concluded, "I think it's fair to say you're a very bad man."[164]

Marcello entered prison in 1983, facing seventeen years behind bars. The Justice Department had sought and obtained an emergency order for his immediate imprisonment, on the basis of a sealed affidavit stating that he planned to flee the country rather than serve his sentence.[165] One wonders if the aging Marcello appreciated the irony. Robert Kennedy's Justice Department had stretched legal boundaries to avoid judicial interference in its efforts to get him out of the country. But the Reagan Justice Department hastily sought court assistance to prevent that very result—which it might instead have treated as the culmination of a quarter-century deportation effort. By this point, however, Marcello may not have noticed much. He suffered from Alzheimer's disease and had also experienced more than one major stroke. He was released from prison in 1989 and was never seen again in public. He died in 1993, in his mansion in the New Orleans suburb of Metairie, cared for by relatives and private nurses, at the age of eighty-three.

The Return of Ideological Deportations

The Saga of Harry Bridges

> Oh, the FBI is worried, the bosses they are scared;
> They can't deport six million men, they know.
> And we're not a-goin' to let them send Harry o'er the sea.
> We'll fight for Harry Bridges, and build the CIO.
>
> —Pete Seeger, Lee Hays, and Millard Lampell,
> "The Ballad of Harry Bridges" (1966)

The case of union leader Harry Bridges illustrates the tensions implicit within the regime of ideological post-entry social control deportation in the mid-twentieth-century United States. Stripped to its essentials, it was a prolonged struggle over the idea that noncitizens, no matter their status or length of residence, could be deported for "subversive" thoughts and association. What is perhaps most fascinating in retrospect is how that fundamental notion itself was never definitively resolved, even as it influenced nearly thirty years of legal proceedings and public discourse.

Harry Bridges, born in Australia in 1901, arrived in the United States in 1920. His deportation problems began in 1934, during a longshoremen's strike that extended from San Francisco along the California coast and from Texas to New Orleans.[166] The workers' main demand was an end to the "shape-up" hiring system, referred to by some as "the employers' slave market," and its replacement by a union-run hiring system.[167] This strike was one of many in a time when "social upheavals of extraordinary importance, drama, and violence . . . ripped the cloak of civilized decorum from society, leaving exposed naked class conflict."[168]

The longshoremen's strike closed down Pacific shipping. In early July, the Industrial Association of San Francisco attempted to force the port open, using strikebreakers and police support.[169] As the situation descended into violence, the Teamsters and then other maritime unions joined the strike; the longshoremen, led by Bridges, refused to return to work until all the strikes were settled.[170] Bridges, who had experienced a similar general strike years before in Australia, which he said had "tied up the whole darn country," was elected as the leader of the Joint Marine Strike Committee. Eventually, some 130,000 workers supported the strike. With federal intervention, the parties eventually agreed to submit to arbitration.[171] The longshoremen achieved most of their goals.[172]

The strike was described by Frances Perkins as "a spontaneous demonstration to vindicate the right of collective bargaining."[173] Others took a rather different view. Bridges, the "alien agitator," became a focal point for attacks against the newly invigorated labor movement. The INS began to receive requests from a variety of sources, including California governor Frank Merriam, to investigate Bridges for possible deportation.[174] In a radio broadcast, Governor Merriam reportedly said, "It is the plotting of such alien and vicious schemers . . . that has intensified, magnified and aggravated our labor problems."[175] Frances Perkins periodically received notes from Franklin Roosevelt asking her to investigate Bridges.[176]

In early 1936, the INS commissioner testified before a subcommittee of the House Appropriations Committee that Bridges had been followed "unremittingly" for many years by local police and federal agents.

Frances Perkins's understanding of the legal standard at that time was that deportation could be ordered if an alien "teaches Communism." She had concluded, however, that either Bridges was not a Communist, "or has so carefully guarded his utterances that there is no legal ground for his deportation."[177] Still, pressure mounted to the point where, three years later, Perkins defensively reported that "neither through fear nor cowardice were any officials of the Department of Labor at any time swayed from their duty in connection with the Bridges matter."[178]

Meanwhile, Bridges was elected president of the local chapter of the American Federation of Labor (AFL), then president of the newly formed International Longshoremen and Warehousemen Union, affiliated with the more radical Congress of Industrial Organizations (CIO). The ILWU was strongly antiracist, a unique posture at the time and especially significant given the racial history of labor struggles in California. Bridges's San Francisco local was fully integrated; indeed at least a quarter of its membership was African American.[179] He was later appointed regional director of the entire California CIO.[180]

In the fall of 1936, Frances Perkins reportedly personally telephoned Bridges and asked him to cooperate with the government by having his men continue to work under a consent agreement but without a contract. She encouraged the fiery union leader to believe that differences with management would be resolved if the parties would "sit around a table and talk it over."[181] This approach seems to have worked for awhile. Negotiations eventually broke down, however, and Pacific Coast ports endured more longshoremen's strikes from late 1936 into 1937. Positions on both sides hardened considerably. In December 1936, it was reported that "employers on the Pacific Coast virtually have completed a coastwise 'vigilante' organization to protect their interests in the event they find themselves unable to obtain redress from the government." Writing in late 1936, Louis Adamic worried that the employers would "get more and more desperate." He surmised that "they may not make their next move, whatever it will be, for some time—unless they decide to attempt to frame Bridges."[182]

In March 1938, the INS district director in Seattle, Washington—apparently without consulting Frances Perkins—brought deportation proceedings against Bridges on ideological grounds. But ideological deportation law was also in some turmoil. The Fifth Circuit held in the 1938 case of Joseph Strecker that a noncitizen who was not currently a member of the Communist Party could not be deported for past membership alone.[183] The Bridges matter was postponed, with the acquiescence of the Department of Justice, until the Supreme Court could resolve this issue. Even after the Supreme Court upheld the Circuit Court, however, Perkins faced strong pressure to proceed against Bridges somehow.[184] The *New York Daily News* reported, "Secretary of Labor Perkins has been battered so ruthlessly for her delay in pushing the charges for Harry Bridges' deportation that reporters displayed almost unique delicacy in quizzing her . . . Finally, a third newspaperman slyly asked: 'Is there any truth in the rumor that London Bridge's falling down?' at which Miss Perkins suffered a spasm of embarrassment."[185]

The Bridges matter was a major political concern within the administration. James Farley reportedly told the cabinet members at a meeting in early 1939 that Perkins's failure to deport Bridges could hurt the Democratic Party and that she should consider this in her evaluation of the evidence.[186] Joseph Kennedy, then chairman of the Maritime Commission, reportedly presaged the later use of deportation by his son Robert against Carlos Marcello: "Bridges has kept West Coast shipping in such turmoil to satisfy his lust for power, that it's immaterial whether he's a Communist, but that he's a trouble-maker and a pest and does not deserve the tender consideration bestowed on him by Madame Perkins."[187]

The Bridges matter also highlighted long-standing tensions between the Roosevelt administration and the Congress over the boundaries of executive and legislative power. Harold L. Ickes wrote in his diary that when Frances Perkins reported at a cabinet meeting that she had forwarded confidential departmental records about Bridges to the Senate Immigration Committee, "the President nearly jumped down her throat." Homer Cummings reportedly agreed that "the administrative departments did not have to produce everything in the way of information that a legislative committee might request."[188] Such structural tensions had, of course, long predated the New Deal. Andrew W. Mellon had once reportedly told President Coolidge, "government by investigation is not government."[189] By the late 1920s, such committees increasingly began to focus on deporting Communists and other allegedly subversive aliens. Grandstanding was common. A House committee chaired by Hamilton Fish of New York publicly asserted in 1930, without disclosing its method of calculation, that there were 500,000 to 600,000 Communists and sympathizers in the United States.[190] Among the recommendations that followed from this insight were new immigration laws to exclude and deport "alien Communists," more funds for the Bureau of Immigration to handle deportation cases, changes to the naturalization laws to prevent grants of citizenship to Communists, and denial of reentry to any noncitizen who went to Russia to study Communism.[191] The country was deeply divided. Many believed that the recommendations were "far more dangerous to liberty and freedom than the pitiful handful of Communists in the United States ever have been."[192] But a contrary view prevailed.

By 1931, the Congress was flooded with bills to combat Communism in every imaginable way.[193] Among the rising stars of this era was Martin Dies, whose particular focus on alien Communists was to be a dominant feature of the American political and legal landscape for two decades. Dies, characterized by the *New Republic* as "physically a giant, very young, ambitious, and cocksure,"[194] repeatedly introduced bills to deport alien Communists and Fascists with no great success until, on June 6, 1938, he was appointed to chair a House Committee to investigate "un-American activities." But what exactly were "un-American activities"? Francis Biddle worried that the phrase was, at best, meaningless and "sterile, reflecting the timid longing to be correct . . . [but] at its worst, narrow, dark, and brutal."[195] Two years later, the Dies committee offered a definition that was clearly aimed at the foreign born: "organizations or groups existing in the United States which are directed, controlled, or subsidized by foreign governments or agencies which seek to change the policies and form of the government of the United States in accordance with the wishes of such foreign governments."[196]

Conflicts between the Roosevelt administration and Dies were bitter and often personal. Harold Ickes felt that Dies was "intent on smearing the New Deal whenever he could." At a press conference in November 1938, Ickes described Dies as "the outstanding zany in all our political history" and said that "no police court judge anywhere in the country would conduct such a hearing as he is conducting." He concluded that the Dies committee investigation was "the most outrageously unfair thing of the sort that has ever taken place."[197] When J. Parnell Thomas began an investigation of the Federal Theatre Project that encompassed allegations against such alleged subversives as Clark Gable, James Cagney, and even Shirley Temple,[198] Frances Perkins said, "Perhaps it is fortunate that Shirley Temple was born an American citizen and that she will not have to debate the issues raised by the preposterous revelations of your Committee."[199] Much of the popular press began to have its doubts as well. *Life* magazine reported that the committee was open to anyone who "cared to come in and call anyone else a red."[200]

But Congressman Dies was, to say the least, energetic and full of new ideas. And why not? In 1938, a Gallup poll showed that 74 percent of those asked were in favor of the committee's investigative work.[201] Father Coughlin's magazine, *Social Justice,* named Dies its "Man of the Week" and said he should be supported by every "honest, American-loving, Red-hating, United States citizen."[202] Dies pressed on. In late 1938, he sent to the State Department a long list of organizations that he wanted excluded from the country as "agents" of foreign governments. The first such organization was the Civil Liberties Union.[203] Dies's committee also maintained its focus on deportation: "the failure of the Labor Department to carry out laws with respect to deportation is a contributing factor to the widespread activities and propaganda carried on by un-American elements in the United States."[204]

On August 30, 1938, Dies sent a letter to Perkins in which he demanded immediate action against Harry Bridges. She replied that he was "attempting to usurp the functions of an executive department." Moreover, she repeated that Bridges would not be deported without "scrupulous regard for the due process of law, the clear and certain ruling of the courts, and the facts in the case."[205] Dies responded by threatening Perkins with impeachment. The matter was widely reported as a developing cause célèbre for the history of labor.[206]

In his diary on January 7, 1939, Harold Ickes reported a discussion about Bridges in a cabinet meeting. He wrote that Bridges, an "objectionable labor leader in the eyes of capital and the employer," had engendered "great pressure . . . upon the Department of Labor to deport him." According to Ickes, none of the various allegations against Bridges would justify his deportation. However, "notwithstanding all this, there is a great clamor throughout the land for his deportation." Still, President Roosevelt told his cabinet that Bridges ought not to be deported, "unless there was a legal justification for it."[207]

The pressure on Perkins to find such justification increased. On January 24, 1939, J. Parnell Thomas told the House that he impeached "Frances Perkins . . . James L. Houghteling [INS Commissioner], and

Gerald Reilly [Department of Labor Solicitor] . . . for high crimes and misdemeanors . . . to wit: . . . failing, neglecting, and refusing to enforce the immigration laws of the United States . . . against [Harry Bridges], an alien, who advises, advocates, or teaches the overthrow by force or violence of the Government of the United States."[208]

The resolution was referred to the House Judiciary Committee for testimony. To the president and many others, this action seemed more a sideshow than a serious legislative action. Harold Ickes viewed it as "an outrageous proceeding." He advised Perkins to "march right up to the Judiciary committee" and "put all her cards upon the table."[209] After some thought, Perkins did so, and the impeachment resolution was soon tabled. But the effect on Perkins was reportedly devastating. She seriously contemplated resignation, believing that the president would be better off without her. J. Parnell Thomas, demanding an investigation into "the sharp decrease in deportation," said that "the Secretary of Labor is endeavoring to replace our immigration statutes with some sort of idealistic philosophy, peculiar to [her]."[210]

Frances Perkins differentiated the external security function of immigration law from its internal deportation aspects and highlighted a "spirit of fair play."[211] She was determined to handle the Bridges matter in this spirit. She appointed a special officer to conduct the proceedings: James M. Landis, dean of the Harvard Law School and a leading expert on the newly developing field of administrative law.[212] Landis would develop the maximum procedural protection ever achieved in a deportation case: a model for future adjudicators to follow. However, he also spurred a furious public reaction that, ironically, inspired even harsher deportation laws.

As Bridges's hearing began in San Francisco on July 12, 1939, he was represented by Carol Weiss King, a highly experienced immigration attorney and a well-known figure of the American Left.[213] False rumors swirled that she was the daughter of Emma Goldman.[214] Dean Landis opened the hearing in a quite remarkable way: he announced that owing to the "seriousness of the consequences of deportation to the alien," the hearing would be governed by "those constitutional standards of fairness in criminal administration set forth in the Sixth Amendment." He did this despite the fact that the Supreme Court had made clear in *Fong Yue Ting* that deportation proceedings are civil, not criminal. Still, he felt that such protections were still required by due process in this case. Although he did not use the terminology of post-entry social control, it is clear that Dean Landis was moved both by Bridges's long residence in this country and by the nature of the charges against him.

Among other innovative rulings, Landis ordered that the proceedings would be open to the press and the public; counsel would be able to obtain a copy of the transcripts; and Bridges would be permitted to subpoena witnesses. He did not, however, have the right to a jury or, apparently, the right not to testify.[215] Bridges was called by the government as its first witness:

Q: Are you an alien?
A: I am.
Q: Are you now a member of the Communist Party?
A: No.
Q: Or have you at any other time in the past been a member of the Communist Party?
A: No.[216]

The defense theory was not subtle. As Attorney King put it, "This case is a product of employer plans and employer money. A conspiracy exists against Bridges." As conspirators she named, among others, Harper Knowles, the chair of the Commission on Subversive Activities of the American Legion in California, as well as various police and other public officials, including the Seattle district director of the INS.[217] The hearings went on for months. Landis was ultimately unimpressed by the government's case, referring to one star witness as "a problem in contumacy," noting that another was "a self-confessed liar," and referring to others with such adjectives as "prejudiced," "intemperate," "overbearing," "corrupt," and "pathological."[218] Following the close of the government's case, Bridges again took the stand in his defense. He admitted readily that he had known and associated with some Communists. "Look," he said, "we took whatever help we could get, and we were grateful for all of it."[219] The defense also called Harper Knowles as a hostile witness.[220] Landis later concluded that in Knowles's committee, "a close differentiation was not always made between labor agitators and those truly engaged in subversive activities."[221]

The Bridges hearing concluded in the fall and Dean Landis's 150-page decision appeared on December 28, 1939. He concluded that there was no valid evidence that Harry Bridges was a member of or even affiliated with the Communist Party. Landis also pointedly noted that "[o]pposition to 'red' baiting is not the equivalent of proof of Communist membership." He elegantly described Bridges's testimony about his own political beliefs as "a fighting *apologia* that refused to temper itself to the winds of caution."[222] Bridges later said in a newspaper interview, "Sometimes I get a little irritated when my views are ascribed to the Communist Party, because I had them before the Communist Party came into being."[223] On January 8, 1940, Secretary Perkins officially cancelled the warrant for Bridges's arrest, apparently ending the matter.

Many continued to be distressed by "the blatant and demagogic Dies." Harold Ickes noted in his diary that "Mussolini rose to absolute power in Italy as a result of a 'communist' hunt; that Hitler did the same thing in Germany; that Japan invaded China in order to suppress 'communism.'"[224] Walter Lippmann wrote that although the committee was attacking a "formidable evil in modern society," its procedure was "itself a violation of American morality."[225] But one can hardly overestimate the power of the antialien sentiment in the House at this time. As one member put it, "The mood of the House is such that if you brought in the Ten Commandments today and asked for their repeal, and attached to that request an alien law you could get it."[226]

The administration, too, moved toward a harsher posture. Following the Nazi-Soviet nonaggression pact, Robert Jackson reported that Franklin Roosevelt became "militantly" anti-Communist.[227] This affected the approach taken to deportation. In May 1940, the president asked Congress to transfer the Immigration Service from the Department of Labor to Justice. In part, this was an attempt to coordinate security measures for potential "enemy aliens." But more general concerns about the perceived softness of Frances Perkins's approach to deportation also played a role.[228]

On the very day that France signed its capitulation Armistice with Nazi Germany, Martin Dies called for strict enforcement of immigration laws against aliens in the United States.[229] In August 1940, Dies stated that he believed there were some 6 million Communist and Nazi sympathizers within the United States—a "real menace."[230] His views were well captured by the title of his 1940 book, *The Trojan Horse in America*.

Harry Bridges remained a high-profile target. The House voted 330 to 42 to authorize and direct the deportation of Bridges "forthwith to Australia" because "the Congress deems hurtful" his presence in the country.[231] Francis Biddle's opinion that the vote amounted to a bill of attainder was ignored.[232] Robert Jackson wrote an extraordinary letter to the *New York Times*, arguing that the bill was unconstitutional and recalling that Bridges "had been accused, investigated, and tried at great length, and . . . had not been proved guilty."[233]

Representative Samuel Hobbs soon proposed another much broader deportation bill, stating, "it is my joy to announce that this bill will do, in a perfectly legal and constitutional manner, what the bill specifically aimed at the deportation of Harry Bridges seeks to accomplish . . . deporting Harry Bridges and all others of similar ilk."[234] The House debate over the bill lasted one half hour and it passed 384 to 4. Though similarly supported by the Senate, the bill was vetoed by President Roosevelt but then passed by override. The Alien Registration Act of 1940 (also known as the Smith Act)[235] was also designed to overturn the *Strecker* decision in which the Supreme Court had held that past membership was not grounds for deportation. The new law authorized the deportation of those who had ever belonged to an organization that advocated the violent overthrow of the government. It also required all noncitizens to register, to notify the government of changes of address, and to state under oath activities in which they had engaged or intended to engage.

Thus, in August 1940, Attorney General Robert Jackson commenced a new investigation into whether Bridges was subject to deportation. FBI Director J. Edgar Hoover, returning to the deportation arena in which he had begun his career, sent a 2,500-page report to the attorney general in November.[236] Bridges, rearrested in February, was not alone. Joseph Strecker was also rearrested and charged with past membership in the Communist Party.[237]

Bridges's second round of deportation hearings was very different from the first. The government had learned important lessons. The idealistic New Dealers, Landis and Perkins, were replaced by government actors of a rather different cast. The new hearing officer was Judge Charles Sears from New York—undoubtedly a competent jurist, having served as a trial judge for many years and on the New York Court of Appeals. But he was not James Landis.

The government had mounted a huge nationwide investigation for witnesses; the American Legion apparently participated.[238] One of the new witnesses against Bridges was Benjamin Gitlow, whose criminal conviction for the distribution of the *Manifesto of the Socialist Party* was upheld in the famous case of *Gitlow v. New York*, sparking Holmes's dissent that "[e]very idea is an incitement."[239] Gitlow was called by the government as a witness on Marxism, the political affiliations of Bridges's lawyers, and a variety of other collateral matters that illustrated the highly charged political backdrop of the case.[240] Deportation law was now, yet again, a public stage on which loyalty and Red Scare fears would be played out, with minimal rights for the accused. On April 29, 1941, the *New York Times* reported that the chief government lawyer said that all of Bridges's lawyers were themselves Communists.[241] A brief excerpt from the cross-examination of Harry Bridges by the government illustrates well the nature of the government's theory of the case as well as the biting wit of Harry Bridges:

> *Q:* You had received orders from the Communist Party to support this strike, and when you realized the asinine mistake you had made you tried to retract, but it was too late, isn't that what actually happened?
> *A:* You are just a fool.
> . . .
> *Q:* Did you also state: "The striking workers should know that they have demonstrated solidarity—"
> *A:* They have to.
> *Q:* You got that from the Communist Manifesto, "Solidarity," didn't you?
> [laughter from the spectators]
> *A:* [no answer][242]

When Adolf Hitler broke his nonaggression pact with the Soviet Union and invaded on July 22, 1941, the focus on Communists in the United States began to diminish, as concern about Nazis increased. Deportation law rather quickly reflected the new reality. Rumors circulated that "all Red cases have been put on ice by the Immigration Service."[243] This was apparently true for some, but not for Harry Bridges. On September 26, 1941, Judge Sears found Bridges deportable. The decision was mostly based on Judge Sears's belief in the testimony of one witness: Harry Lundberg, former secretary-treasurer of the Sailors' Union of the Pacific. Lundberg testified that Bridges had invited him to dinner in 1935 and asked him to join the Communist Party. This testimony contradicted what Lundberg earlier had told the Labor Department and the FBI, and Lundberg and Bridges had apparently long been "bitter enemies." Nevertheless, Judge Sears concluded that Lundberg's bias would not "cause him to deviate from the truth."[244]

Bridges's attorneys filed an appeal to the Board of Immigration Appeals. Excerpts from the government's remarkable brief reveal the tenor of the times: "Bridges was and is a serpent, slithering into the trade union movement from a dark, unwholesome den of the past, to practice in the movement the treacherous tactic of hypocrisy and deceit, and to form with his "comrades" a tyranny therein that might compare in its exercise of power with that most vicious one Soviet Russia, where 9,000,000 human beings were slaughtered as a single project in the most cruel and inhuman program in the history of the world."[245]

The political content of the deportation case was apparent to all. I. F. Stone, referencing the Illinois governor who had pardoned some of the "Haymarket" defendants, wrote, "Attorney General Biddle will need the courage of an Altgeld to reverse Judge Sears." In a time when the United States was beginning to spread abroad propaganda for democracy, said Stone, "[t]he best propaganda will falter if it can be whispered abroad that although America calls itself free it deported Harry Bridges."[246]

The day after the bombing of Pearl Harbor, the Supreme Court handed down its opinion in another case that involved Harry Bridges and his prosecution for contempt of court, arising from a bitter labor dispute.[247] The Court, ironically relying on *Gitlow*, implicitly recognized that Bridges, despite being a noncitizen, had First Amendment rights in the United States. This was a principle that, if taken seriously, could have had profound implications for the state of deportation law. Four justices, however, led by Felix Frankfurter, dissented vigorously. The law on that score soon turned more toward the dissenters' position.

As the country mobilized for war, the administration's attitude toward some noncitizens took a more generous turn. The president said, "there are no foreigners now that we are United Nations" in the war effort. The nominee for INS commissioner, Earl Harrison, reaffirmed that immigrants had built the United States. Loyalty was the key concern for all. Indeed, the American Committee for the Protection of Foreign Born supported efforts to "enable Americans of Foreign birth to contribute to [the] war effort" while working to "eliminate Axis agents and fifth-column elements from their ranks."[248]

The Board of Immigration Appeals overturned Bridges's deportation case in 1942.[249] This seemed to end the matter, as the only possible avenue of appeal for the government would be to Attorney General Francis Biddle, who was widely recognized as a supporter of civil liberties and due process protections for noncitizens. Moreover, it was virtually unheard-of at that time for the attorney general to overturn a decision of the specialized board. Thus, it came as a major shock when Biddle, without a hearing, overruled the board and found Bridges to be subject to deportation on the grounds that he had been a member of, and affiliated with, the Communist Party and "a Communist organization." Indeed, the general counsel to INS, Edward Ennis, refused to support the decision before the Supreme Court, and it was handled by the criminal division of the Justice Department. One commentator noted Biddle's "blind spot that prevented him from foreseeing [the decision's] effects." It fell "like a shower of bombs along the West Coast waterfront."[250] Eleanor Roosevelt wrote to Franklin in support of Bridges, apparently without positive effect. On the other hand, Radio Berlin applauded Biddle's decision as "a very good *resumé* of the Communist Party's policy to overthrow the U.S. Government."[251]

Biddle's decision was upheld in district court.[252] The Ninth Circuit then also ruled against Bridges, 3 to 2, applying a deferential "some evidence" standard.[253] The dissenters furiously noted the "paucity" of evidence and bitterly asserted that "no amount of philosophizing can make a silk purse out of this obvious sow's ear."[254] Then, some twenty-five years after Bridges had first come to the United States, his deportation case finally came before the U.S. Supreme Court. The political stakes could hardly have been higher. I. F. Stone wrote that the decision would be "of worldwide significance." If the Court were to rule against Bridges, he suggested, it would provide "a sardonic background for the forthcoming international security conference at San Francisco" (that ultimately led to the creation of the United Nations).[255] However, in his argument to the Court, Solicitor General Fahy pointed out that "this petitioner has had more due process of law than perhaps any one of the numerous ones who have been deported in the past, including the Chinese laborer, the prostitutes and others."[256]

The Court, in an opinion authored by Justice Douglas, took a closer look at the evidence than had the lower courts and found that the order of deportation could not be sustained.[257] Justice Douglas offered important guidance on the meaning of "affiliation" as a basis for deportation: "Certainly those who joined forces with Russia to defeat the Nazis may not be said to have made an alliance to spread the cause of Communism. An individual who makes contributions to feed hungry men does not become 'affiliated' with the Communist cause because those men are Communists."[258] Justice Murphy, in concurrence, wrote, "The record in this case will stand forever as a monument of man's intolerance of man. Seldom if ever in the history of this nation has there been such a concentrated and relentless crusade to deport an individual because he dared to exercise the freedom that belongs to him as a human being and that is guaranteed to him by the Constitution."

Bridges had won. But, amazingly, his legal trials were still not over. When he applied for naturalization, he testified that he had never joined the Communist Party or any organization that advocated the overthrow of the government by force or violence. He was then admitted to citizenship.[259] Some three years later, a federal grand jury indicted Bridges for "conspiracy to defraud the United States by impairing, obstructing and defeating the proper administration of its naturalization laws" on the basis of his allegedly fraudulent statement that he had never belonged to the Communist Party in the United States. He was also charged with "willfully and knowingly making a false statement under oath."[260] Following a jury trial in November 1949, he was convicted and sentenced to prison. His citizenship was revoked. *Time* magazine reported in 1950, "Unless higher courts come to his rescue, Bridges, already under sentence of five years for perjury, will presumably be deported to his native Australia, which doesn't want him either."[261] In July 1950, while his case was on appeal, Bridges's bail was revoked, allegedly because he had called for a cease-fire in Korea.[262] But the Supreme Court ultimately did "come to his rescue," in 1953, finding that his prosecution was barred by the statute of limitations.[263] The Court also reversed his denaturalization.[264] The government still did not give up, however, pursuing civil denaturalization proceedings until finally losing in 1955.[265]

In the end, Bridges achieved iconic and symbolic status. He died peacefully at home in 1990. There is at least one institute in his name and an academic chair and center at the University of Washington. The city of San Francisco even declared a Harry Bridges Day in July 2001.[266]

As Bridges put it, upon his retirement: "I got to play a small part in some of the great events of this century. I got the testimonials, I got to meet all kinds of famous people. I was also the one that got attacked, red-baited, called every name under the sun . . . The praise I got really belonged to the members of this union, and the attacks on me were all directed at them."[267]

"A Bucketful of Terror and Travesty": Cold War Ideological Deportation

[A]s world convulsions have driven us toward a closed society the expulsion power has been exercised with increasing severity.

—*Harisiades v. Shaughnessy*, 342 U.S 580, 598 (1952)

In late 1948, Carol Weiss King described the incredible deportation saga of her client, Gerhart Eisler, in a letter to her cousin. King wrote, "Only Lewis Carroll or James Thurber could really tell this incredible tale in appropriate fashion. The one is dead. I wish the other would try." King's cousin apparently forwarded the letter to Thurber, who wrote, "It is just one item in a bucketful of terror and travesty, and somebody should do a comprehensive story or book on the whole subject."[268]

Thurber's "bucketful of terror and travesty" poured into the wake of World War II much as the Palmer Raids had followed World War I. The third wave of ideological deportation lacked a single charismatic champion from the executive branch—a Pickering or a Palmer. This was probably due mostly to the fact that the Roosevelt and Truman administrations tended toward liberal immigration policies. Those liberal policies, however, generally focused much more on the elimination of racial quotas and facilitating family immigration and refugee admissions than on softening deportation laws.

In June of 1946, Attorney General Tom Clark addressed the Chicago Bar Association.[269] He claimed that the United States faced a plot by Communists, "outside ideologists," and "small groups of radicals" who sought to divide the country. Clark suggested that no one was "more subject to censure than the revolutionary who enters our ranks, takes the solemn oath of our calling, and then uses every device in the legal category to further the interests of those who would destroy our government by force, if necessary."[270] Clark soon turned his attention to deportation. In September 1947, speaking to the National Conference of United States Attorneys, he said, "If any alien in your district engaged in

Communist activity, there is no place for him in the United States."[271] In the year that followed, more than seventy people were arrested for post-entry social control political deportations. This was not, of course, a large number, but many of the targets were high-profile figures. The deportation system quickly became an essential weapon in the new Cold War. The exclusion system also was used to ban an increasing number of alleged subversives, a practice that continued well into the 1980s, barring such well-known figures as Charles Chaplin and Gabriel García Márquez.[272]

These were dangerous, politically charged times for some citizens as well as noncitizens. But an especially harsh Cold War deportation regime emerged, supplemented by criminal prosecutions and denaturalization.[273] In July 1948, prosecutions for alleged violations of the Alien Registration Act were commenced against a dozen national leaders of the Communist Party. On December 7, 1948—the anniversary of the attack on Pearl Harbor—the Department of Justice announced that it planned to arrest some 500 noncitizens on political grounds, to delay and investigate some 500 other applications for citizenship, and to revoke the citizenship of 228 naturalized citizens. In early 1950, the Immigration Service reported active investigations into some 1,000 naturalizations, owing to current or past membership in the Communist Party.[274]

Labor and political leaders were, as before, among the most important targets. John Williamson, a leader of the U.S. Communist Party, was deported, as was Ferdinand C. Smith, a West Indian-born labor leader who at the time was fifty-four years old, had lived in the United States for thirty years, and had a wife and daughter who were U.S. citizens. Smith's request for bail was denied, and he was sent along with other political deportees to Ellis Island, which had been transformed from a welcoming entry point to a deportation detention center.[275] A similar fate awaited Charles A. Doyle, international vice president of the United Chemical Workers Union-CIO. Doyle was forty-four, had entered the United States legally in 1924, was married, and was the father of four American-born children.

Many artists and writers were targeted for deportation as well. Hanns Eisler, a world-famous musician and composer, had fled the Nazis and settled in Hollywood, where he lived a productive, nonpolitical life until he declined to testify against his brother, Gerhart, before the House Un-

American Activities Committee. Eisler was first blacklisted and then placed in deportation proceedings. Notwithstanding protests from Pablo Picasso, Henri Matisse, Jean Cocteau, and many others, Eisler ultimately was forced to leave the United States. Gerhart was also arrested for deportation in 1948.

These four deportees—Eisler, Williamson, Smith, and Doyle—were isolated from the general population and held in solitary cells. They were allowed only thirty minutes of outside exercise per day. After their attorneys protested, the four were placed in one large cell together and allowed one hour of exercise on the roof. From this perch, they reportedly could see only the back of the Statue of Liberty.[276]

The detainees vigorously pursued justice in the U.S. administrative and legal systems, though the days of James Landis were now a distant memory. The courts were ambivalent about whether they even had a right to bail.[277] In *Carlson v. Landon,* the Supreme Court upheld the detention of noncitizens without bail, pending deportation proceedings based on Communist Party membership.[278] The Court, noting the "civil" nature of deportation, per *Fong Yue Ting,* held that "[d]etention is necessarily a part of this deportation procedure." Although due process applied, the attorney general's discretion to deny bail could be overridden only when it was "clearly shown that such discretion was without a reasonable foundation."[279] The practical result was that the government could now generally detain whomever it wanted for however long deportation proceedings lasted.

This detention mandate was combined with important substantive changes to ideological deportation law. Under the 1940 act, to deport someone for membership in the Communist Party the government had been required to prove that the party actually advocated the violent overthrow of the government. The Internal Security Act of 1950 removed the requirement for such proof. Present or former membership in the Communist Party was now grounds for deportation. The government seized this opportunity quickly. In October 1950, the Justice Department announced plans to arrest some 3,400 noncitizens for deportation.[280] It was apparent to all that another powerful ideological deportation episode was emerging and that the legal system would again be called on to establish constitutional baselines. What happened, however, was another period of judicial capitulation, in some ways even more astonishing than that of the Chinese cases.

In the *Carlson* case, Justice Reed wrote, for a 5 to 4 majority, that the issue of the power to deport "presently undesirable aliens" required "no reexamination." Endorsing a probationary view of even long-term lawful permanent residents, the Court indicated that all such aliens "remain subject to the plenary power of Congress to expel them under the sovereign right to determine what non-citizens shall be permitted to remain within our borders."[281] The Court cited *Fong Yue Ting* and *Bugajewitz*. Legality of entry, length of residence, or family ties mattered little. The Court rather blithely recounted the history of one of the detainees in a footnote:

> Appellant was seventeen years of age when he arrived in this country from Poland in 1913. Since then he has lived continuously in the State of Michigan. He has been a waiter in an English speaking restaurant in Hamtramck, Mich., for seventeen years and for a great part of that time he was head waiter. He owns his own home in Detroit and has a family consisting of his wife, two sons, a daughter, and five grandchildren. Both sons served in the armed services of the United States in World War II. His children and grandchildren were born in this country and his daughter married here. During World War II while appellant was head waiter in the restaurant he sold about $50,000.00 worth of U.S. War Bonds and during that period he donated blood on seven occasions to the Red Cross for the United States Army . . . The record fails to disclose that he has violated any law or that he is engaged or is likely to engage in, any subversive activities.[282]

Much of the opinion concerned the Court's view of the "doctrines and practices" of Communism and the reasonableness of congressional concern about these aliens, an inquiry not unlike Justice Field's anti-Chinese musings in *Chae Chan Ping*. As to the questionable legitimacy of post-entry social control deportation of long-term legal residents, the Court was unmoved: "[T]he fact that [these aliens] . . . were made deportable after entry is immaterial . . . Otherwise, when an alien once legally became a denizen of this country he could not be deported for any reason of which he had not been forewarned at the time of entry."[283]

Harisiades v. Shaughnessy, another signature deportation case of this era, embodied similar values.[284] Peter Harisiades, born in Greece in 1901, came to the United States as a teenaged lawful permanent resident alien. In 1928, he worked as an organizer for the Communist Party in the Massachusetts textile mills. Following the *Kessler v. Strecker* decision, Harisiades was dropped from the party in 1939. In December 1944, he was raising two American-born children and working as the editor of a newspaper in New York City. He decided to apply for naturalization.[285] This was a serious mistake. Two years later he received an innocuous letter from the Immigration Service to come in for an interview. He was arrested immediately, on the basis of a warrant that had apparently been issued nearly two decades earlier, in 1930. The government's case was based on Harisiades's former membership in the Communist Party.

As Ann Fagan Ginger has recounted, Peter Harisiades himself had poignantly framed the underlying issues of justice and fairness in late 1947: "I came to this country from Greece as a young boy 31 years ago . . . I worked with my hands in railroads, in shops and factories. I joined unions and I helped to organize unions. I participated in strike struggles. I faced and I actually felt the club and the brutality of the police in different industrial towns and I was thrown into jails. I helped to organize unemployed workers and participated in hunger marches for relief and for unemployment insurance. This is the way my ideas were formed, that I began to understand America and to become an American . . . What is my 'crime'?"[286]

The ultimate resolution of his case was a tragic exemplar of Cold War reasoning for Harisiades. Special Inquiry Officer Zimmerman found Harisiades to be deportable and his finding was sustained by a special three-member board constituted to hear the appeal. Harisiades' case, consolidated with a few others, eventually came before the U.S. Supreme Court. The Court, in an opinion by Justice Jackson, expressly rejected what it termed a "vested right" argument that "the alien is entitled to constitutional protection . . . to the same extent as the citizen."[287] This much was to be expected, as the alternative would have been an extraordinary break with the past. The Court, however, also denied that long-term permanent residents had a due process right to a judicial determination of whether a deportation law is even minimally reasonable. As in *Carlson*, however, the opinion contained much purely political discussion of the reasonableness of the law at issue.[288]

It is interesting to note that Justice Jackson later called deportation "an almost useless security mechanism." He also said, "If people have committed acts for which they should be punished, we should make it our business to punish them . . . [D]eportation for conduct occurring in the country after the alien is lawfully admitted is a very dubious policy."[289] However, his *Harisiades* opinion stated that the "privilege" to remain in the United States "is a matter of permission and tolerance," rather than one of right. The power to deport—apparently for any reason and even retroactively—was not limited: "Congressional apprehension of foreign or internal dangers short of war may lead to its use."[290] Peter Harisiades left the United States in November 1952 for Poland, where he was granted asylum because of his fear of being put to death in his native Greece, which was controlled at the time by right-wing generals.[291]

The *Harisiades* opinion had relied on late-nineteenth-century precedent, disregarded the difference between the two types of deportation laws, depreciated the "permanence" of permanent residence, invoked the right-privilege distinction, relegated rights claims raised by noncitizens to essentially political questions, and dabbled in ideological argument. In effect, it gave the government virtually unlimited power to deport whomever it wanted. Herbert Brownell told the nation that 22,000 Reds would be deported and that such "snakes" must be driven out.[292] By July 1953, nearly 300 political deportations were in process. The INS also announced that it planned to denaturalize more than 1,500 citizens under the new McCarran-Walter Act.

The harshness of some of these deportations did not go unrecognized. A National Lawyers Guild study of 219 political deportation cases reported that about half of the deportees had children who were U.S. citizens, about one quarter were married to U.S. citizens, and that 80 percent were over forty-six years old.[293] But the legal system seemed incapable of doing more than occasionally bemoaning these facts. In the 1954 case of *Galvan v. Press,* for example, Justice Frankfurter poignantly recalled from earlier cases that deportation may "deprive a man of all that makes life worth living" and may be "at times the equivalent of banishment or exile."[294] Because "the intrinsic consequences of deportation are so close to punishment for crime," Justice Frankfurter recognized that "it might fairly be said also that the Ex Post Facto Clause, even though applicable only to punitive legislation, should be applied to deportation."[295] But then the Court retreated to one of the least reflective constitutional denouements in the history of American jurisprudence: "But the slate is not clean . . . [T]hat the formulation of these policies is entrusted exclusively to Congress has become about as firmly imbedded in the legislative and judicial tissues of our body politic as any aspect of our government."[296] Justice Black, in dissent, offered a different view: "Petitioner has lived in this country thirty-six years, having come here . . . when only seven years of age . . . For joining a lawful political group years ago—an act which he had no possible reason to believe would subject him to the slightest penalty—petitioner now loses his job, his friends, his home, and maybe even his children, who must choose between their father and their native country."[297]

Nancy Morawetz has noted that it may have been too much to expect the Court that overturned *Plessy v. Ferguson* to tackle, in the same year, "a second line of ingrained precedent," although "the task before the Court in the two cases was remarkably similar."[298] Nevertheless, in the half century since *Carlson, Harisiades,* and *Galvan,* these Cold War cases, together with the earlier precedents, have withstood virtually every challenge. The maximum oversight the Court has been able to muster has been the "clear statement" interpretive method, a complex and deferential substitute for substantive constitutional line drawing.

The Japanese Internment: Aberration or Culmination?

[A] grave injustice was done to both citizens and permanent residents of Japanese ancestry by the evacuation, relocation, and internment of civilians during World War II . . . [which] were motivated largely by racial prejudice, wartime hysteria, and a failure of political leadership.

—Civil Liberties Act of 1988 (enacted August 10, 1988)

The forced relocation and internment of some 120,000 people of Japanese ancestry was, without doubt, "one of the most sweeping and complete deprivations of constitutional rights in the history of this nation."[299] More than 70,000 U.S. citizens and 40,000 noncitizens (mostly lawful permanent residents) were compelled to abandon their homes, farms, and businesses, to store or sell their possessions, and to be marked with numbers like convicts or livestock.[300] Then, under armed guard, they were removed to "assembly centers" and shipped on trains to camps, euphemistically called "relocation centers," far from the coast, where they would be held as prisoners for years. There can be no question that this shameful episode was deeply linked to the history of deportation. It exemplifies how the deportation system is better understood when it is functionally decoupled from the formal citizenship-alienage line and viewed as a system of extraordinary majoritarian power operating outside of well-accepted legal norms. Also, the techniques of deportation—its administrative mechanisms and its legal justifications—provide models for government actions against citizens. As David Cole has written, "the close interrelationship between anti-Asian racism and anti-immigrant sentiment made the transition from 'enemy alien' to 'enemy race' a disturbingly smooth one."[301]

Consider how internment and relocation applied first to "aliens" and then to citizens. In 1940, according to the census, some 127,000 people of Japanese ancestry lived in the United States.[302] With only a very limited exception for World War I veterans, none of them could naturalize because of the racial restrictions of the 1790 Naturalization Act, though those born in the United States were citizens.[303] In the run-up to the Pearl Harbor attack, there were thus many Japanese noncitizens living on U.S. soil who undoubtedly would have become citizens had they been permitted by law to do so.[304]

When the United States entered World War II, the 1798 Enemy Aliens Act—still on the books—provided the executive branch with broad authority to summarily apprehend, restrain, secure, or remove all "[non-U.S. citizen] natives, citizens, denizens, or subjects of a hostile government."[305] On December 7–8, 1941, President Roosevelt issued three proclamations that rendered Japanese, German, and Italian aliens subject to immediate arrest and detention.[306] According to J. Edgar Hoover, of 1,771 "enemy aliens" arrested within the first twenty-four hours, 1,212 were Japanese. By December 15, some 1,430 Japanese and 1,150 Germans were in custody.[307]

Those arrested as enemy aliens had hearings before "Alien Enemy Hearing Boards." A hearing was given to each, "not as a matter of right, but in order to permit him an opportunity to present facts in his own behalf." The "aliens" were permitted to have "a relative or other adviser" attend the hearing, but such advisers were not allowed to "act in the capacity of an attorney."[308] As Edward J. Ennis, head of the Alien Enemy Control Unit, described it, "every effort has been made to get away from costly time consuming judicial procedures."[309] Indeed, the model was the exact opposite of the ethos of the criminal justice system in which the accused is presumed innocent and the government must prove its case beyond a reasonable doubt: "every doubt . . . must be resolved

against [the accused] and in favor of the government."[310] Those found
to be enemy aliens were delivered to the custody of the INS to be "in-
terned." As of October 1943, some 14,807 persons (including 5,303 Japanese and 5,977 Germans) had been arrested as enemy aliens by the FBI
with, as J. Edgar Hoover put it, "the excellent cooperation of local law
enforcement officers." Of this total, 2,909 were "promptly released" before hearings, "when they were able to produce concrete evidence of
their loyalty . . . and to satisfactorily explain their actions." A further
1,374 were released after hearings, and 4,265 were placed on parole.
Forty died after apprehension, and 44 were "repatriated."[311] The program continued to grow throughout the war years. By 1945, the total of
enemy aliens under INS jurisdiction was some 24,886, with 5,264 Japanese noncitizen men, women, and children in INS custody.[312]

Although the enemy alien detentions were limited to aliens, citizenship status did not completely protect all suspects. Hoover expressed
concern about "the naturalized citizen whose cloak of citizenship is a
sham and who is dangerous to the nation's security."[313] By mid-1943,
over 2,000 denaturalization investigations had been commenced, resulting in 75 denaturalizations in fiscal year 1943 and more thereafter. If
citizenship had been fraudulently or illegally procured, then the government could immediately intern the person as an enemy alien.

The program against enemy aliens and, in particular, the apparent
numbers of false arrests and parolees are quite interesting in light of
what was to follow. Even a system of FBI arrests that undoubtedly erred
on the side of arresting anyone remotely thought to be suspicious and
summary hearing boards released a rather large percentage of those arrested. These safeguards, minimal though they were, were not available
to the Japanese—citizens and noncitizens—who later faced "relocation." Everyone was incarcerated.

On February 19, 1942, President Roosevelt issued Executive Order
9066, which authorized the U.S. Army to take complete control of all
persons of Japanese ancestry in California and parts of Oregon, Washington, and Arizona. "Civilian Exclusion Orders" issued by General De-
Witt, pursuant to the president's order, were aimed at "all persons of Japanese ancestry, both alien and non-alien."[314] This peculiarly inverted
phrasing has caught the eye of many observers as a clear indicator of how
" 'foreignness' was imposed on U.S.-born citizens of Asian descent."[315]

Whether one refers to the remote centers with the historically charged term "concentration camps" or names them "relocation centers" and whether one calls the affected people "evacuees," "internees," or "impounded people" matters little at this juncture.[316] The most important point is what Carey McWilliams noted in the 1940s: "A precedent of the gravest possible significance has been established in ordering the removal and internment of this one racial minority." In 1945, Eugene Rostow argued that what he termed the Japanese "exclusion" program was sustained by propositions of the "utmost potential menace": that protective custody is permissible, political opinions may justify imprisonment, ethnic groups—whether citizens or not—may be presumed to possess ideas that justify imprisonment, that the military may decide what political opinions require imprisonment and which ethnic groups are infected with these opinions, and that such decisions can be taken outside the safeguards of the Bill of Rights.[317] The similarity between such concerns and those raised by various aspects of the current "war on terror," especially the use of the deportation system, is obvious.[318]

A 1982 government report concluded, "The broad historical causes which shaped these decisions were race prejudice, war hysteria, and a failure of political leadership."[319] "Race prejudice" connects the internment to the half-century of exclusion and deportation that preceded it.[320] The internment was facilitated and inspired by well-entrenched patterns of discrimination that rendered Asian Americans perpetually "foreign" and therefore more susceptible to such government action than, say, Italian or German citizens were.[321] This was certainly the attitude of the military leader of the evacuation and internment. General DeWitt once wrote, "the Japanese race is an *enemy race* and while many second and third generation Japanese born on United States soil, possessed of United States citizenship, have become 'Americanized,' the racial strains are undiluted."[322] General DeWitt also reportedly testified in 1943 that "[a] Jap's a Jap. It makes no difference whether he is an American citizen . . . You can't change him by giving him a piece of paper."[323]

The full racial history runs much deeper. The internment was more than an unfortunate by-product of "racial prejudice and wartime hysteria." It was also an example of how the norms that were allowed to take hold in exclusion and removal cases, stretching back to *Chae Chan Ping* and *Fong Yue Ting,* confirmed Jefferson's fear that if practices are allowed to take root against "the friendless alien," then, eventually, "the citizen will soon follow." Carey McWilliams noted that "[f]or nearly fifty years prior to December 7, 1941, a state of undeclared war existed between California and Japan."[324] Japanese immigrants began coming to the United States in the late nineteenth century. As their numbers rose, the Japanese began to face the same kind of reaction from whites that had led to laws of exclusion and deportation against Chinese laborers. The first anti-Japanese mass meeting was organized in San Francisco in 1900.[325] A resolution urged the immediate extension of the Chinese Exclusion Act to the Japanese. Edward A. Ross, professor of sociology at Stanford University, was quoted as saying that "should the worst come to the worst it would be better for us to turn our guns on every vessel bringing Japanese to our shores rather than to permit them to land."[326] Over time, a rather rabid anti-Japanese campaign developed in California, led by various politicians and newspapers. The patterns of this movement—its opportunistic, racist fearmongering, its habits of thought, and its episodic movement east to inspire national laws—were all clearly redolent of the anti-Chinese campaigns of the late nineteenth century. Indeed, some of the same people were involved. In 1892, Dennis Kearney had attempted to regain past glory with a new slogan: "The Japs Must Go!"[327] Also, Japan was a much more powerful country than China. Thus, in addition to labor concerns and xenophobia, anxiety about Japanese power and aggressive intentions began to spread throughout the country. Senator Selvage referred to Japan as "a serious menace not only to California, but to the nation."[328]

Such fears escalated with the Japanese victory in the Russo-Japanese War. In March 1905, the California Senate and Assembly unanimously passed a resolution urging the Congress to exclude the Japanese as it had the Chinese.[329] The Japanese and Korean Exclusion League reported more than 78,000 members a year after its formation in 1905. In 1906, the San Francisco School Board, responding to pressure from this group and others like it, agreed to segregate all Chinese, Korean, and Japanese children in the public schools, sparking international concern and federal intervention. Still, many on the West Coast sought Japanese immigrants as fruit growers and for other types of labor, and anti-Japanese sentiment ebbed and flowed through the first decade of the twentieth century.[330] In part because of the strength of Japan and efforts by the Japanese government to regulate immigration, U.S. attempts to recreate the Chinese Exclusion Laws failed. In 1907, a "Gentlemen's

Agreement" negotiated by President Roosevelt with the Japanese government promised to curtail the movement of Japanese nationals from Hawaii to the U.S. mainland and to restrict further entry of laborers. The agreement, however, allowed further immigration of wives and children and the Japanese population in the United States continued to grow. Thus, it did not succeed in quieting anti-Japanese agitation in California. Indeed, it may have exacerbated it.[331]

As war fears and "yellow peril" anxiety increased in California, the first official legal response was the 1913 Alien Land Act.[332] Couched in ostensibly race-neutral language, but grounded in immigration and citizenship laws (it was aimed at "aliens ineligible to citizenship"), the law precluded the Japanese from purchasing land.[333] Its sponsors made quite clear that their ultimate goal was to drive the Japanese from the state entirely. Carey McWilliams has suggested that it was intended as " 'an irritant'—a warning to the Japanese, a step in the campaign for exclusion."[334] It clearly recalled the welter of state and local legal mechanisms used earlier against the Chinese.

During World War I, anti-Japanese sentiment subsided somewhat in California, as Japan joined the United States as an ally. A notable exception, however, was the Hearst press, which maintained a hysterical anti-Japanese campaign replete with fraudulent allegations of secret invasion plans, racist songs, and movies, and other propaganda that, though well described by one contemporary observer as "so ridiculous that only children and morons could take them seriously," kept the low-burning flame of anti-Japanese attitudes alive.[335] Following the war, as national attention turned to Mitchell Palmer's aggressive raids against alien radicals, California politicians aimed again at the Japanese. A 1920 revision of the Alien Land Act passed as a ballot initiative by a 3–1 margin.[336] Other western states passed similar laws, to be ultimately upheld by the Supreme Court with the observation that "the State properly may assume that the considerations upon which Congress made [Asians ineligible to naturalize] are substantial and reasonable."[337]

A 1921 meeting of senators and representatives from thirteen western states illustrated the developing mood. The west faced "invasion by an alien people . . . unassimilable by marriage . . . who are a race unto themselves." Because "economically we are not able to compete with them . . . [and] racially we cannot assimilate with them . . . we must exclude them from our shores . . . and prohibit them from owning land."[338] Albert

Johnson of Washington emerged as the leading proponent of the racist immigration quota laws of 1921 and 1924. The latter contained, in effect, a Japanese exclusion law in that it barred "aliens ineligible to citizenship" from immigrating. It thus prevented even the 100 Japanese who would have been permitted under the restrictive quota system, had the quota applied, from immigrating to the United States. When President Coolidge signed the 1924 law, he specifically noted his disapproval of the exclusion provision, which was a clear insult to Japan. The American ambassador to Japan resigned a few days later, stating that "the immigration bill has struck a blow to their national pride."[339] But others were thrilled. Former California State Senator James D. Phelan, a leader of anti-Japanese agitation said at the time, "I am repaid for my efforts. The Japs are routed."[340]

There remained, however, a large and growing population of Japanese native-born U.S. citizens. Demographic and political differences began to emerge between the first generation, the rather Japan-focused *Issei,* and their children, the increasingly Americanized native-born *Nisei.* By 1940, some 63 percent of Japanese-descended people in the United States were native-born citizens, and their average age was in the twenties.[341]

In the chaotic aftermath of the attacks on Pearl Harbor, anti-Japanese public opinion hardened immediately, especially on the West Coast. Elsewhere, extremists such as John Rankin of Mississippi called for the deportation of "every Jap who claims, or has claimed Japanese citizenship, or sympathizes with Japan in this war."[342] The actions taken by the FBI and INS against Japanese "enemy aliens" migrated quickly to U.S. citizens. On December 30, 1941, Attorney General Biddle authorized the application for search warrants for any house in which an "enemy alien" lived if there was "reasonable cause" to believe that contraband was present. These searches naturally implicated many U.S. citizens of Japanese ancestry. They also fed a growing public perception that where there was smoke there must be fire. The military soon began to pressure civilian authorities, many of whom—New Deal liberals—were uncomfortable with such developments. A distinctive feature of the military approach became its lack of differentiation between Japanese citizens and "aliens." As General DeWitt put it, "We are at war and this area . . . has been designated as a theatre of operations . . . I have no confidence in [the] loyalty of the native born Japanese."[343] He reported "a tremendous volume of public opinion now developing against the Japanese of all classes, that's aliens and non-aliens [sic], to get them off the land." Following the release of a report by Supreme Court Justice Owen J. Roberts that included inaccurate allegations of Japanese spies, the majority of West Coast residents, wrote General DeWitt, "feel that they are living in the midst of a lot of enemies."[344] Many of the West Coast Japanese certainly felt the same way. Military leaders planned the removal and internment of all Japanese from large areas of the West Coast. The sense of panic in the region was illustrated in a column written by Walter Lippmann: "the Pacific Coast is in imminent danger of a combined attack from within and without . . . There is an assumption [in Washington] that a citizen may not be interfered with unless he has committed an overt act . . . [but] nobody ought to be on a battlefield who has no good reason for being there. There is plenty of room elsewhere for him to exercise his rights."[345]

The Lippmann piece seems to have influenced many in the government. Francis Biddle acquiesced soon thereafter. He suggested that "the result might be accomplished by evacuating all persons in the area and then licensing back those whom the military authorities thought were not objectionable."[346] Biddle thus apparently envisioned a discretionary system, insulated from judicial scrutiny, as an end run around implicit equal protection problems. But such niceties were not required. On February 13, 1942, the Pacific Coast congressional delegation sent the president a recommendation for "the immediate evacuation of all persons of Japanese lineage and all others, aliens and citizens alike, whose presence shall be deemed dangerous or inimical to the defense of the United States from all strategic areas."[347] Six days later, President Roosevelt issued Executive Order 9066.

Many have noted the remarkable acquiescence of the legal system in the internment.[348] One is struck by a judicial passivity that is highly reminiscent of the majority opinions in *Chae Chan Ping* and *Fong Yue Ting*. Some, including former Chief Justice Rehnquist, have argued that the main legal problem of the internment was that it applied racial stereotypes to U.S. citizens.[349] Implicit in this view is an acceptance of racial stereotyping and detention of noncitizens. But history teaches that such formal lines may fall rather easily in hard times.

Mexican Removals, 1930–1965

We died in your hills, we died in your deserts,
We died in your valleys and died on your plains.
We died 'neath your trees and we died in your bushes,
Both sides of the river, we died just the same.

—Woody Guthrie, "Deportees" (1961)

[T]he Mexican . . . is less desirable as a citizen than as a laborer.

—"Report of the Dillingham Commission" 61st Cong.,
3rd sess., S. Doc. No. 758 (1911)

Mexican Removals during the Depression

The mass deportation of a particular ethnic or racial group would seem to be among the most "un-American" phenomena imaginable.[350] It plainly contradicts pillars of our constitutional legal structure of which we are rightly proud. In his dissent in *Fong Yue Ting*, Justice Stephen Field described the outrage caused by the banishment by Russia of thousands of Jews, with the apparent intention of "the expulsion of the whole race." Field characterized that government action as "an act of barbarity which has aroused the indignation of all Christendom." He argued that "even if that power were exercised by every government of Europe," the United States, as a government of limited and delegated powers, simply could not do such things in the name of sovereignty.[351]

The modern Supreme Court would not likely uphold such government action. Some national-origin discrimination may be permissible, indeed inherent, in immigration law.[352] But one would certainly hope that the U.S. government, in peacetime, could not legally target large numbers of people for deportation on the basis of their race, nationality, or ethnicity. And yet, in effect, it has happened twice in living memory to Mexicans.

As we have seen, the modern archetype of Mexican border crossers as "illegal aliens" tends to ignore the fact that large-scale migration of Mexicans into the United States has occurred continuously for more than a century.[353] The great majority of such Mexican entrants, motivated by vast wealth disparities, recruited by U.S. businesses, and sometimes encouraged by their own government, have long come to the United States seeking an escape from generations of grinding poverty. They have faced a historically ambivalent U.S. attitude: a recurrent pattern of recruitment, restriction, and expulsion.[354] The formal model of sovereign border control is peculiarly ill-suited to the realities of Mexican immigrants. Indeed, much of the workings of the deportation system as it relates to Mexicans recalls the maxim that "if the only tool you have is a hammer, everything tends to look like a nail."

By the late 1920s, a small number of farms dominated agriculture in the Southwest, through "a dismal story of labor-baiting, private strike-breaking armies and arsenals, collusion with local officials in exploiting labor, and violations of workers' civil liberties."[355] The use of transient Mexican labor was a crucial element of the "dismal story." During the Great Depression, however, the dominant fact in California was the arrival of millions of "Okies" and other "dust bowl refugees."[356] Of this mass migration John Steinbeck poignantly wrote: "And then the dispossessed were drawn west . . . Carloads, caravans, homeless and hungry; twenty thousand and fifty thousand and a hundred thousand and two hundred thousand . . . The kids are hungry. We got no place to live."[357]

What is less well-known is how this vast, tragic movement of (mostly) white people led to the systematic deportation of Mexican workers.[358] More than 1 million people of Mexican ancestry were forcibly removed from the United States during the Depression years. The harsh and, in many cases, illegal nature of these deportations prompted a California legislative commission to later call them "unconstitutional, tyrannic, and oppressive."[359]

Though aimed at local economic and social conditions, the ostensible legal basis for deportation in most cases was extended border control: lack of proof of legal residency. Ironically, for long-term residents, such proof was difficult to obtain. Recall that no visa had been necessary for Mexican immigration until well into the twentieth century. This, then, was essentially a form of selective prosecution: the Mexican deportees were in fact "illegal," but that is clearly not why they were targeted for deportation as a group.

William Doak, secretary of labor from 1930 to 1933, believed that deportation enforcement was a good way to create jobs for unemployed Americans during the Depression. He asserted that there were some 400,000 "illegal aliens" in the United States, of whom 100,000 could be immediately deported under existing law. He sought, as one commentator noted, to turn deportation into a "gladiatorial spectacle."[360] As the commissioner general of immigration put it in his 1931 annual report, "It is the purpose of the Department of Labor . . . to [support] the wage earner of the United States." It was thus a "mere corollary of this duty" to spare "no reasonable effort to remove the menace of unfair competition." The key was to focus on "the vast number of aliens who have in one way or another, principally by surreptitious entries, violated our immigration laws."[361] What this primarily meant, in practice, was the removal of tens of thousands of Mexicans.

The surge in deportations was impressive.[362] The total number of aliens removed from the United States increased from 2,762 in 1920 to 38,795 in 1930.[363] To conduct full hearings in such a large number of cases would be prohibitively expensive, however. Thus, many tens of thousands of these removals, especially those of Mexicans, were done "voluntarily." The advantages of voluntary departure were considerable for both the government and the deportee: no arrest warrant would issue, no records of a formal hearing were generated, and the individual did not face a legal bar to future reentry. Such pragmatic flexibility was available even for Mexican nationals accused of criminal conduct in the United States. Many were offered deals in criminal courts in which they accepted deportation in return for charges being dropped—or at least deferred—if they remained outside of the United States. Convicted criminals were also sometimes offered reprieves if they accepted deportation. For example, in 1932, ninety prisoners at the McNeil Federal Penitentiary in Washington were sent to Mexico.[364]

Formal deportation proceedings were thus rather rare for Mexicans, then as now. But the few that were reported illustrate the complicated interweaving of deportation, voluntary departure, criminal law enforcement, and administrative discretion that marked many Mexican deportations during this era. A 1941 Board of Immigration Appeals case involved a citizen of Mexico, "Mr. "T—," aged forty-nine, who was a widower and a farm laborer. He had first entered the United States around 1895 at the age of two years. He had lived in the United States continuously for all of his adult life, until 1934, when he returned to Mexico "as a repatriate."[365] However, as one could have predicted, he soon reentered the United States, in September 1936. Since that date, he had been deported three times, the last of which occurred in 1940. Again, he had reentered, near Tres Jacales, Texas, "to seek work and to see his children." We should not let the laconic recitation of these facts

dilute their poignancy. Indeed, the opinion recounts that he had no relatives in Mexico and that he had six American-born children, ages
eleven to twenty-six (all of whom presumably were U.S. citizens) and
that "he supports some of them when he is working."[366] Nevertheless,
after having been rendered a deported alien in the 1934 wave, apparently because he had "no assets and was on relief in 1933 and 1934," he
repeatedly risked his life and freedom to return to the United States. But
what was his case? How did the law of deportation understand him? Primarily, it understood him as a law breaker: he had already been sentenced twice for periods of thirty days "for reentry in violation of the Act
of March 4, 1929." A third prosecution was pending.[367]

The case ultimately benefited from the generous, humane discretion
exhibited by one of Frances Perkins's most enlightened agents, Jack
Wasserman (later to represent Carlos Marcello). Wasserman offered an
important, eloquent, and precedential interpretation of the term "good
moral character," a prerequisite for discretionary relief from deportation: "Good moral character does not mean moral excellence. A good
moral character is one that measures up as good among the people of
the community in which the party lives; that is, up to the standard of the
average citizen."[368]

Mr. T's case was remanded so that he might apply for relief—and possibly permanent legal residence—in the "discretion" of the hearing officer. This was obviously a good result for him. Given his powerful equities, he may well ultimately have been allowed to stay. But consider as
well how much was missed in the consideration of this case in this way.
How many thousands of others were deported without hearings, due to
the way the system worked near the border? How many cases never got
to Jack Wasserman? More fundamentally; why was this man subject to
deportation in the first place? Why was there was no place in our deportation law to examine the circumstances of his life and his first "repatriation"? As we have seen, discretionary "relief" mitigated the harshness
of some deportations. It allowed for a humane balancing of factors by an
experienced fact finder. It legitimated a modicum of mercy and forgiveness in an otherwise rigid system. But it also obscured fundamental
truths about the deportation system itself.

Carey McWilliams has well described the remarkable transformation
of attitudes that led to the removal of many Mexicans in the 1930s:
"When it became apparent last year that the programme for the relief of

the unemployed would assume huge proportions in the Mexican quarter, the community swung to a determination to oust the Mexicans . . . He was in default in his rent . . . a burden to the taxpayer. At this juncture, an ingenious social worker suggested the desirability of a wholesale deportation."[369]

One major problem for those seeking such deportations, however, was that many of the younger Mexicans in Southern California were American citizens: U.S.-born children of immigrants.[370] Further, for those who could be deported, the law required formal deportation hearings. From the perspective of many Californians, such a procedure was unduly cumbersome and expensive. As McWilliams noted, "it could not be used to advantage in ousting any large number." Thus, a more efficient plan was crafted: "Social workers reported that many of the Mexicans who were receiving charity had signified their 'willingness' to return to Mexico. Negotiations were at once opened with the . . . Southern Pacific Railroad. It was discovered that, in wholesale lots, the Mexicans could be shipped to Mexico City for $14.70 per capita . . . less than the cost of a week's board and lodging."[371]

The repatriation thus combined stepped-up federal enforcement with state and local practices designed to encourage—or to compel—Mexicans to leave the United States. William Doak launched what one historian has termed a national "scare" campaign. Doak encouraged local immigration officers, law enforcement agencies, and repatriation-sympathetic newspapers to join forces to publicize deportation raids, frightening many Mexicans into self-deportation.[372]

In early 1931, a first trainload of Mexicans was sent from California to Mexico. Dozens more were to follow. The *Los Angeles Times* estimated that some 11,000 were removed in this manner in 1932. By the end of 1933, the *Times* estimated that California had been relieved of more than 200,000 such "repatriados." Indeed, the Mexican population in the United States dropped some 40 percent between 1930 and 1940.[373]

Many of those who experienced the repatriation describe it in stark, terrifying terms. Emilia Castaneda was born in Los Angeles in 1926. She recalls that, as a nine-year-old child, she came home from school one day to hear her father tell the family that they had to leave for Mexico "right away." As Ms. Castenada reports, "the only thing my dad said was—pack a trunk with what little belongings we had and we were there at dawn . . . it was real dark in this train station."[374]

On February 26, 1931, U.S. immigration agents and Los Angeles Police surrounded some 400 men, women, and children in La Placita (the Alvera Street plaza near downtown Los Angeles). The police and immigration agents cornered off with trucks an area in which many people were sitting on benches or resting from shopping. A mass round-up followed, and hundreds of captured people were "shipped straight to Mexico with no word to their families."[375] There have been recent attempts through both litigation and public hearings to catalogue and to redress the almost incalculable costs of what could well be called an ethnic cleansing.[376] The predominant U.S. perspective at the time, however, was clearly encapsulated by a cynical prediction reported by Carey McWilliams: "the Mexican can be lured back, 'whenever we need him.' "[377] This instrumentalist vision turned out to be prescient, as Mexican laborers again began to cross the border in large numbers after the Depression.

From the Bracero Program to "Operation Wetback"

In 1942, the United States began an experiment with what would now be called a program for Mexican "guest workers."[378] The Bracero Program—*bracero* in Spanish means a day laborer or a farmhand—was formally initiated by a 1942 agreement between Mexico and the United States "for the Temporary Migration of Mexican Agricultural Workers to the United States."[379] Spurred by wartime labor needs, it continued, in various forms, until 1964 and facilitated the legal entry into the United States of some 4.5 million Mexican workers.[380] The program mandated minimum working conditions and wages for the workers. Its defining immigration law feature was the contractual requirement for the worker to return to Mexico at the immediate end of a specific period—generally one year.

The program had some benefits for all concerned.[381] But it also had the more subtle and pernicious effect of legitimizing a particularly instrumentalist view of Mexican immigrant workers. Moreover, it internalized the border control feature of immigration law into the very being of Mexican workers. In effect, any Mexican in the United States would now be presumed to be, at best, temporary and, at worst, illegal. Unlike any other discrete group in the United States, then, to be Mexican was to be presumed legally tenuous.

Some large employers supported the broad outlines of the program.[382] Others—long accustomed to relatively unregulated control of agricultural workers—saw the government oversight of the Bracero Program as a dangerous precedent and resisted it.[383] No Texas farmers requested braceros in 1942.[384] Many growers also continued to hire undocumented workers, who were less expensive and involved fewer regulations than did a bracero contract. The protective requirements of the Bracero Program were thus violated by many employers.[385] A broad coalition of groups came to oppose the program for rather different reasons. Opposition came from organized labor (including both the AFL and the CIO), human rights groups, religious organizations, and the National Association for the Advancement of Colored People.[386] The Mexican worker was caught between powerful contending forces. His desire to work was supported by those who viewed him only as a worker; those who tended to support his human rights were allied with a more ambivalent approach to his right to work in the United States.

The contradiction between the legal regime and social reality led to an ironic outcome: the Bracero Program, intended to regularize and legalize Mexican labor immigration, in the long run actually had the opposite effect. The first major problems began in late 1947 when the program was temporarily discontinued.[387] Before it was reinstated, there was again massive illegal immigration countered by various arrangements with employers and an ad hoc "legalization" program designed primarily to meet the needs of large agricultural employers. The U.S. Immigration Service implemented a creative scheme in which thousands of undocumented Mexican workers who had crossed the border illegally were arrested and then brought to border crossing posts where they were granted legal entry as temporary workers.[388] Thousands of workers were brought to the Texas Employment Commission, which dutifully delivered them to work for growers in Texas and elsewhere. This process, sometimes referred to as "drying out the wetbacks" or "storm and drag immigration," was a boon to the growers, who cooperated closely with government authorities in its use.[389] But it relegated the Mexican workers to an ever more murky status: less legal than former braceros, not quite "illegal," but completely subject to the combined power of the growers, the INS, and the Border Patrol. An estimated 142,000 Mexican workers were temporarily legalized in this way from 1947 to 1949.[390] This approach itself may well have inspired further illegal migration, as more workers continued to cross the border, with the added hope of subsequent legalization, in addition to the historical pull of possible work and generations of migration patterns.[391] Employers actively recruited workers and developed mechanisms, such as withholding "deposits" of their wages, to encourage them to return the next year.[392]

The crash of a plane, in January 1948, returning Mexican workers from Oakland to the El Centro Deportation Center inspired Woody Guthrie to write the poem that was later to become the song "Deportees."[393] The poignancy of the crash has struck many over the years. As one witness recounts, "It was a cold and damp day and even though the reports were that the site had been cleaned up, this was not the case. The sadness of seeing those meager possessions of the passengers and the total lack of respect by those who had the task of removing the bodies, will be something I will never forget or forgive."[394]

Guthrie originally simply chanted the song, but it was later set to music by Martin Hoffman.[395] As performed by Pete Seeger, it became one of the staple songs of the civil rights movement and inspired many people, including myself, to think of deportation as a civil (and human) rights matter. For it was during this period, as we have seen, that many of the worst elements of U.S. policy coalesced.

In the postwar period, the deportation system developed large-scale measures to confront the Mexican border problem. Between 1944 and 1954, which is sometimes still referred to in Texas as "the decade of the wetback," the number of "illegal aliens" coming from Mexico increased by some 6,000 percent.[396] In 1951, the Presidential Commission on Migratory Labor reported, "The . . . wetback traffic . . . is virtually an invasion. It is estimated that at least 400,000 of our migratory farm labor force of 1 million in 1949 were wetbacks."[397] For many in the Truman administration, the predominant concerns were the exploitation of the Mexican workers and the effect on domestic labor. In 1951, President Truman said that a "steady stream of illegal immigrants from Mexico, the so-called 'wetbacks,' . . . are coming into our country in phenomenal numbers—and at an increasing rate." He noted that "these unfortunate people . . . are subject to deportation if caught by our immigration authorities. They have to hide and yet must work to live. They are thus in no position to bargain with those who might choose to exploit them. And many of them are exploited, I regret to say, and are left in abject poverty."

Moreover, their presence had "a seriously depressing effect on wages and working conditions in farm areas throughout the southwest."[398]

Public attitudes toward the Mexicans hardened, however. Stringent "rule of law" discourse ascended—championed by the INS, which had much to gain institutionally. According to one INS official, the Mexican migration distinguished itself as the "greatest peacetime invasion ever complacently suffered by another country under open, flagrant, contemptuous violation of its laws."[399] The deportation system grew dramatically. The number of deportations and voluntary departures grew from 29,000 in 1944 to 565,000 in 1950.[400] By 1954, total apprehensions of illegal immigrants had increased to 1,089,583.[401] Moreover, the threat of deportation was as integral to the labor system as it was to the ideological Cold War and to the war on crime. As the 1951 Commission reported, "Once on the United States side of the border . . . numerous devices are employed to keep the wetback on the job . . . [T]he wetback is a person of legal disability who is under jeopardy of immediate deportation if caught. He is told that if he leaves the farm, he will be reported to the [INS, which] will surely find him if he ventures into town or out onto the roads."[402]

Criminal provisions relating to "harboring" of illegal aliens illustrate how law served the interests of employers. The Supreme Court had ruled that the Immigration Act of 1917 did not criminalize concealing or harboring undocumented noncitizens. It only applied to assisting border crossing.[403] A proposed bill sought to permit prosecution for anyone who would transport an "illegal alien" within the United States or "willfully induce an alien . . . to reside in the United States."[404] However, an exception—the "Texas Proviso"—provided that "the usual and normal practices incident to employment shall not be deemed to constitute harboring." This exemption was included in the bill, which became law in 1952.[405] Until the law was changed in 1986, U.S. employers were essentially given leave to hire whomever they wished, while being able to use the threat of deportation against noncitizen workers.

A 1951 law authorized the Labor Department to negotiate a new bracero agreement with Mexico to admit seasonal Mexican workers to work in "essential" areas of agriculture until December 31, 1953.[406] The law required that no Mexican workers would be supplied unless the Department of Labor certified that there were no domestic workers who were "able, willing, and qualified" to do the work. It mandated "reasonable" recruitment efforts and a further finding that the presence of Mexican workers would not "adversely affect the wages and working conditions of domestic agricultural workers similarly employed." Still, Gladwin Hill, writing in the *New York Times*, noted in 1953 that "illegal immigration from Mexico . . . has reached such overwhelming proportions that officers of the United States Immigration Service admit candidly . . . that there is nothing to stop the whole nation of Mexico moving into the United States, if it wants to."[407] Hill, later writing for the *Nation*, reported that illegal entries across the Mexican border were proceeding "at the rate of two or more a minute, day and night, seven days a week, but they are tacitly encouraged by Senator McCarran and many of his colleagues." A consensus emerged that something drastic needed to be done. As Hill noted, "[t]he reason the farmers want the wetbacks is that as fugitives from justice they have to work for whatever they can get."[408] The commission reported, as had Carey McWilliams a generation earlier, "When the work is done, neither the farmer nor the community wants the wetback around."[409]

In August 1953, Attorney General Herbert Brownell called for an increase in congressional appropriations for border patrols, for the United States to work closely with Mexico to develop a mutual solution to the problem of illegal immigration, for the Department of Justice to investigate ways to create tougher federal laws to curb illegal entry, and for individual state district attorneys to make similar changes in state laws.[410] The action that Brownell actually took, however, was much more extreme. On June 9, 1954, with President Eisenhower's approval, Brownell initiated Operation Wetback: aggressive, large-scale round-ups and deportations of Mexican laborers.[411] The military structure of the campaign fit the style of INS Commissioner Joseph Swing, nicknamed the "General."[412] The operation involved the Border Patrol, municipal, county, and state agents, and the military. The very name of Operation Wetback embodied its contradictions.[413] The term "operation" implies a short-term action with a specifically defined goal and a reasonable prospect of immediate success. But the problem at which this operation was aimed had deep and complex roots. The second part of the name— "wetback"—reveals its racial and ethnic complexity. An ostensibly race-neutral term, its use by government and by many whites transformed it into a racial epithet with stereotypical images of law-breaking Mexican border crossers, the archetypal "illegal alien."

Beginning in the lower Rio Grande valley, the operation moved quickly north. Sites of deportation were chosen in part by considering how workers could be most quickly moved to the Mexican interior, to discourage reentry. Some 4,800 noncitizens were arrested the first day. After that, the operation caught approximately 1,100 people per day. Initially, most deportations were by train, then by truck and buses. Eventually, however, ships, including one ironically called the *Emancipation,* took deportees to Veracruz. When seven deportees jumped ship and drowned, the use of ships was discontinued. Some deportees, caught in the midwestern states, were transported by air to Brownsville, Texas, and taken from there to Mexico. The INS reported apprehension at the time of some 1,100,000 Mexicans.[414] Indeed, the INS stated in 1955 that it had ended the "wetback problem."

The Bracero Program ended in December 1964. By then, however, "the symbiosis between Mexican migrants and employers in the Southwest was well-entrenched, the product of over fifty years of formal and informal policy-making."[415] The remarkably symmetrical relationship between labor recruitment and the deportation system is illustrated by the fact that, up to 1964, the number of braceros, nearly 5 million, was almost exactly the same as the number of deportees.

Conclusion

After his veto of the McCarran-Walter Act was overridden, President Truman appointed a commission to study the immigration policies of the United States. In its 1953 report, entitled "Whom We Shall Welcome," the commission wrote that the immigration laws "flout fundamental American traditions and ideals, [and] display a lack of faith in America's future."[416] The commission predicted that laws that "fail to reflect the American spirit must sooner or later disappear from the statute books." One is left to wonder whether the deportation system that had crystallized by then rendered the commission's prediction naive or revealed the complexity of "the American spirit" itself.

6

Discretion, Jurisdiction Stripping, and Retroactivity, 1965–2006

Crackdowns and Special Protections

The 1965 Immigration Act was a watershed moment in U.S. history.[1] A dramatic centerpiece of the civil rights initiatives of the Johnson administration, and an homage to John F. Kennedy, it finally ended the national origins quota system that had stamped immigration law since the 1920s.[2] It also created a seven-category "preference system" that strongly prioritized family unity and certain occupational skills for the issuance of immigrant visas. As he signed the bill, President Johnson referred to the fairness of the newer system as "self-evident." In the arena of deportation policy, however, the 1965 law had few liberalizing features. Indeed, one of its most enduring legacies has been the creation of a numerical quota of 120,000 per year on Western Hemisphere immigration.[3] This has led to huge backlogs in legal visa-processing times for Mexican and other Latin American immigrants, thereby increasing pressure to enter without inspection and leading to unprecedented expansion of extended border control deportation. As the House Judiciary Committee noted in 1976, the result of the new quota, "completely unforeseen and unintended," was "considerable hardship for intending immigrants from this hemisphere."[4]

Taken as a whole, U.S. immigration and deportation laws of the last four decades have had a rather schizophrenic cast. Some aspects are humane and generous by most comparative or historical measures. The 1965 act, for example, included a "seventh preference" category, designated for the admission of refugees. Limited in its early definitions to those fleeing Communism, the "general area of the Middle East," and "catastrophic natural calamity," and implemented largely through discretionary "parole power," the law was regularized with the passage of the 1980 Refugee Act.[5] Since then, tens of thousands of otherwise deportable noncitizens have been granted political asylum.[6] Millions of "illegal" noncitizens were also granted "legalization" in 1986, and a welter of specific laws have been passed to protect battered spouses and children, victims of crime and human trafficking, and those who would face torture if deported. In addition, special laws have been passed for various national groups, including Cubans, certain Chinese opponents of family planning, some Central Americans, and Haitians.[7]

But the general countertrend in deportation has been laws that are harsher, less forgiving, and more insulated from judicial review. In effect, what has emerged is an exceptionally rigid legal regime, mediated by legislative special case exemptions—some ad hoc, some more durable—riven with discretionary executive authority, and increasingly immune from meaningful oversight.

Laws passed in the 1980s illustrate the tensions of modern deportation law. The decade began with the passage of the generous Refugee Act. But colder enforcement currents also emerged. In 1978, Congress had established a Select Commission on Immigration and Refugee Policy. Its final report recommended, among other things, sanctions against employers who knowingly and willfully employ undocumented aliens and a legalization program for certain undocumented noncitizens.[8] Eventually, these proposals rose to the top of the legislative agenda. The Immigration Reform and Control Act of 1986 (IRCA) achieved wide bipartisan support.[9] IRCA was envisioned by its sponsors, and widely heralded, as a "carrot and stick" law that would end most of the problems of illegal immigration in the United States.[10] It would finally enable the United States, said President Reagan, "to regain control of our borders."[11]

On the "stick" side, IRCA imposed sanctions on employers who knowingly hired, or continued to employ, noncitizens who did not have federal authorization to work. Employers and employees were required to complete forms, the employee attesting, under penalty of perjury, that he or she was authorized to work in the United States. Employers had to attest that they saw documentation and that they believed that the applicant was authorized to work. The "carrot" was legalization for those who had resided in the United States continuously, in unlawful status, since January 1, 1982. Also, a "Special Agricultural Worker" program legalized certain farm workers. Though many were deeply concerned at the time about an unprecedented expansion of federal oversight into employer-employee relations, the grant of amnesty to some 3 million noncitizens certainly marks it historically as a pragmatic compromise. But it had an odd feature: IRCA was designed to be confidential in order to overcome the natural fear of the undocumented to come forward. However, the law precluded judicial review of an administrative denial of a claim unless claimants turned themselves in for deportation proceedings. Thus, a generous law utilized a restrictive and portentous method: judicial review of amnesty denials was conditioned upon the acceptance of risk in deportation proceedings.[12]

In 1986, Congress also addressed long-standing concerns about marriage fraud. The Immigration Marriage Fraud Amendments of 1986 (IMFA) created a "conditional permanent resident status" for those married less than two years.[13] The status could be revoked if it was found to have been improperly obtained or if the marriage was legally terminated, other than through the death of a spouse. The conditional resident and the petitioner were required to file a special application before the second anniversary of the conditional grant and to appear for another interview. The IMFA, in effect, rendered such persons subject to a new kind of immigration probation.[14]

Attention also began to turn, again, to "criminal aliens."[15] It sometimes seemed that frustration over the apparently insoluble border problem fueled energy to get tough on a more tractable one. The new deportation law regime began to emerge in 1988 with the passage of the Anti-Drug Abuse Act, which created the "aggravated felony" category.[16] The 1988 law defined an aggravated felony with a short, sharp list of very serious offenses: murder, drug trafficking, and illicit trafficking in firearms. A noncitizen convicted of an aggravated felony at any time after entry would be "conclusively presumed" to be subject to deportation, taken into custody by the attorney general upon completion of his or her jail term, and held without bond. Voluntary departure was precluded. After deportation as an aggravated felon, anyone who reentered or tried to reenter the United States without obtaining the attorney general's permission faced severe criminal sanctions.

During the next few years, it sometimes seemed as if a tsunami had been unleashed against "criminal aliens." A relentless crackdown ensued. The Immigration Act of 1990 expanded the definition of "aggravated felony" to include money laundering and (nonpolitical) "crimes of violence," for which the term of imprisonment (even if it was suspended) was at least five years.[17] A person convicted of an aggravated felony was precluded from obtaining asylum or withholding of deportation. An aggravated felony conviction also meant a lack of "good moral character," which, in effect, eliminated most forms of discretionary relief from deportation and from naturalization. The long-standing power of criminal court judges to prevent deportation through "Judicial Recommendations against Deportation" was also eliminated, retroactively. Those deported because of an aggravated felony were now barred from returning for twenty years.[18]

In 1994, the law got tougher still. The attorney general was authorized to bypass regular deportation procedures for certain aggravated felons who were not lawful permanent residents and who appeared ineligible for any relief from deportation. Judicial review in such cases was severely limited.[19] The 1994 law also enhanced a variety of immigration-related criminal penalties and created a criminal alien tracking center to identify and locate noncitizens convicted of aggravated felonies. Then came the 1996 deluge. Though the specific political reasons for each step in this harsh turn were complex, this much is clear: the post-entry social control deportation system was a perfect vehicle for politicians to demonstrate toughness on crime at virtually no political cost. Moreover, the turn toward "criminal aliens" offered an easy way to appear to be doing something meaningful about the more intractable, resurgent problem of undocumented immigration. Those individuals, families, and communities who bore the brunt of these policies and those who feared their implications and trends went largely unheard.

Deportation and Discretion

Discretion is only to be respected when it is conscious of the traditions which surround it and of the limits which an informed conscience sets to its exercise.

—*Carlson v. Landon*, 342 U.S. 524, 562 (1951) (Frankfurter, J., dissenting)

Many of the harsh recent changes to deportation law depend on the extraconstitutional status of the whole enterprise. Largely unfettered from substantive constitutional restraint, the political branches have long felt free to enact disproportionate, retroactive laws, with mandatory detention and little or no judicial oversight. And yet, as we have seen, a counterdiscourse, with subconstitutional judicial oversight, has long existed. This complex *pas de deux* was challenged by the extreme 1996 laws that pushed the outer boundaries of what our legal and moral traditions could accept. Much of that challenge, not yet resolved, has centered around the related issues of executive discretion and judicial review.

If judicial review of deportation orders is an essential part of the rule of law, then 1996 could well have been the year in which the rule of deportation law died. Cresting a wave of get-tough sentiment, still unsatisfied by the 1988, 1990, and 1994 laws, a Republican Congress and a Democratic administration fundamentally restructured immigration and deportation law. The Antiterrorism and Effective Death Penalty Act and the Illegal Immigration Reform and Immigrant Responsibility Act, designed in large part to stifle the dialogue between the judiciary and the executive branch enforcers of deportation laws, were a bold assertion that deportation law was outside the mainstream of the U.S. rule of law. In 1997, I wrote, optimistically, that "the complete preclusion of a judicial role in decisions of this magnitude . . . will come to be seen . . . as the transitory excess of government actors who, as Henry Hart once put it, 'knew not Joseph.' "[20]

This prediction was partly correct—the judiciary has indeed resisted the complete elimination of judicial review of deportation cases with strict interpretations of some of the laws' provisions.[21] In *Zadvydas v. Davis*, for example, Justice Breyer wrote for a majority that was willing to adopt a creative reading of the statute governing posthearing detention and import a presumptive limit to it of six months.[22] But the opinion is inconsistent. The Court holds that indefinite postremoval detention of noncitizens would raise "a serious constitutional problem" under the due process clause, and that plenary power is "subject to important limitations." But one page later comes this: "Despite this constitutional problem, if 'Congress has made its intent' in the statute clear, 'we must give effect to that intent.' "[23] It is hard to see how both of these ideas can simultaneously be true. But such contradictions flow inevitably from the anomalous state of deportation.

Also perplexing are cases that deal with the preclusion of judicial review of certain "discretionary" agency decisions, among the more subtle features of the otherwise unsubtle 1996 laws.[24] Despite extensive Supreme Court consideration, two basic questions remain unanswered: What, exactly, are "discretionary" immigration agency decisions? And may such decisions legitimately be rendered unreviewable by courts? Because of the harshness and rigidity of our current deportation laws and the powerful role historically played by discretion in deportation law—often as the last repository of mercy in an otherwise merciless system—the issues are crucially important.

Discretion, as we have seen, has been deeply intertwined with deportation law for many years. Indeed, much of modern immigration law could fairly be described as a fabric of discretion.[25] A noncitizen seeking admission, permanent residence, or citizenship can lay claim to precious few rights along the way. At every step, discretionary power awaits: not only as the power to dispense mercy, but also as a hurdle to overcome. Deportation law, as we have seen, allows immense prosecutorial discretion. The government has enormous flexibility to choose whom to deport from a vast array of potential charges. Then, the so-called relief provisions are expressly discretionary. Certain other aspects of deportation law—such as the interpretation of statutory terms and procedural decisions—have been considered by courts to be discretionary, though there is wide disagreement about what this means.

After many years of discretionary accretion, we now face a rather strange legal situation. Congress has recently passed laws that prevent the judiciary from reviewing discretionary decisions. The Supreme Court has implied that courts may indeed be precluded from reviewing the exercise of administrative discretion.[26] But we lack fundamental agreement on what discretion actually means. Discretion remains an extremely amorphous concept—a kind of shadow standard, a contentless gap filler, and often simply a euphemism for allocation of authority. The 2005 REAL ID Act put a fine point on this problem.[27] It provides that "no court shall have jurisdiction to review" most "discretionary" decisions in deportation cases, though it permits the courts of appeals to review "constitutional claims or questions of law."[28] Of course, compared with the cruder approach taken by the 1996 laws, the REAL ID Act opens the possibility of a more nuanced, better system. But it impedes the genuinely fertile judicial-legislative-executive conversation that has sometimes led in the past to a more tempered regime.[29] Important legal and factual issues are buried beneath the jargon of discretionary preclusion. Louis Jaffe once wrote that "the availability of judicial review is the necessary condition, psychologically if not logically, of a system of administrative power which purports to be legitimate, or legally valid."[30] This is what is now at stake for much deportation law.

The Definitional Problem

> Even discretion . . . has its legal limits.
>
> —*INS v. Doherty*, 502 U.S. 314, 330
>   (1992) (Scalia, J., concurring
>   in part and dissenting in part)

The roots of the deportation discretion problem are deeply intertwined with our understanding of the nature of law. One might distinguish discretion from rules: the core of the "rule of law." Even so basic a dichotomy is problematic, though. Indeed, the term "rule" is itself ambiguous.[31] Because the definition of discretion is derived residually from that of rules, this ambiguity hinders a precise definition. Discretion, as Ronald Dworkin once famously put it, "like the hole in a doughnut, does not exist except as an area left open by a surrounding belt of restriction."[32] A rough, pragmatic definition is simply "power to make a choice between alternative courses of action."[33] The implication in either case is that there is no such thing as a uniquely correct discretionary decision. There may, however, certainly be *incorrect* discretionary decisions, such as those that are unauthorized or arbitrary. The most basic theoretical problems of discretion are thus how to define and restrain its abuse without destroying its non-rulelike character.

Immigration and deportation law have proven particularly resistant to any consistent understanding of discretion. The term describes choices of whom to prosecute; adjudication of claims for "discretionary" relief; whether bond should be granted; whether a motion to reopen proceedings has established a prima facie case; whether new evidence is material, was not available, and could not have been presented at a former hearing; various "policy-based" decisions; factual determinations; interpretations of statutory terms; and more.[34]

One of the most well-known and best attempts to grapple with this problem is that of Judge Henry Friendly in a 1966 case, *Wong Wing Hang v. INS.*[35] The case was an appeal from a denial of suspension of deportation relief. Judge Friendly considered the apparent conflict between APA section 701(a)(2) ("committed to agency discretion by law") and section 706 ("arbitrary, capricious, an abuse of discretion, or otherwise not in accordance with law"). Following the lead of professors Hart and Sacks, he rejected the idea of discretion "not subject to the restraint of the obligation of reasoned decision."[36] He offered a useful formula: "The denial of suspension to an eligible alien would be an abuse of discretion if it were made without a rational explanation, inexplicably departed from established policies, or rested on an impermissible basis such as an invidious discrimination against a particular race."[37] More recently, Justices Scalia, Stevens, and Souter have distinguished "merits-deciding" discretion from other forms.[38] But the Supreme Court has not gone much further than this.[39] And lower courts are wildly inconsistent.[40] Some courts review cases merely to ensure that "discretion" (however defined) was *actually* exercised rather than to review *how* it was exercised.[41] Many judges agree that "there is no place for unreviewable discretion in a system such as ours."[42] In deportation law, however, a notion of nonreviewability has also long percolated through the federal judiciary. In a particularly chilling pre-1996 decision, one court held that there is "no law to be applied" in relief-from-deportation cases.[43]

Prosecutorial Discretion

Deportation prosecutorial discretion has been largely immune from judicial scrutiny. Immigration authorities establish enforcement priorities on the basis of various, often contradictory, factors. Some considerations—such as efficiency and the apprehension of violent "terrorists"—raise few conceptual difficulties. Others—such as the targeting of certain racial or national groups or those who may simply oppose the policies of a current administration—are much more problematic. The general disinclination of courts to second-guess such decisions follows patterns established by the criminal justice system. But in the deportation realm, this deferential posture is exacerbated by the plenary power doctrine—if noncitizens have no substantive right to challenge deportation laws on equal protection grounds, then how can they challenge enforcement decisions based on national origin or race? As we have seen, plenary power has been mitigated somewhat in deportation law by the tacit recognition of some First Amendment protections, as well as by fluid norms of procedural due process and creative statutory interpretation techniques.[44] The majority opinion in *AADC v. Reno*—rejecting the selective prosecution claim—did not actually rely directly on plenary power but, first, on the demanding standard required in criminal law to inquire into the "special province of the Executive."[45] This disinclination was magnified, wrote Justice Scalia, by special factors in deportation cases, such as how delay could "permit and prolong a continuing violation of United States law." Justice Scalia also returned to a leitmotif that had loomed large in the 1950s cases: that courts might require "the disclosure of foreign-policy objectives and . . . foreign-intelligence products and techniques."[46]

Neither of these concerns seems especially compelling in most post-entry social control cases generally involve legal residents.[47] When a legal resident faces deportation, one does not normally think of "an ongoing violation of United States law."[48] This is particularly true of retroactive deportations. Visa overstayers and border crossers present a tougher call. But in the end, such cases would be better served by an equitable balancing of the noncitizen's violation, mitigating factors, if any, and the nature of the government's targeting. Dismissal of all charges might not be the only available remedy.[49] And surely the judiciary could use the same mechanisms developed in criminal cases to avoid revealing foreign intelligence matters.[50]

Ultimate Discretion

Because of the severe hardship that could be caused by exclusion or deportation, Congress, over the years, has enacted an array of discretionary measures to waive inadmissibility or deportability. Examples include (former) suspension of deportation, cancellation of removal, voluntary departure, registry, adjustment of status, and asylum. As Kenneth Davis once noted, "[t]he underlying scheme of the Act is to avoid conferring legal rights on aliens."[51] Such ultimate discretion is sometimes seen as immune from judicial scrutiny. Judge Frank Easterbrook once wrote, "The power to . . . grant an adjustment of status is a power to dispense mercy. No one is entitled to mercy, and there are no standards by which judges may patrol its exercise."[52]

A classic example of ultimate discretion is now called "cancellation of removal," formerly known as suspension of deportation. Since 1952, the statute has embodied a doubled discretionary delegation: "The Attorney General may, in his discretion, suspend deportation."[53] Immigration authorities had been authorized to suspend deportation as early as 1903.[54] Indeed, even the 1798 Aliens Act, aimed at "any alien judged dangerous to the peace and safety of the nation," authorized the president to grant "license to such alien to remain . . . for such time as he shall judge proper."[55] In the later statutes, such grants of authority to the executive were similarly broad, but limited by race. The 1917 act allowed such generosity only for certain "white" aliens who were not "ineligible for naturalization" (a euphemism that primarily meant "not Asian") and could show "good moral character" and hardship if deported.[56]

For many years, a rather complicated but judicially unregulated system of administrative discretion flourished *sub silentio*.[57] The Alien Registration Act of 1940 brought this process into the open, in conformity with emerging concerns about administrative regularity. The statute permitted the attorney general to suspend deportation of an alien who had shown "good moral character" for the preceding five years, and whose citizen or permanent-resident spouse, parent, or minor child would suffer "serious economic detriment" as a result of deportation.[58] Suspension was unavailable to anarchists, convicted narcotics dealers, and certain delineated "immoral classes," including prostitutes and the mentally ill.[59]

In the 1940s, as we have seen, a relatively tolerant administrative regime took hold for a while.[60] Liberal discretion was then stridently criticized in the debates leading to the passage of the 1952 McCarran-Walter Act.[61] As the Senate Judiciary Committee put it, "To continue in the pattern existing under the present law is to make a mockery of our immigration system."[62] As a result, applicants were required to meet a new standard: "exceptional and extremely unusual hardship."[63] Discretion was now vested in the Department of Justice, not Labor, and the phrase "in [the Attorney General's] discretion" was added, apparently to render the discretionary action more insulated from judicial scrutiny.[64]

In light of such signals, it is not surprising that the case law on judicial review of the exercise of ultimate discretion represents a high (or low) point of judicial deference. Consider the 1956 case of *Jay v. Boyd*.[65] Cecil Jay had entered the United States in 1914. His only absence from the United States had occurred during World War I when he served in the armed forces of Canada. He was a member of the U.S. Communist Party from 1935 to 1940, a period during which that party was widely recognized as a bona fide political organization, fielding candidates in many state elections. Although membership in the Communist Party was not completely clarified as a ground of deportation until ten years after Jay's membership had ceased, he, like many others, was held subject to deportation retroactively. Jay was over sixty years of age at the time he applied for suspension. He had been out of the Communist Party for many years. He had no criminal record. The special inquiry officer who heard his case found, in fact, that he was a person "of good moral character" and acknowledged Jay's testimony that "if he were deported . . . he would be separated from relatives and friends, and . . . he would find it almost impossible to maintain himself because of lack of funds." His application for suspension, however, was denied on the basis of certain "confidential information."[66]

The Supreme Court, in an opinion authored by Justice Reed, declined to consider the propriety of such secret proceedings and focused instead on the discretionary nature of suspension.[67] The determination was left to the "sound discretion of the Attorney General." The "unfettered discretion" of the attorney general in suspension cases was deemed most analogous to the parole power over convicted criminals. Not only would the Court import no substantive standards into this realm, but there would not even be found a right to a hearing or full disclosure of the considerations entering into a decision. In a formulation that echoes the power of a monarch, relief was said to be "in all cases a matter of grace."[68]

The decision provoked four strong dissents, all of which were animated by concerns about fairness and the "rule of law."[69] The most basic argument was that of Chief Justice Warren.[70] He could not "in conscience" agree with the majority opinion because it sacrificed "too much of the American spirit of fair play." He saw discretion as having been given by Congress not as a carte blanche but in the "interest of humanity."[71] His dissent implicates the most basic questions: May ultimate discretion be dispensed arbitrarily? Does "grace" really mean "exempt from all legal norms"?[72] As Justice Black noted, this was "a strange case in a country dedicated by its founders to the maintenance of liberty under law."[73] Nevertheless, the *Jay* majority's understanding of discretion was very influential. Indeed, although the use of secret procedures in deportation cases has waned somewhat since the Cold War, the concept of ultimate discretion in deportation law has remained fairly constant: an applicant may meet the statutory requirements but may still be denied if there are insufficient "equities" to merit relief. The ultimate discretionary decision is not often said to be completely unreviewable, but the "matter of grace" formulation is a powerful signal in that direction. Courts strain mightily to avoid a direct confrontation with the attorney general's ultimate discretionary decision.

Interpretive Discretion

Much confusion about discretion in deportation law derives from the unusual complexity of the statutory scheme. The immigration statute exceeds 500 pages and contains a welter of terms, such as "crimes of moral turpitude," that often strike the nonspecialist (and many specialists as well) as quaint and archaic, if not vague and opaque. Many statutory terms have been subjected to decades of sometimes contradictory agency interpretive discretion. As one court noted, "we are in the never-never land of the Immigration and Nationality Act, where plain words do not always mean what they say."[74] If undertaken by courts, much of this process would simply be called statutory interpretation. However, as Alex Aleinikoff has noted, "Agencies are the captains of the ship of state, and they are constantly giving meaning to statutes as they write regulations, bring enforcement actions, adjudicate claims, or issue interpretive guidelines."[75]

In *INS v. Jong Ha Wang*, the Supreme Court crafted a standard approach to agency interpretive discretion in deportation law.[76] At issue was the meaning of the words "extreme hardship," which the Court held were "not self-explanatory, and reasonable men could easily differ as to their construction." However, the definition was committed "in the first instance to the Attorney General and his delegates." A court was not to overturn the agency's interpretation "simply because it may prefer another interpretation of the statute."[77] *Jong Ha Wang* was not an ultimate discretion case. Deciding what is extreme hardship is not the same thing as administering grace. Rather, the Court deferred to a "permissible interpretation" by the agency, implicitly assuming that there was no single correct interpretation.

But the path of the law has not been straight in this area. Contrast *Wang* with *INS v. Phinpathya*, which—three years later—considered the "continuous presence" requirement for suspension.[78] Rather than deferring to the interpretive discretion of the Board of Immigration Appeals (BIA), the Court determined the "plain meaning" of the statute. This was especially interesting in that the board had in fact read the provision similarly to the Court and had been overruled by the court of appeals. One could perhaps resolve this inconsistency by concluding that the phrase "continuous presence" has some sort of inherently clear content that is lacking in "extreme hardship," though this seems problematic.[79] *Wang* mandated deference to agency interpretive discretion while *Phinpathya* empowered courts (or at least the Supreme Court) to interpret statutory terms de novo. The two cases thus demonstrate how an anterior decision about method can obscure doctrinal clarity, a major problem for deportation law given its reliance on subconstitutional methods to preserve rights.[80]

Another variant of discretion is procedural interpretive discretion by which agencies control practice in the deportation system. It involves changes of venue, continuances, procedural motions, and so forth.[81] The standard of review for such decisions is often said to be "abuse of discretion," but the field is replete with a variety of highly discretionary formulae.[82] Recent criticism of certain administrative deportation practices—many of which faced only minimal judicial oversight—rose to a sufficient crescendo that Attorney General Alberto Gonzales felt compelled to admonish immigration judges that for the "aliens" before them, they were "the face of American justice" and that "each [must] be treated with courtesy and respect."[83] The effect of such administrative controls remains to be seen.

Finally, there is factual interpretive discretion, which involves "adjudicative and legislative fact" determinations, credibility, and more complex hybrid inquiries.[84] Administrative findings of fact are required to be "conclusive unless any reasonable adjudicator would be compelled to conclude to the contrary."[85] Beyond the natural variance in how courts interpret even this deferential standard, there lies a deeper problem. When, for example, an adjudicator determines whether a marriage (which might lead to permanent residence) is bona fide, that determination is not simply a matter of deciding who did what, or when, or why. Rather, it is a mix of law and fact: a much more fluid process, the exact methods of which are extremely difficult to define and monitor. While the outer bounds of this sort of discretion may be policed by constitutional requirements of due process, there is a vast gray area that eludes consistent rules and standards. The law of asylum offers a good example of factual interpretive discretion. As David Martin has written, "the asylum determination rests on uniquely elusive grounds. It will usually turn on facts which are strikingly inaccessible . . . by U.S. courts and agencies . . . [and will] often revolve critically around a determination of the applicant's credibility."[86] This elusiveness of fact is only part of the discretionary problem, however. There is another elusive area: where legal definition meets fact. In the asylum process, the tail end of this discretion is what Martin called "an informed prediction (not truly a finding) about the degree and type of danger the particular applicant is likely to face upon return."[87] As this last step is critical in the often life-and-death asylum process, a lack of clarity about how it should be judicially reviewed is troubling.[88] As Martin noted, echoing Hart and Sacks, the best we seem to be able to do is to recognize that "success consists . . . in achieving sufficient acceptance of the process, including respect for the judgment and fairness of the decision-makers, so that final grants and denials are regarded as authoritative."[89]

But how much respect is due such "judgment and fairness"? Some federal judges have recently become quite scathing in their criticism of immigration judges' decisions, especially in asylum cases.[90] Judge Richard Posner has written, "the adjudication of these cases at the administrative level has fallen below the minimum standards of legal justice."[91] Part of the reason for this is increasing appeals court caseloads following "streamlining" of the BIA by former Attorney General John Ashcroft. On August 23, 2002, the attorney general restructured the organization and procedures of the BIA. The size of the board was reduced from twenty-three to eleven members. The reported goal was to improve timeliness and reduce backlogs while continuing to ensure the quality of adjudications.[92] The regulation allowed the BIA to make greater use of single board member adjudications. "Summary affirmances"—without written opinions—are now common.[93] Much of the backlog has shifted to the federal courts, tempting judges to rely on preclusionary mechanisms to reduce caseloads.[94]

Still, aspects of the deportation process that had previously been insulated from judicial review are now exposed. Judge Julio Fuentes referred to one immigration judge's conduct of a hearing as "more appropriate to a court television show than a federal court proceeding."[95] Though most immigration judges work hard to exercise their power responsibly and professionally, the combination of harsh laws, broad discretion, lack of counsel, reduced administrative review, and limited judicial oversight has been a formula for what former BIA member Lory Rosenberg has called "a pattern of unfettered misuse of authority."[96]

These basic types of discretion—*prosecutorial, ultimate,* and *interpretive*—form a distinctive pattern in U.S. deportation law. Legal proceedings with the highest possible stakes for the participants, literally sometimes life and death, take place in a complex, very well-insulated, discretionary legal environment. Of the nearly 600,000 cases adjudicated by immigration judges in 2003–2004, more than 30 percent involved applications for discretionary relief of one sort or another.[97] To be sure, many immigration judges welcome the chance to be generous where they can. But they also face real pressures not to grant too many discretionary relief cases.[98] Of some 36,000 "defensive" asylum cases presented to immigration courts in 2004, about 74 percent were denied.[99] The grant rate for claims made pursuant to the Convention Against Torture, a matter of interpretive discretion, was some 3 percent in 2004.[100] As troubling, exceptionally wide variations appear from region to region and from judge to judge.[101]

The problem of discretion merged with two other long-standing deportation law questions—retroactivity and preclusion of judicial review—in the 2001 (pre–September 11) case of *INS v. St. Cyr.*[102] Enrico St. Cyr, a lawful permanent resident since 1986, had pled guilty to a criminal charge that made him deportable. At the time of his criminal conduct and plea, he would have been eligible for discretionary "Section 212(c)" relief. Until 1996, 212(c) relief was available to long-term lawful permanent residents facing deportation for many types of criminal convictions. Mr. St. Cyr's removal proceedings, however, began too late. The government asserted that he was no longer eligible for relief and, in effect, had no defense to deportation and no right to judicial review. To challenge this, St. Cyr filed a habeas corpus petition.

The issues that came to the Supreme Court were jurisdictional (whether habeas review remained available to review questions relating to discretionary relief) and substantive (retroactivity). In brief, the Court concluded that "leaving aliens without a forum for adjudicating claims such as those raised in this case would raise serious constitutional questions."[103] It construed the jurisdiction-stripping provisions of the statute not to preclude habeas jurisdiction. Substantively, the Court held that deportation laws—indeed, even discretionary "relief from deportation" laws—cannot be applied retroactively absent meticulous clarity on the point by the legislature. The *St. Cyr* opinion thus exemplified the sort of subconstitutional reasoning that has long dominated U.S. deportation law. But in *St. Cyr,* as in *Zadvydas,* the Court seemed close to jettisoning the plenary power doctrine. That it did not do so is especially poignant in light of what developed post–September 11.

The problem of discretion also arose again. Against the government's assertion that habeas courts could not review discretionary matters, the Court noted that habeas courts had "regularly answered questions of law that arose in the context of discretionary relief." Echoing *Jay v. Boyd,* the Court labeled ultimate discretion "a matter of grace."[104] The opinion thus left us with a rather binary and formal view of the rule-of-law/discretion dichotomy.[105] Essentially, the threshold characterization of an issue as either a "pure question of law" or "a matter of grace" (discretion) may now be dispositive as to judicial review.[106] Imagine that when Mr. St. Cyr went back before the immigration judge, she denied his case not because he was statutorily barred, but because, on balance, the "equities" were not in his favor. In her decision, she would weigh various factors. What if she speculated that Mr. St. Cyr would "probably be better off in Haiti, anyway." Would this be reviewable by a federal court? Apparently not, as it is a "discretionary" decision.

The congressional delegation of discretionary authority in deportation law is exceedingly broad, and in some cases standardless. But this does not mean that the judiciary should—or may—cede the field completely to administrative actors. Messy though this all may be, it has interbranch conversational attributes that are of great value to the government as well as to the people affected by these cases. But the conversations of the past will be silenced if such action is rendered immune from review. This could be a profoundly painful and unjust outcome for many noncitizens, their families, and our legal system as a whole. Discretion will be a dustbin of a jurisprudential category: the place where—as triples were once said to do in the glove of Joe Jackson—complicated legal questions go to die. Surely we can do better in cases in which long-term legal residents may be separated forever from their families than simply to say, "The Board did not take mercy on Achacoso-Sanchez, but it has the discretion to be cold-blooded . . . [N]o one is entitled to mercy."[107]

The Civil-Criminal Line and Retroactivity

The *St. Cyr* Court's analysis of retroactivity reflected powerful subconstitutional norms. The Court made clear that, as a matter of statutory interpretation (but not ex post facto clause or due process analysis), it was deeply concerned that the "[l]egislature's unmatched powers allow it to sweep away settled expectations suddenly and without individualized consideration."[108] Moreover, the Court specifically applied to noncitizens the insight that legislatures "may be tempted to use retroactive legislation as a means of retribution against unpopular groups or individuals."[109] Though the Court demurred as to the ultimate constitutional validity of retroactive deportation laws, its requirement of an "unambiguous direction" from Congress was "a demanding one." A retroactive deportation law will now require statutory language that is "so clear that it could sustain only one interpretation."[110] The Court explicitly declined the government's invitation to rule that deportation laws can never be retroactive because deportation is inherently prospective.[111]

I quite clearly recall the moment I read this. "Interesting," I thought, "may we tell that to Mr. Mahler, Mr. Galvan, or Mr. Harisiades or their descendants wherever they may be?"[112] More important, may we tell it to the hundreds, if not thousands, of noncitizens who have recently found themselves in removal proceedings based on criminal dispositions that were not grounds for deportation when they entered?[113] Well, not so fast. The problem is that the *St. Cyr* Court also reiterated the *Fong Yue Ting* doctrine that "deportation is not punishment for past crimes" The Court imported an antiretroactivity norm redolent of criminal law into the nominally civil deportation realm. One might, and I did, applaud the result of this approach for Mr. St Cyr. But the Court's reasoning tends to sustain retroactivity in other deportation statutes. Indeed, says the Court, "our decision today is fully consistent with a recognition of Congress' power to act retrospectively"[114] That is an outcome that portends at least as much hardship and injustice as did the elimination of Section 212(c).

Whatever value the civil retroactivity "default" rule may have in other settings, it seems strange in deportation cases. Can a retroactive change from possible to certain deportation truly be thought only to require a "clear statement" by Congress to be constitutionally permissible? It is true that such clarity is rarely found. Still, this approach renders much of the most powerful normative underpinnings of civil retroactivity cases bitterly irrelevant. Let us assume, for example, that one is truly concerned—as a matter of principle—about "the legislature's unmatched powers . . . to sweep away settled expectations suddenly." Let us further assume that one recognizes how a legislature's "responsivity to political pressures poses a risk that it may be tempted to use retroactive legislation as a means of retribution against unpopular groups or individuals."[115] Can it be seriously maintained that a constitutional court properly addresses such problems simply by requiring the legislature to be clear about it? Indeed, a legislature that is truly aiming at an unpopular group may be, if anything, more likely to be meticulously clear than one that retroactively deprives a more empowered group of something. The link between countermajoritarian concerns and the remedy of a requirement of a clear statement of legislative intent may make sense in the context of a civil suit for money damages. But it works much less impressively in the arena of deportation laws, where—as we have seen—legislative majorities have repeatedly targeted noncitizen social groups and political dissidents quite clearly. A more functional view of some forms of deportation as punishment provides a more solid—and no more complicated—analytic framework.

Post-entry social control deportation of long-term residents could well be considered punishment for ex post facto clause purposes.[116] Strong historical and functional arguments sustaining this view may be traced back as far as 1798 in *Calder v. Bull*.[117] Retroactive deportation laws also implicate accepted norms of substantive due process.[118] Had the Court considered the nature of the deportation proceedings even a bit more functionally, had it been willing to grapple even a bit more directly with basic questions of justice and fairness, it might well have achieved a better, more durable outcome.[119]

Still, the *St. Cyr* opinion could be read expansively. The Court's apparent recognition of the similarities between the constitutional protections in criminal cases and deportation subtly bridges the civil and criminal categories. Even were the Court to continue explicitly to reject the argument that deportation is punishment, the opinion offers a constitutional middle way. As to retroactive deportation laws, the Court could continue to import the norms of ex post facto analysis more fully and directly, without necessarily resolving the entire civil-criminal issue. It would, however, eventually have to invoke a rich theory of due process in order to do so convincingly. Such an analysis would provide a better path out of the civil retroactivity forest by returning our attention to the trees on which we should gaze: the real interests at stake for real people considered in the light of history, justice, and fairness. It was undoubtedly a good thing that some civil retroactivity chickens came home to roost in *St. Cyr.* Perhaps it is time to renovate the coop.

Conclusion

FRIAR LAURENCE:
A gentler judgment vanish'd from his lips,
Not body's death, but body's banishment.
ROMEO:
Ha, banishment! be merciful, say "death;"
For exile hath more terror in his look,
Much more than death: do not say "banishment."

—William Shakespeare, *Romeo and Juliet*, Act 3, Scene 3

As a 100-plus years social experiment, the U.S. deportation system has caused considerable harm and done little demonstrable good. It is poorly planned, irrationally administered, and, as a model on which to base other enforcement systems, dangerous. The dramatic recent increase in post-entry social control deportation warrants special concern. If proportionality is a fundamental component of justice,[120] then is it not unjust to deport and banish for life long-term legal permanent residents with family here and no contacts in their country of birth who commit a single minor crime? A conviction for petty larceny or simple assault can now be an aggravated felony.[121] A noncitizen convicted of an aggravated felony is subject to removal from the United States with virtually no possibility of relief on humanitarian or other grounds. That person will be banned for life from the United States. Length of residence is irrelevant. Family ties here are meaningless. Hardship is immaterial. To contest such a deportation case, one must remain incarcerated for however long such appeals last. The discretionary "relief" system is an inconsistent mess even in the limited cases for which it is still available. Worse, it is a mess that has now been rendered largely immune from judicial oversight. Equally worrisome is the easy acquiescence to radically expedited procedures of arrest, detention, and removal along a 100-mile swath of U.S. territory along every land and sea border, including many major cities. This is hardly a healthy legal system.

The basic argument against reform proposals—such as a statute of limitations or revisitation of the civil-criminal dichotomy—is that noncitizens who come to the United States are, in effect, on probation until they become citizens. If they violate their terms, they face the consequence they always knew was there: deportation. But this argument proves too much. It is one thing to say to a person, "you are on probation." It is quite another to say, "you may be deported at any time for almost any reason, even if it's a single marijuana offense and you've lived here for fifty years and have no family elsewhere." There have to be limits beyond which the probation metaphor breaks down. What if we were to say to people, "you may enter the United States and live here, but if you litter you will be shot?" It is hardly a sufficient justification of such a law to say that it is merely part of their "probation" as noncitizens. Madison's insight that the "favor" of admission cannot be revoked "at pleasure" remains apt.

Of course, the Supreme Court is far from concluding that there is anything *constitutionally* wrong with a harsh deportation law aimed at minor crimes. If a citizen can get life in prison for petty larceny in a "three strikes" jurisdiction, why can't we deport a permanent resident for littering? The argument reduces to whether there is an implicit constitutional right to proportionality in penal laws. The Supreme Court seems inclined to answer this general question negatively, though it has been somewhat more receptive to such claims in the past.[122] But in the legal deportation realm, no such reasoning takes place, as a result of the persistence of the plenary power doctrine. A more forthright approach would analyze deportations to determine whether—under the circumstances in which they are imposed—they are punishment. It is hardly inspiring to say that deportation is not punishment because the Court has not historically considered it to be punishment.[123] This becomes especially clear when one looks closely at the historical contexts of those precedents and the unique harshness of the current regime. The label of punishment should be applied, if appropriate, to deportation as the product of a functional, historical, and intentional analysis. The deportation of long-term legal residents for post-entry conduct is imposed as a direct consequence of a prior "bad" act. Its purpose can hardly be said to be compensatory. Congress was clearly aiming at retribution or deterrence. These are predominantly indicia of punishment, not of regulation.[124]

Retroactivity also calls for a constitutional solution. The use of exceedingly nice techniques of statutory interpretation tends to free the political branches from the clear constitutional dialogue that might actually restrain proposals for such laws. The Court could either expand the reach of the ex post facto clause or rely on substantive due process.[125] Is it not important to discourage retroactive punitive lawmaking against those least able to invoke the political process against government overreaching?[126] Who has less such ability than noncitizens?

Such an approach does not necessarily require that all of the procedures of a criminal trial be available in deportation cases. A "quasi-criminal" model could reasonably impart some rights and not others, as has been done in the past.[127] The right to appointed counsel, bail, and recognition by courts that a lawyer's failure to consider deportation consequences can be ineffective assistance of counsel are very strong claims. This is both because of the punitive nature of some deportations and because of the increasing convergence between the criminal and deportation systems.[128]

As for extended border control deportation, history shows how poorly that system has actually worked. It has functioned primarily as a labor control device, a kind of extra tool in the hands of large businesses (and, for that matter, American families seeking nannies, gardeners, and so forth) to provide a cheap, flexible, and largely rightless labor supply.[129] Worse, it has facilitated selective enforcement against particular racial and ethnic groups. The rejection by the Court of a selective prosecution defense gives a dangerously free hand to government agents. To permit an enforcement agency to use racial profiling, and to ignore the "chilling effect" when people are chosen for investigation or arrest because they have criticized the government violates our most precious politico-legal ideals. As David Cole has noted, "chilling effects are particularly severe in immigrant communities, partly because immigrants are less likely to have grown up with a strong First Amendment tradition, and partly because they have so much to lose."[130] Could such a chilling effect be confined to noncitizens? Everyone in any mixed citizen-noncitizen group would live in fear of deportation. It would also contradict some of the most eloquent and persuasive critiques made of the Alien and Sedition Acts by Jefferson and Madison. I suspect that all of this explains why, in the end, the Court at least declined to "rule out the possibility of a rare case in which the alleged basis of discrimination is so outrageous that the foregoing considerations can be overcome."[131] But that is a thin reed of support for so fundamental a right.

While it may be true, generally, that "distinctions in federal law among aliens on the basis of their country of current nationality are not constitutionally suspect," we should not conflate two distinct types of discrimination.[132] It is one thing to favor nationals of selected foreign countries. It is more problematic to explicitly disfavor others. And it is most problematic to disfavor one group through selective enforcement of punitive laws. This difference between positive and negative effects, long recognized in retroactivity analysis, is especially important in times of fear, like the present, when the government tends to rely on administrative processes instead of the formal criminal system and to target individuals for action often on the basis of questionable predictions about what they might do.[133] Finally, as the history of deportation shows so clearly, we simply cannot easily disaggregate nationality discrimination from its racial and ethnic aspects. Imagine a decision by the attorney general to prosecute only white-collar crimes in California committed by Mexican Americans or by Israeli Americans in New York. Should such an enforcement choice be dismissed as merely permissible nationality discrimination?

Woody Guthrie wrote a poem in the late 1940s about a plane crash that killed a number of Mexican workers who were being removed from California. The poem ultimately became the song "Deportees."[134] One of Guthrie's stanzas refers to the bodies of the deportees killed in the plane crash as "these dear friends scattered like dry leaves."[135] I do not know whether he was aware that Henry Wadsworth Longfellow had used essentially the same metaphor in his 1847 poem "Evangeline," a romantic depiction of the Acadian deportation from Nova Scotia in the 1750s.[136] But even if Guthrie did not consciously echo Longfellow, it points to a fascinating cultural connection. It is more than coincidental that both Thomas Jefferson and Abraham Lincoln used the term "deportation" to describe massive plans to remove freed slaves from America and that similar terminology was used to describe the forced movement of the Cherokee and the particularly vicious 1917 "Bisbee deportation" of IWW workers. It is evidence of a long understudied subterranean stream. In the end, the history of deportation law shows us how integral the removal impulse has been to our nation of immigrants. It also shows the importance of choosing its best principles to guide us. In the words of Justice Frank Murphy in Harry Bridges's case; "Only by zealously guarding the rights of the most humble, the most unorthodox and the most despised among us can freedom flourish and endure in our land."[137]

Notes

Index

Notes

Preface

1. Thomas Paine, *Common Sense* (1776); Thomas Jefferson, 1801 Annual Message to Congress; Ronald Reagan, Acceptance Speech, Detroit, Michigan, July 17, 1980, reported in *New York Times,* July 18, 1980, A8.

1. Introduction

1. U.S. Department of Justice, Executive Office for Immigration Review (EOIR), "FY 2005 Statistical Yearbook," at C3, Table 3, and G1, Figure 9. Removal proceedings encompass what were formerly differentiated as exclusion and deportation proceedings.
2. Dianne Schmidley, "Current Population Reports," U.S. Department of Commerce, Economics and Statistics Administration, U.S. Census Bureau, February 2003.
3. Kelly Jefferys and Nancy Rytina, "U.S. Legal Permanent Residents: 2005," Department of Homeland Security (DHS), Office of Immigration Statistics, April 2006.
4. DHS, Office of Immigration Statistics, "2004 Yearbook of Immigration Statistics," Table 26 ("DHS 2004 Yearbook"). Tens of thousands of people also enter the United States each year as refugees who are eligible to become lawful permanent residents after one year. See 8 U.S.C. §1101(a)(42); 8 U.S.C. §1157, 1159.
5. Some 14 million persons, including 4.7 million children, live in families in which the head of the household or the spouse is an unauthorized migrant. Over 3 million of those family members are U.S. citizens by birth. Jeffrey S. Passel, "Unauthorized Migrants; Number and Characteristics," June 14, 2005; David Martin, "Twilight Statuses: A Closer Examination of the Unauthorized Population" (Migration Policy Institute, June 2005, no. 2). Background Briefing Prepared for Task Force on Immigration and America's Future, Pew Hispanic Center, available at http://pewhispanic.org/reports/report.php?ReportID=46.
6. See DHS 2004 Yearbook, Table 36.

7. 8 U.S.C. §1227(3)(A).

8. 8 U.S.C. §1227(4)(A) (emphasis added).

9. 8 U.S.C. §1427.

10. See, e.g., 8 U.S.C. §1424 (naturalization precluded for anyone "who advocates or teaches, or who is a member of or affiliated with any organization that advocates or teaches, opposition to all organized government; or . . . who is a member of or affiliated with . . . the Communist Party of the United States").

11. DHS 2004 Yearbook, Tables 31, 35, and 40. These statistics include "voluntary departures" (recorded since 1927) and "formal removals," which include deportations, exclusions of arriving "aliens," and removal proceedings (which were created in 1996 as a unified system to include both exclusions and deportations).

12. EOIR reported over 100,000 absconders in 2005. More than half were from two courts in Texas. EOIR, "FY 2005 Statistical Yearbook," H1–H4. DHS estimates that there may be 500,000 absconders at large in the United States. Brian Friel, "Busted," 38 *National Journal* 20–26 (2006).

13. Mary Dougherty, Denise Wilson, Amy Wu, DHS, Office of Immigration Statistics, "Immigration Enforcement Actions: 2004," November 2005.

14. See The Intelligence Reform and Terrorist Prevention Act, 108 Public Law 458, sec. 5204.

15. DHS Secretary Michael Chertoff referred to children who accompany their families as "window dressing for smugglers" and has touted the family detention center as humanitarian, in that it will discourage people from bringing children on the dangerous journey across the border. DHS: "Charting a Path Forward," Heritage Foundation Reports, April 3, 2006.

16. Indeed, the arrest may also be due to a mistake. A Migration Policy Institute study conducted in 2005 concluded that more than 8,000 people may have been wrongly entered into a national crime database. Some law enforcement agencies had error rates as high as 90 percent. "Blurring the Lines: A Profile of State and Local Police Enforcement of Immigration Law Using the National Crime Information Center Database, 2002–2004," December 2005.

17. *I.N.S. v. Lopez-Mendoza,* 468 U.S. 1032, 1033 (1984) (exclusionary rule generally does not apply in deportation hearings).

18. *United States v. Silva,* 715 F.2d, 43, 46 (2d Cir. 1983); *United States v. Moody,* 649 F.2d 124, 127 (2d Cir. 1981); *Babula v. I.N.S.,* 665 F.2d 293, 297 (3d Cir. 1981); see 8 U.S.C. 1356(a)(1) (1996); 8 U.S.C. 1357(a)(2) (1996).

19. 8 C.F.R. 287.3 (2004); 8 C.F.R. 1292.2 (2004).

20. *Reno v. American-Arab Anti-Discrimination Committee,* 525 U.S. 471, 491 (1999).

21. 8 U.S.C. 1361 (1994); *In re Ponce-Hernandez,* 22 I&N Dec. 784 (B.I.A. 1999); *In re Castro,* 16 I&N Dec. 81 (B.I.A. 1976).

22. See Chapter 5.

23. See, e.g., *Mendez-Moranchel v. I.N.S.,* 338 F.3d 176, 176 (3d Cir. 2003); *Mendes v. I.N.S.,* 197 F.3d 6, 11 (1st Cir. 1999).

24. E. P. Hutchinson, *Legislative History of American Immigration Policy, 1798–1965* 443 (1981).

25. It is one of the ways that we may "make foreign those whom we persecute." Bonnie Honig, "A Legacy of Xenophobia," 27 *Boston Review* (December 2002). Available at http://www.bostonreview.net/BR27.6/honig.html.

26. See, e.g., Linda S. Bosniak, "Membership. Equality, and the Difference That Alienage Makes," 69 *N.Y.U. L. Rev.* 1047 (1994).

27. See Roscoe Pound, *Social Control through Law,* 16 (1942): "I begin with the ideas of civilization, of social control as the means of maintaining civilization, and of law as an agency . . . of social control."

28. An immigrant may be told, for example, not to obtain public benefits for five years. Such conditions may be viewed as contractual, though they do not require positive action.

29. Report to the General Assembly of Virginia (Jan. 7, 1800), vol. 4 *Elliot's Debates on the Federal Constitution* 541, 556 (Lippincott, 2d ed. 1907).

30. See *Campos v. I.N.S.,* 961 F.2d 309, 315 (1992).

31. Statement of Edward Livingston, quoted in James Morton Smith, *Freedom's Fetters; The Alien and Sedition Laws and American Civil Liberties* 85 (1956); see also 88.

32. See Thomas Jefferson, The Kentucky Resolution, in *Documents of American History* 181 (6th ed. 1958).

33. See Ali Behdad, "Nationalism and Immigration to the United States," 6 *Diaspora* 155–178 (1997).

34. Zechariah Chafee, Jr., *Freedom of Speech* 229 (1919).

35. Reported in testimony before the Senate Judiciary Committee in December 2001 by Attorney Michael Boyle http://www.aila.org/contentViewer.aspx ?bc=9,576,971,978; see also Richard A. Serrano, "Response to Terror; The Detainees," *Los Angeles Times,* November 4, 2001, A.1.

36. Ashcroft is quoted in Office of the Inspector General, The September 11 Detainees: A Review of the Treatment of Aliens held on Immigration Charges in Connection with the Investigation of the September 11 Attacks, April 2003 ("OIG Report") at 12; see also 13. Some 762 persons, about whom there was at least some "suspicion," were held by the INS in a scattered network of federal, local, and private detention facilities throughout the country *Id.* at 1–2. Detainees were subjected to a "hold until cleared by the FBI" policy, resulted in an average detainment of eighty days from the time of arrest to clearance, with considerable numbers of people being held for more than six months. *Id.* at 46, 64.

37. Registration and Monitoring of Certain Nonimmigrants. 67 Fed. Reg. 40,581. The rule became final on August 12, 2002, effective September 11, 2002. 67 Fed. Reg. 52,584. The Immigration and Naturalization Service (INS) was dissolved in 2003, and its functions were transferred to DHS.

38. INS confirmed that "officers conducting these interviews may discover information which leads them to suspect that specific aliens on the list are unlaw-

fully present or in violation of their immigration status." Memorandum from Michael A. Pearson, INS Executive Associate Commissioner (Nov. 23, 2001). See generally Kevin R. Johnson, "The End of 'Civil Rights' as We Know It?: Immigration and Civil Rights in the New Millennium," 49 *UCLA L. Rev.* 1481, 1481–1511 (2002).

39. Diane Cardwell, "Threats and Responses: The Immigrants; Muslims Face Deportation, but Say U.S. Is Their Home," *New York Times,* June 13, 2003, A22.
40. See Nina Bernstein, "Questions, Bitterness and Exile for Queens Girl in Terror Case," *New York Times,* June 17, 2005, A.1.
41. DHS 2004 Yearbook, Table 42.
42. Dougherty et al.
43. Public Law 104–132, 110 Stat. 1214 (1996) (codified as amended in scattered sections of 8, 18, 22, 28, 40, 42 U.S.C.); Public Law 104–208, Div. C, 110 Stat. 3009–546 (1996) (codified as amended in scattered sections of 8, 18 U.S.C.).
44. 8 U.S.C. §1182 (1999); 8 U.S.C. §1227 (1999); 8 U.S.C. §1101(a)(43) (adding retroactive aggravated felony grounds). See Nancy Morawetz, "Rethinking Retroactive Deportation Laws and the Due Process Clause," 73 *N.Y.U. L. Rev.* 97 (1998); 8 U.S.C. §1229(b) (replacing §212[c] and former suspension of deportation with more restricted forms of relief known as "cancellation of removal"); 8 U.S.C. §1226 (listing rules governing apprehension and detention of aliens); see generally Margaret H. Taylor, "Promoting Legal Representation for Detained Aliens: Litigation and Administrative Reform," 29 *Conn. L. Rev.* 1647 (1997): The USA PATRIOT Act also authorizes the attorney general to incarcerate and detain noncitizens if the government has "reasonable grounds to believe" that the individual may be a threat to national security. Such a person may be held for seven days pending the commencement of criminal or removal proceedings. Act of 2001, Public Law 107–156, 115 Stat. 272 (2001) §412; 8 U.S.C. §1228 (1999); 8 U.S.C. §1252 (1999); 8 U.S.C. §1103(a)(8) (1999); 8 U.S.C. §§1531–1537 (1999).
45. See, e.g., American Bar Association, "American Justice through Immigrants' Eyes" (2004); Peter H. Schuck, *Citizens, Strangers, and In-Betweens: Essays on Immigration and Citizenship,* 143–145 (1998).
46. *Demore v. Kim,* 538 U.S. 510 (2003); see also *id.* at 521, citing *Mathews v. Diaz,* 426 U.S. 67, 79–80 [1976]).
47. I was a consultant to the defense team in Ms. Borges's case, which was widely reported in the press.
48. Amy Otten, quoted in Theo Emery, "Shoplifting Conviction Comes Back to Haunt Portuguese Mom," *Associated Press,* August 6, 2003.
49. See 8 U.S.C. §1228(b).
50. Some of these nonimmigrants have so-called conditional permanent resident status.
51. Indeed, the number of undocumented Mexican immigrants exceeds the number of all Asian immigrants (27 percent) and of all immigrants from Eu-

rope and Canada (17 percent). Jeffrey Passel, "Mexican Immigration to the U.S.: The Latest Estimates," in *Selected Readings on US–Mexico Immigration* 14–16 (Migration Policy Institute, 2004).

52. See Maia Jachimowicz, "Bush Proposes New Temporary Worker Program," in *Selected Readings on US–Mexico Immigration* 38–40 Migration Policy Institute, 2004.

53. Public Law 99–603, 100 Stat. 3359; see Nancy Rytina, "IRCA Legalization Effects," Office of Policy and Planning, Statistics Division, U.S. INS (2002); DHS 2004 Yearbook, Table 4.

54. See H.R. Rep. No. 682(I), 99th Cong., 2d sess., 1986, 46.

55. DHS 2004 Yearbook, Table 38.

56. The Border Patrol defines two categories: Mexicans and "OTMs" (other than Mexicans). In 2004, some 155,000 OTMs were caught near the southern border. They are subject to detention and then forced removal, most to Central America and Brazil. This category includes those who leave "voluntarily" after arrest. "Border Security: Apprehensions of 'Other than Mexican' Aliens," Congressional Research Service Report, September 22, 2005.

57. DHS 2004 Yearbook, Table 42.

58. *Id.*

59. "Immigration Raid at Plant Leaves Children in Limbo," *Associated Press,* July 31, 2005, 1.22.

60. *Almeida-Sanchez v. INS,* 413 U.S. 266 (1973).

61. 8 CFR 287.3.

62. Quoted in Peter Andreas, *Border Games: Policing the U.S.–Mexico Divide* 87 (2000); see also *id.* at 106.

63. See, e.g., Ken Ellingwood, *Hard Line: Life and Death on the U.S.–Mexico Border* (2004); Luis Alberto Urrea, *The Devil's Highway: A True Story* (2004).

64. See K. Sullivan and M. Jordan, "7 Days of Desperation along Mexican Border; Migrants' Dreams Die in Brutal Crossing," *Washington Post,* May 26, 2003, A1.

65. Andreas, *Border Games* at 108.

66. *Binational Study: Migration Between Mexico and the United States* 28 (Mexico City and Washington, D.C.: Mexican Foreign Ministry and U.S. Commission on Immigration Reform 1997).

67. Indeed, much of the border itself was contested until well into the twentieth century. See Leon Metz, *Border: The U.S.–Mexico Line* 20–40 (1989); Oscar Martinez, *Troublesome Border* 17–21 (1988).

68. Demetrios G. Papademetriou, "The Mexico Factor in U.S. Immigration Reform," in *Selected Readings on US–Mexico Immigration* 7 (Migration Policy Institute, 2004).

69. From 1993 to 2002, the Border Patrol more than doubled in size from 4,036 agents to nearly 10,000. ABA, "American Justice through Immigrants' Eyes" 84 (2004).

70. One of the most compelling concerns about this system has been its effect on potential asylum seekers. See United States Commission on International Reli-

gious Freedom, "Report on Asylum-Seekers in Expedited Removal" (2005) (Washington, D.C.)

71. 8 U.S.C. §1182(a)(9)(a)(i). There are exceptions for those who express a fear that they may be persecuted if excluded; who ask to apply for asylum; or who claim to be U.S. citizens, lawful permanent residents, refugees, or asylees. See 8 U.S.C. §1335(b)(1)(A)(i) and (ii), 8 C.F.R. §§235.3(b)(4) and (b)(5).

72. ABA report at 9.

73. 69 Fed. Reg. 48,877 (Aug. 11, 2004).

74. *Id.;* "Department Of Homeland Security Streamlines Removal Process along Entire U.S. Border," *US Fed News,* January 30, 2006.

75. Those who return to the United States without permission after having been deported face the administrative "reinstatement" of their previous orders without a hearing. No judge will hear their case, and they are barred from any relief, even if their circumstances have changed dramatically. See 8 U.S.C. 1231(a)(5).

76. That is some 21 percent of the total number of removals. DHS, Office of "Immigration Statistics, "Immigration Enforcement Actions: 2004," November 2005.

77. Noncitizens, of course, also have been granted important rights under statutory and regulatory law.

78. Gerald Neuman, *Strangers to the Constitution: Immigrants, Borders, and Fundamental Law* 162 (1996).

79. *McCulloch v. Maryland,* 17 U.S. (4 Wheat.) 316, 324 (1819).

80. U.S. Const. art. I, §8, cl. 4.

81. Some drafters may have viewed the clause as authorizing federal control of immigration. See, e.g., 1 *Annals of Cong.* 1147–1164 (Joseph Gales ed., 1790) (discussing the 1790 naturalization act); see also James H. Kettner, *The Development of American Citizenship, 1608–1870* 236–239 (1978).

82. U.S. Const. art. I, §9, cl. 1. Thomas Jefferson argued that the clause barred Congress from regulating immigration prior to 1808. See *Kentucky Resolution,* 4 *Elliot's Debates* 541. See also, *Gibbons v. Ogden,* 22 U.S. 1, 216–217; (clause relevant to free immigration); but see *New York v. Compagnie Generale Transatlantique,* 107 U.S. 59, 62 (1883) ("There has never been any doubt that this clause had exclusive reference to persons of the African race"). See Sarah H. Cleveland, "Powers Inherent in Sovereignty: Indians, Aliens, Territories, and the Nineteenth Century Origins of Plenary Power over Foreign Affairs," 81 *Tex. L. Rev.* 1 (2002).

83. See Stephen Legomsky, *Immigration and the Judiciary* 181–191 (1987).

84. *Yick Wo v. Hopkins,* 118 U.S. 356 (1886).

85. T. Alexander Aleinikoff, *Semblances of Sovereignty* 172 (2004).

86. See *Graham v. Richardson,* 403 U.S. 365 (1971); Aleinikoff, *Semblances* at 151. The Court has held that the Fifth Amendment protects "aliens," even those

whose presence in this country is unlawful, from invidious discrimination by the federal government. *Mathews v. Diaz,* 426 U.S. 67, 77 (1976).

87. 457 U.S. 202, 218–219 (1982).

88. Indeed, the majority cited the attorney general's assertion that such action was impossible in support of its holding.

89. 130 U.S. 581 (1889.)

90. See *Ekiu v. United States,* 142 U.S. 651 (1892) (executive fact-finding in "public charge" exclusion unreviewable); *Fong Yue Ting v. United States,* 149 U.S. 698 (1892).

91. *Yamataya v. Fisher,* 189 U.S. 86 (1903).

92. See Hiroshi Motomura, "Immigration Law after a Century of Plenary Power: Phantom Constitutional Norms and Statutory Interpretation," 100 *Yale L. J.* 545 (1990).

93. Aleinikoff, *Semblances* at 167–169. As the Supreme Court once put it, "Aliens are by definition those outside of this community." *Cabell v. Chavez-Salido,* 454 U.S. 432, 440 (1982).

94. *Harisiades v. Shaughnessy,* 342 U.S. 580 (1952).

95. *Id.* at 600. (Douglas, J., dissenting).

96. See Aleinikoff, *Semblances* at 173.

97. *Hamdi v. Rumsfeld,* 124 S. Ct. 2633 (2004).

98. This is a process that recalls the Book of Job: "The serving maids look on me as a foreigner, a stranger, never seen before." See Bonnie Honig, *Democracy and the Foreigner* 34 (2001).

99. Aleinikoff, *Semblances* at 5.

100. Neuman, *Strangers* at 136–138.

101. See, e.g., *Padilla v. Hanft,* 2005 U.S. App. LEXIS 28229 (4th Cir. December 21, 2005); *Reno v. AADC, supra.*

102. 142 *Congressional Record* S4600 (statement of Sen. Roth) (emphasis added); see also 142 *Congressional Record* H2376–87, H2458–59 (statement of Rep. Becerra) (arguing that although deportation is an acceptable punishment, permanent exile is too harsh).

103. One might, however, consider the long-term consequences of deporting parents of U.S. citizen children who may remain behind.

104. See, e.g., Charles A. Radin, "A Homeland but Not Home: Young Cape Verdeans Face Grim Realities," *Boston Globe,* Sept. 6, 1999, A1; Larry Rohter, "In U.S. Deportation Policy, a Pandora's Box," *New York Times,* Aug. 10, 1997, A1.

105. Margaret H. Taylor and T. Alexander Aleinikoff, "Deportation of Criminal Aliens: A Geopolitical Perspective," §III.C, http://www.iadialog.org (June 1998) (on file with the Harvard Law School Library).

106. See, e.g., Peter H. Schuck and John Williams, "Removing Criminal Aliens: The Pitfalls and Promises of Federalism," 22 *Harv. J. L. & Pub. Pol'y* 367 at 368–376.

107. 8 U.S.C. §§1101(a)(43)(G) and 1101(a)(48), taken together, could result in a

permanent resident convicted of petty larceny and given a one-year suspended sentence being deported as an aggravated felon.

108. The scapegoat, as Bonnie Honig notes, need not be a foreigner, "but rather anyone whom the community can successfully . . . cast as one." *Democracy and the Foreigner* 34.

109. Emile Durkheim, *The Division of Labor in Society* 102 (George Simpson trans., 1960).

2. Antecedents

1. Romantic depictions of the ideal tend to ignore this fact. See, e.g., J. Hector St. John de Crèvecœur, *Letters from an American Farmer,* 1782 (London: J. M. Dent & Sons, 1971, Letter III, 42), describing how Europeans who had been "mowed down by want, hunger and war" could take root and flourish.

2. "Address to the Members of the Volunteer Association and Other Inhabitants of the Kingdom of Ireland Who Have Lately Arrived in the City of New York, December 2, 1783," in *The Writings of George Washington,* vol. 27, 254 (John C. Fitzpatrick ed., 1938).

3. See T. H. Marshall, *Class, Citizenship, and Social Development* (1964); K. Karst, *Belonging to America: Equal Citizenship and the Constitution* (1989); Linda Bosniak, "Citizenship Denationalized," 7 *Indiana Journal of Global Legal Studies* 447–509 (2000); Linda Bosniak, "Universal Citizenship and the Problem of Alienage," 94 *Nw. U. L. Rev.* 963–982 (2000); Leti Volpp, " 'Obnoxious to Their Very Nature': Asian Americans and Constitutional Citizenship," 5 *Citizenship Studies* 57 (2001); Kunal M. Parker, "Citizenship as Refusal. 'Outing' the Nation of Immigrants: State, Citizenship, and Territory: The Legal Construction of Immigrants in Antebellum Massachusetts," 19 *Law and Hist. Review* 583 (2001).

4. See Moon Ho-Jung, *Coolies and Cane: Race, Labor, and Sugar in the Age of Emancipation* (2006).

5. *New York Times,* December 10, 1852 (quoted in Moon Ho-Jung, "Outlawing 'Coolies': Race, Nation, and Empire in the Age of Emancipation," 57 *American Quarterly.* 677, 682 (2005).

6. The primary politico-legal orientation of Fuller, Brewer, and Field was laissez-faire capitalism. They were strong believers in substantive due process as a protection for business interests. David Brewer said in 1891 that "absolute and eternal justice forbid that any private property [be] destroyed in the interests of public health, morals or welfare." Henry J. Abraham, *Justices and Presidents: A Political History of Appointments to the Supreme Court* 148 (2d ed. 1985); Melvin I. Urofsky, *A March of Liberty: A Constitutional History of the United States* 61–65 (1988).

7. *Fong Yue Ting,* 149 U.S. 698, 740–756 (Brewer, J., dissenting); 756–757 (Field, J., dissenting).

8. Kettner, *Development* at 4 (before the Tudor period, "there appears to have been no firm sense of a 'fixed' national status identified with a more or less specific complex of rights from which 'non-nationals' were excluded." See also J. Mervyn Jones, *British Nationality Law* 1–4 (1956).

9. Kettner, *Development* at 5. An important legal distinction between the two groups was a restriction on the rights of aliens to hold land and to pass it to their descendants. A corollary to this was that aliens could not exercise franchises or hold offices for which the ownership of real property was a prerequisite.

10. Blackstone had suggested that aliens were "such persons as are of so mean a situation as to be esteemed to have no will of their own." Quoted in Chilton Williamson, *American Suffrage from Property to Democracy, 1760–1860* 11 (1960); see also Judith N. Shklar, *American Citizenship: The Quest for Inclusion* 37 (1991).

11. William S. Holdsworth, *History of English Law,* ix, 72, 93–99 (1926).

12. Kettner, *Development* at 8.

13. *Id.* at 173; see also Rogers M. Smith, *Civic Ideals: Conflicting Visions of Citizenship in U.S. History* 70–86 (1997) (analyzing the evolution of conceptions of citizenship throughout the colonial period).

14. Shklar, *Quest* at 37

15. See, e.g., Jill Lepore, *New York Burning: Liberty, Slavery, and Conspiracy in Eighteenth-Century Manhattan* xi (2005).

16. Kettner, *Development* at 65.

17. The Virginia Charter of 1606, for example, stated that "all and every Persons being our Subjects, which shall dwell and inhabit within . . . [the] several Colonies and Plantations, and every of their children, which shall happen to be born within any of the Limits and Precincts of the said several Colonies and Plantations, shall HAVE and enjoy all Liberties, Franchises, and Immunities . . . as if they had been abiding and born, within this our Realm of England." "Virginia Charter of 1606," in *The Federal and State Constitutions, Colonial Charters, and Other Organic Laws* vol. 7, 3788 (Francis Newton Thorpe ed., 1909); Kettner, *Development* at 65.

18. See, e.g., the 1620 Charter of New England, in 3 Thorpe, *Federal and State Constitutions* at 1839 (guaranteeing "liberties, and franchises, and Immunities of free Denizens and natural Subjects"); 1622 Charter of Connecticut, reprinted in 1 *id.* at 5 (guaranteeing "liberties and Immunities of free and natural Subjects"); 1629 Charter of the Massachusetts Bay Colony, in 3 *id.* at 1857 (guaranteeing the "liberties and Immunities of free and natural subjects"); 1632 Charter of Maine, in 3 *id.* at 1635 (guaranteeing "liberties[,] Franchises and Immunityes of or belonging to any of the natural borne subjects"); 1632 Charter of Maryland, in 3 *id.* at 1682 (guaranteeing "Privileges, Franchises and Liberties"); 1663 Charter of Carolina, in 5 *id.* at 2747 (holding "liberties, franchises, and privileges" inviolate); 1663 Charter of the Rhode Island and Provi-

dence Plantations, in 6 *id.* at 3220 (guaranteeing "libertyes and immunityes of free and natural subjects"); and 1732 Charter of Georgia, in 2 *id.* at 773 (guaranteeing "liberties, franchises and immunities of free denizens and natural born subjects").

19. "A denizen of England by letters patent for life, in tayl or in fee, whereby he becomes a subject in regard of his person." *Craw v. Ramsey,* Vaughan's Reports, 278. This status, as we shall see, was later unsuccessfully invoked by Chinese noncitizens in support of their claims of rights.

20. Blackstone's Commentaries on the Laws of England 374. The term was roughly interchangeable with "subject" in some parts of America. The Virginia Resolves, for example, provided that "The Colonists aforesaid are declared entitled to all Liberties, Privileges, and Immunities of Denizens and natural Subjects, to all Intents and Purposes, as if they had been abiding and born within the Realm of *England*". See *United States v. Villato,* 2 U.S. 370 (1797). In 1832, the U.S. Supreme Court wrote of denizenship: "It sometimes means a natural born subject; and sometimes a person who, being an alien, has been denizenized [*sic*] by letters patent of the crown." *Levy v. M'Cartee,* 31 U.S. 102, 118 (1832). Justice McLean made a powerful argument in favor of the concept of denizenship for "free people of color" in his dissent in the *Dred Scott* case. *Scott v. Sandford,* 60 U.S. 393, 562 (1857) (McLean, J., dissenting).

21. Naturalization could be granted only by Parliament, and it conferred a somewhat higher status and a greater array of rights than royal denization. It was difficult to obtain and legally unavailable to some groups, including Catholics and Jews. Kettner, *Development* at 67, 96.

22. *Id.* at 66–71, 78, 101; Lords of Trade to the Lords Justices, Oct. 27, 1698, Cal. State Paper, Col., vol. 16, 510–511 (cited in Kettner, *Development* at 95).

23. Baseler, *Asylum for Mankind: America, 1607–1800* 62 (1998).

24. Preamble to "an Act for naturalizing such foreign Protestants, and others therein mentioned, as are settled, or shall settle, in any of his Majesty's Colonies in America." 13 Geo. II, c. 7 (1740); Leo F. Stock, ed., *Proceedings and Debates of the British Parliaments Respecting North America, 1452–1754* vol. 5, 15, 17–18n (1924); Kettner, *Development* at 74.

25. In 1756, Parliament also granted authority to the king to commission foreigners as officers and engineers in colonial regiments. In 1761, Parliament granted a right to special naturalization to certain foreign Protestants who had served or would serve for two years in North America. 2 Geo III, c. 25 (1761); Kettner, *Development* at 77.

26. James Hamilton of Pennsylvania (referring to Germans). See Baseler, *Asylum* at 64 (quoting Sally Schwartz, *A Mixed Multitude: The Struggle for Toleration in Colonial Pennsylvania* 204, 258 (1987).

27. Joseph Willard, *Naturalization in the American Colonies,* 9–10 (1859); Kettner, *Development* at 103–104. The order forbade royal governors either from naturalizing any aliens or from establishing title of any person "to Lands, Tene-

ments & real estates . . . originally granted to, or purchased by Aliens antecedent to naturalization."

28. Distinctions did exist between native-born citizens and naturalized foreigners. After 1701, naturalized aliens were precluded from military commissions, could not sit in Parliament, and could not receive land grants from the king. Baseler, *Asylum* at 55. Catholics could neither vote nor hold office until the end of the eighteenth century, and Jews were disenfranchised until the mid-nineteenth century. Kettner, *Development* at 98–99.

29. Kettner, *Development* at 111.

30. N.C. Col. Recs., I, 639 (cited in Kettner, *Development* at 122).

31. See generally Jamin B. Raskin, "Legal Aliens, Local Citizens: The Historical, Constitutional and Theoretical Meanings of Alien Suffrage," 141 *U. Pa. L. Rev.* 1391, 1399 (1993).

32. Expulsion from England, though never as common a practice as in many other places, had been used against Jews as early as the thirteenth century. W. Cunningham, *Alien Immigrants to England,* 70–89 (Frank Cass 1969) (1897); Baseler, *Asylum* at 28.

33. See, e.g., Walter Raleigh, "A Discourse of the Original and Fundamental Cause of Natural, Arbitrary, Necessary, and Unnatural War," in *The Works of Sir Walter Raleigh, Kt.* vol. 8, 256 (William Oldys and Thomas Birch eds., 1829) (cited in Baseler, *Asylum* at 24).

34. Strong arguments refuting Raleigh's position were also made, and specific concerns were raised about the negative economic effects of rural depopulation.

35. Bernard Bailyn, *Voyagers to the West: A Passage in the People of America on the Eve of the Revolution* 24–27 (1986).

36. Baseler, *Asylum* at 23–25. From 1689 to 1727, at least fifteen English veterans of the Irish wars later served as royal governors. Stephen Saunders Webb, "Army and Empire: English Garrison Government in Britain and America, 1569 to 1763," 34 *William and Mary Quarterly* 15 (1977).

37. Baseler, *Asylum* at 25.

38. *Id.* at 29–30.

39. William Penn, quoted in Walter Allen Knittle, *Early Eighteenth Century Palatine Emigration: A British Government Redemption Project to Manufacture Naval Stores* 27 (1937); Mildred Campbell, "'Of People Too Few or Too Many': The Conflict of Opinion on Population and Its Relation to Emigration," in William Appleton Aiken and Basil Duke Henning, eds., *Conflict in Stuart England: Essays in Honour of Wallace Notestein* (London: Jonathan Cape, 1960) 172, 188–194; Baseler, *Asylum* at 34.

40. Transportation involved forced movement to another territory of the same sovereign. Stock, *Proceedings and Debates,* vol. 1, 288–290, 293, 305; Baseler, *Asylum* at 35.

41. Bailyn, *Voyagers* at 166–189.

42. *Nova Britannia,* p. 23, in Peter Force, *Tracts* vol. 1, quoted in Abbot Emerson

Smith, *Colonists in Bondage: White Servitude and Convict Labor in America, 1607–1776* 9 (1965).

43. Susan M. Kingsbury, ed., *Records of the Virginia Company of London* vol. 3, 221, cited in Smith, *Colonists* at 12; see also Smith, *Colonists* at 12–17, 21.

44. Jones, *American Immigration* at 34.

45. Edmund S. Morgan, *The Puritan Dilemma: The Story of John Winthrop* 136 (2d ed. 1998); Josiah Henry Benton, *Warning Out in New England* 46 (1911).

46. Benton, *Warning Out* 18.

47. *Id.* at 19.

48. Morgan, *Puritan Dilemma* at 85, 92, 169.

49. Cotton Mather had referred to Irish Catholic immigration as the work of Satan. Jones, *British Nationality* at 38.

50. Baseler, *Asylum* at 150.

51. Morgan, *Puritan Dilemma* at 103–114, 131–137.

52. Act LI, 1643, in William Waller Hening, ed., *Statutes at Large of Virginia: Being a Collection of All the Laws of Virginia from . . . 1619*, vol. 1, 268–269 (1809); Baseler, *Asylum* at 73.

53. Kettner, *Development* at 109. A 1729 Pennsylvania law aimed at "lewd, idle and ill-affected persons' and imposed a per capita head tax on immigrants, with a special fee also charged to importers of Irish servants and redemptioners.

54. *Conn. Col. Recs.*, V, 405–406, VII, 521; X, 450–451 (cited in *id.* at 108).

55. Baseler, *Asylum* at 8.

56. *Jours. Cont. Cong.*, 49. Resolutions in June of 1776 provided that "no man in these colonies, charged with being a tory, or unfriendly to the cause of American Liberty" should be injured or otherwise disturbed, unless the proceedings were authorized by Congress or local governments. Kettner, *Development* at 178 (citing *Jours. Cont. Cong.*, IV, 205).

57. Gerald Neuman has pointed out to me that the notion that aliens owe allegiance and could be guilty of treason was standard English law as well.

58. *Jours. Cont. Cong.*, V, 475–476.

59. Kettner, *Development* at 180.

60. Thomas Jefferson, *Notes on the State of Virginia*, 281 (Merrill D. Peterson ed., 1984): "Proceedings as to Tories The measures taken with regard of the estates and possessions of the rebels, commonly called Tories."

61. Kettner, *Development* at 183–184.

62. See Baseler, *Asylum* at 199–208.

63. Act of 1782, in Allen D. Candler, ed., *The Colonial Records of the State of Georgia* vol. 19, pt. 2, 162–164 (1904–1916) (quoted in Baseler, *Asylum* at 147). The law provided "that no Person a native of Scotland, shall be permitted or allowed to emigrate into this State with intent to Settle within the same, or to carry on Commerce or other trade, Profession or business."

64. Moses Coit Tyler, *Patrick Henry* 257–259 (1899).

65. The Treaty of 1783 provided for the payment of debts to "real British subjects."

The British approach (that the Tories were British subjects) was eventually accepted by the Continental Congress, but the cost of returning confiscated estates and repaying debts fell on state and local governments. See generally Kettner, *Development* at 184.

66. Baseler, *Asylum* at 202, n. 30.

67. Kettner, *Development* at 160–170.

68. The idea was that in a revolution each person has the right to take a side, but one must do so within a reasonable period of time. *Id.* at 194.

69. *Martin v. Commonwealth,* 1 Mass. 347, 391, 392 (Mass. 1805). See generally Kettner, *Development* at 198.

70. Act of March 26, 1790, 1 Stat., section 1.

71. See generally John Higham, *Send These to Me: Immigrants in Urban America* 71–80 (rev. ed. 1984); Mark Gibney, "United States Immigration Policy and the 'Huddled Masses' Myth," 3 *Geo. Imm. L. J.* 361 (1989)(contrasting the myth with then-current immigration policies); Gerald Neuman, *Strangers* at 19 (viewing Lazarus's work as a "poetic fiction").

72. The Supreme Court has, however, held that states may not discriminate against nonresident citizens for purposes of providing public benefits. *Saenz v. Roe,* 526 U.S. 489 (1999).

73. "Report of George Goode . . . on the Law of Settlement and Removal of the Poor," H.C. no. 675 of 1851, 11, quoted in S. and B. Webb, *English Poor Law History* pt. 1, 318 (1927), cited in Jane Perry Clark, *Deportation of Aliens from the United States to Europe* 33 (1969).

74. Webb and Webb, *id.* at 322–323; Clark, *Deportation* at 34.

75. See Ruth Wallis Herndon, *Unwelcome Americans: Living on the Margins in Early New England* at 1, 2 (2001); see also Benton, *Warning Out*.

76. Part of the rationale for banishment was that no police force existed to monitor potentially dangerous vagabonds. Douglas Lamar Jones, "The Strolling Poor: Transiency in Eighteenth-Century Massachusetts," 8 *Journal of Social History* 28–54 (1975).

77. Benton, *Warning Out* at 19, 22–26, 29.

78. Benjamin J. Klebaner, "State and Local Immigration Regulation in the United States before 1882," 3 *International Review of Social History* 271 n., 270, 290–295 (1958), citing David Pulsifer, ed., *Records of the Colony of New Plymouth . . . Laws 1623–1682* (1861); see also Clark, *Deportation* at 35.

79. See generally Emberson Edward Proper, *Colonial Immigration Laws: A Study of the Regulation of Immigration by the English Colonies in America* (1900).

80. It is interesting to note that this statute was repealed in 1797 and replaced by one that banned only the immigration of convicts. Klebaner, "Regulation" at 292.

81. See generally Lamar Jones, "Strolling Poor."

82. Moreover, in many colonies, aliens could not vote.

83. Lamor Jones, "Strolling Poor" at 29.

84. Herndon, *Unwelcome* at 5. To be a bit more technical, this distinction is perhaps most similar to that between nonimmigrants and lawful permanent resident aliens. See also *id.* at 85–86.
85. Benton, *Warning Out* at 58.
86. Herndon, *Unwelcome* at 6.
87. Benton, *Warning Out* at 42.
88. Herndon, *Unwelcome* at 6.
89. *Id.* at 8.
90. Lamar Jones, "Strolling Poor" at 46, citing *Mass. Acts and Resolves* ch. 23, 52–53 (1796–1797).
91. Herndon, *Unwelcome* at 18–21, Appendix Figure A5 at 205;
92. *Id.* at 39–41.
93. Lamar Jones, "Strolling Poor" at 46.
94. *Mass. Acts and Resolves* ch. 28, 64–68 (1692–1714).
95. Lamar Jones "Strolling Poor" at 47, citing *Town Records of Salem,* vol, 112.
96. *Id.* at 48, citing *Mass. Acts and Resolves* ch. 59, 479–493 (1792–1793); see also *id.* at 49.
97. Parker, "Citizenship as Refusal" at 586. Article 4 of the Articles of Confederation expressly excluded "paupers, vagabonds and fugitives from justice" from the guarantee of "all privileges and immunities of free citizens in the several States." Neuman, *Strangers* at 23. Indeed, it was not until the twentieth century that U.S. law recognized a right to mobility for poor people. See *Edwards v. California,* 314 U.S. 160 (1941); *Shapiro v. Thompson,* 394 U.S. 618 (1969) (state residence requirements for welfare benefits held unconstitutional).
98. See Baseler, *Asylum* at 198 (citing "Act for the Better Settlement and Relief of the Poor" (1788, ch. 62), Laws of the State of New York Passed at the Sessions of the Legislature Held in the Years 1785, 1786, 1787, and 1788, Inclusive 731–744 (Albany: Weed Parsons and Company, 1886).
99. Klebaner, "Regulation" at 290.
100. *The Laws of Massachusetts, 1780 to 1800* vol. 2, 628–629. (1886).
101. Neuman, *Strangers* at 25, citing Act of Feb. 26, 1794, ch. 32, §§10, 13, 1794 Mass. Acts & Laws 375, 379, 383.
102. It was not until 1859, however, that the reach of this law was explicitly limited to U.S. noncitizens. Neuman, *Strangers* at 201 n. 70, citing Mass. Gen. Stat. ch. 71, §52 (1859).
103. See statistics cited by Baseler, *Asylum* at 198 fn. 20.
104. Smith, *Colonists* at 90.
105. J. M. Beattie, *Crime and the Courts in England 1660–1800* 473 (1986). Though forced "abjuration of the realm" would be the more direct analogy to modern deportation, it was much less common during this period.
106. *Id.* at 479–480.
107. 4 GEO. I, c. II.
108. Smith, *Colonists* at 111, 117.

109. Some attempts at regulation of the trade were made as early as 1718 in Maryland and 1722 in Virginia. Pennsylvania and New Jersey levied duties, which were ultimately disallowed by the Privy Council. *Id.* at 120.

110. See, e.g., Benjamin Franklin, "Felons and Rattlesnakes," printed in the *Pennsylvania Gazette,* May 9, 1751; *The Papers of Benjamin Franklin* vol. 4, 130 (Leonard W. Labaree ed., 1961).

111. See Baseler, *Asylum* at 5.

112. *Executive Journal of the Council of Colonial Virginia,* IV, 281–282 (quoted in Smith, *Colonists* at 128).

113. Smith, *Colonists* at 129.

114. *Id.* at 130.

115. "Felons and Rattlesnakes," printed in the *Pennsylvania Gazette,* May 9, 1751. Reprinted in *The Papers of Benjamin Franklin* vol. 4, 130 (Labaree ed., 1961).

116. Baseler, *Asylum* at 125.

117. Smith, *Colonists* at 124.

118. "Congress to the British Secretary for Foreign Affairs," *Journals of the Continental Congress,* vol. 34, 528–529 (quoted in Baseler, *Asylum* at 164).

119. "On Sending Felons to America" in Benjamin Franklin, *Writings,* 1142–1144 (J. A. Leo Lemay ed., 1987).

120. *Journals of the Continental Congress,* vol. 34, 528. (quoted in Baseler, *Asylum* at 164).

121. See Gerald Neuman, "The Lost Century of American Immigration Law (1776–1875)" 93 *Colum. L. Rev.* 1833 at 1843 (1993), citing Act of Oct. 1788, 1788 Conn. Acts & Laws 368; *Id.,* citing Pa. Act of Amr. 27, 1789, ch. 463. New Jersey emulated this provision in 1797. Act of Jan. 28, 1797, ch. 611, §3, 1797 N.J. Acts 131, 131.

122. Banishment as a criminal sanction is now prohibited in at least fifteen state constitutions and almost invariably overruled by courts in other states. See generally Gerald R. Miller, "Note, Banishment—A Medieval Tactic in Modern Criminal Law," 5 *Utah L. Rev.* 365 (1957); Wm. Garth Snider, "Banishment: The History of Its Use and a Proposal for Its Abolition under the First Amendment," 24 *N.E. J. on Crim. & Civ. Con.* 455 (1998). Conditional pardons have been rejected when a defendant is ordered to leave the United States. See, e.g., *United States v. Jalilian,* 896 F.2d 447, 448–449 (10th Cir. 1990) (requiring defendant to leave the country as a condition of probation exceeds the authority of the sentencing judge, as a "*de facto* deportation").

123. See Neuman, *Strangers* at 23.

124. See, e.g., *Aldridge v. Commonwealth,* 4 Va. 447; 1824 Va. LEXIS 60; 2 Va. Cas. 447 (1824)("it is undeniable that [the Bill of Rights] never was contemplated, or considered . . . to apply to our slave population [nor to] free blacks and mulattoes . . . [N]obody has ever questioned the power of the Legislature, to deny free blacks and mulattoes [the right to vote]").

125. Neuman, *Strangers* at 23 (citing Alabama, 1819, and Mississippi, 1817).

126. Carl A. Brasseaux, *The Founding of New Acadia: The Beginnings of Acadian Life in Louisiana, 1765–1804* (1987); Warren A. Perrin, "The Petition to Obtain an Apology for the Acadian Deportation: 'Warren A. Perrin, et al. versus Great Britain, et al.,'" 27 *S.U. L. Rev.* 1 (1999).

127. The Treaty of Utrecht provided that "All Nova Scotia or Acadia . . . are yielded and made over to the queen of Great Britain, and to her crown for ever" (April 13, 1713).

128. Naomi E. S. Griffiths, *The Contexts of Acadian History 1686–1784* 35 (1992) (quoting Treaty of Utrecht); Bona Arsenault, *History of the Acadians* 75 (1988). A royal letter, issued on June 23, 1713, had further instructed the governor of the colony of the rights due the Acadians. The governor's commission had made clear that the Acadians could "retain and Enjoy their said lands . . . as fully and freely as the others our Subjects do, or may possess their lands and Estates, or to sell the same if they shall rather chose to remove elsewhere." See Griffiths, *Contexts of Acadian History* at 35.

129. Arthur G. Doughty, *The Acadian Exiles* 69 (1920).

130. Sally Ross and Alphonse Deveau, *The Acadians of Nova Scotia: Past and Present* 57–60 (1992). Brasseaux, *Founding* at 89. The oath, as taken, was in fact unqualified, but Governor Phillips reportedly gave verbal assurances that in the event of war, the Acadians would not have to bear arms against the British, French, or Indians.

131. Naomi E. S. Griffiths, *The Acadians, Creation of a People* 27 (1973).

132. *In re Halladjian,* 174 F. 834 (1st Cir. D. Mass. 1909).

133. Griffiths, *Contexts of Acadian History* at 36.

134. Georges Arsenault, *The Island Acadian 1720–1980* 33 (1989).

135. The Grand-Pré National Historic Site, operated by Parks Canada, contains a memorial church, a statue of Evangeline—heroine of Longfellow's poem about the Acadians—and a commemorative deportation cross. Apparently, the order had never actually been made by the king.

136. Fred Anderson, *Crucible of War: The Seven Years' War and the Fate of the Empire in British North America, 1754–1766* 113 (2000).

137. The war began on May 18, 1756. Rene Babineau, *Brief History of Acadia 1604–1988* 6–7, 8–9, 32–33 (1988).

138. The precise number of Acadians who were expelled is unknown. By some accounts, a number of Acadians were sheltered by local indigenous peoples who had sided with the French during the war. See Daniel N. Paul, *We Were Not Savages: A Micmac Perspective on the Collision of European and Aboriginal Civilization* 142 (1993).

139. Quoted in 2 Justin Winsor, *Memorial History of Boston* 125 (1880–1881).

140. See "The Petition to Obtain an Apology for the Acadian Deportation: 'Warren A. Perrin, et al. versus Great Britain, et al.'" (asserting that Pitt said it was "an outrageous action and a violation of the human rights and liberties of the Acadians").

141. Carl A. Brasseaux, *Scattered to the Wind: Dispersal and Wanderings of the Acadians, 1755–1809* (1991).

142. On July 9, 1756, a special act was passed to empower the justices to "bind out" Acadian children younger than twenty-one, for service from three to twelve weeks. Doughty, *The Acadian Exiles* 139. See also Pierre Daigle, *Tears, Love, and Laughter: The Story of the Cajuns* 49–50 (1987) (asserting that "[m]any of the Acadians, particularly the children, were sold into slavery").

143. See James Oldham and Michael J. Wishnie, "The Historical Scope of Habeas Corpus and *INS v. St. Cyr*," 16 *Geo. Immigr. L. J.* 485, 498 nn. 66–68 (2002) (citing *The Colonial Records of South Carolina: Journal of the Commons House of Assembly, 1755–1757* xii (Terry W. Lipscomb ed., 1989).

144. See Geoffrey Gilbert Plank, *An Unsettled Conquest: The British Campaign against the Peoples of Acadia* 152–153, 156 (2001). Miquilon is an island off the coast of Newfoundland.

145. See Oldham and Wishnie, "Historical Scope" at 498 n. 67.

146. Eventually, the governor did send those Acadians considered the most dangerous to North Carolina and Virginia.

147. Plank, *Unsettled* 120–121.

148. Plank, *Unsettled* 104 (the Acadians were uniformly referred to as "French"); Griffiths, *Contexts of Acadian History* at 36 (Acadians were considered "border people of the English empire" and viewed as "temporarily conquered people" or "prospective British subjects"); see generally Oldham and Wishnie, "Historical Scope."

149. *Act for the Quieting of Possessions of the Protestant Grantees of the Lands Formerly Occupied by the French Inhabitants,* S.N.S. 1759, c. 3; see generally D. H. Brown, "Foundations of British Policy in the Acadian Expulsion: A Discussion of Land Tenure and the Oath of Allegiance" 55 *Dalhousie Rev.* 709 (1978).

150. J. B. Brebner, *New England Outpost: Acadia before the Conquest of Canada* (1927).

151. Nova Scotian Archives, 4 *Council*, 24 Mar., 1764, at B13.

152. William F. Rushton, *The Cajuns* 319 (1979).

153. Laws of quarantine developed early in the New World as concerns grew about the health of newcomers. After the Revolution, many states continued such laws in force. See Kettner, *Development* at 110.

154. *Id.* at 127.

155. For a discussion of this issue in the current era, see Aleinikoff, *Semblances* at 147–152,

156. See Baseler, *Asylum* at 196, quoting Drew R. McCoy, *The Elusive Republic: Political Economy in Jeffersonian America* (1980).

157. "Lieutenant Governor Colden to the Board of Trade, New York, Sept. 25, 1761," *N.Y. Col. Docs.,* vol. 7, 469–470 (quoted in Kettner, *Development* at 110).

158. See Baseler, *Asylum* at 192.

159. Jones, *British Nationality* at 37.
160. Edmund S. Morgan, *American Slavery, American Freedom: The Ordeal of Colonial Virginia* 376 (1975).
161. See generally Smith, *Freedom's Fetters*.
162. See *N.Y. Times v. Sullivan,* 376 U.S. 254, 275 (1964) ("although the Sedition Act was never tested in this Court, the attack upon its validity has carried the day in the court of history" [footnote omitted]).
163. A subtler version of this sort of argument may differentiate the rights of short-term visitors from those of permanent residents.
164. See David Cole, "Jurisdiction and Liberty: Habeas Corpus and Due Process as Limits on Congress's Control of Federal Jurisdiction" 86 *Geo. L.J.* 2481 (1998).
165. See Thomas Jefferson, "The Kentucky Resolution," in *Documents of American History* 181 (6th ed. 1958).
166. See generally Daniel Kanstroom, "Crying Wolf or a Dying Canary," 25 *N.Y.U. Rev. L. & Soc. Change* 435 (1999).
167. Joanne B. Freeman, *Affairs of Honor: National Politics in the New Republic* (2001).
168. There were also, of course, "ancient disagreements between commercial and agrarian forces, creditors and debtors and New Englanders and Virginians." See *id.* at 10.
169. See generally Baseler, *Asylum*.
170. *Id.*
171. Smith, *Freedom's Fetters* at 12. Among the concerns of the Federalists, the "society of illuminati" loomed especially large. A purportedly secret organization that extended throughout the world, it was thought by some Federalists to have as its aim the destruction of all religion and all governments and to have provoked events ranging from the French Revolution to the revolution led by former slaves in Santo Domingo. See John C. Miller, Crisis in Freedom: The Alien and Sedition Acts 11 (1951).
172. Miller, *Crisis* at 15 (quoting the *Salem Gazette,* Nov. 30, 1798). The more strident Federalists, with a mission of saving the United States from the "evils of unlimited Democracy," viewed extreme democracy as essentially incompatible with order.
173. Quoted in Smith, *Freedom's Fetters* at 159.
174. The Jay Treaty adopted the British position that goods belonging to belligerent nations were subject to seizure even if found on neutral ships. The Franco-American Treaty, conversely, held that free ships made free goods. France, therefore, could not seize British goods on American vessels. See Gerald H. Clarfield, *Timothy Pickering and American Diplomacy, 1795–1800* (1969); Samual Flagg Bemis, *Jay's Treaty: A Study in Commerce and Diplomacy* 265, 269–273 (1962).
175. See Miller, *Crisis* at 46.

176. See generally Albert H. Bowman, *Struggle for Neutrality: Franco-American Diplomacy during the Federalist Era* 285 (1974).

177. Adet sent a diplomatic note to Timothy Pickering announcing a new French policy to treat neutrals "as they allow themselves to be treated by the British." Pickering's response, drafted under time pressure at the behest of Washington, was indignant, legalistic, and politically inept. Clarfield, *Pickering and Diplomacy* at 51–66. See Adet to Pickering, October 27, 1796, in Clarfield, *Pickering and Diplomacy* 67 n. 76.

178. Oliver Wolcott, Jr., for example, had written to Hamilton that it would be a disgrace to bend any more to the will of the French than had already been done. Wolcott to Hamilton, March 31, 1797, *Hamilton Papers;* Clarfield, *Pickering and Diplomacy* at 102 n. 31. Hamilton, however, was quite concerned about the consequences of war with France. See Clarfield, *Pickering and Diplomacy* at 103 n. 33.

179. The Directory was composed of five men who held executive power in France pursuant to the constitution of year III (i.e., 1795) after the French Revolution. See Martyn Lyons, *France under the Directory* (1975).

180. When Adams learned of the attempted coup d'état on September 4, 1797, in which a Royalist plot was averted by the Directory, his concerns about the unfriendly attitude in Paris toward the United States became even greater. John Ferling, *John Adams: A Life* 351 (1992).

181. Ferling, *Adams* at 355, 357. See generally David McCullough, *John Adams* (2001). See also Broadus Mitchell, 2 *Alexander Hamilton: The National Adventure, 1788–1804* 223–236 (1962). Adams, fearing Hamilton's ultimate agenda and his growing influence, described him as "the most restless, impatient, artful, indefatigable and unprincipled Intriguer in the United States." Ferling, *Adams* at 361.

182. A resolution to that effect was introduced by the Republicans on March 30, 1798. Clarfield, *Pickering and Diplomacy* at 153.

183. Ferling, *Adams* at 354.

184. Clarfield, *Pickering and Diplomacy* at 6.

185. *Id.* (quoting *Albany Sentinel*, Oct. 12, 1798; *Porcupine's Gazette*, July 27, 1798; and *Pennsylvania Herald and York General Advertiser*, Aug. 1, 1798).

186. Miller, *Crisis* at 21.

187. See "President's Proclamation on National Day of Prayer and Remembrance for the Victims of the Terrorist Attacks on Sept. 11," *U.S. Newswire*, Sept. 13, 2001 ("Civilized people around the world denounce the evildoers who devised and executed these terrible attacks.").

188. A prominent Federalist noted in January 1799 that "our Constitution and Administration are marked with mildness, and evildoers are encouraged to think coercion is not a characteristic of either." Miller, *Crisis* at 20 n. 81 (quoting Uriah Tracy to Jonathan Trumbull, Jan. 2, 1799).

189. *Id.* at 41 (quoting *Albany Sentinel,* Aug. 7, 1798; *Porcupine's Gazette,* July 3, 1798; and Letter from James McHenry to Timothy Pickering, Sept. 10, 1798).
190. Miller, *Crisis* at 41, 42 (quoting Letter from Noah Webster to Timothy Pickering, July 7, 1797), 44.
191. Jefferson's ultimate victory in the election of 1800 was an example of a successful political strategy based in part on immigrants' votes.
192. Miller, *Crisis* at 43.
193. Aleine Austin, *Mathew Lyon; "New Man" of the Democratic Revolution, 1749–1822* 95 (1981).
194. Robert Goodloe Harper said, "the time is now come when it will be proper to declare that nothing but birth shall entitle a man to citizenship in this country." Smith, *Freedom's Fetters* at 27 n. 16.
195. Ch. 54, 1 Stat. 566 (repealed by Act of Apr. 14, 1802, ch. 28, 2 Stat. 153). It also required noncitizens to register within forty-eight hours of their entry. Resident aliens were to report within six months after the bill became law.
196. A major difficulty for the Federalists, however, was that the states implemented naturalization during this time. Pennsylvania, for example, permitted naturalization and granted a right to vote after two years residence. Differentiation between native-born and naturalized citizens was proposed by Harrison Gray Otis, who sought to exclude in the future all foreign born from "all offices of honor, trust or profit in the government of the United States." See Frank George Franklin, *The Legislative History of Naturalization in the United States* 70–71 (1969). The legislatures of Massachusetts and Connecticut set forth a proposed constitutional amendment that would render any foreigners who had been naturalized since the Declaration of Independence ineligible to become a representative, senator, or president. The amendment was aimed at Albert Gallatin, who had been born in Switzerland. As the *Albany Sentinel* saw it, "if the French had an agent in that House it would have been impossible for him to act his part better" (May 25, 1798). Miller, *Crisis* at 48–50.
197. In March 1798, Pickering wrote that nothing would "satisfy the ambitious and rapacious rulers of that nation but universal dominion of the sea as well as of the land with the property of all nations at their disposal, to seize and keep what portion they please." Letter from Pickering to Higginson (Mar. 6, 1798) in *The Timothy Pickering Papers* vol. 8, 187 (1966). Clarfield, *Pickering and Diplomacy* at 144 n. 11.
198. Ferling, *Adams* at 357 n. 22.
199. Alien Enemies Act, ch. 66, 1 Stat. 577 (1798).
200. See 50 U.S.C. §21–24 (2002). The act was upheld by the Supreme Court against constitutional challenge in *Ludecke v. Watkins,* 335 U.S. 160, 171–72 (1948).
201. See Miller, *Crisis* at 51 (citing Harrison Gray Otis).
202. *Abridgement of the Debates of Congress* vol. 2, 257 (New York, 1857); Miller, *Crisis* at 51.

203. Smith, *Freedom's Fetters* at 36–38.

204. Alien Friends Act, ch. 58, 1 Stat. 570, 571 (1798) (expired June 25, 1800).

205. See generally Smith, *Freedom's Fetters* at 51 (Smith citing Senate Records, 5C, 2S, RG, 46 [National Archives].

206. Miller, *Crisis* at 53; Smith, *Freedom's Fetters* at 51–53 (quoting *Aurora,* May 11, 1798).

207. Letter from Jefferson to Madison (May 31, 1798), in *Jefferson's Writings* vol. 7, 261. See also Smith, *Freedom's Fetters* at 53 n. 9.

208. See Smith, *Freedom's Fetters* at 56 (quoting Benjamin Bache, *Aurora,* June 14, 1798).

209. *Id.* at 64 n. 2, quoting *Debates and Proceedings in the Congress of the United States, 1789–1825* 5C, 2S (June 19, 1798) (1985–1986). Opponents of the bills downplayed the assertions of danger cited by the Federalists, seeking proof for their fears and finding none. They also highlighted their confidence in the "upright judges and vigilant magistrates" of the United States who could deal with any actual attempts at treason or sedition by either aliens or citizens under existing laws. See Smith, *Freedom's Fetters* at 63–64.

210. See generally Adrienne Koch and Harry Ammon, "The Virginia and Kentucky Resolutions: An Episode in Jefferson's and Madison's Defense of Civil Liberties," 5 *William & Mary Q.* 145 (1948).

211. James Madison, Speech before the Virginia Assembly (Dec. 21, 1798) 6 *The Writings of James Madison* 360–361 (Gaillard Hunt, ed., 1906).

212. Of course, the normative underpinnings of some Republican opposition to the Alien and Sedition Laws were extremely complex. Representative Baldwin and then-Senator Abraham of Georgia expressed the not atypical Republican fear that the Aliens Act might be the leading edge of an attack by the federal government against slavery: "Congress would again be appealed to . . . for an abolition of slavery." Indeed, some feared that the president might ultimately be authorized to deport slaves from the country as aliens. Miller, *Crisis* at 164 (quoting *Philadelphia Gazette,* Feb. 2, 1799).

213. Smith, *Freedom's Fetters* at 83, 56 (citing *Aurora,* May 29, 1789), 85.

214. *Debates and Proceedings* 5C, 2S, 2007–2010. See Smith, *Freedom's Fetters* at 86.

215. Sewall said that "sovereignty must reside in the government of the United States" and that Congress must have the power "to control public peace and tranquility." *Debates and Proceedings* 5C, 2S, 1957, June 16, 1798.

216. Letter from Pickering to Upham, 1873, in *Life of Pickering* 475 (1867–1873).

217. See generally Neuman, *Strangers* at 3, 54–55 (arguing that this became the dominant approach).

218. *Debates and Proceedings* 2012 (June 1798).

219. See generally Neuman, *Strangers* at 57 n. 34 (quoting John Taylor).

220. See Smith, *Freedom's Fetters* at 85 (quoting *Debates and Proceedings* 5C, 2S, 2008). (June 1798).

221. James Madison, "Report on the Virginia Resolutions, vol. 4 *Debates, Resolutions*

and Other Proceedings, in *Convention on the Adoption of the Federal Constitution* 556 (Jonathan Elliot ed., 2d ed. 1836). See generally Neuman, *Strangers* at 58.

222. Miller, *Crisis* at 163 n. 8 (quoting St. George Tucker, A Letter to a Member of Congress, Virginia, 1799).

223. Smith, *Freedom's Fetters* at 85 (quoting *Debates and Proceedings* 5C, 2S, 2007–2008) (June 1798).

224. The *Hartford Courant* wrote of the new laws, "[T]he only thing that it is wanting to establish their complete popularity, is a prompt and faithful execution of them." *Porcupine's Gazette,* July 31, 1799, quoted in Miller, *Crisis* at 186.

225. Indeed, a substantial number of French refugees did leave the United States during this period. See generally Frances S. Childs, *French Refugee Life in the United States, 1790–1800* (1940).

226. James Morton Smith, "The Enforcement of the Alien Friends Act of 1798," 41 *Miss. Valley Historical Rev.* 85, 87 (1954).

227. His full name was Constantin Francois Chasseboeuf, Comte de Volney. See Smith, *Freedom's Fetters* at 87.

228. See Smith, *Freedom's Fetters* at 161 n. 6 (reporting that some fifteen ships sailed in two months). See generally Childs, *French Refugee Life.*

229. See generally George W. Kyte, "A Spy on the Western Waters: the Military Intelligence Mission of General Collot in 1796," 34 *Miss. Valley Historical Rev.* 427, 427–442 (1947).

230. Smith, *Freedom's Fetters* at 167–169. Collot was apparently a British prisoner of war, though somehow at liberty. Pickering suggested that he might be compelled to place himself under British jurisdiction. See Letter from Pickering to the President, Aug. 1, 1799, in *Pickering Papers* vol. 9, 525 (1966). Although Collot's activities were closely monitored, he was neither arrested nor deported. He remained in North America until sometime in August 1800. See Kyte, "The Detention of General Collot," 3 *William and Mary Q.* 628, 630 (1949).

231. Letter from Jean-Antoine B. Rozier to Moreau de St. Mèry, June 27, 1798, in *Moreau de St. Mèry, 1793–1798,* 253 (1947).

232. Letters from Rozier to St. Mèry, 253 (citing diary entry of July 14, 1798). See also Smith, *Freedom's Fetters* at 100.

233. See generally Smith, *Freedom's Fetters* at 100.

234. See Miller, *Crisis* at 99 (citing Letter from Richard Harrison to Pickering, July 13, 1798).

235. *Id.* at 100.

236. Smith, *Freedom's Fetters* at 173. If so, it was part of a successful strategy that paid off for the Republicans in the elections of 1800.

237. Miller, *Crisis* at 102.

238. Letter from Adams to Pickering, Aug. 13, 1799, in C. F. Adams, *The Works of John Adams, with Life* vol. 9, 13–14 (1854).

239. Smith, *Freedom's Fetters* at 175.

240. Jefferson, *Works,* vol. 7, 310; *William and Mary Q.* 147 (April 1948); Miller, *Crisis* at 134.

241. Federalists such as Joseph Hopkinson Miller, *Crisis* at 192 worried about the future effects of this trend: "the American knee shall bend before the footstool of foreigners and the dearest rights and interests of our country await on their nod." Miller, *Crisis* at 192.

242. Miller, *Crisis* at 75.

243. William Blackstone, *Commentaries on the Laws of England* 150 (repr. ed. 1979).

244. Aleinikoff, *Semblances* at 99.

245. See, e.g., Phillip P. Frickey, "Domesticating Federal Indian Law," 81 *U. Minn. L. Rev.* 31, 63 (1996); Aleinikoff, *Semblances* at 18–21, 27–28, 95–150.

246. Much removal was ostensibly voluntary, but over time, its voluntarist aspect devolved more and more into force.

247. Native Americans did not achieve full citizenship until 1924. See Act of June 2, 1924, ch. 233, 43 Stat. 253 (codified at 8 U.S.C. 1401[b]).

248. The phrase "plenary power" has been used to describe several distinct concepts: exclusive power; power that may preempt state law; and, most extremely, unlimited power. In the final category, one might distinguish between power unlimited by other constitutional provisions and power unlimited as to the objectives Congress might pursue. See Nell Jessup Newton, "Federal Power over the Indians, Its Sources, Scope, and Limitations," 132 *U. Pa. L. Rev.* 195, 196 n. 3 (1984); see also Felix S. Cohen, *Felix S. Cohen's Handbook of Federal Indian Law* (1982).

249. Frickey, "Domesticating" at 63; Robert N. Clinton, "There is No Federal Supremacy Clause for Indian Tribes," 34 *Ariz. St. L.J.* 113, 116 (2002). Clinton writes: "The . . . doctrine under which Congress claims complete, virtually unlimited, legislative control over any matter involving Indians, including the very continued existence of the Indian tribes, merely constitutes a racist American relic of 'white man's burden' arguments employed to justify American colonialism."

250. Philip P. Frickey, "Marshalling Past and Present: Colonialism, Constitutionalism, and Interpretation in Federal Indian Law," 107 *Harv. L. Rev.* 381 (1993).

251. Treaty with the Delawares, Sept. 17, 1778, 7 Stat. 13. For similar language, see Treaty with the Cherokee Nation, July 2, 1791, art. V, 7 Stat. 39.

252. Treaty of Greenville with the Wyandots and Other Tribes, Aug. 3, 1795, 7 Stat. 49.

253. Treaty of Hopewell with the Cherokee Nation, Jan. 3, 1786, art. IV, 7 Stat. 21. See also Treaty of Hopewell with the Chickasaw Nation, Jan. 3, 1786, art. IV, 7 Stat. 24; Treaty on the Great Miami with the Shawnee, Jan. 31, 1786, art. 7, 7 Stat. 26; Treaty of Fort Harmar with the Wyandot Nation and other tribes, Sept. 27, 1789, art. 9, 7 Stat. 28; Treaty of New York with the Creek Nation,

Aug. 7, 1790, art. 6, 7 Stat. 35; Treaty of Holston with the Cherokee Nation, July 2, 1791, art. 8, 7 Stat. 39. See Clinton, "Federal Supremacy" at 123.

254. 21 U.S. (8 Wheat.) 543 (1823). See generally Robert A. Williams, Jr., *The American Indian in Western Legal Thought* 312–317 (1990); Robert N. Clinton, "The Proclamation of 1763: Colonial Prelude to Two Centuries of Federal-State Conflict over the Management of Indian Affairs," 69 *B.U. L. Rev.* 329, 367–368 (1989); and Robert N. Clinton and Margaret T. Hotopp, "Judicial Enforcement of the Federal Restraints on Alienation of Indian Land: The Origins of Eastern Land Claims," 31 *Me. L. Rev.* 17, 19–37 (1979).

255. *Johnson,* 21 U.S. (8 Wheat.) at 568.

256. *Id.,* citing Vattel, 1.1, c. 19.

257. *Johnson,* 21 U.S. (8 Wheat.) at 573, 587.

258. *Id.* at 574, 587.

259. Frickey, "Marshalling" at 386, 388. See also Aleinikoff, *Semblances* (adopting this phrase to describe the Court's deferential posture in immigration law).

260. *Marbury v. Madison,* 5 U.S. (1 Cranch) 137, 177 (1803).

261. *Johnson,* 21 U.S. (8 Wheat.) at 589.

262. Act of May 28, 1830, ch. 148, 4 Stat. 411; see generally Robert V. Remini, *Andrew Jackson and His Indian Wars* (2001).

263. *A Compilation of the Messages and Papers of the President* vol. 3, 1082 (1897).

264. 130 U.S. 581, 594, 595.

265. *Compilation* at 1083.

266. McKenney is quoted in Patricia Nelson Limerick, *The Legacy of Conquest* 193 (1987); see also *id.* at 194.

267. The law affected only "such tribes or nations of Indians as may choose to exchange the lands where they now reside, and remove there." Indian Removal Act of 1830, ch. 148, 4 stat. 411, 412. See also Clinton, "Federal Supremacy" at 137 n. 63.

268. Rudyard Kipling, "The White Man's Burden," in *Rudyard Kipling's Verse; Inclusive Edition, 1885–1932* at 373 (1938); see Clinton, "Federal Supremacy" at 163 n. 138.

269. 60 U.S. (19 How.) 393, 403 (1856).

270. 112 U.S. 94, 99–102 (1884).

271. 30 U.S. (5 Pet.) 1 (1831); *id.* at 16–20.

272. *Id.* at 15.

273. *Worcester v. Georgia,* 31 U.S. (6 Pet.) 515, 557 (1832); 543.

274. *Id.* at 561. Phillip Frickey has noted that it seems impossible to determine the degree to which this decision resulted from Marshall's "evolving normative perspectives on federal Indian law, rather than from his instinct to centralize in the federal government the authority to resolve questions of national importance." Frickey, "Marshalling" at 405.

275. *Worcester,* 31 U. S. at 561.

276. Frickey, "Marshalling" at 396.

277. Horace Greeley, *The American Conflict* 106 (1864). See also Joseph C. Burke, "The Cherokee Cases: A Study in Law, Politics, and Morality," 21 *Stan L. Rev.* 500 (1969).

278. See generally Grant Foreman, *Indian Removal* 251–312 (1932) (discussing the removal of the Cherokee from Georgia and other southeastern states).

279. See Fergus M. Bordewich, *Killing the White Man's Indian* 47 (1996).

280. See generally Cohen, *Handbook* at 74–92.

281. Actually, there were at least four separate forced marches. See generally J. P. Dunn, *Massacres of the Mountains* (1886); Peter Iverson, *Diné: A History of the Navajos* (2002).

282. See David Roberts, "The Long Walk To Bosque Redondo," *Smithsonian*, Dec. 1997. Available at http://www.smithsonianmag.com/issues/1997/december/bosque.php.; L. R. Bailey, *The Long Walk* (1964).

283. See generally Frederick E. Hoxie, *A Final Promise: The Campaign to Assimilate the Indians, 1880–1920* (1984); Newton, "Federal Power" at 205–206.

284. Act of Mar. 3, 1871, ch. 120, §1, 16 Stat. 566. See also *Antoine v. Washington*, 420 U.S. 194, 201–203 (1975) (discussing the history of the 1871 rider).

285. 31 U.S. at 589.

286. Newton, "Federal Power" at 206, citing H. Jackson, *A Century of Dishonor* 26 (1881); see also James B. Thayer, "Report of the Law Committee," in *Americanizing the American Indians: Writings by the "Friends of the Indian," 1880–1900* 172–174 (Francis Paul Prucha ed., 1973) (1888 report by then-dean of Harvard Law School on the legal status of Indians).

287. See Cohen, *Handbook* at 138.

288. Frickey, "Domesticating" at 45.

289. Act of Mar. 3, 1849, ch. 108, §5, 9 Stat. 395; Newton, "Federal Power" 216.

290. Clinton, "Federal Supremacy" at 165.

291. See William Bradford, "With a Very Great Blame on Our Hearts: Reparations, Reconciliation, and an American Indian Plea for Peace with Justice," 27 *Am. Indian L. Rev.* 1, 24 (2002) (noting that by the 1870s, many thousands had succumbed to starvation as a result of the loss of the buffalo).

292. See, e.g., Bradford at 90, n. 104. (describing the murder of 105 Cheyenne and Arapaho women and children in the village of Sand Creek, Colorado, on Nov. 29, 1864, by Col. Chivington and 700 troops of the U.S. Cavalry); See also Stan Hoig, *The Sand Creek Massacre* (1987); Carol Chomsky, "The United States-Dakota War Trials: A Study in Military Injustice," 43 *Stan L. Rev.* 13 (1990).

293. Donald E. Worcester, *The Apaches: Eagles of the Southwest* 167 (1979).

294. See generally Michael Lieder and Jake Page, *Wild Justice: The People of Geronimo vs. the United States* (1997).

295. *Ex parte Crow Dog*, 109 U.S. 556 (1883); Act of Mar. 3, 1885, ch. 341, §9, 23 Stat. 362, 385.

296. *United States v. Kagama*, 118 U.S. 375 (1886).

297. Frickey, "Domesticating" at 35; Laurence M. Hauptman, "Congress, Plenary

Power, and the American Indian, 1870–1992," in *Exiled in the Land of the Free* 317 (Oren Lyons et al. eds., 1992).

298. *Kagama* at 381–382.

299. See *Benner v. Porter,* 50 U.S. (9 How.) 235 (1850) (territorial courts lack power over exclusive federal cases after statehood).

300. "[W]e think it would be a very strained construction of this clause, that a system of criminal laws for Indians living peaceably in their reservations . . . was authorized by the grant of power to regulate commerce with the Indian tribes." *Kagama,* 118 U.S. 375.

301. See generally Newton, "Federal Power" at 213–214.

302. As Nell Jessup Newton has noted, some aspects of *Kagama* seem positive: the states were in fact "enemies of the Indian tribes," the federal government had always insisted on the exclusive right to deal with the tribes, and the holding "did no violence to the allocation of powers between nation and states in the Constitution." But the Court in *Kagama* failed to consider tribal rights. Indians were not citizens and could not vote. Thus, the principle of consent of the governed was completely ignored. Newton, "Federal Power" at 215–216.

303. Ultimately, *Kagama* was also a pragmatic decision regarding federal power: "It must exist in that government, because it never has existed anywhere else, because the theatre of its exercise is within the geographical limits of the United States, because it has never been denied, and because it alone can enforce its laws on all the tribes." *Kagama* at 384–385.

304. *Kagama,* 118 U.S. 356, 374 (1886).

305. David E. Stannard, *American Holocaust: Columbus and the Conquest of the New World* 11, 261–268 (1992). *Rep. on Indians Taxed and Indians Not Taxed in the U.S. (Except Alaska),* H.R. Misc. Doc. No. 340, pt. 15, at 24 (1st sess., 1894).

306. See William Bradford, "With a Very Great Blame on Our Hearts: Reparations, Reconciliation, and an American Indian Plea for Peace with Justice," 27 *Am. Indian L. Rev.* 1 (2002); Jared Diamond, *Guns, Germs, and Steel: The Fates of Human Societies* (1997); Russell Thornton, *American Indian Holocaust and Survival: A Population since 1492* (1992); E. Wagner Stearn and Allen E. Starn, *The Effect of Smallpox on the Destiny of the Amerindian* 44–45 (1945); Rennard Strickland, "Genocide-at-Law: An Historic and Contemporary View of the Native American Experience," 34 *Kan. L. Rev.* 713, 718 (1986); M. Annette Jaimes, ed., *The State of Native America: Genocide, Colonization, and Resistance* (1992).

307. 187 U.S. 553 (1903). *Sioux Nation v. United States,* 601 F.2d 1157, 1173 (Ct. Cl. 1979) (Nichols, J., concurring), aff'd, 448 U.S. 371 (1980).

308. See also *The Cherokee Tobacco,* 78 U.S. 616, 620–622 (1870) (treating Indian treaties and federal statutes as equivalent sources of law, such that a treaty may be abrogated by a subsequent statute).

309. 187 U.S. 553 at 565.

310. See Ira Berlin, *Generations of Captivity* 3 (2003): "Slavery's moral stench cannot

mask the design of American captivity: to commandeer the labor of the many to make a few rich and powerful. Slavery thus made class as it made race, and in entwining the two processes it mystified both."

311. See, e.g., Sally E. Hadden, *Slave Patrols: Law and Violence in Virginia and the Carolinas* (2001)(considering the slave patrols and pass systems from colonial times through the Civil War).

312. Henry N. Sherwood, "Early Negro Deportation Projects," 2 *Miss. Valley Hist. Rev.* 484, 486 (1916).

313. See generally, Gerald L. Neuman, *Strangers* at 34–40, 208.

314. See generally Ira Berlin, *Slaves without Masters: The Free Negro in the Antebellum South* (1974).

315. See Leon F. Litwack, *North of Slavery: The Negro in the Free States, 1790–1860* 67 (1961); Paul Finkelman, "Prelude to the Fourteenth Amendment: Black Legal Rights in the Antebellum North," 17 *Rutgers L.J.* 415 (1986).

316. See Philip J. Schwarz, "The Transportation of Slaves from Virginia, 1801–1865," 7 *Slavery and Abolition* 215 (1986) (use of sale and transportation abroad against slaves).

317. See, e.g., Ark. Act of Jan. 20, 1843, §3; Va. Act of Mar. 2, 1819, ch. 111, §§67–77; Miss. Code, ch. 37 §81 (1848); Berlin, *Slaves without Masters* at 93–94, 327–332.

318. Act of Feb. 21, 1823 ch. 32, 1823 Va. Acts 35. Virginia courts, though repeatedly asserting that free blacks were not protected by the Constitution or the Bill of Rights, were careful not to impose such punishments retroactively. See *Attoo v. the Commonwealth*, 4 Va. 382; 1823 Va. LEXIS 69; 2 Va. Cas. 382 (1823)("there was no Law in force for the punishment of the offence, whereof the said Attoo was convicted at the time of the said conviction . . . the judgment of the Superior Court was therefore erroneous, and must be reversed; and the prisoner acquitted and discharged").

319. See, e.g., 8 U.S.C. 1227 (a) (2) (A) (i) (II) ("a crime for which a sentence of one year or longer may be imposed").

320. *John Aldridge v. the Commonwealth*, 4 Va. 447, 1824 Va. LEXIS 60 (1824).

321. Berlin, *Slaves without Masters* at 96–97, 304–305.

322. James Madison, *Writings* vol. 2, 15 (Hunt, ed., 1901), cited in Sherwood, "Negro Deportation" at 484.

323. Before being transported, the offender was to be flogged and branded. Laws of Pennsylvania (Lancaster, Pa. 1801), 1: 45, 46. Sherwood, "Negro Deportation" at 484–485.

324. William W. Hening, *Statutes at Large; Being a Collection of All the Laws of Virginia from the First Session of the Legislature in 1619* vol. 3, 87 (1821). This law also forbade emancipation of slaves unless the owner provided for transportation within six months after manumission.

325. See *Annals of Congress,* 16th Cong., 2d sess., 1820–1821. The privileges and immunities clause is found in Article IV. This question, of course, was not de-

cisively resolved by the legal system until Justice Taney's infamous opinion in the *Dred Scott* case.

326. In 1821, following the Missouri Compromise, Attorney General William Wirt considered the legal question whether a free African American could legally command a ship operating out of Norfolk, Virginia. The law required commanders to be citizens of the United States. Wirt, a Virginian, concluded, "No person is included in the description of citizen of the United States who has not the full rights of a citizen in the State of his residence." The implication of this view was that a free African American from Massachusetts might have the right to command a vessel, while one from Virginia would not. See generally Don Fehrenbacher, *Slavery, Law, and Politics: The Dred Scott Case in Historical Perspective* (1981).

327. See Kettner, *Development* at 315–320.

328. *Amy (a woman of colour) v. Smith,* 11 Ky. Rep. (1 Littell) 326 (1822) (cited in Schuck and Smith, *Citizenship without Consent: Illegal Aliens in the American Polity* 69 (1985).

329. See Berlin, *Slaves without Masters* at 93–94, 327–332.

330. See Neuman, *Strangers* at 35 n. 180 (citing various state statutes from 1811 to 1835). The relationship between the first state attempts to bar Chinese labor and anti-black attitudes has been noted by historians. See, e.g., Neuman, *Strangers;* Charles J. McClain, Jr., "The Chinese Struggle for Civil Rights in Nineteenth Century America: The First Phase, 1850–1870," 72 *Cal. L. Rev.* 529 (1984).

331. See Paul Finkelman, "The Constitution and the Intentions of the Framers: The Limits of Historical Analysis," 50 *U. Pitt. L. Rev.* 349, 385–390 (1989).

332. See W. E. B. Du Bois, *The Suppression of the African Slave Trade* 84–85 (repr. ed. 1969) (1896). Despite their evident desire for federal help with this sort of border control, Southerners resisted erosion of what John C. Calhoun later called "the very important right, that the States have the authority to exclude the introduction of such persons as may be dangerous to their institutions." Indeed, Calhoun made clear his view that this principle was applicable "to other persons as well as blacks" and "may hereafter occupy a prominent place in the history of our legislation." John C. Calhoun, "Speech in Reply to Criticisms of the Bill to Prohibit the Circulation of Incendiary Publications through the Mail (April 12, 1836)," in 13 *The Papers of John C. Calhoun* 147, 156 (Clyde N. Wilson ed., 1980), cited in Neuman, *Strangers* at 36.

333. Act of Feb. 28, 1803, ch. 10, 2 Stat. 205. As Gerald Neuman notes, the exception was deemed necessary because of the accepted view that free African American citizens had the right to travel.

334. See Sanford Levinson, "Slavery in the Canon of Constitutional Law," in *Slavery and the Law* 101 (Paul Finkelman ed., 1997).

335. 8 F.Cas. 493 (C.C.D.S.C. 1823) (No. 4,366). Vesey was a former slave who had purchased his own freedom.

336. William Wirt concurred the following year. Fehrenbacher, *Slavery, Law, and Politics* at 38.

337. *Gibbons v. Ogden*, 22 U.S. (9 Wheat.) 1 (1824). See Neuman, *Strangers* at 44–45.

338. *The Nation*, April 17, 1902, 303.

339. The 1850 law actually merged private and public enforcement, providing that "all good citizens are hereby commanded to aid and assist in the prompt and efficient execution of this law, whenever their services may be required." Ch. 60, 9 Stat. 462, 463 (1850).

340. Art. 4, Sec. 2, clause 3.

341. The 1793 federal statute dealt both with the interstate rendition of fugitives from justice and with fugitive slaves. Fugitive Slave Act of 1793, Law of Feb. 12, 1793, ch. 1, 1 Stat. 302 (repealed 1864); Stanley W. Campbell, *The Slave Catchers: Enforcement of the Fugitive Slave Law, 1850–1860* 9 (1968). See also C. W. A. David, "The Fugitive Slave Law of 1793 and Its Antecedents," 9 *Journal of Negro History* 18–25 (1924); Paul Finkelman, "The Kidnapping of John Davis and the Adoption of the Fugitive Slave Law of 1793," 56 *Journal of Southern History*, 397–422 (1990).

342. It is interesting to note that one of the most debated aspects of the 1793 law was whether "certificates of removal" would be granted for alleged fugitives who had been born in, or had lived for a long time in, the states where they were captured. The slave owners won an important victory on this point. See Finkelman, "The Kidnapping of John Davis" at 417.

343. Campbell, *Slave Catchers* at 8.

344. *Acts of the General Assembly of Virginia, 1849–1850*, 251–253. (quoted in Campbell, *Slave Catchers* at 8.

345. Campbell, *Slave Catchers* at 10.

346. 41 U.S. 539 (Pet.) (1842).

347. Act. Pa., Mar. 26, 1826.

348. Henry Wilson, *History of the Rise and Fall of the Slave Power in America*, vol. 1, 471 (1872).

349. *Prigg*, 41 U.S. 539, 577. As the lawyers for the state put it, "Pennsylvania says: Instead of preventing you from taking your slaves, we are anxious that you should have them; they are a population we do not covet, and all our legislation tends toward giving you every facility to get them."

350. *Id.*

351. Story, the year before, had grappled with the famous *Amistad* case.

352. Story interpreted the purpose of this clause broadly—"to secure to the citizens of the slaveholding states the complete right and title of ownership in their slaves, as property, in every state in the union into which they might escape." 41 U.S. 539, 540.

353. See also *Jones v. Van Zandt*, 5th Howard Rep. 215 (1847) (upholding constitu-

tionality of 1793 Fugitive Slave Law and affirming conviction of one who aided fugitive slaves).

354. 41 U.S. at 542–543.

355. See, e.g., *Henderson v. New York,* 92 U.S. 259, 264 (1876) (in which counsel cites *Prigg).* The *Prigg* decision, in effect, reversed the usual states'-rights debate. It was now the Southern states that sought increased federal authority and power in support of what they viewed as their property rights. See Campbell, *Slave Catchers* at 14.

356. *Congressional Globe,* 31st Cong., 1st sess., 21:99, 103; Appendix, p. 79 (1850).

357. In a well-publicized 1836 opinion, *State v. the Sheriff of Burlington,* Chief Justice Hornblower of New Jersey had highlighted the problem of where such a trial should take place: "What, first transport a man out of the state, on a charge of his being a slave, and try the truth of the allegation afterwards—separate him from the place, it may be of his nativity—the abode of his relatives, his friends and his witnesses—transport him in chains to Missouri or Arkansas, with the cold comfort that if a freeman he may there assert and establish his freedom! No, if a person comes into this state, and here claims the servitude of a human being, whether white or black, here he must prove his case, and here prove it according to law." Paul Finkelman, "Chief Justice Hornblower of New Jersey and the Fugitive Slave Law of 1793," in *Slavery and the Law* 114.

358. *Congressional Globe,* 31st Cong., 1st sess., 21:210 (1850).

359. *Congressional Globe,* 31st Cong., 1st sess., Appendix, p. 274 (1850); see also Campbell, *Slave Catchers* at 18.

360. *Congressional Globe,* 31st Cong., 1st sess., Appendix 421 (1850).

361. 31st Cong. ch. 60, September 1850, 9 Stat. 462–465.

362. See Allen Johnson, "The Constitutionality of the Fugitive Slave Acts," 31 *Yale L. J.* 161 (1921). This argument, however, had been decisively rejected by the Court in *Prigg.* See also Campbell, *Slave Catchers* at 28.

363. See, e.g., Trial of Thomas Sims, an issue of Personal Liberty, on the Claim of James Potter of Georgia Against Him, as an alleged Fugitive From Service. Arguments of Robert Rantoul, Jr., and Charles G. Loring, With the Decision of George T. Curtis . . . 31 (1851) (cited in Campbell, *Slave Catchers* at 32).

364. An obvious problem with this analogy is that extradition of criminals is a state governmental process, whereas in the case of a fugitive slave, the claimant was an individual whose interest was in the complete deprivation of the rights of his captive. See Horace Mann, *Slavery: Letters and Speeches* 443 (1853) (cited in Campbell, *Slave Catchers* at 35).

365. One specific concern was the extent to which the decision of the authority in the sending state would be considered binding or persuasive on the courts of the slave states. As Wisconsin Judge Whiton put it, "the alleged fugitive from labor is taken back to the state from which he is said to have escaped, as a person who has been proved and adjudged to be a slave." *In re Booth,* 3 Wisconsin 71 (1854) (cited in Campbell, *Slave Catchers* at 37).

366. Similarly, Justice Scalia has recently opined that noncitizens may be held without bail pending removal for alleged criminal activity because they have had full criminal process before the removal proceedings have begun. *Demore v. Kim* 538 U.S. 510 (2003).

367. As the *Prigg* Court had seen it, the former cases involved "a challenge by a man of the propriety or ownership of a thing [sic] which he has not in his possession, but which is wrongfully detained from him." *Prigg*, 41 U.S. at 614.

368. Chief Justice Chase served until 1873. See Henry J. Abraham, *Justices and Presidents: A Political History of Appointments to the Supreme Court* 120–122 (1974); Melvin I. Urofsky, *A March of Liberty: A Constitutional History of the United States* 101–106 (1988). Stephen Field, who authored the *Chinese Exclusion Case* but dissented in *Fong Yue Ting*, served with Chase for many years on the court. See also *In re Neagle* 135 U.S. 1 (1890); *Ex Parte Clarke* 100 U.S. 399, 412 (1880) (dissent of Justices Field and Clifford).

369. Of course, following *Dred Scott*, this became explicit.

370. Emma Lou Thornbrough, *The Negro in Indiana: A Study of a Minority* 65 n. 15 (1957) (cited in Campbell, *Slave Catchers* at 59).

371. Beginning with Vermont, in 1850, a number of states passed strong personal liberty laws throughout the 1850s. Campbell, *Slave Catchers* at 85–87.

372. He saw this as part of "the general acquiescence in these measures of peace which has been exhibited in all parts of the Republic . . . [that have] given renewed assurance that our liberty and our Union may subsist together for the benefit of this and all succeeding generations." Campbell, *Slave Catchers* at 102.

373. James Buchanan's attorney general, Jeremiah S. Black, instructed his marshals in the clearest terms: "You will of course see to it that your prisoners are not rescued out of your custody either by the void process of Judges who have no jurisdiction or by open and undisguised violence." Jeremiah S. Black to Matthew Johnson, April 26, 1959, Letter Book, B/2, Attorney General's Office, 1859–1861, National Archives, Justice and Executive Branch, Washington, D.C., cited in Campbell, *Slave Catchers* at 108. The marshals were also told to "respectfully decline to produce the bodies before the State Court" even if it issued a writ of habeas corpus. President Lincoln, with some reservations, had initially adopted this view. He reportedly stated, in 1858, "I have never hesitated to say, and I do not now hesitate to say, that I think, under the Constitution of the United States, the people of the Southern States are entitled to a Congressional Fugitive Slave Law." Reported in *New York Weekly Tribune,* June 2, 1860 (cited in Campbell, *Slave Catchers* at 189).

374. Roy Franklin Nichols, *Franklin Pierce: Young Hickory of the Granite Hills* 361 (1931) (citing *National Intelligencer,* May 29, 1854)

375. See, e.g., Campbell, *Slave Catchers* at 111 ("The views which hold that the Fugitive Slave Law was not enforced may have been based upon inconclusive research, and the criteria of measurement have not always been clear").

376. Indeed, the law was apparently enforced by federal marshals during the Civil War as late as June 1863, some six months after the Emancipation Proclamation had taken effect. Campbell, *Slave Catchers* at 192–194.
377. As Paul Finkelman has noted, drawing such historical parallels is tricky. Nevertheless, the functional similarities are worth noting. See Paul Finkelman, "Fugitive Slaves, Midwestern Racial Tolerance, and the Value of "Justice Delayed," 78 *Iowa L. Rev.* 89 n. 45 (1992).
378. Canada was often a safe haven for the fugitives. In one famous case in the early 1860s, a former slave named John Anderson successfully defeated extradition to the United States for his alleged involvement in the murder of a slaveholder that had occurred while Anderson was escaping. Fred Landon, "The Anderson Fugitive Case," *Journal of Negro History* 233–244 (1922). Mexico had prohibited the slave trade in 1824 and abolished slavery in 1829. Indeed, the fugitive slave issue had been a long-standing source of tension between the United States and Mexico. See Alleine Howren, "Causes and Origin of the Decree of April 6, 1830," 16 *S.W. Hist. Q.* 387–390 (1913). See also Ethan A. Nadelmann, *Cops across Borders: The Internationalization of United State Criminal Law Enforcement* 62 (1993).
379. Fred Landon, "The Negro Migration to Canada after the Passing of the Fugitive Slave Act," 5 *Journal of Negro History* 22 (1920).
380. *The Liberator,* October 18, 1850 (cited in *id.* at 23).
381. Such fears were well founded. See Gerald G. Eggert, "The Impact of the Fugitive Slave Law on Harrisburg: A Case Study," 109 *P.A. Mag. Hist. & Biography* 537 (1985) (describing cases of wrongful kidnapping of free people by slave catchers).
382. James O. Horton and Lois E. Horton, "A Federal Assault: African Americans and the Impact of the Fugitive Slave Law of 1850," 68 *Chi.-Kent L. Rev.* 1179, 1188 (1993).
383. Michael F. Hembree, "The Question of 'Begging': Fugitive Slave Relief in Canada, 1830–1865," 37 *Civ. War Hist.* 314, 315 (1991); Horton and Horton, "Federal Assault" at 1188.
384. In the midst of the Civil War, the Fugitive Slave Law was finally repealed, effective June 28, 1864, 38 Cong. ch. 166, 13 Stat. 200.
385. Campbell, *Slave Catchers* at 193.
386. *National Intelligencer,* October 3, 1862; cited in Campbell, *Slave Catchers* at 194.
387. Don B. Kates, Jr., "Abolition, Deportation, Integration: Attitudes toward Slavery in the Early Republic," 53 *Journal of Negro History* 33, 39 (1968).
388. Henry Adams, *The Life of Albert Gallatin* 109–110 (1879); Kates, "Attitudes" at 44.
389. Quoted in Matthew T. Mellon, *Early American Views on Negro Slavery* 29 (1963); Kates, "Attitudes" at 41.
390. Robert McColley, *Slavery and Jeffersonian Virginia* 133 (1973).

391. See Thomas Jefferson, Notes on Virginia, Query and Answer XIV in *Thomas Jefferson* 264 (Merrill D. Peterson, ed., 1984).

392. St. George Tucker, *Dissertation on Slavery* 93, 94 (1796); Sherwood, "Negro Deportation" at 487.

393. Brissot de Warville, *New Travels in the United States of America* vol. 1 237 (1796); see also La Rochefoucauld-Liancourt, *Travels through the United States,* vol. 2 357 (1799).

394. Kates, "Attitudes" at 45.

395. William W. Henry, *Patrick Henry; Life, Correspondence and Speeches* vol. 1, 114 (1891); Sherwood, "Negro Deportation" at 487.

396. Noah Webster, *Effects of Slavery on Morals and Industry* 35–36 (1793).

397. Kates, "Attitudes" at 42.

398. P. J. Staudenraus, *The African Colonization Movement, 1816–1865* (1961).

399. Berlin, *Slaves without Masters* at 200.

400. American Colonization Society, *African Repository and Colonial Journal* 5 (March 1829) (cited in Berlin, *Slaves without Masters* at 201).

401. Kates, "Attitudes" 42 (citing *Annals of Congress*, 13th Cong.).

402. See Nathaniel Weyl and William Marina, *American Statesmen on Slavery and the Negro* 132–134 (1971).

403. Henry N. Sherwood, "The Formation of the American Colonization Society," 2 *Journal of Negro History* 209–228 (1917).

404. See generally Penelope Campbell, *Maryland in Africa: The Maryland State Colonization Society* 1831–1857 (1971). *Id.* at 30–38, citing Md. Laws, c. 281, c. 323.

405. Berlin, *Slaves without Masters* at 203.

406. *Richmond Daily Dispatch,* March 9, 1853 (quoted in Berlin, *Slaves without Masters* at 363).

407. Orville Taylor, *Negro Slavery in Arkansas* 255–258 (1958); Act Passed at the Twelfth Session of the General Assembly of the State of Arkansas 1858, c. 151.

408. Roy P. Basler, ed., *Collected Works of Abraham Lincoln* 2, 255–256 (1953).

409. The Kansas-Nebraska Act would have admitted Kansas into the Union as a slave state.

410. Basler, *Collected Works* vol. 2, 405, 408, 409.

411. Philip Foner, *History of Black Americans* vol. 3, 163 (1983). The Haitian government had sent a delegation seeking immigrants to the United States two years earlier.

412. Paul J. Scheips, "Lincoln and the Chiriqui Colonization Project," 37 *Journal of Negro History* 418–420 (1952).

413. The plan had the additional asserted benefit of securing U.S. power and control in the region. See 36th Cong., 1st sess., House of Representatives, Report no. 568: Report of the Hon. F. H. Morse, of Maine, from the Committee on Naval Affairs, H.R. in Relation to the Contract made by the Secretary of the Navy for Coal and Other Privileges on the Isthmus of Chiriqui.

414. Scheips, "Lincoln and the Chiriqui Colonization Project" at 420–421.

415. Basler, *Collected Works* vol. 5, 48.

416. See Michael Vorenberg, "Abraham Lincoln and the Politics of Black Coloniza-tion," 14 *Journal of the Abraham Lincoln Association* 22–28 (1993).

417. R. Basler, *Collected Works* vol. 5, 192.

418. Reprinted in Ira Berlin et al., eds, *Free at Last: A Documentary History of Slavery, Freedom, and the Civil War* 38–41 (1992).

419. *Id.* at 40–41.

420. Scheips, "Lincoln and the Chiriqui Colonization Project" at 426–427; James Mitchell to A. Lincoln, May 18, 1862. *The Robert Todd Lincoln Collection of the Papers of Abraham Lincoln* vol. 76, f. 16044 (1947).

421. Scheips, "Lincoln" at 426–427. A "Bureau of Emigration" was later proposed. See *Congressional Globe*, House, 37th Cong., 3d sess., 1029 (1863). In 1864, Congress created the position of commissioner of immigration, under the au-thority of the secretary of state. 38th Cong., 1st sess., 3546. It seems that by this time, "immigration" was beginning to be applied to incoming persons, whereas "emigration" also referred to proposed resettlement plans. Lincoln, however, used the term "emigration" in his address to the Second Session of the 38th Congress interchangeably with "immigrants." *Congressional Globe*, House, 37th Cong., 3rd sess., Appendix, 2 (1863).

422. As conditions in Union detention camps for detained African Americans were well-known to be deplorable and life threatening, one must use the word "vol-untary" carefully.

423. "Address on Colonization to a Committee of Colored Men, Washington, D.C.," in *Abraham Lincoln: Speeches and Writing, 1859–1865* 353–357 (Don E. Fehrenbacher ed., 1989).

424. *Id.*

425. *Id.* See also "The Colonization Scheme," *Detroit Free Press*, August 15 (or 27), 1862 (cited in Scheips, "Lincoln" at 437–438). The Lincoln administration also funded efforts for a colony in Haiti, which failed due in part to massive embezzlement, resulting in eventual instructions to the War Department to offer to return the Haitian colonists to the United States.

426. *Id.*

427. Also, on August 26, 1862, Kansas Senator Pomeroy published an appeal, "To the Free Colored People of the United States," in which he suggested that "it is within your own power to take one step that will secure, if successful, the ele-vation, freedom, and social position of your race upon the American conti-nent." That step was to leave the United States. Pomeroy reported that by Oc-tober, he had received nearly 14,000 applications for emigration. Scheips, "Lincoln and the Chiriqui Colonization Project" at 436–438.

428. James Mitchell, Commissioner of Emigration, to United States Ministers of the Colored Race (1862), The Robert Todd Lincoln Collection of the Papers of Abraham Lincoln (1947) vol. 98 ff. 20758–20759. Apparently, these argu-

ments had some resonance. Revenue Edward Thomas, the chairman of the black delegation, wrote to President Lincoln on August 16, 1862, to say that he now favored colonization and to ask permission to travel among his black friends and coworkers to convince them of the same. Edward M. Thomas to A. Lincoln, Aug. 16, 1862, *Lincoln Collection* vol. 84 ff. 17718–17719.

429. Reprinted in Basler, *Collected Works* vol. 5, 433–436 (1953).

430. Unknown to Joseph Henry, Sept. 5, 1862, *Lincoln Collection* vol. 86 ff. 18226–18227 (cited in Scheips, "Lincoln" at 430–431).

431. James R. Partridge to William Seward, Aug. 26, 1862, A. B. Dickinson to W. Seward, Sept. 12, 1862, and Pedro Zeledon to A. B. Dickinson, Sept. 12, 1862, *Papers Relating to Foreign Affairs,* 891–892, 897–898 (cited in Scheips, "Lincoln" at 443–444); see also N. Andrew Cleven, "Some Plans for Colonizing Liberated Negro Slaves in Hispanic America," 6 *Southwestern Political and Social Science Quarterly* 157 (1925).

432. Basler, *Collected Works* 519.

433. N. Weyl and W. Marina, *American Statesmen on Slavery and the Negro* 228–229 (1971).

434. Scheips, "Lincoln" at 419.

435. Charles H. Wesley, "Lincoln's Plan for Colonizing the Emancipated Negroes," 4 *Journal of Negro History* 17–19 (1919).

436. In fact, Lincoln continued to talk of "exporting" African Americans as late as April 15, 1865, fearing race wars in the South. He asked General Butler, "what shall we do with the negroes after they are free? . . . I can hardly believe that the South and North can live in peace, unless we can get rid of the negroes . . . I believe that it would be better to export them all to some fertile country with a good climate, which they could have to themselves." The president sought investigation as to how "our very large navy" could be used to send "the blacks away." See Benjamin Butler, *Autobiography and Personal Reminiscences of Major-General Benjamin F. Butler* 903–908 (1892) (quoted in Wesley, "Lincoln's Plan" at 20); but see Mark Neely, "Abraham Lincoln and Black Colonization: Benjamin Butler's Spurious Testimony," 25 *Civil War History* 77–83 (1979) (questioning Butler's statement).

437. Scheips, "Lincoln" at 439, citing Tyler Dennett, ed., *Lincoln and the Civil War in the Diaries and Letters of John Hay* 203 (1930).

438. Statutes at Large, XIII, p. 352.

439. See generally Allan Nevins, *The War for the Union* vol. 2, *War Becomes Revolution, 1862–1863* 10 (1960).

3. Chinese Exclusion

1. Alexis de Tocqueville, *Democracy in America* vol. 1, 70 (1835).

2. Stephen Skowronek, *Building a New American State: Expanding National Administrative Capabilities, 1877–1920* 5 (1982).

3. 11 Peters 102 (1837).
4. 48 U.S. 282 (1849).
5. *The Passenger Cases,* 48 U.S. at 283. Owing in part to absences and deaths on the Court and to many rearguments, the nearly 300 pages of text were preceded by a headnote stating that "there was no opinion of the court." See generally Mary Sarah Bilder, "The Struggle over Immigration: Indentured Servants, Slaves, and Articles of Commerce," 61 *Mo. L. Rev.* 743, 813 (1996) (suggesting that "the Court's nineteenth-century opinions on immigration under the Commerce Clause reveal the shadows of slaves and indentured servants").
6. Bilder, "The Struggle" at 813, citing Carl B. Swisher, *The Taney Period: 1836–64* 381 (1974).
7. See generally Bilder, "The Struggle."
8. The 1862 Morrill Act for the Suppression of Polygamy, Act of July 1, 1862, ch. 126, 12 Stat. 501 (repealed 1910) (outlawing polygamy in the territories) was another important assertion of federal authority during this era. See Sarah Barringer Gordon, *The Mormon Question: Polygamy and Constitutional Conflict in Nineteenth-Century America* 81 (2002).
9. National exclusion laws had been proposed as early as 1836, when Senator Davis of Massachusetts encouraged the Congress to pass a law "to prevent the introduction of foreign paupers into this country." *Register of Debates in Congress,* 12, pt. 2:1378. A successful resolution to direct the secretary of the treasury to investigate the problem soon followed. See E. P. Hutchinson, *Legislative History of American Immigration Policy, 1798–1965* 25–26 (1981). Similar measures appeared periodically during the next two decades, without inspiring significant federal action. The issues raised by the immigration of "paupers" and criminals, however, were often on the congressional agenda. Indeed, an 1856 House report concluded that increases in crime and poverty throughout the country were "traceable to the immense influx of foreigners within the last ten years." House Report 359, 34th Cong., 1st sess. 2188 (cited in Hutchinson, *Legislative History* at 42).
10. Act of Feb. 19, 1862, 12 Stat. 340, 8 USC 331 (repealed 1974).
11. John Higham, *Strangers in the Land: Patterns of American Nativism, 1860–1925* 18 (1992).
12. *Congressional Globe,* 38th Cong., 1st sess., Appendix, 1–2 (1863) (cited in Hutchinson, *Legislative History* 48).
13. Act of July 4, 1864, ch. 246, 13 Stat. 385 (repealed 1868).
14. *Id.,* Sec. 2; see Hutchinson, *Legislative History* at 49.
15. *Congressional Globe,* 38th Cong., 2d sess., Appendix (1863).
16. 18 Stat. 477. For an interesting argument that the Page Act's concern about preserving traditional American conceptions of marriage lies at the root of our federal immigration system, see Kerry Abrams, "Polygamy, Prostitution, and the Federalization of Immigration Law," 105 *Colum. L. Rev.* (2005).

17. *Henderson, et al. v. Mayor of New York, et al.*, 92 U.S. 259 (1876); *Chy Lung v. Freeman*, 92 U.S. 275 (1876).

18. *Chy Lung* at 278, 280.

19. *Henderson*, 92 U.S. at 259, 270.

20. *Chy Lung* at 280.

21. See Higham, *Strangers*; Hutchinson, *Legislative History* at 79.

22. 18 Stat. 477.

23. Immigration Act of Aug. 3, 1882, 22 Stat. 214.

24. 112 U.S. 580 (1884). See Sarah H. Cleveland, "Powers Inherent in Sovereignty: Indians, Aliens, Territories, and the Nineteenth Century Origins of Plenary Power over Foreign Affairs," 81 *Tex. L. Rev.* 111 (2005).

25. Brief for the United States at 2–3, *Edye v. Robertson*, 112 U.S. 580 (1884) (No. 772).

26. *Id.*, citing Thomas M. Cooley, *A Treatise on the Constitutional Limitations Which Rest upon the Legislative Power of the States of the American Union* 197 (5th ed., Little, Brown 1883).

27. 112 U.S. at 600.

28. Sec. 206; see Clark, *Deportation* at 40.

29. 130 U.S. 581.

30. See, e.g., Louis Henkin, "The Constitution and United States Sovereignty: A Century of Chinese Exclusion and Its Progeny," 100 *Harv. L. Rev.* 853 (1987).

31. See James A. R. Nafziger, "The General Admission of Aliens under International Law," 77 *Am. J. Int'l L.* 804, 809 (1983) (collecting views of international publicists).

32. 2 Samuel Pufendorf, *Of the Law of Nature and Nations* bk. 3, ch. 3, 9, at 365 (1703).

33. Emer de Vattel, *The Law of Nations* bk. 1, ch. 19, 213, at 101 (Joseph Chitty ed., T. & J. W. Johnson 1876) (1758).

34. 1 Robert Phillimore, *Commentaries upon International Law* pt. 3, ch. 18, at 347 (1854).

35. Edward S. Creasy, *First Platform of International Law* 200–201 (1876).

36. David Dudley Field, *Outlines of an International Code* 165 (photo. reprint 2001) (2d ed. 1876), citing James Kent, *Commentary on International Law* 35 (J. T. Arby ed., 1878).

37. Theodore Ortolan, *Règeles Internationales et Diplomatie de la Mer* bk. 2, ch. 14, at 297 (Author trans., Paris, H. Plon, 4th ed. 1864) (1845).

38. 1 Robert Phillimore, *Commentaries upon International Law* pt. 3, ch. 10, at 233 (1854). See also pt. 3, ch. 21, at 407 (describing "the right of the State, into which he has migrated, to send the foreign citizen back to his own home").

39. James Reddie, *Inquiries into International Law* 208 (1842).

40. Skowronek, *Building* at ix.

41. Woodrow Wilson, *The Study of Administration* (1887).

42. See, e.g., Robert McCloskey, *The American Supreme Court* 101–136 (1960);

Arnold M. Paul, *Conservative Crisis and the Rule of Law: Attitudes of the Bar and Bench, 1887–1895* (1976); Skowronek, *Building* at 41.

43. Higham, *Strangers* at 131, 134.

44. See Dan Caldwell, "The Negroization of the Chinese Stereotype in California," 53 *Southern California Quarterly* 123–132 (1971).

45. See generally Patricia Nelson Limerick, *The Legacy of Conflict: The Unbroken Past of the American West* 269 (1987).

46. Ronald Takaki, *Strangers from A Different Shore: A History of Asian Americans* 101 (1989).

47. See generally Stephen H. Legomsky, *Immigration and the Judiciary: Law and Politics in Britain and America* 177–222 (1987); Stephen H. Legomsky, "Immigration Law and the Principle of Plenary Congressional Power," 1984 *Sup. Ct. Rev.* 255, 256 (University of Chicago Press, 1985); Hiroshi Motomura, "The Curious Evolution of Immigration Law: Procedural Surrogates for Substantive Constitutional Rights," 92 *Colum. L. Rev.* 1625 (1992); Hiroshi Motomura, "Immigration Law after a Century of Plenary Power: Phantom Constitutional Norms and Statutory Interpretation," 100 Yale L. J. 545 (1990); Peter H. Schuck, "The Transformation of Immigration Law," 84 *Colum. L. Rev.* 1, 5–34 (1984); Herbert Hill, "The Problem of Race in American Labor History," 24 *Reviews in American History* 189–208 (1996); Peter Kwong, *Forbidden Workers: Illegal Chinese Immigrants and American Labor* (1997); Charles J. McClain, *In Search of Equality: The Chinese Struggle against Discrimination in Nineteenth-Century America* (1994); David R. Roediger, *The Wages of Whiteness: Race and the Making of the American Working Class* (rev. ed. 1999); Lucy E. Salyer, *Laws Harsh as Tigers* (1995); John Kuo Wei Tchen, *New York before Chinatown: Orientalism and the Shaping of American Culture, 1776–1882* (1999).

48. Robert S. Chang, "Toward an Asian American Legal Scholarship: Critical Race Theory, Post-Structuralism, and Narrative Space," 81 *Calif. L. Rev.* 1243, 1291 (1993).

49. Act of Apr. 16, 1850, ch. 99, §14, 1850 Cal. Stat. 229, 230, amended by Act of Mar. 18, 1863, ch. 70, 1863 Cal. Stat. 69, repealed by omission from codification, Cal. Penal Code §1321 (1872) (officially repealed, Act of Mar. 30, 1955, ch. 48, §1, 1955 Cal. Stat. 488, 489). A similar provision applied to civil cases. Civil Practice Act of 1851, ch. 5, §394(3), 1851 Cal. Stat. 51, 114, amended by Act of Mar. 16, 1863, ch. 68, 1863 Cal. Stat. 60, repealed by omission from codification, Cal. Civ. Proc. Code §§8, 1880 (1872) (officially repealed, Act of Mar. 30, 1955, ch. 33, §1, 1955 Cal. Stat. 475, 475).

50. *People v. Hall*, 4 Cal. 399 (1854).

51. *Id.* at 400.

52. See generally, Charles J. McClain, Jr., "The Chinese Struggle for Civil Rights in Nineteenth Century America: The First Phase, 1850–1870," 72 *Cal. L. Rev.* 529 (1984). A year after Murray wrote the court's opinion in *People v. Hall*, he was elected to the California Supreme Court bench as a candidate of the Know

Nothing" party. See Gerald Uelmen, "The Know Nothing Justices of the California Supreme Court," 2 *Western Legal History* 89–106 (1989).

53. George F. Seward, *Chinese Immigration* 126 (1881), quoting from Rep. Ch. Im. P. 586.

54. Act of Feb. 19, 1862, 12 Stat. 340, 8 USC 331.

55. David Montgomery, *Beyond Equality: Labor and the Radical Republicans, 1862–1872* 391 (1967).

56. *Congressional Globe,* 40th Cong. 2d sess., 1868, Appendix, 505.

57. David Montgomery, *The Fall of the House of Labor: The Workplace, the State, and American Labor Activism, 1865–1925* 67–68 (1987).

58. *Id.* at 85.

59. Gwendolyn Mink, *Old Labor and New Immigrants in American Political Development: Union, Party, and State, 1875–1920* 67–73 (1986).

60. See Mary Roberts Coolidge, *Chinese Immigration* 270 (1969, first published in 1909).

61. Matthew Frye Jacobson, *Whiteness of a Different Color: European Immigrants and the Alchemy of Race* 13–90 (1998); David R. Roediger, *Towards the Abolition of Whiteness: Essays on Race, Politics, and Working Class History* 21–38, 181–198 (1994).

62. Marcus Lee Hansen, *The Atlantic Migration, 1607–1860: A History of the Continuing Settlement of the United States* 241–251 (1961); Maldwyn Allen Jones, *American Immigration* 130–131 (1960); Alexander Saxton, *The Indispensable Enemy: Labor and the Anti-Chinese Movement in California* 28 (1971).

63. Saxton, *Indispensable Enemy* at 29.

64. Noel Ignatiev, *How the Irish Became White* (1995).

65. See Wei Tchen, *New York before Chinatown.*

66. See Saxton, *Indispensable Enemy* at 269–348.

67. Reprinted in Coolidge, *Chinese Immigration* at 66.

68. Seward, *Chinese Immigration* at 243.

69. Seward, *Chinese Immigration* at 247–248.

70. Coolidge, *Chinese Immigration* at 425.

71. Saxton, *Indispensable Enemy* at 7.

72. The clearance would come from the Six Companies.

73. Saxton, *Indispensable Enemy* at 8.

74. See generally Abrams, *"Polygamy."*

75. A California law had declared (only) Chinese houses of prostitution to be public nuisances in 1866. Act of Mar. 21, 1866, ch. 505, 1866 Cal. Stat. 641. The law was applied to all such houses eight years later.

76. *Congressional Globe,* 39th Cong., 1st sess., 1866, 1056.

77. In 1880, California extended its 1850 general antimiscegenation law to Asians. See Abrams, *"Polygamy"* at 663 n. 125.

78. Cornelius Cole, "The Senator Interviewed by a Chronicle Reporter," *San Francisco Chronicle,* October 23, 1870, at 1 (quoted in Abrams, *"Polygamy"* at 663 n. 123).

79. See, e.g., *People v. Downer,* 7 Cal. 169 (1857)(invalidating passenger tax aimed at the Chinese as a violation of the federal commerce power). Act of Mar. 18, 1870, ch. 230, 1870 Cal. Stat. 330. See Abrams, *"Polygamy"* at 674–676.

80. 1873–1874 Acts Amendatory of the Codes of California §70 at 39.

81. *In re Ah Fong,* 1 F. Cas. 213, 216 (C.C.D. Cal. 1874)(No. 102).

82. 18 Stat. 477.

83. 3 *Congressional Record,* House, 43rd Cong., 2d sess., Appendix at 44.

84. See Abrams, *"Polygamy"* at 692–698, 700–701.

85. Ronald Takaki, *Strangers from a Different Shore: A History of Asian Americans* 40 (rev. ed. 1998).

86. *New York Times,* September 3, 1865, quoted in Stuart C. Miller, *The Unwelcome Immigrant: The American Image of the Chinese, 1785–1882* 170 (1969); see also Lawrence H. Fuchs, *The American Kaleidoscope: Race, Ethnicity, and the Civic Culture* 113 (1990).

87. Saxton, *Indispensable Enemy* at 6.

88. Saxton, *Indispensable Enemy* at 100–101; Miller, *Unwelcome Immigrant* at 175–184.

89. September 24, 1870, quoted in *Andrew Gyory, Closing the Gate: Race, Politics, and the Chinese Exclusion Act* 60 (1998).

90. Samuel Gompers, *Seventy Years of Life and Labor: An Autobiography* vol. 1, 216–217 (1925).

91. Saxton, *Indispensable Enemy* at 110. See also Sucheng Chan, "European and Asian Immigration into the United States in Comparative Perspective, 1820s to 1920s," in *Immigration Reconsidered: History, Sociology, and Politics* 37–75 (Virginia Yans-McLaughlin ed., 1990).

92. Higham, *Strangers* at 30–32.

93. Saxton, *Indispensable Enemy* at 112.

94. Quoted in Higham, *Strangers* at 31.

95. Saxton, *Indispensable Enemy* at 118 (quoting *San Francisco Evening Bulletin,* November 5, 1877).

96. *Id.* at 128 (quoting Henry George, "Kearney Agitation in California," *Popular Science,* 17, 445, 448–449.

97. California Constitution of 1879, art. II, §1, and art. XIX, §2, 3.

98. See Ralph Kauer, "The Workingmen's Party of California," 13 *Pacific Historical Review* 278, 285–286 (1944).

99. Saxton, *Indispensable Enemy* at 129.

100. See, e.g., Stanford M. Lyman, "The 'Chinese Question' and American Labor Historians," 7 *New Politics* 113–148

101. See Miller, *Unwelcome Immigrant* at 150–154.

102. See Him Mark Lai, Joe Huang, and Don Wong, *The Chinese of America, 1785–1980* (1980) 18.

103. Liping Zhu, *A Chinaman's Chance: The Chinese on the Rocky Mountain Mining Frontier* 33 (1997).

104. See Coolidge, *Chinese Immigration* at 50–54.

105. Saxton, *Indispensable Enemy* at 17, 18.

106. Quoted in Saxton, *Indispensable Enemy* at 273.

107. See Eugene H. Berwanger, *The Frontier against Slavery: Western Anti-Negro Prejudice and the Slavery Extension Controversy* 60–77 (1967); Saxton, *Indispensable Enemy* at 19–20.

108. See Saxton, *Indispensable Enemy* at 105.

109. See Takaki, *Strangers from a Different Shore* at 198.

110. Higham, *Strangers* at 48; see also Herbert Gutman, "The Workers' Search for Power in the Gilded Age," in *Power and Culture: Essays on the American Working Class* 90–91 (Ira Berlin ed., 1987); Gyory, *Closing the Gate* at 66.

111. See Gyory, *Closing the Gate* at 66.

112. See Lucy M. Cohen, *Chinese in the Post–Civil War South: A People without a History* 124 (1984); Eric Foner, *Reconstruction: America's Unfinished Revolution, 1863–1877* 419 (1988).

113. Gyory, *Closing the Gate* at 66.

114. Ch. 114, §16, 16 Stat. 140, 144 (1869–1870); McClain, "The Chinese Struggle" at 567.

115. Jacob A. Riis, *How the Other Half Lives: Studies among the Tenements of New York* 76 (1957).

116. Part of the reason for this was the perceived nature of the Chinese immigrants. Most Chinese laborers were understood to be "birds of passage" or "sojourners." Their intention was to work in the United States for awhile, save as much money as they could, and then return to China. Saxton, *Indispensable Enemy* at 17. See also Gunther Barth, *Bitter Strength: A History of the Chinese in the United States, 1850–1870* 1–4 (1964).

117. See Gyory, *Closing the Gate* at 111, 116

118. Saxton, *Indispensable Enemy* at 127–132; see also Carl Brent Swisher, *Motivation and Political Technique in the California Constitution, 1878–79* (1930).

119. Saxton, *Indispensable Enemy* at 132.

120. Quoted in Milton R. Konvitz, *The Alien and the Asiatic in American Law* 10 fn. 29 (1946). Field's pronouns are noteworthy.

121. 8 *Congressional Record,* 1312–1315 (1879); Konvitz, *Alien and the Asiatic* 10.

122. Konvitz, *Alien and the Asiatic* 10.

123. "A Breach of National Faith," *Harper's Weekly*, March 8, 1879, at 182 (editorial).

124. Saxton, *Indispensable Enemy* at 134.

125. House executive doc. no. 102, 45th Cong., 3d sess.

126. Elmer C. Sandmyer, *The Anti-Chinese Movement in California* 91–92 (1973).

127. Gyory, *Closing the Gate* at 177.

128. Elmer C. Sandmyer, *Anti-Chinese Movement;* see also *Harper's Weekly*, March 8, 1879, at 182 (editorial) ("what is the secret of this summary and hurried action? The answer is equally plain—the Presidential election").

129. *Congressional Record,* Senate 3625, Apr. 25, 1892.

130. Quoted in Coolidge, *Chinese Immigration* at 168.
131. 13 *Congressional Record*, 3264; Coolidge, *Chinese Immigration* at 177.
132. 22 Stat. 58.
133. Sec. 12. The law also prevented "any state court or court of the United States" from granting citizenship to any Chinese person; Sec. 14.
134. See, e.g., *In re Chin Ah Sooey*, 21 F. 393 (D. Cal. 1884).
135. H.R. 1798, with H. Rept. 614, 15 *Congressional Record*, 154, 240, 3752.
136. 23 Stat. 115.
137. *San Francisco Call*, November 22, 1885 (quoted in Saxton, *Indispensable Enemy* at 202).
138. See Shih-shan Henry Tsai, *The Chinese Experience in America* 67–76 (1986); see also anon., *The Chinese Massacre at Rock Springs, Wyoming Territory, September 2, 1885* (1886); Paul Crane and Alfred Larson, "The Chinese Massacre," 12 *Annals of Wyoming* 47–55 (1940), reprinted in Roger Daniels, ed., *Anti-Chinese Violence in North America* (1978); Craig Storti, *Incident at Bitter Creek: The Story of the Rock Springs Chinese Massacre* (1991); William Wei, "The Anti-Chinese Movement in Colorado: Interethnic Competition and Conflict on the Eve of Exclusion," in *Chinese America: History and Perspectives* 179–197 (Marlon K. Hom et al., eds., 1995).
139. Saxton, *Indispensable Enemy* at 202.
140. "The Rock Springs Massacre," *The Nation*, September 24, 1885, 252, 253.
141. Salyer, *Laws Harsh as Tigers* at 21. Gerry Neuman has pointed out to me that this fact might make one wonder about the practical value one might have gained from a jury trial requirement in deportation cases.
142. Saxton, *Indispensable Enemy* at 207 (citing the *San Francisco Call*, February 8, 9, 12, 1886).
143. Higham, *Strangers* at 37, 39; see also Josiah Strong, *Our Country* (1885); Richmond Mayo-Smith, *Emigration and Immigration: A Study in Social Science* (1890).
144. Higham, *Strangers* at 48.
145. Act of Feb. 26, 1885, 23 Stat. 332; Act of Feb. 23, 1887, 24 Stat. 414, c. 220.
146. See generally Paul Avrich, *The Haymarket Tragedy* (1984).
147. The number of casualties among the crowd is unknown.
148. On November 11, 1887, Albert Parsons, August Spies, George Engel, and Adolph Fischer were hanged. Louis Lingg committed suicide in his cell the day before he was scheduled to be executed. Illinois governor Richard Oglesby commuted the sentences of Samuel Fielden and Michael Schwab to life in prison. Finally, in 1893, Governor John Peter Altgeld pardoned the three surviving defendants, an act that is widely regarded as having destroyed his political career.
149. Editorials are quoted in Higham, *Strangers* at 54–55.
150. Saxton, *Indispensable Enemy* at 207.
151. Higham, *Strangers* at 56.

152. Saxton, *Indispensable Enemy* at 209 (quoting the *San Francisco Call*, February 16, 1886).

153. *Congressional Record*, 47th Cong., 1st sess., Mar. 22, 1882, 2139, Appendix 63; Gyory, *Closing the Gate* at 237.

154. Coolidge, *Chinese Immigration* at 203.

155. "There is no distinction in this respect, between citizens and the subjects of other nations. Liberty is the birthright and inalienable possession of all men, as men. For this proposition an American lawyer disdains to cite authority. Neither the fundamental law of the United States, nor of any one of the States, recognizes any such distinction." 130 U.S. 581, 584.

156. 83 U.S. 36 (1873) (the federal Constitution held only to apply to "privileges or immunities of a national character," such as the right to petition the government, the right of assembly, or the right of habeas corpus).

157. For a strong critique of this holding, see Henkin, "The Constitution."

158. Henkin, "The Constitution" at 862–863.

159. U.S. Congress, House, Select Committee on Immigration and Naturalization, Report, 51st Cong., 2d sess. (1891), ii.

160. 26 Stat. 1084.

161. See 26 Stat. 1084, Section 8. Another important doctrinal feature of the 1891 law was its mandate that decisions of immigration inspectors "touching the right of any alien to land" were to be "final." The law stated that such finality would apply "unless appeal be taken to the superintendent of immigration . . . subject to review by the Secretary of the Treasury." Over time, this provision spawned a great deal of federal case law requiring highly deferential judicial review of immigration and deportation cases.

162. U.S. Cong., *Congressional Record*, 47th Cong., 1st sess., 1881, 3266 (quoted in Takaki, *Strangers from a Different Shore* at 217).

163. 142 U.S. 651, 659 (citing Vattel and Phillimore) See James A. R. Nafziger, "The General Admission of Aliens under International Law," 77 A. J. I. L. 804 (1983) (describing this expansion of doctrine as "tendentious, and its talismanic dictum ill-founded").

164. See Siegfried Hesse, "The Constitutional Status of the Lawfully Admitted Permanent Resident Alien: The Pre-1917 Cases," 68 *Yale L.J.* 1578, 1590 (1959).

165. An 1893 amendment changed this requirement to "at least one credible witness other than Chinese." Sec. 6, 28 Stat. 7. See also *Congressional Record*, Senate, May 4, 1892, at 3872, for discussion of the original provision.

166. *Congressional Record*, Senate, April 25, 1892, at 3609.

167. *Congressional Record*, Senate, April 25, 1892, at 3628.

168. *Congressional Record*, Senate, April 25, 1892, at 3610.

169. *Congressional Record*, Senate, April 25, 1892, at 3628.

170. *Congressional Record*, Senate, April 25, 1892, at 3629.

171. *Id.*

172. *Congressional Record*, Senate, May 3, 1892, at 3874.

173. Salyer, *Laws Harsh as Tigers* at 48–51 (quoting *Appellants' Brief of J. Hubley Ashton* 69–83).
174. *Brief for Respondents* at 59; Salyer, *Laws Harsh as Tigers* at 52.
175. 149 US 698 (1892).
176. 149 U.S. at 707, 713, 724.
177. Justice Field, author of the *Chinese Exclusion Case*, dissented, writing that such a statute as this invited the exercise of a "dangerous and despotic power."
178. *Id.* at 730.
179. See Hesse, "The Pre-1917 Cases" at 1596.
180. *Fong Yue Ting,* 149 U.S. at 730.
181. See *id.* at 709, citing L. Bar, *International Law: Private and Criminal* 708 n.2, 711 (G. R. Gillespie trans., 1883) (internal quotation marks omitted). For a historical analysis of transportation that supports the idea of deportation as punishment, see Javier Bleichmar, "Deportation as Punishment: A Historical Analysis of the British Practice of Banishment and Its Impact on Modern Constitutional Law," 14 *Geo. Immigr. L.J.* 115 (1999).
182. The approach taken by the dissenters, including Justice Field, who had authored the *Chinese Exclusion Case*, tends to support the broadest reading of the majority opinion—that it applies to both types of deportation laws. Justice Field accepted a power to deport for crime or "in view of existing or anticipated hostilities," but not for lawfully resident nationals of countries with which the United States is at peace. *Fong Yue Ting,* 149 U.S. at 757 (Field, J., dissenting). Justice Brewer argued that the doctrine of inherent sovereign powers was both "indefinite and dangerous" and that lawful residents were entitled to a panoply of constitutional protections, including those of the Fourth, Fifth, Sixth, and Eighth Amendments. *Id.* at 737 (Brewer, J., dissenting). Chief Justice Fuller argued that "limitations exist or are imposed upon the deprivation of that which has been lawfully acquired." *Id.* at 763 (Fuller, C. J., dissenting).
183. Salyer, *Laws Harsh as Tigers* at 55 (quoting *Congressional Record*, 53rd Cong., 1st sess., 2422) (1893).
184. *Id.* (quoting *San Francisco Call,* Sept. 16, 1893).
185. *Id.* at 86.
186. Coolidge, *Chinese Immigration* at 219, 223.
187. *In re Ny Look,* C. C. New York (1893), 56 Fed. 81. Some of these defects were addressed by the so-called McCreary Amendment, passed in 1893, which reaffirmed the requirements of the Geary Act while giving the Chinese an additional six months to register. 53rd Cong., ch. 14; 28 Stat. 7.
188. Higham, *Strangers* at 68.
189. Saxton, *Indispensable Enemy* at 229 (quoting *Pacific Rural Press,* August 26, 1893).
190. *Id.* at 234 (quoting *Los Angeles Times,* September 2, 1893).
191. Terence Powderly, "The Chinese Evil, Master Workman Powderly Speaks Out,

Urges Reenactment of the Exclusion Law by Congress," *San Francisco Chronicle,* Jan. 8, 1892, quoted in Jules Becker, *The Course of Exclusion, 1882–1924: San Francisco Newspaper Coverage of the Chinese and Japanese in the United States* 13, 99–100 (1992).

192. Coolidge, *Chinese Immigration* at 230.

193. Salyer, *Laws Harsh as Tigers* at 89.

194. 163 U.S. 228 (1896).

195. See Act of May 5, 1892, ch. 60, 4, 27 Stat. 25 (expired by its own terms in 1902).

196. *Wong Wing v. United States,* 163 U.S. at 235, 237.

197. See *Boyd v. United States,* 116 U.S. 616 (1886) ("We are . . . clearly of opinion that proceedings instituted for the purpose of declaring the forfeiture of a man's property by reason of offences committed by him, though they may be civil in form, are in their nature criminal").

198. See *Wong Wing,* 163 U.S. at 233. The government, conversely, argued that punishment at hard labor did not render the proceeding to be for an "infamous crime." *Id.* at 234.

199. *Wong Wing,* 163 U.S. at 237.

200. *Id.*

201. 118 U.S. 356 (1886).

202. See *Wong Wing,* 163 U.S. at 238.

203. See Henry M. Hart, Jr., "The Aims of the Criminal Law," 23 *Law & Contemp. Probs.* 401, 404–405 (1958) (distinguishing military service from imprisonment as punishment because imprisonment expresses the moral condemnation of society).

204. For example, the Court noted that "a judicial trial [was necessary] to establish the guilt of the accused." *Wong Wing,* 163 U.S. at 237.

205. See Gerald Neuman, "Wong Wing v. United States," in *Immigration Stories* (David A. Martin and Peter H. Schuck eds., 2005).

206. See Legomsky, "Plenary" at 256, 278.

207. See generally Fuchs, *American Kaleidoscope* at 54–79; Higham, *Strangers* at 87–330.

208. See, e.g., *Fong Yue Ting,* 149 U.S. at 743 (1893) (Brewer, J., dissenting) (referring, perhaps ironically, to "obnoxious Chinese").

209. See Konvitz, *Alien and the Asiatic* at 10 n. 29.

210. See Legomsky, "Plenary" at 261 (describing how the plenary power doctrine involved foreign affairs concerns); Aleinikoff, *Semblances.*

211. Peter H. Schuck, "The Transformation of Immigration Law," 84 *Column. L. Rev.* 5–7 (1984).

212. See Legomsky, "Plenary" at 269.

213. Act of Mar. 3, 1875, ch. 141, 18 Stat. 477 (repealed 1974).

214. Act of Mar. 3, 1891, ch. 551, 26 Stat. 1084; id. at sec. 11, superseded by Act of Mar. 3, 1902, ch. 112, 20, 36, 32 Stat. 1213, 1218, 1221 (repealed 1907).

215. Act of Mar. 3, 1903, ch. 1012, 21, 32 Stat. 1213, 1218 (repealed 1917).
216. See Hesse, "The Pre-1917 Cases" at 1615.
217. See Hutchinson, *Legislative History* at 101.
218. Act of Feb. 20, 1907, ch. 1134, 3, 34 Stat. 898, 900, amended by Act of Mar. 26, 1910, ch. 128, 2, 36 Stat. 263, 265 (repealed 1917).
219. 2 U.S. Immigration Commission, *Abstracts of Reports of the Immigration Commission,* S. doc. no. 61–747, at 339 (3rd sess. 1910).
220. See Hesse, "The Pre-1917 Cases" at 1618.
221. See Act of Mar. 26, 1910, ch. 128, 2, 36 Stat. 263, 265 (repealed 1917). Note that it was based on the status of being a prostitute, not necessarily a criminal conviction.
222. 228 U.S. 585 (1913).
223. *Bugajewitz v. Adams,* 228 U.S. at 590.
224. *Id.* See Hesse, "The Pre-1917 Cases" at 1622 (arguing that Holmes may well have meant that her post-entry conduct proved her inadmissibility as a prostitute at entry).
225. See *Bugajewitz,* 228 U.S. at 586–589.
226. See *id.* at 591.
227. See, e.g., Hesse, "The Pre-1917 Cases" at 1621–1625; Schuck, *Transformation* at 25.
228. 228 U.S. 549 (1913).
229. See *id.* at 554, 556–557. (internal citations omitted). Holmes may well have interpreted the question in light of his general acceptance of the so-called right-privilege distinction. If a policeman has no right to talk politics if he wants to continue to be a policeman, then an alien should surely have no basis on which to claim a "right" to reside in the United States.
230. William C. Van Vleck, *Administrative Control of Aliens* 241 (1923).
231. 189 U.S. 86 (1903).
232. The *Yamataya* court used what in modern terms we would call a "clear statement" method—with which the Court interpreted a statute in a certain way to avoid a constitutional problem. ("This is the reasonable construction of the acts of Congress here in question, and they need not be otherwise interpreted. In the case of all acts of Congress, such interpretation ought to be adopted as, without doing violence to the import of the words used, will bring them into harmony with the Constitution.") 189 U.S. 86, 101.
233. *Whitfield v. Hanges,* 222 F. 745, 748. (8th Cir. 1915).
234. See Skowronek, *Building.*
235. See, e.g., Robert W. Gordon, "Legal Thought and Legal Practice in the Age of American Enterprise, 1870–1920" in *Professions and Professional Ideologies in America* 70–110 (1983).
236. *Lem Moon Sing v. United States,* 158 U.S. 538, 549 (1895).
237. See Salyer, *Laws Harsh as Tigers* at 98. A district court in California held that

the "finality clause" of the statute did not apply to such claims. *In re Tom Yum,* 64 F. 485 (1894).

238. *United States v. Wong Kim Ark,* 169 U.S. 649 (1898).
239. Salyer, *Laws Harsh as Tigers* at 100.
240. *United States v. Sing Tuck,* 194 U.S. 161, 168–170 (1904).
241. *United States v. Ju Toy* 198 U.S. 253 (1905).
242. Quoted in Salyer, *Laws Harsh as Tigers* at 113.
243. 198 U.S. 45 (1905).
244. See *Murray's Lessee v. Hoboken Land & Improvement Co.,* 18 How. 272 (1855).
245. *Ju Toy* at 268, 273, 279–280. As in *Fong Yue Ting,* it is unclear whether Brewer's use of the word "obnoxious" was ironic.
246. The Geary Act vested authority in courts to oversee deportation decisions involving Chinese people. Ironically, this led to greater judicial intervention in those cases than in others.
247. *Chin Yow v. United States,* 208 U.S. 8, 12 (1908).
248. Salyer, *Laws Harsh as Tigers* at 177–179. Chin Yow, however, dispirited and demoralized after two years of detention while his case worked its way through the courts, had already chosen to accept deportation back to China. When informed of his victory, he reportedly said that he would rather die than risk detention in the United States again.
249. *Low Wah Suey v. Backus,* 225 U.S. 460 (1912).
250. *Gegiow v. Uhl,* 239 U.S. 3, 10 (1915). (The agency had claimed the interpretive authority to base exclusions under the "likely to be become a public charge" ground on its own conclusions about the labor market and other general factors. Justice Holmes denied the agency this "amazing claim to power.")
251. 71 U.S. 277 (1867). (A priest was indicted and convicted of the crime of teaching and preaching as a priest and minister of the Roman Catholic Church without having first taken a post–Civil War "test oath." The Court held that the oath had no possible relation to fitness for various pursuits and professions and constituted punishment under the federal Constitution). It should be noted that Cummings was represented by David Dudley Field, Justice Field's brother.
252. *Id.* at 320.

4. The Second Wave

1. Morton Keller, *Regulating a New Society: Public Policy and Social Change in America, 1900–1933* 4 (1994), citing John Martin, "Social Reconstruction Today," 102 *Atlantic Monthly* 293–294 (1908).
2. Fifth Annual Message, December 5, 1905, 40 *Congressional Record* 101 (1905). Some of these suggestions were incorporated into the Immigration Act of 1907, 34 Stat. 898.

3. Frederic C. Howe, "Lynch Law and the Immigrant Alien," *The Nation* (February 14, 1920).
4. Act of Feb. 5, 1917; 39 Stat. 874.
5. The zone excluded Japan and the Philippines, which was a U.S. territory.
6. The first quota law, the Act of March 19, 1921, set an annual quota for each nationality group, defined by country of birth, at 3 percent of the number of foreign-born persons of that group counted in the 1910 census.
7. Immigration Act of 1924, 43 Stat. 153. It moved the benchmark measure for quotas back to the 1890 census, reducing the Italian quota from 42,000 to about 4,000; the Polish from 31,000 to 6,000; and the Greek from 3,000 to 100. See Select Commission on Immigration and Refugee Policy (SCIRP), U.S. Immigration Policy and the National Interest, Staff Report (1981).
8. This was largely due to the perceived failure of a diplomatic initiative known as the Gentlemen's Agreement by which the Japanese government had agreed to prevent labor immigration.
9. See Mae Ngai, *Impossible Subjects: Illegal Aliens and the Making of Modern America* 37–39 (2004), citing Yuji Ichioka, *The Issei: The World of First Generation Japanese Immigrants, 1880–1924* 71–72, 251–254 (1988); Bill Ong Hing, *Making and Remaking Asian America through Immigration Policy, 1850–1990* 29 (1993).
10. See, e.g., Clark, *Deportation* at 241 (recounting the case of Vilma Megyi, who came to the United States with her father in 1913 at the age of 7 and was deported in December 1925).
11. Homer Cummings and Carl McFarland, *Federal Justice: Chapters in the History of Justice and the Federal Executive* 475 (1937), citing Wayne L. Morse and Raymond C. Morley, "Crime Commissions as Aids in the Legal Social Field," 145 *Ann. Am. Acad. Pol. & Soc. Sci.* 68 (1929); John M. Pfiffner, "The Activities and Results of Crime Surveys," 23 *Am. Pol. Sci. Rev.* 930 (1929); John H. Wigmore, "The National Crime Commission," 16 J. Am. Inst. Crim. L. Grim. 312 (1925).
12. U.S. Immigration Commission of 1911, Report 1:45–48 (1911); Hutchinson, *Legislative History* at 148.
13. In March 1916, the house accepted a committee proposal for deportation, without any time limit, of aliens who had been convicted of certain crimes prior to entry. *Congressional Record,* 6th Cong., 1st sess. (1916) 53:5169.
14. Act of Feb. 5, 1917, ch. 29, 19, 39 Stat. 874, 889 (repealed 1952).
15. S. Rep. No. 81–1515, at 54–55 (1950).
16. Act of Feb. 5, 1917, ch. 19, 39 Stat. 874 (repealed 1952).
17. This latter provision, the so-called JRAD (Judician Recommendation against Deportation), was repealed in 1990.
18. May 10, 1920, 41 Stat. 593.
19. May 26, 1922, 42 Stat. 596.
20. Clark, *Deportation* at 9.
21. Edwin E. Grant, "Scum from the Melting-Pot," 30 *American Journal of Sociology* 641–651 (1925).

22. *United States ex rel. Bilokumsky v. Tod,* 263 U.S. 149, 153–154 (1923). See generally Daniel Kanstroom, "Hello Darkness: Involuntary Testimony and Silence as Evidence in Deportation Proceedings" 4 *Geo. Immigr. L.J.* 599 (1990).
23. *Mahler v. Eby,* 264 U.S. 32, 39 (1924).
24. See, e.g., *Coykendall v. Skrmetta,* 22 F.2d 120, 121 (5th Cir. 1927).
25. *Tillinghast v. Edmead,* 31 F.2d 81, 83 (1929).
26. *Iorio v. Day,* 34 F.2d 920 (2d Cir. 1929)
27. Note, "Crimes Involving Moral Turpitude," 43 *Harv. L. Rev.* 117, 121 (1929).
28. See Hutchinson, *Legislative History* at 173.
29. Act of May 26, 1922, 42 Stat. 596. The grounds of deportation for narcotics were made more comprehensive in 1931 (46 Stat. 1171); marijuana was added to the list in 1940 (54 Stat. 673); and even addicts were to be deported after 1952 pursuant to § 241(a)(11) of the Immigration and Nationality Act.
30. *Jordan v. DeGeorge,* 341 U.S. 223 (1951).
31. 41 Stat. 305 (1919) (also known as the National Prohibition Act).
32. Although ushered in with an optimistic tone, it became evident that these agents were in many ways inferior to most of the urban police they supplemented. The federal agents were widely seen as poorly disciplined, badly organized, underpaid, and often corrupt. Clair Bond Potter, *War on Crime: Bandits, G-men, and the Politics of Mass Culture* 16 (1998); Cummings and McFarland, *Federal Justice* at 475.
33. See Mary M. Stolberg, *Fighting Organized Crime: Politics, Justice, and the Legacy of Thomas E. Dewey* 17 (1995).
34. Cummings and McFarland, *Federal Justice* at 475.
35. David M. Kennedy, *Over Here: The First World War and American Society* 11 (1980).
36. See generally Higham, *Strangers.*
37. Although Czolgosz styled himself an anarchist, it is generally accepted that he was mentally ill. Louis Post termed him "an American lunatic with a foreign name." Louis F. Post, *The Deportations Delirium of the Nineteen–Twenties* 61 (1923). See Act of March 3, 1903, 32 Stat. 1213, c. 1012.
38. See Sections 2 and 38 of the Act of March 3, 1903, 32 Stat. 1213, c. 1012.
39. *United States ex rel. Turner v. Williams,* 194 U.S. 279, 280 (1904).
40. The reported speech was a combination of an anarchist lecture and a labor rally. Certain papers were also found on Turner, including one that stated, "It may be interesting to all that Turner has recently refused to accept a candidacy to Parliament because of his anarchistic principles." *Id.*
41. Their appeal cited *Ex parte Sing* (C. C.), 82 Fed. Rep. 22; *Wong Wing v. United States,* 163 U.S. 228 (1896); and *Yick Wo v. Hopkins,* 118 U.S. 356 (1886). They also raised an Article III challenge.
42. 149 U.S. 286 (1903).
43. *Id.* at 287.
44. *Id.* at 290.

45. Howe, "Lynch Law," *supra.*
46. Kennedy, *Over Here* at 12.
47. Hutchinson, *Legislative History* at 164; 53 Congressional Record, 6th Cong., 1st sess. 99 (1915).
48. Woodrow Wilson, Message to the Congress, April 12, 1917, 65th Cong., 1st sess., Sen. Doc. 5, serial no. 7264.
49. Higham, *Strangers* at 200.
50. As Wilson had noted, it was upon the executive branch that "the responsibility of conducting war and safeguarding the nation will most directly fall." Kennedy, *Over Here* at 14.
51. *Id.* at 165, 166.
52. *Id.* at 157.
53. H. Rept. 127, Aug. 4, 1917, p. 2 (cited in Hutchinson, *Legislative History* at 168).
54. Kennedy, *Over Here* at 17.
55. *Id.* citing Chase C. Mooney and Martha E. Lyman, "Some Phases of the Compulsory Military Training Movement, 1914–1920," 38 *Miss. Valley Historical Rev.* 41 (1952).
56. Kennedy, *Over Here* at 17–18, citing *Congressional Record,* House, 65th Cong., 1st sess., Apr. 5, 1917, 319.
57. Higham, *Strangers* at 205.
58. Kennedy, *Over Here* at 23, 25.
59. Albert Shaw, ed., *Messages and Papers of Woodrow Wilson* vol. 1, 151 (1924).
60. Act of Feb. 5, 1917, 39 Stat. 874; Act of Oct. 16, 1918, 40 Stat. 1012.
61. 40 Stat. 217, June 15, 1917.
62. Act of May 16, 1918, 40 Stat. 553–554.
63. Cummings and McFarland, *Federal Justice* at 420.
64. Kennedy, *Over Here* at 82; Keller, *Regulating* at 97. It was joined by, among others, "the Terrible Threateners" and the "Sedition Slammers."
65. Cummings and McFarland, *Federal Justice* at 420 (quoting John Lord O'Brian, *Civil Liberty in War Time,* January 1919, published by 42nd annual meeting of the New York Bar Association).
66. Kennedy, *Over Here* at 82.
67. See Ernst Freund, "Freedom of Speech and the Press" 25 *New Republic* (1921); Samuel Walker, *In Defense of American Liberties: A History of the ACLU* (1990).
68. Higham, *Strangers* at 247.
69. Keller, *Regulating* at 99, citing Edward S. Corwin, "Freedom of Speech and the Press under the First Amendment: A Resumé," 30 *Yale L.J.* 48 (1921).
70. Higham, *Strangers* at 213.
71. Kennedy, *Over Here* at 67, quoting *Hearing before a Special Committee of the House of Representatives,* 65th Cong., 3d sess., 2013 (1919).
72. Kennedy, *Over Here* at 67–68.
73. Cummings, *Federal Justice* at 427, citing Ann. Rep. Atty Gen. 1918, 39; Ann. Rep. Atty Gen. 1918, 25–26.

74. Thomas E. Campbell, "The I.W.W. in Arizona, True Copy of the original notes of Thomas E. Campbell, former Governor of Arizona" (c.1934–1939), University of Arizona Digital Lib., Arizona Historical Society Library, MS 132, Campbell and family papers, Folder 6, ftp://digital.library.arizona.edu/bisbee/docs2/rec_camp.htm (accessed June 21, 2004) [hereinafter Campbell, "Notes"].

75. See generally Sheila Bonnand, *Historical Context of the Bisbee Deportation,* http://digital.library.arizona.edu/bisbee/main/history.php; see also Lynn R Bailey, *Bisbee, Queen of the Copper Camps* (1983); Ann M. Cox, *History of Bisbee, 1877 to 1937* (1938); Rob E. Hanson, *The Great Bisbee I.W.W. Deportation of July 12, 1917* (1989).

76. James W. Byrkit, *Forging the Copper Collar: Arizona's Labor-Management War of 1901–1921* 21 (1982), citing "Writers' Program of the Work Projects Administration," in *Arizona: A State Guide* 175 (1940); Will H. Robinson, *The Story of Arizona* 397 (1919); Louis Levine, "The Development of Syndicalism in America," 28 *Political Science Quarterly* 451–479 (1913).

77. Ann M. Cox, *History of Bisbee, 1877 to 1937* (1938), citing "Bisbee's Early History," *Copper Queen Bulletin* 7 (1922).

78. Byrkit, *Forging* at 29.

79. Campbell, "Notes" at 9.

80. In 1916, the International Union of Mine, Mill and Smelter Workers successfully organized some 1,800 miners. See Bonnand, *Bisbee Deportation.*

81. Byrkit, *Forging* at 158.

82. Robert W. Bruere, "Copper Camp Patriotism," 106 *The Nation* 202 (Feb. 21, 1918).

83. "The Sheriff's Call," July 12, 1917, http://digital.library.arizona.edu/bisbee/docs2/deport.php (University of Arizona Special Collections H9791 B621 A51).

84. Byrkit, *Forging* at 184.

85. *New York Times,* June 29, 1917, 17.

86. "The Great Wobbly Drive," *Bisbee Daily Review,* July 13, 1917 (capitals as in the original), reprinted at http://www.I.W.W.iww.org/~iw/feb/stories/bisbee.html.

87. *Id.,* "The Deportation."

88. Bonnand, *Bisbee Deportation.*

89. "Report and Recommendations of President's Mediators on the Underlying Causes and Remedy for Labor Unrest," *The Official Bulletin,* Feb. 11, 1918, 9–14.

90. Byrkit, *Forging* at 173–174.

91. *Id.,* citing Alexander M. Bing, *War-Time Strikes and Their Adjustment* 265 (1955); see also John Caughey, *Their Majesties, the Mob* 9 (1960); Wayne Gard, *Frontier Justice* (1949).

92. Writing in hindsight about Bisbee, Governor Campbell suggested that the first "deportation" in Arizona was the ouster not of strikers but of mining management from the Clifton-Morenci Mining District in 1915 when then-Governor

Hunt boasted how he had "run the 'Foreigners' out of the State." Campbell, "Notes" at 2–5.

93. See Byrkit, *Forging* at 226–227.

94. Kennedy, *Over Here* at 73, citing H. C. Peterson and Gilbert C. Fitye, *Opponents of War, 1917–1918* 57–60, 79 (1968).

95. Cited in Byrkit, *Forging* at 225.

96. *Id.* at 148.

97. See Anthony Caminetti, U.S. Congress, House, *Exclusion and Expulsion of Aliens of Anarchistic and Similar Classes,* Doc. No. 7652, 65th Cong., 2d sess., H.R. 504 (Dec. 16, 1919), 4.

98. Higham, *Strangers* at 220.

99. Bruere, "Copper Camp Patriotism."

100. Higham, *Strangers* at 220.

101. *State of Arizona v. H. E. Wooton.* See John D. Lawson, ed., *American State Trials,* vol. 17, 8–11 (1936).

102. J. O. Calhoun of Douglas (foreman of the jury), *In the Superior Court of Conchise County, State of Arizona (Plaintiff) v. H. E. Wooton (Defendant), in the Law of Necessity as Applied in the State of Arizona, Bisbee I.W.W. v. Deportation Case H. E. Wooton.* Available from the University of Arizona Special Collections H9791 B621 L41, http://digital.library.arizona.edu/bisbee/docs/lawnec.php.

103. George Soule, "Law and Necessity in Bisbee," 113 *The Nation* (August 31, 1921). http://digital.library.arizona.edu/bisbee/docs/nation.php.

104. See John D. Lawson, ed., *American State Trials* vol. 17, 8–11 (1936); see also "Legal Aspects," http://digital.library.arizona.edu/bisbee/main/deposit.php.

105. The purchasing power of the dollar more than halved from 1913 to 1919. Costs for food, clothing, and housing skyrocketed. The cost of living in 1919 was some 99 percent higher than it had been five years earlier. Robert K. Murray, *Red Scare, a Study in National Hysteria, 1919–1920* 7 (1955).

106. Higham, *Strangers* at 221.

107. Murray, *Red Scare* at 8–9.

108. *Id.* at 67.

109. *Id.* at 167–168, citing "What Is Back of the Bombs?" 61 *Literary Digest* 9–11 (June 14, 1919).

110. *Id.* at 121.

111. *Id.* at 169, quoting the poem entitled "Bol-she-veek!" by Edmund Vance Cooke, 22 *Public* 722 (July 19, 1919).

112. Hoover was appointed to this position in 1917. See Cummings and McFarland, *Federal Justice* at 429, citing *A Digested History of the Federal Bureau of Investigation* (mimeographed document of the bureau); Murray, *Red Scare* at 193. See also "Investigation Activities of the Department of Justice," 66th Cong., 1st sess., Sen. Doc. 153, 5, 8, 10–12, 14 (1919).

113. *Attorney General A. Mitchell Palmer on charges made against Department of Jus-*

tice by Louis F. Post and others, hearings before the committee on rules, House of Representatives, Washington, D.C., 157–158 (1920).

114. Cummings and McFarland *Federal Justice* at 428; "Palmer and Family Safe," *New York Times,* June 3, 1919, 1.

115. Mitchell Palmer was a Quaker, a fact that was well-known at the time—he was sometimes known as the "fighting Quaker" and years later would be mocked as "the quaking fighter." Murray, *Red Scare* at 192, citing James Kerney, *The Political Education of Woodrow Wilson* 301–303 (1926).

116. "Attorney General Palmer Warns the Anarchists," *New York Times,* June 4, 1919, 1.

117. Cummings and McFarland *Federal Justice* at 429, quoting from *Charges of Illegal Practices of the Department of Justice, Sen. Jud. Subcomm. Hearings,* 66th Cong., 3d sess., 580.

118. See Mark Ellis, "J. Edgar Hoover and the 'Red Summer' of 1919," 28 *Journal of American Studies* 39–59 (1994).

119. Murray, *Red Scare* at 196.

120. Quoted in Charles H. McCormick, *Seeing Reds: Federal Surveillance of Radicals in the Pittsburgh Mill District, 1917–1921* 188 (1997).

121. Murray, *Red Scare* at 196.

122. "Reds Are Working among Negroes," *New York Times,* Oct. 19, 1919, 1.

123. The report apparently was written by Robert Bowen of the Post Office, Ellis, "J. Edgar Hoover" at 53, citing Robert A. Bowen, "Radicalism and Sedition among the Negroes as Reflected in Their Publications," Oct. 28, 1919, File OG 3056, Bureau of Investigation Records, Record Group 65, National Archives.

124. U.S. Senate, *Investigation Activities of the Department of Justice,* 66th Cong., 1st sess., Nov. 15, 1919, at 328; Ellis, "J. Edgar Hoover" at 54.

125. Ellis, "J. Edgar Hoover" at 49 (emphasis added); see also Robert A. Hill, "'The Foremost Radical Among His Race': Marcus Garvey and the Black Scare, 1918–1921," 16 *Prologue* 214–231 (1984).

126. Ellis, "J. Edgar Hoover" at 49; Tony Martin, *Race First: The Ideological and Organizational Struggles of Marcus Garvey and the Universal Negro Improvement Association* 191–200 (1976).

127. Keller, *Regulating* at 105; see Oswald G. Villard, "The New Fight for Old Liberties," 151 *Harper's Monthly* 440 (1925).

128. See "Johnstown's Flood of Negro Labor," 79 *Literary Digest* 178 (Oct. 6, 1923); "Rioting Negroes Kill Police in Johnstown, *New York Times,* Sept. 1, 1923, 11; "Johnstown Expels 2000 Working men," *New York Times,* Sept. 15, 1923, 17. Cauffield, who reportedly also permitted only pro-Fascist speakers to hold public meetings, lost the next election.

129. Post, *Delirium* at 30–31 (quoting in part from *New York Times* account).

130. *Id.* at 31–32.

131. *Id.* at 167.

132. *Id.* at 66, 69.
133. *Id.* at 100.
134. *Id.* at 18, 100. The law required deportees to be returned "to the country [from] whence they came." For Russian immigrants, this presented at least two rather serious problems. First, there were no regular channels of communication open to facilitate the return of people to Russia. Second, the alternative of sending them to "White Russia" might well result in immediate execution for many of those who were alleged to be "Reds." An arrangement was thus made with Finland, then at war with Russia, to send the deportees there and to have them somehow transported from there to Russia under a flag of truce.
135. *Id.* at 3.
136. Alexander Berkman and Emma Goldman, *Deportation, Its Meaning and Menace: Last Message to the People of America, Ellis Island, New York, U.S.A.* (December 1919), Goldman Archive, Anarchy Archives; courtesy of International Institute for Social History; reprinted at http://sunsite.berkeley.edu/Goldman/Exhibition/plea.html.
137. See generally Ernest Hover, "Citizenship of Women in the United States," 26 *American Journal of International Law* 700–719 (1932).
138. Emma Goldman, *Living My Life* 712 (1931).
139. Post, *Delirium* at 14. Post was puzzled when Goldman did not take this issue to the courts. She, in turn, expressed outrage that he had not accepted her legal arguments. Indeed, in her memoirs, she plaintively recalled that she had dined with the Posts years before and felt deeply betrayed by him. She wrote that Post had "covered himself with ignomy." Goldman, *Living My Life* at 712.
140. Statement by Emma Goldman at her deportation hearing, New York, Oct. 27, 1919, reprinted in *The Emma Goldman Papers*, Berkeley Digital Library, http://sunsite.berkeley.edu/cgi-bin/imagemap/emma.
141. *Id.*
142. *Id.*
143. Post, *Delirium* at 14–15.
144. *Id.* at 61.
145. *Id.* at 16.
146. *Id.* at 34.
147. *United States ex rel. Bosny et al. v. Williams*, 185 Fed. 598, 599 (SDNY 1911).
148. *Id.*
149. Murray, *Red Scare* at 211. The new rule stated, "At the beginning of the hearing under the warrant of arrest, the alien shall be permitted to inspect the warrant . . . and shall be apprised that he may be represented by counsel."
150. Post, *Delirium* at 87.
151. 8 CFR 287.3.
152. U.S. Comp. Stat., 1918, §42891/4 jj.
153. See, e.g., Louis Post, "Administrative Decisions in Connection with Immigration," 10 *Pol. Sci. Rev.* 261 (1916).

154. Chafee, *Freedom of Speech* at 234.
155. The doctrinal reason for this rule, as noted, was said to be that deportation proceedings were essentially "Executive not Judicial" and "not in the same legal category with proceedings to punish crimes." Post, "Administrative Decisions" at 52–53.
156. Chafee, *Freedom of Speech* at 253–254.
157. Murray, *Red Scare* at 206, citing *Congressional Record*, 66th Cong., 2d sess., 1920, 37, 990, 1334, quoting Senator McKellar.
158. *Id.* at 219, citing "Extent of the Bolshevik Infection Here," 64 *Literary Digest* 13 (January 17, 1920), and *Attorney General A. Mitchell Palmer on Charges,* 27.
159. Louis Post had resisted some aspects of Palmer's deportations. Indeed, Post began his 1923 book about the period with a clear statement of what he thought was at stake: "The question is whether the people of this country really believe in their own principles." In an act of considerable courage, Post had ordered the cancellation of hundreds of warrants. See Post, *Delirium* at ix. Palmer felt that Post had improperly "nullified" the intent of Congress and released "among the people the very public enemies" that Congress had intended the country "to be rid of." Cummings and McFarland, *Federal Justice* at 430.
160. Frederic C. Howe, *The Confessions of a Reformer* 267 (1967).
161. A contemporary poll of union leaders indicated that 305 favored the deportations of "Reds," while 176 were opposed, 22 were divided, and 16 reportedly asked what a "Red" agitator was. Keller, *Regulating* at 102.
162. Howe, *Lynch Law and the Immigrant Alien* at 195.
163. Keller, *Regulating* at 103. See also Lewis S. Gannett, "A Yankee Verdict: Judge Anderson's Decision," 111 *The Nation* 7 (July 3, 1920).
164. See Matt S. Meier, "North from Mexico," in Carey McWilliams, ed., *North from Mexico* 309, 310 (1990). Statistics about Mexicans in the United States have been subject to frequent criticism. As one 1930 survey noted, there was a sharp distinction between the number of reported immigrants and the actual numbers admitted. Abraham Hoffman, Unwanted Mexican Americans in the Great Depression 13 (1974).
165. See *id.* at 6–7; Ernesto Galarza, *Merchants of Labor: The Mexican Bracero Story* (1964).
166. For that matter, Mexicans were also seen as less threatening than African American workers.
167. Lawrence Cardoso, *Mexican Emigration to the United States, 1897–1931* 21 (1980).
168. Philip Martin, "Guestworkers: Past and Present," in *Migration Between Mexico and the United States: Binational Study* 878 (1998).
169. Charles A. Thomson, "The Man from Next Door," 111 *Century Magazine* 276 (1926) (cited in Hoffman, *Unwanted*, at 9).
170. "Using Chinese Labor," *Los Angeles Times,* Jan. 15, 1920, 2.4. (cited in Martin, "Guestworkers" at 878).

171. Hoffman, *Unwanted* at 10.
172. Joseph Nevins, *Operation Gatekeeper: The Rise of the "Illegal Alien" and the Making of the U.S.-Mexico Boundary* 32–33 (2002), quoting Wayne Cornelius, *Mexican Migration to the United States: Origins, Consequences, and Policy Options* (1989).
173. Nevins, *Operation Gatekeeper* at 33.
174. Three weeks later, President Wilson called the U.S Congress into special session to propose that the Congress "formally accept the status of belligerent which has thus been thrust upon it." Kennedy, *Over Here* at 10–13.
175. Hoffman, *Unwanted* at 11.
176. Ngai, *Impossible* at 56–89.
177. See generally Ngai, *Impossible*.
178. The 1924 law, as noted above, also adopted quotas for the Eastern Hemisphere.
179. Immigration Act of 1924, 43 Stat. 153. One month later, the Act of June 7, 1924 (43 Stat. 669) provided that certain aliens who had entered the country in excess of the quota could, if otherwise not subject to deportation, be allowed to remain.
180. Ngai, *Impossible* at 60, citing U.S. Bureau of the Census, *Historical Statistics of the U.S. Colonial Times to 1970* 114 (Washington, D.C.: GPO, 1975). The figures include deportation under formal warrant and voluntary departures.
181. Office of Immigration Statistics, *2004 Yearbook of Immigration Statistics,* Table 45.
182. This changed in 1965. See Immigration and Nationality Act of 1965, 79 Stat. 911.
183. 39 Stat. 874.
184. Ngai, *Impossible* at 64.
185. Hoffman, *Unwanted* at 32.
186. Ngai, *Impossible* at 67.
187. George Sanchez, *Becoming Mexican American* 59–61 (1993) (cited in Ngai, *Impossible* at 67–68 fn. 43).
188. Ngai, *Impossible* at 68, fn. 44. The Border Patrol was created in 1924, with a budget of one million dollars. By 1930, its size exceeded 780 employees, and it had reported the capture of some 100,000 "illegal aliens." Hoffman, *Unwanted* at 31.
189. Ngai, *Impossible* at 70 fn. 52.
190. By 1929, illegal entry was a federal misdemeanor, and illegal reentry of a previously deported person was a felony. 45 Stat. 1551.
191. Ngai, *Impossible* at 67–70.
192. Ernesto Galarza, "Life in the United States for Mexican People: Out of the Experience of a Mexican," in *Proceedings of the National Conference of Social Work, 56th Annual Session* (1929).
193. Ngai, *Impossible* at 71.

194. Post, *Delirium* at 250, quoting Mrs. William Hard.
195. Quoted in Post, *Delirium* at 271.

5. The Third Wave

1. Gardner Jackson, "Doak the Deportation Chief," 132 *The Nation* 295 (March 18, 1931).
2. "The Cooling Melting Pot," review of Clark, *Deportation,* 133 *The Nation* 366 (October 7, 1931).
3. Potter, *War* at 13.
4. Mary M. Stolberg, *Fighting Organized Crime: Politics, Justice, and the Legacy of Thomas E. Dewey* 40 (1995); William Keller, *The Liberals and J. Edgar Hoover: The Rise and Fall of a Domestic Intelligence State* 156 (1989).
5. See, e.g., David A. Orebaugh, *Crime, Degeneracy, and Immigration* 2 (1929) ("superior germ plasms of various superior races have gone to form the American type"); see also Linda C. Bowler, "Law Enforcement and the Alien," *National Conference of Social Work Proceedings* 479–494 (1931).
6. Stolberg at 47, citing Bella Rodman, *Fiorello La Guardia* 147 (1962).
7. Keller, *Hoover* at 157, citing Richard Enright, "Our Biggest Business—Crime" 228 *North American Review* 385–388 (1929).
8. Orebaugh, *Crime* at 86.
9. Homer Cummings, "Progress Toward a Modern Administration of Criminal Justice in the United States," 22 *A. B. A. J.* 476 (1936); *Congressional Record* LXXI 4–5, 417, 3100; LXII, 27, 1501.
10. House of Representatives, *Summary Report of the National Commission on Law Observance and Enforcement,* House Document No. 722 (Washington, D.C.: GPO, 1931) 54–55, 43.
11. U.S. National Commission on Law Observance and Enforcement, *Report on the Enforcement of the Deportation Laws of the United States* (Washington, D.C.: GPO, 1931).
12. See Potter, *War* at 22 (citing testimony of journalist Walter Liggett).
13. Potter, *War* at 12 (citing Skowronek, *Building*).
14. J. Edgar Hoover, *Persons in Hiding* 312 (1941).
15. Keller, *Hoover* at 5.
16. *Id.* at 155, citing Edward Rubin, "A Statistical Study of Federal Criminal Prosecutions," 1 *Law and Contemporary Problems* 494–503 (1934).
17. As Kristen Potter has noted, the enforcement philosophy "displaced the principles of social critique and corrective intervention that had originally produced the idea of the modern policeman." Potter, *War* at 184.
18. See, e.g., Act of Feb. 18, 1931, 46 Stat. 1171 (deportation for violation of federal laws relating to "opium, coca leaves, heroin" or derivatives). In 1940, the requirement of a sentence was eliminated, marijuana was added, and state, ter-

ritory, and District of Columbia laws were included. Act of June 18, 1940, 54 Stat. 673.

19. Cummings, "Progress" at 478, citing *Address before the Law School Association of the University of Minnesota,* April 15, 1931, D.J. File 44–06–4; *Address in the National Radio Forum,* Columbia Broadcasting System, May 13, 1931, D.J. File 44–06–4; Ann. Rep. Atty. Gen. 1932, 4.

20. 47 Stat. 326, June 22, 1932. This statute in many ways echoed the first such federal law, the "Mann Act," also known as the "White Slave Act," which had prohibited the interstate or international transportation of women and girls for "immoral purposes."

21. Quoted in Potter, *War* at 123.

22. *Id.,* Louis M. Howe to Eleanor Roosevelt, July 27, 1933, "crime" box 72, LMH, FDR Library. Louis M. Howe, "Uncle Sam Starts after Crime," July 29, 1933, box 72 LMH, FDR Library.

23. Cummings, "Progress" at 483.

24. Potter, *War* at 110.

25. Capone had an interesting view of his place in U.S. society. In a 1931 interview by Cornelius Vanderbilt, Jr., he said, "Us fellas has gotta stick together . . . I think we both speak the same language; and I think we're both patriots." "How Al Capone Would Run This Country," *Liberty* October 17, 1931, quoted in Potter, *War* at 58.

26. Stolberg, *Fighting* at 73, citing *William B. Herlands Interview* 36–38 in University of Rochester, Thomas E. Dewey papers).

27. *United States ex rel. Klonis v. Davis,* 13 F.2d 630 (2d Cir. 1926).

28. Some 115,000 people benefited from this law between 1933 and 1940. U.S. Secretary of Labor, "Annual Reports, 1933–1940."

29. The Bureau of Immigration and Naturalization had been housed in the Treasury Department since 1891. It was moved to the Commerce and Labor Department in 1903; then it became part of the new Department of Labor in 1913. Carl Brent Swisher, *American National Government* 362 (1951).

30. Emphasis added.

31. See William C. Van Vleck, "Administrative Justice in the Enforcement of Quasi-Criminal Law," 1 *Geo. Wash. L. Rev.* 18, 19 (1932); Charles Enslow, "Alien Deportation Law," 19 *Lawyer and Banker,* 146–153, 233–247 (1925).

32. Lillian Homlen Mohr, *Frances Perkins, That Woman in FDR's Cabinet!* 131 (1979).

33. Reuben Oppenheimer, "The Deportation Terror," 69 *New Republic* 231–234 (1932); Reuben H. Klainer, "Deportation of Aliens," 15 *B.U. Law Rev.* 663–722 (1935).

34. Mohr, *Perkins* at 125, quoting Franklin J. Carter, *The New Dealers* 174 (1934).

35. *Id.* at 110.

36. *Id.* at 37.

37. *Id.* at 125, quoting Arthur M. Schlesinger, *The New Deal in Action 1933–1937* 299–300 (1938).

38. *Id.* at 132.

39. *Id.*, citing Carter, *The New Dealers,* 176–177.

40. Of longer lasting duration were certain technical mechanisms designed to mitigate the harshness of deportation. For example, the so-called Seventh Proviso of the 1917 act, which allowed permanent residents to overcome grounds of exclusion following short trips abroad, was used creatively by Perkins's agency as a discretionary mechanism to allow long-term residents to overcome criminal grounds of deportation.

41. Alan Block, *East Side-West Side: Organizing Crime in New York, 1930–1950,* 1 (1983).

42. William Howard Moore, *The Kefauver Committee and the Politics of Crime* 115 (1974).

43. Drew Pearson, "Background of Mysterious Mafia," *Washington Post,* Oct. 10, 1950, 13. Cited in Moore, *Kefauver Committee* at 125.

44. Moore, *Kefauver Committee* at 117.

45. Harold B. Hinton, "Senators Again Start on Underworld Trials," *New York Times,* Nov. 12, 1950, 158.

46. Moore, *Kefauver Committee* at 132. There were still doubters. Legislative counsel Rufus King referred to the Mafia conclusions as "romantic myth." Moore, *Kefauver Committee* at 133; see also Rufus G. King "The Control of Organized Crime in America," 4 *Stan. L. Rev.* 52 (December 1951).

47. O. W. Holmes, Jr., "The Path of the Law," 10 *Harv. L. Rev.* 457, 459 (1897).

48. See generally John H. Davis, *Mafia Kingfish: Carlos Marcello and the Assassination of John F. Kennedy* (1989); see also Thomas L. Jones, *Carlos Marcello: Big Daddy in the Big Easy* http://www.crimelibrary.com/gangsters/marcello/.

49. Davis, *Mafia* at 18; John E. Coxe, "The New Orleans Mafia Incident," 20 *Louisiana Historical Quarterly* 1067–1110 (1937); J. Alexander Karlan, "The New Orleans Lynchings of 1890 and the American Press," 24 *Louisiana Historical Quarterly* 187–203 (1941); John H. Kendall, "Who Killa De Chief," 22 *Louisiana Historical Quarterly* 492–530 (1939).

50. Davis, *Mafia* at 21–23.

51. Davis, *Mafia* at 28.

52. *Id.* at 37.

53. Well, maybe. Carolla himself apparently reentered the United States illegally at least once. He died in New Orleans in 1972. G. Robert Blakey and Richard N. Billings, *The Plot to Kill the President* 241 (1981).

54. Davis, *Mafia* at 58.

55. *Id.* See "Inquiry Asks Term for 'Top Criminal,'" *New York Times,* January 30, 1951, 18.

56. Davis, *Mafia* at 60.

57. See *United States ex rel. Marcello v. Ahrens,* 113 F. Supp. 22 (E.D. La. 1953).
58. 66 Stat. 214, 8 U.S.C. §1254(a)(5). For an explanation of how restrictive this standard was meant to be, see H. Rept. 1365 in *U.S. Code Congressional* and *Administrative News,* 82d Cong., 2d sess., 1951, vol. 2, 1718.
59. Though no formal application for suspension of deportation had been filed, the board considered whether relief was merited but exercised its discretion against it. *Matter of M—,* A-2669541, 5 I&N Dec. 261 (June 1, 1953).
60. See generally Walter Gellhorn, "The Administrative Procedure Act: The Beginnings," 72 *Va. L. Rev.* 219 (1986). 58 A.B.A. Rep. 197, 203 (1933). The committee thought that such functions should either be transferred to an independent tribunal or that "judicial-type" agency decisions should be subject to full factual and legal review by an independent tribunal. 59 A.B.A. Rep. 539 (1934). Gellhorn, "Administrative Procedure Act" at 220.
61. See, e.g., Louis L. Jaffe, "Invective and Investigation in Administrative Law," 52 *Harv. L. Rev.* 1201, 1233–1234 (1939).
62. Jacob M. Lashly, "Administrative Law and the Bar," 25 *Va. L. Rev.* 641, 658 (1939).
63. "Final Report of the Attorney General's Committee on Administrative Procedure," Administrative Procedure in Government Agencies, 77th Cong., 1st sess., S. Doc. 8, 1941, 1 [Final Committee Report]; Gellhorn, "Administrative Procedure Act" at 225.
64. Gellhorn, "Administrative Procedure Act" at 231.
65. Martin Shapiro, "APA: Past, Present, and Future," 72 *Va. L. Rev.* 447 (1986).
66. See generally Peter L. Strauss, "Changing Times: The APA at Fifty," 63 *U. Chi. L. Rev.* 1389 (1996).
67. 339 U.S. 33 (1950).
68. 60 Stat. 237, 240 §5(c), 5 U.S.C. §1004(c); 60 Stat. 244 §11, 5 U.S.C. §1010.
69. The requirements of the APA as to inquisitorial process were a little less clear: it seemed to forbid a hearing examiner from protecting the government's interests while adjudicating. But it could also be construed more narrowly—forbidding only a behind-the-scenes role for a clearly designated "prosecutor" in advising or influencing a hearing examiner in a particular case.
70. See *Yamataya v. Fisher,* 189 U.S. 86, 100, 101 (1903).
71. 60 Stat. 237, 241, 5 U.S.C. §1006.
72. "One purpose was to introduce greater uniformity of procedure and standardization of administrative practice among the diverse agencies whose customs had departed widely from each other." 339 U.S. at 41 (footnote omitted).
73. Cf. *Harisiades v. Shaughnessy, infra.*
74. The Secretary of Labor's Committee on Administrative Procedure, the Immigration and Naturalization Service, 77, 81–82 (Mimeo. 1940) (cited in 339 U.S. at 43).
75. 339 U.S. at 45, 47.
76. 339 U.S. at 49–50.

77. 339 U.S. at 52. The statutory language did "direct them to conduct border inspections of aliens seeking admission . . . [and to] administer oaths and take, record, and consider evidence."

78. Supplemental Appropriation Act of 1951, ch. 1052, 64 Stat. 1044, 1048 (1950), exempting deportation and exclusion proceedings from the Administrative Procedure Act, ch. 324, §§5, 7–8 60 Stat. 237, 239 (1946), repealed by Immigration and Nationality Act of 1952, ch. 477, §403(a)(47), 66 Stat. 163, 280.

79. S. 3455, introduced Apr. 20, 1950. McCarran, born in Reno, Nevada, in 1876, was a state district attorney from 1907 to 1909 and Nevada Chief Justice from 1917 to 1918, periods during which, as we have seen, "labor deportations" of radical union organizers were not uncommon.

80. Public Law 81–831, 22, 64 Stat. 987, 1006–1007 (1950); see generally Charles Gordon, "The Immigration Process and National Security," 24 *Temp. L. Q.* 302 (1950) (describing the act). For McCarran's explication and justifications, see Patrick A. McCarran, "The Internal Security Act of 1950," 12 *U. of Pitt. L. Rev.* 481 (1951).

81. The Internal Security Act also declared it unlawful to conspire to establish a totalitarian dictatorship, to conceal membership in the American Communist Party when seeking government employment, or to use a United States passport. President Truman vetoed it, saying that it "would betray our finest traditions" in its attempt to "curb the simple expression of opinion." The Congress, however, overrode Truman's veto. See generally Robert John Frye, *Deportation of Aliens: A Study in Civil Liberties,* Ph.D. Dissertation, University of Florida (1959).

82. H.R. Rep. No. 81–2980 (1950), reprinted in 1950 U.S.C.C.A.N. 3886, 3886–3890.

83. Reported by Oscar Handlin, "The Golden Door (Book Review)," by J. Campbell Bruce, *Commentary* 509 (May 1954).

84. Laurent B. Frantz, "Deportation Deliriums," *The Nation* 258 (March 26, 1955).

85. I doubt that I am the first person to notice that this mixed metaphor amounts to a wet blanket.

86. U.S. Congress, *Revision of Immigration, Naturalization, and Nationality Laws, Joint Hearings before the Subcommittees of the Committee on the Judiciary,* 82nd Cong., 1st sess. (1951), 2.

87. 98 *Congressional Record* 2140 (1952); Frye, *Deportation of Aliens* at 275–279.

88. 98 *Congressional Record* 2141 (1952).

89. 98 *Congressional Record* 5239 (1952).

90. The Humphrey-Lehman bill also would have created a statutory basis for the Board of Immigration Appeals.

91. 98 *Congressional Record* 5316 (1952).

92. 98 *Congressional Record* 4320 (1952).

93. *New York Times,* May 24, 1952, 4. Frye, *Deportation of Aliens* at 283.

94. U.S. Congress, House, Message from the President of the United States, 82nd Cong., 2d sess., H. Doc. 520, 6–7 (1952).
95. C. P. Trussell, "Immigration Bill Passed by House over Truman Veto," *New York Times,* June 26, 1952, 1; Frye, *Deportation of Aliens* at 284.
96. An alternative method was permitted by the statute, under which an additional immigration officer presented the evidence while the special inquiry officer presided. See 8 CFR §242.53 (1955).
97. INA Sec. 242(b).
98. 113 F. Supp. at 22.
99. *Marcello v. Ahrens,* 212 F.2d 830 (5th Cir. 1954).
100. *Id.,* citing the rather different case of *United States v. Morton Salt Company,* 338 U.S. 632, 644 (1950) (the APA created safeguards even narrower than the constitutional ones, against arbitrary official encroachment on private rights).
101. The prejudgment argument was based on the recently decided case of *United States ex rel. Accardi v. Shaughnessy,* in which the Supreme Court had held that Accardi was entitled to a hearing on his allegations that his name had appeared on a list of "unsavory characters" whom the attorney general wished to have deported. 347 U.S. 260 (1954).
102. For the text of the release, see *Marcello v. Bonds,* 349 U.S. at 312.
103. *Id.* at 839.
104. 212 F.2d at 833.
105. *Id.;* see also *Matter of M—, supra.*
106. The fact that he had received a pardon and that some of his contempt convictions had been reversed did not preclude the board from considering them as a matter of discretion. 212 F.2d at 840. See also *Marcello v. United States,* 196 F.2d 437 (5th Cir. 1952).
107. 212 F.2d. at 836 (citing *Harisiades v. Shaughnessy,* 342 U.S. 580, 587–588).
108. 349 U.S. at 308.
109. *Id.*
110. *Id.* at 314.
111. Id., citing *Galvan v. Press,* 347 U.S. 522 (1954); *Harisiades,* 342 U.S. 580 (1952).
112. For a favorable review of Justice Douglas's position, see John Hart Ely, "Legislative and Administrative Motivation in Constitutional Law," 79 *Yale L.J.* 1205, 1312 (1970).
113. See *Bridges v. Wixon,* 326 U.S. 135, 154 (1945); *Delgadillo v. Carmichael,* 332 U.S. 388, 391 (1947).
114. *Ng Fung Ho v. White,* 259 U.S. 276, 284 (1922).
115. 349 U.S. at 321.
116. *Id.* at 311.
117. See Louis B. Boudin, "The Settler within Our Gates" (pts. 1–3), 26 *N.Y.U. L. Rev.* 266, 451, 634 (1951); Will Maslow, "Recasting Our Deportation Laws: Proposals for Reform," 56 *Colum. L. Rev.* 309 (1956); Hesse, "The Pre-1917

Cases"; Siegfried Hesse, "The Constitutional Status of the Lawfully Admitted Permanent Resident Alien: The Inherent Limits of the Power to Expel," 69 *Yale L. J.* 262 (1959).

118. See, e.g., 2 Davis, *Administrative Law Treatise* 5 §10.02 (1958).

119. Commission on Organization of the Executive Branch of the Government, *Task Force Report on Legal Services and Procedure* 273 (1955). See Bernard Schwartz, "Administrative Law," *N.Y.U. Ann. Surv. Am. L.* 93 (1955). See also 20 Fed. Reg. 5729 (1955), amending 8 C.F.R. §242 (1952). See generally Note, "The Supreme Court, 1954 Term," 69 *Harv. L. Rev.* 165 (1955). In 1956, comprehensive regulations substantially revised deportation hearing procedures and provided for an examining officer to present the government's case and made clear that the only role for the special inquiry officer was to hear and decide the case. 21 Fed. Reg. 97–102 (1956); see 1955–1956 INS Ann. Rep. 15–16. See generally Note, "The Special Inquiry Officer in Deportation Proceedings," 42 *Va. L. Rev.* 803 (1956); Maslow, "Recasting" at 352 (1956).

120. 48 Fed. Reg. 3038–3040 (Feb. 25, 1983).

121. 8 U.S.C.A. §1253. See *Marcello v. Kennedy, et al.,* 194 F. Supp. 750; 1961 U.S. Dist. LEXIS 5775 (U.D.D.C., May 22, 1961).

122. Robert Blakey alleges that Marcello paid a $25,000 bribe to "a high ranking official of the Italian court." Blakey and Billings, *Plot* at 242.

123. See H.R. Rep. No. 565, 87th Cong., 1st sess. 1961, 9.

124. Davis, *Mafia* at 76.

125. Blakey and Billings, *Plot* at 242.

126. Robert F. Kennedy, *The Enemy Within* 265 (1960).

127. Davis, *Mafia* at 88.

128. Blakey and Billings, *Plot* at 242.

129. Davis, *Mafia* at 90, 91.

130. See H.R. Rep. No. 565, 87th Cong., 1st sess. 1961, 8, for the history of the three-day notice issue. See also *Marcello v. Kennedy,* 312 F.2d 874 (D.C. Cir. 1962).

131. Davis, *Mafia* at 91.

132. Davis, *Mafia* at 92, 93 (Marcello before a congressional committee).

133. *Marcello v. Kennedy, et al.,* 194 F. Supp. 750; 1961 U.S. Dist. LEXIS 5775 (U.D.D.C., May 22, 1961); opinion vacated by *Marcello v. Kennedy,* 114 U.S. App. D.C. 147; 312 F.2d 874 (D.C. Cir. 1962).

134. 194 F. Supp. at 753.

135. *Id.* at 754.

136. Trafficante was a racketeer who had worked for Meyer Lansky in Cuba and then moved to Florida, where he rose to prominence as a Mafia leader.

137. Frank Ragano and Selwyn Raab, *Mob Lawyer* 130 (1994). The last part of this story is corroborated by the fact that Marcello was later indicted for illegal entry and use of an invalid passport.

138. Ed Reid, *The Anatomy of Organized Crime in America; The Grim Reapers* (1969) 154–155.

139. *Id.* at 161.
140. The House Select Committee on Assassinations was established in September 1976 by House Resolution 1540, 94th Congress, 2d Session, to conduct a full and complete investigation of the circumstances surrounding the deaths of President John F. Kennedy and Dr. Martin Luther King, Jr., The committee's final report is available at http://www.archives.gov/research_room/jfk/house _select_committee/committee_report.html.
141. Reid, *The Grim Reapers* at 161–162.
142. *House Assassination Committee Hearings,* vol. 9H at 82–83. David E. Scheim, *Contract on America* (1988) 80–81.
143. Davis, *Mafia* at 110.
144. Ragano and Raab, *Mob Lawyer* at 135.
145. Seth Kantor, *Who Was Jack Ruby?* 136 (1978).
146. *Id.* at 144.
147. *Id.* at 146.
148. *Id.* at 150.
149. Ragano and Raab, *Mob Lawyer* at 356.
150. See, e.g., Gerald Posner, *Case Closed* (1993).
151. Report of the Select Committee on Assassinations of the U.S. House of Representatives; section I.C., at 147, 169.
152. *Id.* See also Kantor, *Who Was Jack Ruby?,* concluding that Ruby was a Mafia hit man. Posner disputes this vigorously in *Case Closed.* The committee established that Oswald and Ferrie apparently first came into contact with each other during Oswald's participation as a teenager in a Civil Air Patrol unit for which Ferrie served as an instructor, although Ferrie, when interviewed by the FBI after the assassination, denied any past association with Oswald. Ferrie stated that he may have spoken "in an offhand manner of the desirability of having President Kennedy shot," though he denied actually wanting it to be done. On the morning of the day of the assassination, Ferrie and Marcello were together at a courthouse in New Orleans, awaiting a jury verdict in Marcello's criminal trial on conspiracy and perjury charges. In his testimony before the committee, Marcello acknowledged that Ferrie did work for his lawyer, G. Wray Gill.
153. Report of the Select Committee on Assassinations, 172.
154. See also, H.R. Rep. 1086, 87th Cong., 1st sess. (1961), 28–32.
155. Act of Sept. 26, 1961, Public Law 87–301, §5, 75 Stat. 651.
156. See, e.g., *United States ex rel. Marcello v. District Director,* 634 F.2d 964 (5th Cir. 1981), cert. denied 452 U.S. 917.
157. See Davis, *Mafia* at 432 (recounting an FBI wiretap in which Marcello was informed that then-Commissioner of INS Mario Noto had agreed to lift travel restrictions against him).
158. Davis, *Mafia* at 299.
159. *Id.* at 323.
160. Wilfred Sheed, "Everybody's Mafia," *New York Review of Books,* July 20, 1972.

161. David Chandler, "Louisiana's Unshaken Mobster Boss," *Life,* April 10, 1970, 30.

162. Davis, *Mafia* at 375.

163. *Id.* at 471.

164. *Id.* at 501.

165. See "Racketeering Figure Jailed in New Orleans" *New York Times,* Apr. 16, 1983, A6. (Thanks to David Martin for bringing this to my attention.)

166. He apparently had once applied for naturalization but had not pursued the matter.

167. Louis Adamic, "Harry Bridges: Rank-and-File Leader," *The Nation* 576 (May 6, 1936). See also Irving Bernstein, *Turbulent Years; a History of the American Worker, 1933–1941* 252 (1969); Charles P. Larrowe, *Harry Bridges: The Rise and Fall of Radical Labor in the United States* 62–94 (1972); Howard Kimeldorf, *Reds or Rackets: The Making of Radical and Conservative Unions on the Waterfront* 100–114 (1988); Bruce Nelson, *Workers on the Waterfront: Seamen, Longshoremen, and Unionism in the 1930s* 127–155 (1988).

168. Bernstein, *Turbulent* at 217–220. The longshoremen's action was the seventh strike in 1934 that involved 10,000 or more workers and the fifty-fifth strike that year. Ann Fagan Ginger, *Carol Weiss King, Human Rights Lawyer 1895–1952* 253–254 (1993).

169. Ginger, *King* at 254.

170. See Kimeldorf, *Reds or Rackets*; Nelson, *Workers.*

171. Larrowe, *Harry Bridges.*

172. Brace Minton and John Stuart, *The Men Who Labor* (1937), reprinted at http://www.ilwu19.com/history/biography.htm.

173. Frances Perkins, *The Roosevelt I Knew* 314 (1946); Mohr, *Perkins* at 169.

174. Mohr, *Perkins* at 172; Ginger, *King* at 255 (he asked the federal government to rid the state of "alien reds").

175. Minton and Stuart, *The Men Who Labor.*

176. Mohr, *Perkins* at 249, citing memo from Roosevelt to Perkins, marked confidential, Aug. 29, 1935, and from Roosevelt at Hyde Park, Sept. 18, 1935, in Misc., FDR Library.

177. Ginger, *King* at 255, 256.

178. Mohr, *Perkins* at 250, quoting Secretary of Labor, *Twenty-Seventh Annual Report,* Fiscal year ended June 30, 1939, 12–13, 213–221.

179. Bruce Nelson, *Divided We Stand: American Workers and the Struggle for Black Equality* 96–97 (2001).

180. Ginger, *King* at 259; see Mike Quin, *The Big Strike* 3, 47, 91, 159 (1949).

181. Mohr, *Perkins* at 249, 250, citing letter from Harry Bridges to Mohr, Aug. 5, 1969. Bridges, however, later denied completely that the call, asking him to be a "good boy," ever took place at all.

182. Adamic, "Harry Bridges" at 578.

183. *Strecker v. Kessler,* 95 F.2d 976 (5th Cir. 1938) (referring to the deportation of

Strecker as "a kind of Pecksniffian righteousness, savoring strongly of hypocrisy and party bigotry").

184. *Kessler v. Strecker,* 307 U.S. 22 (1939).

185. Mohr, *Perkins* at 251 quoting *New York Daily News,* Apr. 24, 1939. Some believed that Bridges would never be deported because he was secretly employed by the British government, which wanted to know what the United States was shipping to the Orient.

186. Harold L. Ickes, *The Secret Diary of Harold L. Ickes,* vol. 5, part II, *The Inside Struggle, 1936–1939* 550 (1954); Mohr, *Perkins* at 251.

187. Ickes, *Secret Diary* at 312.

188. *Id.*

189. August Raymond Ogden, *The Dies Committee: A Study of the House Committee for the Investigation of Un-American Activities, 1938–1944* 3 (1945). As one writer put it, the congressional investigating committee was at its best a kind of grand jury, but at its worst, it was "a scavenger of the private drains responsible for public malady." Leland Hamilton Jenks, "The Control of Administration by Congress," 2 *American Review* 599 (Nov. 1924).

190. U.S. Congress, House, *Special Committee on Communist Activities in the United States, Investigation of Communist Propaganda,* 71st Cong., 3rd sess., Report No. 2290 at 4–22 (1930).

191. *Id.* at 63–65.

192. Jerome Davis, "Capitalism and Communism: Menace of Communism," *Annals of the American Academy of Political and Social Science* 156 (1931).

193. Ogden, *Dies* at 31.

194. *New Republic,* June 15, 1938, at 158 (quoted in Ogden, *Dies* at 47).

195. Francis Biddle, *Fear of Freedom* 124 (1951).

196. U.S. Congress, House, *Special Committee to Investigate Un-American Activities and Propaganda in the United States, Investigation of Un-American Activities and Propaganda* 76 Cong., 3rd sess., Report No. 1476, 2 (Jan. 3, 1940).

197. Ickes, *Secret Diary* at 507.

198. J. B. Matthews, a voluntary witness before the committee, who was later to become its lead investigator, stated in public hearing that these actors had featured their greetings in the first anniversary publication of *Ce Soir,* an allegedly "French Communist" paper. See Ogden, *Dies* at 64.

199. Mohr, *Perkins* at 252.

200. Biddle, *Fear of Freedom* at 116 citing "A Congressional Committee Investigates the Reds," *LIFE,* September 5, 1938, 11–13.

201. Ogden, *Dies* at 101.

202. Biddle, *Fear of Freedom* at 116.

203. Ickes, *Secret Diary* at 529.

204. U.S. Congress, House, *Special Committee to Investigate Un-American Activities and Propaganda in the United States, Investigation of Un-American Activities and Propaganda,* 76 Cong., 1st sess., Report No. 2, 90–91 (1939).

205. Mohr, *Perkins* at 252.

206. *Id.*, citing John O'Donnell and Doris Fleeson, "Bridges' Deportation Likely Cause Célèbre," *New York Daily News,* Feb. 14, 1938.

207. Ickes, *Secret Diary* at 549–550.

208. *Congressional Record,* 76th Cong., 1st sess., Jan. 24, 1939, vol. 84, pt. 1, 703–711; see also, "Miss Perkins Tells Committee Bridges Gets No Favoritism," *New York Times,* Feb. 9, 1939, 1, 14; Mohr, *Perkins* at 252–253.

209. Ickes, *Secret Diary* at 567–568.

210. Mohr, *Perkins* at 257, citing NBC radio address, Mar. 29, 1939.

211. Mohr, *Perkins* at 255, citing "Miss Perkins's Defense before House Committee in the Bridges Case," *New York Times,* Feb. 9, 1939, 14.

212. Landis had served on the Federal Trade Commission and had chaired the Securities and Exchange Commission.

213. King, Richard Gladstein and Aubrey Grossman also represented Bridges. Ginger, *King,* at 260.

214. In fact, King was the daughter of a well-known New York corporate lawyer. *Id.* at 262.

215. See Kanstroom, "*Hello Darkness.*"

216. Ginger, *King* at 267.

217. Ginger, *King* at 267.

218. *Id.* at 277.

219. *Id.* at 281.

220. Apparently, the defense team had somehow acquired material from his office, including correspondence and "secret" codes used by undercover agents, that were used to cross-examine him with devastating effect.

221. Ginger, *King* at 284.

222. *Id.* at 301.

223. *Id.* at 302.

224. Ickes, *Secret Diary* at 573.

225. Walter Lippman, "Today and Tomorrow," *Washington Post,* Jan. 11, 1940, 9 (quoted in Ogden, *Dies* at 180).

226. Ginger, *King* at 318.

227. "The Reminiscences of Robert Jackson," *Columbia Oral History Archives,* 1040 (on file with author).

228. See H.R. Report No. 2269, 76th Cong., 3rd sess., 1940; *History of the Immigration and Naturalization Service,* report for the House Committee on the Judiciary, 96th Cong., 2d sess., 1980, 47; *Congressional Record,* 76th Cong., 3rd sess., May 27, 1940, 6916–6918; May 31, 1940, 7199–7202, 7259–7290; June 13, 1940, 12380–12407.

229. Ogden, *Dies* at 210, citing *Congressional Record,* 76th Cong., 3d sess., June 18, 1940, 8640–8641.

230. "Dies Asks U.S. Ban on Bund and Reds," *New York Times,* Aug. 27, 1940, 13.

231. 86 *Congressional Record* 8203.

232. Ginger, *King* at 319.
233. "Jackson Opposes Bridges Ouster," *New York Times*, June 20, 1940, 12.
234. 86 *Congressional Record* 9031.
235. Ch. 439, §23(b), 54 Stat. 673.
236. Ginger, *King* at 325–327.
237. Ginger, *King* at 328.
238. U.S. Department Of Justice, *Memorandum Of Decision in the Matter of Harry Renton Bridges* (1941); See generally Larrowe, *Harry Bridges* at 226–237; Ginger, *King* at 330.
239. 268 U.S. 652, 673 (1925).
240. Ginger, *King* at 332. Gitlow had also appeared before the Dies committee. Ogden, *Dies* at 136.
241. Ginger, *King* at 334.
242. *Id.* at 340.
243. *Id.* at 349–351.
244. I. F. Stone, "Next Steps on Bridges," *The Nation* 329 (October 11, 1941).
245. Quoted in Ginger, *King* at 352.
246. Stone, "Next Steps" at 330.
247. *Bridges v. State of California,* 314 U.S. 252 (1941).
248. Ginger, *King* at 359.
249. One member of the board was Jack Wasserman.
250. Freda Kirchwey, "Biddle and Bridges," *The Nation* 646 (June 6, 1942).
251. *Id.* at 360.
252. *Ex parte Bridges,* 49 Supp. 292, 306 (1934); see also *U.S. ex rel. Vajtauer v. Commissioner of Immigration at Port of New York,* 273 U.S. 103 (1927).
253. *Bridges v. Wixon,* 144 F.2d 927, 932 (1944) (finding it "unnecessary to consider the question [of the burden of proof], as we think the record taken as a whole . . . presents some evidence supporting the deportation order"). 273 U.S. 110.
254. 144 F.2d at 943.
255. I. F. Stone, "Bridges and Some Broader Issues," *The Nation* 350 (March 31, 1945).
256. Ginger, *King* at 413.
257. The author of the brief in support of Bridges was Nathan Greene, who, as a law student, had coauthored *The Labor Injunction* with Felix Frankfurter in 1930. *Id.* at 412.
258. Quoted in Ginger, *King* at 417.
259. *Bridges v. United States,* 346 U.S. 209, 212 (1953).
260. *Id.* at 213.
261. "Man without a Country?," *Time* (June 26, 1950).
262. Fowler Harper, "The Crusade against Bridges," 323 *The Nation* (April 5, 1952).
263. His case was argued by Telford Taylor, who had worked with the American prosecution team at Nuremberg under Robert H. Jackson. See Telford Taylor,

Nuremberg: The Modern Law of War and Its Limitations: The Anatomy of the Nuremberg Trials: A Personal Memoir (1992). *Bridges,* 346 U.S at 228.

264. 345 U.S. 979 (1953).

265. *United States v. Bridges,* 133 F. Supp. 638 (N.D. Cal. 1955).

266. See "Harry and the ILWU," http://www.harrybridges.com/index.html (retrieved Oct. 2, 2006).

267. See "The Harry Bridges Chair," http://www.harrybridges.com/harryb.htm (retrieved Oct. 2, 2006).

268. Ginger, *King* at 487.

269. President Harry S. Truman nominated Clark to the Supreme Court in 1949, where he served as associate justice until resigning in 1967 to avoid a potential conflict of interest when Lyndon Johnson appointed his son Ramsey as attorney general. See http://www.oyez.org/oyez/resource/legal_entity/86/biography.

270. Ginger, *King* at 426.

271. *Id.* at 445.

272. See former Sections (a) (27)–(29) of the 1952 McCarran-Walter Act. According to a 1984 internal INS report, more than 8,000 people from ninety-eight countries were excluded from the United States for their political beliefs or associations between 1952 and 1984. See David Cole, "The 1952 McCarran-Walter Act: Is It Irrelevant in Today's World?" *Nat'l. L. J.* 22 (May 29, 1989). See also Burt Neuborne and Steven R. Shapiro, "The Nylon Curtain: America's National Border and the Free Flow of Ideas," 26 *Wm. & Mary L. Rev.* 719, 723 (1985).

273. President Truman's "loyalty order" required federal employees to testify about their associations and statements; some were fired. See Executive Order 9835. The attorney general also promulgated a list of more than 250 proscribed organizations. Membership would lead to loss of federal employment, inability to secure a passport, forfeiture of an array of federal benefits, and, for noncitizens, deportation.

274. Ginger, *King* at 494, 507.

275. *Id.* at 449.

276. As Ann Fagan Ginger has noted, "very appropriately." *Id.* at 449.

277. *United States ex rel. Potash v. District Director of Immigration and Naturalization at Port of New York,* 149 F.2d. 747, 751 (2d Cir. 1948) ("the general spirit of our institutions make[s] it improbable that Congress intended to give the Attorney General unlimited power over the admission to bail of aliens").

278. 342 U.S. 524 (1952). The detainees had argued that the attorney general's decision violated procedural due process because it was arbitrary, capricious, and an abuse of discretion, and that Congress's delegation of such power also violated procedural due process. See *Demore v. Kim,* 538 U.S. 510 (2003) (mandatory detention with no right to bail at all does not offend due process).

279. 342 U.S. at 541.

280. Ginger, *King* at 510.
281. *Id.* at 534.
282. 342 U.S. at 533.
283. See *id.* at 535–537 ("We have no doubt that the doctrines and practices of Communism clearly enough teach the use of force to achieve political control to give constitutional basis, according to any theory of reasonableness or arbitrariness, for Congress to expel known alien Communists.") (footnote omitted).
284. 342 U.S. 580 (1952).
285. Ginger, *King* at 435–436.
286. *Id.* at 443.
287. 346 U.S. at 584.
288. See *id.* at 584–591. Justice Jackson dissented on this point in a 1953 case that involved the indefinite detention of a returning lawful permanent resident. See *Shaughnessy v. United States ex rel. Mezei,* 345 U.S. 206, 222 (1953) (Jackson, J., dissenting) (due process requires "reasonable general legislation reasonably applied to the individual").
289. "Reminiscences of Robert Jackson," *Columbia Oral History Archives,* 1024–1025 (on file with author).
290. *Harisiades,* 342 U.S. at 586–587.
291. Ginger, *King* at 538.
292. *Id.*
293. See Laurent B. Frantz, "Deportation Deliriums," *The Nation* 258–262 (March 26, 1955).
294. 347 U.S. 522 (1954). *Id.* at 530, quoting *Ng Fung Ho v. White,* 259 U.S. 276, 284 (1922) (internal quotation marks omitted). *Id.* quoting *Fong Haw Tan v. Phelan,* 333 U.S. 6, 10 (1948) (internal quotation marks omitted).
295. *Id.* at 531 (footnote omitted).
296. 347 U.S. 522, 530–532 (citations omitted).
297. *Id.* at 533 (Black, J., joined by Douglas, J., dissenting) Justice Black may well have felt especially strongly about this issue in light of his personal history. As a young man, he had joined the Ku Klux Klan, later asserting that he thought of it as a social organization. See Peter Irons, *A People's History of the Supreme Court* 326 (1999).
298. Nancy Morawetz, "Rethinking Retroactive Deportation Laws and the Due Process Clause," 73 *N.Y.U. L. Rev.* 97, 98 (1998).
299. *Korematsu,* 323 U.S. at 214, 235 (Murphy, J., dissenting).
300. According to the War Relocation Authority, a total of 120,313 individuals were in custody throughout the war. See Roger Daniels, "A Quantitative Note," in *Japanese Americans: From Relocation to Redress* (Roger Daniels, Sandra C. Taylor, and Harry H. L. Kitano eds., 1991)
301. David Cole, "Enemy Aliens," 54 *Stan. L. Rev.* 953, 992 (2002).
302. In addition, 158,000 lived in the territories of Hawaii and Alaska.

303. See *Ozawa v. United States,* 260 U.S. 178 (1922).

304. Daniels, "A Quantitative Note" at 72.

305. 50 U.S.C. §21 (as amended in 1918). See generally John Christgau, *"Enemies": World War II Alien Internment* (1985).

306. Proclamations 2525, 6 Fed. Reg. 6321; 2526, 6 Fed. Reg. 6323; 2527, 6 Fed. Reg. 6324.

307. J. Edgar Hoover, "Alien Enemy Control," 29 *Iowa L. Rev.* 396, 401, 402 (1944).

308. *Id.* at 403.

309. John J. Culley, "The Santa Fe Internment Camp and the Justice Department Program for Enemy Aliens," in Daniels, *Relocation* at 58.

310. Hoover, "Alien Enemy Control" at 403.

311. *Id.*

312. See Tetsuden Kashima, "American Mistreatment of Internees during World War II: Enemy Alien Japanese," in Daniels et al., *Relocation* at 52.

313. Hoover, "Alien Enemy Control" at 407.

314. See, e.g., Civilian Exclusion Order No. 34, quoted in *Korematsu v. United States,* 323 U.S. 214, 229 n. 6 (1944) (providing that, after 12:00, May 8, 1942, all persons of Japanese ancestry, "both alien and non-alien, were to be excluded from a described portion of Military Area No. 1").

315. Natsu Taylor Saito, "Symbolism under Siege: Japanese American Redress and the 'Racing' of Arab Americans as 'Terrorists,'" 8 *Asian L.J.* 1 n. 44 (2001).

316. See Daniels, "Relocation, Redress, and the Report," in Daniels et al., *Relocation* at 6; see also, Daniels, "Quantitative Note," in Daniels et al., *Relocation* (discussing the implications of each term). The most common comprehensive term in current usage is "internment," although historically this applied to aliens only.

317. Eugene V. Rostow, "The Japanese American Cases: A Disaster," 54 *Yale L.J.* 489, 523 (1945).

318. See Saito, "Symbolism under Siege" at 25; Cole, "Enemy Aliens."

319. *Personal Justice Denied* Report of the Commission on Wartime Relocation and Internment of Civilians 18 (Washington, D.C.: GPO, 1982).

320. See, e.g., Carey McWilliams, *Prejudice; Japanese Americans: Symbol of Racial Intolerance* (1944); Milton R. Konvitz, *The Alien and the Asiatic in American Law* (1946).

321. See Natsu Taylor Saito, "Alien and Non-Alien Alike: Citizenship, 'Foreignness,' and Racial Hierarchy in American Law," 76 *Or. L. Rev.* 261 (1997); Natsu Taylor Saito, "Model Minority, Yellow Peril: Functions of 'Foreignness' in the Construction of Asian American Legal Identity," 4 *Asian L.J.* 71 (1997).

322. "Final Report of General DeWitt," quoted in Jacobus tenBroek, Edward N. Barnhart, and Floyd W. Matson, *Prejudice, War, and the Constitution* 110 (1954).

323. Testimony of Apr. 13, 1943, House Naval Affairs Sub-committee, San Francisco, quoted in McWilliams, *Prejudice* at 116 (emphasis added).

324. McWilliams, *Prejudice* at 15.

325. *Id.* at 16.

326. McWilliams, *Prejudice* at 17.

327. Roger Daniels, *Concentration Camps, North America* 9 (1989).

328. McWilliams, *Prejudice* at 19.

329. *Id.*

330. Both Japanese and American newspapers fomented trouble. As Theodore Roosevelt wrote in a 1907 letter to Henry Cabot Lodge, "The Japanese seems to have about the same proportion of prize jingo fools that we have." *Id.* at 34.

331. Daniels, *Concentration Camps* at 14.

332. For an excellent discussion of how the alien land laws laid the groundwork for the internment, see Keith Aoki, "No Right to Own?: The Early Twentieth-Century 'Alien Land Laws' as a Prelude to Internment," 40 *B.C. L. Rev.* 37 (1998).

333. The first generation of Japanese immigrants, the *issei,* were ineligible to become U.S. citizens. Their children, known as the *nisei,* were U.S. citizens by birth. Most *nisei* knew little of Japanese culture, spoke English, and generally wanted to be "100% American."

334. McWilliams, *Prejudice* at 45, 49.

335. McWilliams, at 53.

336. Daniels, *Concentration Camps* at 16. The law was further strengthened in 1923. Konvitz, *Alien and Asiatic* at 160.

337. *Terrace v. Thompson,* 263 U.S. 197 (1923); see also *Porterfield v. Webb,* 263 U.S. 225 (1923).

338. House Doc. No. 89, 67th Cong., 1st sess. 1921, 4.

339. Y. Ichihashi, *Japanese in the United States* 309–314 (1932).

340. Daniels, *Concentration Camps* at 21.

341. *Id.* at 23.

342. *Id.* at 43.

343. *Id.* at 46, citing notes of Jan. 4, 1942, conference; see Stetson Conn, "The Decision to Evacuate the Japanese from the Pacific Coast," in *Command Decisions* 92 (Kent Roberts Greenfield ed., 1959).

344. Daniels, *Concentration Camps* at 50–51.

345. Lippmann, "The Fifth Column on the Coast," *New York Tribune,* Feb. 2, 1942 (quoted in Daniels, *Concentration Camps* at 68).

346. Letter, Biddle to Henry Lewis Stimson, Feb. 12, 1942, Sec'y of War, Record Group 107, National Archives (cited in Daniels, *Concentration Camps* at 69).

347. "Recommendations" in Sec'y of War, Record Group 107, National Archives (cited in Daniels, *Concentration Camps* at 70).

348. See *Korematsu v. United States,* 323 U.S. 214 (1944); *Hirabayashi v. United States,* 320 U.S. 81 (1943); *Yasui v. United States,* 320 U.S. 115 (1943).

349. William H. Rehnquist, *All the Laws but One: Civil Liberties in Wartime* 208–211 (1998); see Cole, "Enemy Aliens" at 993, for discussion of this point.

350. It also violates international human rights law. See e.g., Rome Statute of the International Criminal Court, Art. 7, U.N. Doc. A/CONF.183/09 (1998), as corrected by the *proces-verbaux* of 10 Nov. 1998 and 12 July 1999 (stating that "crime against humanity" included "[d]eportation or forcible transfer of population"); John Quigley, "State Responsibility for Ethnic Cleansing," 32 *U.C. Davis L. Rev.* 341 (1999).

351. 149 U.S. 698, at 758.

352. See, e.g., *Narenji v. Civiletti,* 617 F.2d 745 (D.C. Cir. 1979), cert. denied, 446 U.S. 957 (1980).

353. See generally M. Barrera, *Race and Class in the Southwest: A Theory of Racial Inequality* (1979); Gerald P. López, "Undocumented Mexican Migration: In Search of a Just Immigration Law and Policy," 28 *UCLA L. Rev.* 615 (1981); Kitty Calavita, "The Immigration Policy Debate: Critical Analysis and Future Options," in *Mexican Migration to the United States: Origins, Consequences, and Policy Options* 155 (W. Cornelius and J. Bustamante eds., 1989).

354. See generally Michael A. Olivas, "The Chronicles, My Grandfather's Stories, and Immigration Law: The Slave Traders as Racial History," 34 *St. Lou. U. L. J.* 425 (1990).

355. Carey McWilliams, *Ill Fares the Land: Migrants and Migratory Labor in the United States* 16–19 (Barnes and Noble 1967) (1942).

356. Woody Guthrie, who had written a well-known song entitled "Dust Bowl Refugees" in 1938, reportedly disliked the term. Often, according to his biographer, he introduced the song by saying, "You know, there are different kinds of refugees. There are people who are forced to take refuge under a railroad bridge because they ain't got no place else to go, and there are those who take refuge in public office." Joe Klein, *Woody Guthrie: A Life* 115 (1981).

357. John Steinbeck, *The Grapes of Wrath* 317 (Viking Critical Library 1972) (1939).

358. Jorge China points to domestic concern over "alien" status, competition with native-born workers, and alleged overrepresentation within the labor force and unemployment ranks, which all served as fanciful justifications for what Carey McWilliams later termed the "getting rid of the Mexican" scheme. Jorge L. China, "Ethnic Prejudice and Anti-Immigration Policies in Times of Economic Stress: Mexican Repatriation from the United States, 1929–1939," *East Wind/West Wind* 9–13 (Winter 1996).

359. Francisco E. Balderrama and Raymond Rodriguez, *Decade of Betrayal: Mexican Repatriation in the 1930s* 121 (1995). A California State Legislative Commission has found that between 1929 and 1944, the total number of removals was as high as 2 million people. See http://info.sen.ca.gov/pub/bill/sen/sb_0401 –0450/sb_427_bill_20040823_amended_asm.html, Chapter 3.2. *The Commission on the 1930's "Repatriation" Program.*

360. Hoffman, *Unwanted* at 39.

361. U.S. Bureau of Immigration, Annual Report 1931.

362. See generally Balderrama and Rodríguez, *Decade of Betrayal*; Hoffman, *Un-*

wanted; Camille Guerin-Gonzales, *Mexican Workers and the American Dream: Immigration, Repatriation, and California Farm Labor, 1900–1939* (1994).

363. U.S. Bureau of the Census, *Historical Statistics of the United States: Colonial Times to 1970* 113 (Washington, D.C.: GPO, 1975).

364. Balderrama and Rodríguez, *Decade of Betrayal* at 51.

365. *In the Matter of T—* (No. 55910/216); 1941 BIA LEXIS 30; 1 I. & N. Dec. 158 (Sept. 4, 1941).

366. *Id.*

367. *Id.* at 159.

368. *Id.*

369. Carey McWilliams, "Repatriados," *American Mercury,* March 1933, available from http://www.digitalhistory.uh.edu/mexican_voices/voices_display.cfm?id=96

370. See Balderrama and Rodríguez, *Decade of Betrayal* at 216.

371. McWilliams, "Repatriados."

372. Chinea, "Ethnic Prejudice" at 5, 6.

373. Id. at 6, 7

374. NPR: Profile: Efforts by California to compensate victims of a 1930s campaign to repatriate millions of Mexicans and Mexican-Americans back to Mexico, September 13, 2003 (Transcript on file with author).

375. Hoffman, *Unwanted* at 2–3; Balderrama and Rodriguez, *Decade of Betrayal* at 57–58.

376. See, e.g., "Painful Past," *The News Hour with Jim Lehrer,* Nov. 27, 2003; Edward Hegstrom, "Repatriation Issue Is Revived," *Houston Chronicle,* Sept. 29, 2003, A14; Gregg Jones, "Reparations Sought for '30s Expulsion Program," *Los Angeles Times,* July 16, 2003, pt. 2, 8; Gregg Jones, "Apology Sought for Latino 'Repatriation' Drive in '30s," *Los Angeles Times* July 15, 2003, pt. 2, 1. See also California State Senate Select Committee on Citizen Participation, *Hearings on the Examination of the Unconstitutional and Coerced Emigration of Legal Residents and U.S. Citizens of Mexican Descent during the 1930's,* July 15, 2003, at http://www.calchannel.com/july2003.htm. In late 2004, California Governor Schwarzenegger vetoed a bill that would have opened a window in the statute of limitations to allow victims of the repatriation to sue for damages. See www.nbcsandiego.com/politics/3760305/detail.html.

377. McWilliams, "Repatriados."

378. See generally Kitty Calavita, *Inside the State: The Bracero Program, Immigration, and the I.N.S.* (1992); Ernest Galarza, *Merchants of Labor: The Mexican Bracero Story* (1964).

379. It was formally entitled "Agreement of August 4, 1942 For the Temporary Migration of Mexican Agricultural Workers to the United States as Revised on April 26, 1943, by an Exchange of Notes Between the American Embassy at Mexico City and the Mexican Ministry for Foreign Affairs." The original agreement was formalized on July 23, 1942, but was later modified. The final version was released on Apr. 26, 1943.

380. U.S. Congress, House Committee on the Judiciary, *Illegal Aliens*, 92d Cong., 1st and 2d Sess., 1971–1972, 5 vols. (Washington, D.C.: GPO, 1972); Lawrence A. Cardoso, *Mexican Emigration to the United States, 1897–1931* (1980); Juan Ramón García, *Operation Wetback: The Mass Deportation of Mexican Undocumented Workers in 1954* 23–61 (1980).

381. The braceros had been permitted under the 1942 agreement to bring their families with them. In practice, however, virtually no family members were actually admitted. Philip Martin, "Guest Workers: Past and Present," *Migration between Mexico and the United States: Binational Study* 878–881 (1998).

382. Richard B. Craig, *The Bracero Program: Interest Groups and Foreign Policy* 24 (1971).

383. In November 1942, the American Farm Bureau, the National Grange, and the National Council of Farmers Cooperation protested the rules and regulations contained in the agreement. Garcia, at 26.

384. Martin, at 880.

385. See Kitty Calavita, "U.S. Immigration Policy: Contradictions and Projections for the Future," 2 *Ind. J. Global Leg. Studs.* 143, 146 (1994). The widespread failure to withhold 10 percent of the workers' wages, to be eventually returned to the workers by the Mexican government, has led to litigation (to date unsuccessful) in the United States. See *Cruz v. United States*, 219 F. Supp. 2d 1027, 1032 (N.D. Cal. 2002); see also 387 F. Supp. 2 1057 (2005); 2005 U.S. Dist. LEXIS 21204.

386. Racial tensions in California, including the infamous "Zoot-suit Riots" in Los Angeles in which many Mexican Americans were attacked, beaten, and incarcerated by bands of whites and by the police, inspired many to rethink the Bracero Program. Garcia, *Operation* at 31.

387. Eleanor M. Hadley, "A Critical Analysis of the Wetback Problem," *Law and Contemporary Problems* 21 (Spring 1956). In 1948, the United States and Mexico entered into another agreement under which each bracero entered into a contract directly with a U.S. employer. The U.S. government was no longer a signatory to the individual work contract.

388. See Calavita, "The Immigration Policy Debate," describing the Bracero agreement of 1949.

389. *1951 Commission Migratory Labor Report in American Agriculture: Report of the President's Commission on Migratory Labor* 53 (Washington, D.C.: GPO, 1951); Dick J. Reavis, *Without Documents* 39 (1978).

390. *1951 Commission Migratory Labor Report.*

391. Kitty Calavita, *U.S. Immigration Law and the Control of Labor 1820–1924* 34–35 (1984).

392. As the 1951 Commission reported, "Well-established practices . . . range from spreading news of employment in [Mexican] plazas and over the radio to the withholding from wages . . . a 'deposit' which is intended to urge, if not guarantee, the return to the same farm as quickly as possible of a wetback employee who may be apprehended and taken back to Mexico."

393. See "32 killed in crash of charter plane," *New York Times*, Jan. 29, 1948, 5.
394. *milnsue@aol.com*, reported at http://members.nbci.com/_XMCM/elstongunn/deportees.html.
395. Klein, *Woody Guthrie* at 349–350.
396. See, e.g., Texas State Historical Association, *The Handbook of Texas*, http://www.tsha.utexas.edu/handbook/online/articles/view/OO/pqo1.html.
397. *1951 Commission Migratory Labor Report.*
398. "Special Message to the Congress," July 13, 1951. He reported, "Last year 500,000 illegal immigrants were apprehended and returned to Mexico.
399. Quoted in Ernesto Galarza, *Merchants of Labor: The Mexican Bracero Story* (1964).
400. *1951 Commission Migratory Labor Report.*
401. U.S. Immigration and Naturalization Service, *INS Statistical Yearbook 1959*, 54 (Washington, D.C.: GPO).
402. *1951 Commission Migratory Labor Report.*
403. *United States v. Evans*, 333 U.S. 483 (U.S. 1948).
404. S. 1851; see S. Rept. 1145, Feb. 4, 1952.
405. Act of March 20, 1952, 66 Stat. 26. This law also gave authority to INS officers to have access to private lands, though not private dwellings, within twenty-five miles of the border, "to prevent the illegal entry of aliens."
406. Public Law 78, July 12, 1951.
407. Gladwin Hill, "Mexican Border-Jumpers Set Two-a-minute Mark in April, *New York Times*, May 9, 1953, 15.
408. Gladwin Hill, "The Wetbacks: McCarran's Immigrants," *The Nation* 151, 152 (Aug. 22, 1953).
409. *1951 Commission Migratory Labor Report.*
410. García, *Operation* at 158.
411. Nevins, *Operation Gatekeeper* at 35.
412. Ngai, *Impossible* at 153–156.
413. See García, *Operation* at 169–174.
414. *Annual Report of the Immigration and Naturalization Service*, 1959 (Washington, D.C.: GPO).
415. Calavita, "Immigration Policy Debate" at 158.
416. *Whom We Shall Welcome: Report of the President's Commission on Immigration and Naturalization* 179 (Jan. 1, 1953) (Washington, D.C.: GPO).

6. Discretion, Jurisdiction Stripping, and Retroactivity

1. Act of Oct. 3, 1965, 79 Stat. 911.
2. President Kennedy had introduced legislation to eliminate the national origins quota system.
3. A 1976 amendment actually made matters worse by applying 20,000 per country quotas to Western Hemisphere countries, including Mexico, which had exceeded that number consistently since 1965.

4. See SCIRP, Staff Report.

5. The 1980 act created stable mechanisms for refugee aid and admissions, broadened the definition of refugee to a nonideological and nongeographical standard, and provided a clear path from refugee status to lawful permanent residence. See 8 U.S.C. 1101(a)(42)(A).

6. I do not, of course, mean to overlook the many serious problems with the asylum adjudications system that have been revealed over the years.

7. See, e.g., Nicaraguan Adjustment and Central American Relief Act (NACARA), Public Law 105–100, §203, 111 Stat. 2160 (Nov. 19, 1997), as amended by the Nicaraguan Adjustment and Central American Relief Act-Technical Amendments (NACARATA), Public Law 105–139, 111 Stat. 2644 (Dec. 2, 1997). See also Haitian Refugee Immigration Fairness Act of 1998 (HRIFA), enacted as Title IX of the Omnibus Consolidated and Emergency Supplemental Appropriations Act, 1999, Public Law 105–277, §902, 112 Stat. 2681, 2681–538 (Oct. 21, 1998).

8. SCIRP, Staff Report.

9. Public Law 99–603, 100 Stat. 3359 (Nov. 6, 1986).

10. See Robert Bach and Doris Meissner, *Employment and Immigration Reform: Employer Sanctions Four Years Later* 5–6 (1990); Robert H. Gibbs, "It Ain't Over 'Til It's Over: Amnesty Issues Persist a Decade after IRCA," 73 *Interpreter Releases* 1493 (1996).

11. Public Papers of the President, Immigration and Reform Control Act of 1986, 22 Wkly. Comp. Pres. Doc. 1534 (1986).

12. See Daniel Kanstroom, "Judicial Review of Amnesty Denials: Must Aliens Bet Their Lives to Get into Court?" 25 *Harv. C.R.-C.L. L. Rev.* 53 (Winter 1990).

13. Public Law 99–639, 100 Stat. 3537 (Nov. 10, 1986).

14. It also precluded those who married a U.S. citizen while in exclusion or deportation proceedings from gaining any immigration benefits until they had resided outside of the United States for two years after the marriage.

15. See, e.g., Peter H. Schuck and John Williams, "Removing Criminal Aliens: The Pitfalls and Promises of Federalism," 22 *Harv. J. L. & Pub. Pol'y* 367 (Spring 1999).

16. Public Law 100–690, 102 Stat. 4181.

17. Public Law 101–649, 104 Stat. 4978. Certain foreign convictions were also now aggravated felonies.

18. However, the 1990 law modified the mandatory detention of alleged aggravated felons and permitted discretionary bail for lawful permanent residents.

19. Review was limited to questions of whether the person (1) was in fact the "alien" described in the deportation order; (2) was in fact of the requisite status; (3) had been finally convicted of an aggravated felony; and (4) had been afforded certain limited procedural protections.

20. Daniel Kanstroom, "Surrounding the Hole in the Doughnut: Discretion and Deference in U.S. Immigration Law," 71 *Tul. L. Rev.* 703 (1997), citing Henry

M. Hart, Jr., "The Power of Congress to Limit the Jurisdiction of Federal Courts: An Exercise in Dialectic," 66 *Harv. L. Rev.* 1362, 1389–1391 (1953).

21. In *Reno v. AADC, supra,* the Court concluded that 8 U.S.C. 1252(g) imposes jurisdictional limits only on claims addressing "'decisions or actions'" specifically enumerated in the statute. 525 U.S. at 482.

22. 121 S. Ct. 2491 (2001).

23. *Id.* at 2498, 2501, 2502 (quoting *Miller v. French,* 530 U.S. 327 (2000).

24. See 8 U.S.C. §1252(a)(2)(B).

25. See Michael G. Heyman, "Judicial Review of Discretionary Immigration Decisionmaking," 314 *San Diego L. Rev.* 861 (1994); Colin S. Diver, "The Optimal Precision of Administrative Rules," 93 *Yale L.J.* 65 (1983); Arthur C. Helton, "The Proper Role of Discretion in Political Asylum Determinations," 22 *San Diego L. Rev.* 999 (1985); Maurice A. Roberts, "The Exercise of Administrative Discretion under the Immigration Laws," 13 *San Diego L. Rev.* 144 (1975); Abraham D. Sofaer, "Judicial Control of Informal Discretionary Adjudication and Enforcement," 72 *Colum. L. Rev.* 1293 (1972).

26. See discussion of *INS v. St. Cyr, infra.*

27. Public Law 109–13, Div. B, Title I, 119 Stat. 231 (May 11, 2005).

28. 8 U.S.C. §1252(D). This provision was a response to the *St. Cyr* case discussed below.

29. It also channels virtually all deportation appeals to the courts of appeals and away from full evidentiary hearings in district courts.

30. Louis L. Jaffe, *Judicial Control of Administrative Action* 320 (1965).

31. See Diver, "Optimal Precision" at 66–71; see also Cass R. Sunstein, "Problems with Rules," 83 *Cal. L. Rev.* 953, 961–962 (1995) (although a system of rules attempts to set the context of law in advance of its application, legal judgments must be made in deciding actual cases).

32. Ronald M. Dworkin, "Is Law a System of Rules?," in *The Philosophy of Law* 52 (R. M. Dworkin ed., 1977).

33. Stephen H. Legomsky, *Immigration and the Judiciary: Law and Politics in Britain and America* (1987) 12–13, quoting J. M. Evans, *DeSmith's Judicial Review of Administrative Action* 278 (4th ed. 1980); Henry M. Hart, Jr., and Albert M. Sacks, *The Legal Process: Basic Problems in the Making and Application of Law* 162 (tentative ed. 1958) (defining discretion as the power to choose between multiple permissible courses of action).

34. See, e.g., *INS v. Abudu,* 485 U.S. 94, 105–107 (1988) (motion to reopen); *Prado v. Reno,* 198 F.3d 286, 291 (1st Cir. 1999) (review of decision not to grant an adjustment of status is precluded as "discretionary").

35. 360 F.2d 715 (2d Cir. 1966).

36. *Wong Wing Hang,* 360 F.2d at 718, quoting *Hart and Sacks, Basic Problems* at 172, 175–77.

37. *Wong Wing Hang,* 360 F. 2d at 719. Judge Friendly, seeking better "equilibrium" between the judiciary and the attorney general, suggested that "proper admin-

istration would be advanced and reviewing courts would be assisted if the Attorney General . . . were to outline certain bases deemed to warrant the affirmative exercise of discretion and other grounds generally militating against it." *Id.* at 718.

38. 502 U.S. 314, 329–334 (Scalia, J., concurring in part and dissenting in part).

39. See *Lopez v. Davis*, 531 U.S. 230 (2001) (upholding, as permissible use of discretion, a regulation of the Bureau of Prisons that categorically denied early release to certain classes of prisoners).

40. Compare *Romero-Torres v. Ashcroft*, 327 F.3d 887, 892 (9th Cir. 2003), and *Spencer Enterprises, Inc. v. United States*, 345 F.3d 683, 690–691 (9th Cir. 2003).

41. One of the earliest appearances of this idea was in an opinion of the legal realist judge Jerome Frank in *United States ex rel. Adel v. Shaughnessy*, 183 F.2d 371 (2d Cir. 1950).

42. Bernard Schwartz, "Administrative Law Cases during 1985," 38 *Admin. L. Rev.* 392, 310 (1986); see also Kenneth Culp Davis, "No Law to Apply," 25 *San Diego L. Rev.* 1, 2, 10 (1988) (noting that the Court always has a standard of reasonableness to apply); Ronald M. Levin, "Understanding Unreviewability in Administrative Law," 74 *Minn. L. Rev.* 689, 734–735 (1990).

43. *Achacoso-Sanchez v. INS*, 779 F.2d 1260, 1265 (7th Cir. 1985) (denial of relief held unreviewable); see also *Perales v. Casillas*, 903 F.2d 1043, 1048, 1050–1051 (5th Cir. 1990) (denial of voluntary departure and work authorization unreviewable); *Dina v. Attorney General of the United States*, 793 F.2d 473, 476 (2d Cir. 1986) (USIA waiver recommendation is committed to agency discretion).

44. Indeed, the Ninth Circuit opinion in *AADC v. Reno* highlighted decisions that had recognized First Amendment rights of "aliens living in the United States." 70 F.3d 1045, 1064 (9th Cir. 1995).

45. 525 U.S. 471, 489 (1999).

46. *Id.* at 491. Justice Scalia also reiterated that "[w]hile the consequences of deportation may assuredly be grave, they are not imposed as punishment."

47. See David Cole, "Supreme Court Denies First Amendment Rights to Legal Aliens," *Legal Times*, Mar. 8, 1999, 19. Three of the other six became permanent residents by the time the case got to the Supreme Court. See *id.* at 20.

48. See Gerald L. Neuman, "Terrorism, Selective Deportation and the First Amendment after *Reno v. AADC*," 14 *Geo. Immig. L. J.* 342–343 (2000).

49. See, e.g., *United States v. Armstrong*, 517 U.S. 456, 461 n. 2 (1996).

50. Prosecutorial discretion may also allow for the implementation of more humane goals. Following in the tradition of Frances Perkins, former INS Commissioner Doris Meissner encouraged prosecutorial discretion to mitigate—in appropriate cases—the harshest effects of the deportation laws. She generated a fairly specific list of factors that helped to regularize practice, increased predictability, and assuaged some concerns that the system was completely heart-

less. Memorandum from Commissioner Meissner on Exercising Prosecutorial Discretion, Nov. 17, 2000 (on file with author).

51. Kenneth C. Davis, *Administrative Law Treatise* 6 (2d ed. 1979); see also, ch. 8:10, at 200.

52. *Achacoso-Sanchez v. INS*, 779 F.2d 1260, 1265 (7th Cir. 1985) (Easterbrook, J.).

53. INA 244, 8 U.S.C. 1254(a).

54. See Act of Mar. 3, 1903, 32 Stat. 1213, Sec. 19 (prescribing a complex procedure whereby the commissioner-general of immigration and secretary of commerce could suspend deportation of certain noncitizens who had violated contract labor provisions.

55. Act of June 25, 1798, 1 Stat. 570.

56. Section 19(c). The Registry Act of 1929 also allowed regularization of status for those "not ineligible to citizenship" who had entered prior to June 3, 1921, had resided continuously in the United States, could show "good moral character," and were not otherwise subject to deportation. 45 Stat. 1512. Certain types of convictions would render a noncitizen ineligible. Section 19(d). The 1917 act also mandated continuing congressional involvement in suspension cases.

57. See Charles Gordon, "Discretionary Relief from Deportation," *Decalogue J.* 6 (Sept.–Oct. 1960). This system included the 1917 act's seventh proviso and other techniques, such as so-called pre-examination. Pre-examination permitted the regularization of status for those who could not show a lawful admission. It allowed, by regulation, a noncitizen to depart to Canada, obtain an immigrant visa there, and return legally to the United States, saving the risk and expense of a return trip to one's home country.

58. Public Law 76–670, 20, 54 Stat. 670, 671–673 (1940), amending the Immigration Act of 1917, Public Law 64–301, 19(c), 39 Stat. 874, 889–890 (repealed 1952). Other mechanisms, based on the seventh proviso and pre-examination, also continued, though still without clear statutory basis.

59. In 1948, a more generous Congress changed eligibility to include certain noncitizens with seven years residence in the United States, even if they lacked family ties here. Act of July 1, 1948, Public Law 80–863, 62 Stat. 1206, 1206, amending the Alien Registration Act of 1940 (repealed 1952).

60. Congressional critics accused Perkins of "exerting unusual efforts to protect and keep within our borders hundreds of deportable foreigners branded as criminals." Senator Robert Reynolds to James Houghterling, Apr. 4, 1938, file 55819/402B, box 75, accession 58A734, INS; *Congressional Record,* Oct. 10, 1940, 20424–20428, cited in Mae Ngai, "The Strange Career of the Illegal Alien: Immigration Restriction and Deportation Policy in the United States, 1921–1965," 21 *Law and History Rev.* 69, 101 (2003).

61. See, e.g., S. Rep. 82–1137 at 25 (1952); S. Rep. 81–1515 at 600–601 (1950).

62. U.S. Congress, Senate, *Revision of Immigration and Nationality Laws,* 82nd Cong., 2d sess., 1952, Rep. 1137, 25.

63. Immigration and Nationality Act, Public Law 82–414, 244(a), 66 Stat. 163, 214–216 (1952), codified as amended at 8 U.S.C. 1254(a).

64. Because the only cases that would rise to the judicial level were denials of relief, the insulation of the system from review can result only in a harsher regime. Moreover, Congress expected that the attorney general would exercise discretion stringently. Congress also maintained a complicated feature of suspension law: in all cases, the attorney general had to report decisions to grant suspension to the Congress. For some classes of cases, the grant would stand unless the Congress passed a joint resolution disapproving it. In other cases, particularly of criminals, "prostitutes or other immoral persons," and subversives, the grant would not be effective unless the Congress approved it by joint resolution. See INA §244(b) and (c). This system was found unconstitutional in *INS v. Chadha,* 462 U.S. 919 (1983).

65. 351 U.S. 345 (1956).

66. *Id.* at 350.

67. See *Jay,* 351 U.S. at 351–356. Owing to the prevailing view in the 1950s of the parameters of the due process clause, Jay apparently did not argue that this use of secret procedures would itself be unconstitutional. He did, however, argue that to deny him a right to a full hearing would be inconsistent with the "tradition and principles of free government." *Jay,* 351 U.S. at 357. Though conceding that this was "on its face . . . an attractive argument," the Court declared itself bound by the "plain meaning" of the statute, "however severe the consequences." *Id.*

68. 351 U.S. at 353–355.

69. The four dissents came from Chief Justice Warren and Justices Black, Frankfurter, and Douglas.

70. Justice Frankfurter noted that discretionary relief from deportation was designed by Congress to mitigate "a very drastic exercise of its constitutional power to turn aliens out of the country for some past misdeed, often unthinking foolishness, and, it may well be, long after genuine repentance and the evolution of the alien into a worthy member of society." Like Warren, he recognized that by doing so, "Congress plainly responded to the dictates of humanity." Still, he wrote, "just as Congress could have exercised to the utmost its power of constitutional severity, so it could appropriately define the mode for its alleviation." Frankfurter's problem, echoed by Justice Black, was with redelegation of this power of mercy: "Congress has not seen fit to invest his subordinates with such arbitrary authority over the lives of men. 351 U.S. at 372–373.

71. *Jay,* 351 U.S. at 361.

72. Justice Douglas saw the main issue as the propriety of secret hearings. He, like Frankfurter, suggested a strong form of statutory interpretation to avoid such a result: "we should lean over backwards to avoid imputing to Congress a purpose to sanction it." *Id.* at 376.

73. Troubled by the breadth of the attorney general's construction of "confidential information," Black said the Court's holding allowed "exile on the basis of anonymous gossip." *Id.* at 362–365.

74. *Yuen Sang Low v. Attorney Gen.,* 479 F.2d 820, 821 (9th Cir. 1973); see also, Guido Calabresi, *A Common Law for the Age of Statutes* 164 (1982).

75. T. Alexander Aleinikoff, "Symposium, *Patterson v. McLean*: Updating Statutory Interpretation," 87 *Mich. L. Rev.* 42–43 (1988).

76. 450 U.S. 139 (1981).

77. *Id.* at 144.

78. 464 U.S. 183 (1984).

79. Since *Chevron, U.S.A., Inc. v. Natural Resources Defense Council, Inc.,* 467 U.S. 837 (1984), judges have been directed to take a two-step approach to review agencies' statutory interpretation. If the intent of Congress is "clear, that is the end of the matter." But if the court decides that Congress has not directly decided the question, then "the question . . . is whether the agency's answer is based on a permissible construction of the statute." Thus, the *Chevron* architecture changes the judicial analysis from whether the agency construction is correct to whether it is "permissible" or, perhaps, "reasonable." There is a presumption of congressional delegation of interpretive authority to agencies. As many (many) commentators have noted, the clarity of the *Chevron* doctrine may be more apparent than real. See generally Cynthia R. Farina, "Statutory Interpretation and the Balance of Power in the Administrative State," 89 *Colum. L. Rev.* 452, 467–488 (1989); *INS v. Cardoza-Fonseca,* 480 U.S. 421 (1987) (whether the asylum standard was the same as that for withholding of deportation was "a pure question of statutory construction" in which deference to the agency was not required); *United States v. Mead Corp.,* 533 U.S. 218 (2001) (deference depends on whether Congress has delegated authority to the agency generally to make rules carrying the force of law).

80. See, e.g., Mark Kelman, "Interpretive Construction in the Substantive Criminal Law," 33 *Stan. L. Rev.* 591, 591–592 (1981).

81. See, e.g., *INS v. Abudu,* 485 U.S. 94, 107 (1988).

82. See, e.g., *Kin Sang Chow v. INS,* 12 F.3d 34, 39 (5th Cir. 1993).

83. Memorandum of Jan. 5, 2006 (on file with author).

84. "Adjudicative facts . . . usually answer the questions of who did what, where, when, how, why, with what motive or intent." Kenneth Culp Davis and Richard J. Pierce, Jr., *Administrative Law Treatise* 10.5 at 141–149 (3d ed. 1994); David A. Martin, "Reforming Asylum Adjudication: On Navigating the Coast of Bohemia," 138 *U. Pa. L. Rev.* 1247, 1282–1285 (1990).

85. INA §242(b)(4).

86. David A. Martin, *The Refugee Act of 1980: Its Past and Future, in Transnational Legal Problems of Refugees* 91, 115 (1982).

87. Martin, "Reforming Asylum Adjudication" at 1280.

88. See Sarah Ignatius, *National Asylum Study Project: An Assessment of the Asylum*

Process of the Immigration and Naturalization Service 31–37 (1993) (noting various deficiencies in the asylum process).

89. Martin, "Reforming" at 1285.
90. See Adam Liptak, "Courts Criticize Judges' Handling of Asylum Cases," *New York Times,* Dec., 26, 2005, 1.
91. *Benslimane v. Gonzales,* 2005 U.S. App. LEXIS 26048 (7th Cir. 2005).
92. Critics, however, have suggested that liberal BIA members were targeted for removal. See Liptak, "Courts Criticize" at 1, quoting Lory Rosenberg. ("They just hacked off all the liberals.")
93. These orders also are referred to as "affirmances without opinion." The language in such orders is established by regulation and may not be changed.
94. Pursuant to the REAL ID Act, a noncitizen may file a petition for review of a BIA decision to the appropriate federal circuit court. Prior to the new regulation, federal courts were receiving about 125 BIA case appeals per month—that number increased in 2005 to an estimated 1,000–1,200 per month.
95. *Qun Wang v. AG of the United States,* 423 F.3d 260, 2005 U.S. App. LEXIS 20227 (3d Cir. 2005).
96. Liptak, "Courts Criticize" at 2.
97. Executive Office for Immigration Review (EOIR), "FY2005 Statistical Yearbook," at I1, Figure 13; and K3, Figure 18.
98. *Id.* at D2, Figure 5. From 2000 to 2005, the percentage actually granted discretionary relief has fairly consistently been around 15 percent.
99. EOIR, "FY2005 Statistical Yearbook," at K2, Figure 18.
100. *Id.* at M1, Table 10.
101. See, e.g., *id.* at K5, Table 8 (showing extremely wide variations in asylum grant rates).
102. *INS v. St. Cyr,* 121 S. Ct. 2271 (2001). There was a companion case: *INS v. Calcano-Martinez,* 121 S. Ct. 2268 (2001). However, the Court's reasoning was contained in *St. Cyr.*
103. 121 S. Ct. at 2269.
104. *St. Cyr,* 121 S. Ct. at 2283, citing *Jay v. Boyd,* 351 U.S. 345, 353–354 (1956).
105. The opinion also stated that Mr. St. Cyr did not "contend that he would have any right to have an unfavorable exercise of the Attorney General's discretion reviewed in a judicial forum." *Id.* Such a concession is best understood as a prudent, tactical move by St. Cyr's counsel. Brief for the Petitioner at 27, *INS v. St. Cyr,* 121 S. Ct. 2271 (2001) (No. 00–767). The INS, in its opening brief, had strenuously sought to frame the entire suspension clause issue as one of discretion.
106. See generally Daniel Kanstroom, "The Better Part of Valor: The REAL ID Act, Discretion, and the 'Rule' of Immigration Law," 51 *N.Y. L. Rev.* 310 (2006).
107. *Achacoso-Sanchez v. INS,* 779 F.2d 1260, 1265 (7th Cir. 1985).
108. *INS v. St. Cyr,* 121 S. Ct. 2271, 2287 (2001), citing *Landgraf v. USI Film Products,* 511 U.S. 244, 266 (1994). (Courts must review legislation to determine

whether the statute itself indicates a retroactive congressional design. They must then consider the nature of the retroactive operation and apply a default rule against retroactive application.)

109. *Id.* at 2287 n. 39, citing Stephen H. Legomsky, "Fear and Loathing in the Congress and Courts: Immigration and Judicial Review," 78 *Tex. L. Rev.* 1615, 1626 (2000); see also Daniel Kanstroom, "Deportation and Punishment: A Constitutional Dialogue," 51 *B.C. L. REV.* 771, 784 n. 64 (2000); Harold J. Krent, "The Puzzling Boundary between Criminal and Civil Retroactive Lawmaking," 84 *Geo. L. J.* 2143, 2167 (1996).

110. *St. Cyr,* 121 S. Ct. at 2288, citing *Lindh v. Murphy,* 521 U.S. 320, 328 n. 4 (1997).

111. For a critique of this argument, see Kanstroom, "Deportation and Punishment." See also *Mojica v. Reno,* 970 F. Supp. 130, 174 (E.D.N.Y. 1997).

112. In *Mahler v. Eby,* 264 U.S. 32 (1924), the Court upheld a deportation for violation of draft laws at a time when such a conviction was not grounds for deportation. In *Galvan v. Press,* 347 U.S. 522 (1954), the Court held constitutional the retroactive application of the Subversive Activity Control Act, ch. 1024, 64 Stat. 1006 (1950). In *Harisiades,* the Court upheld the retroactive application of a deportation law proscribing membership in the Communist Party.

113. In a peculiarly harsh move, many of the criminal removal grounds in the Illegal Immigration Reform and Immigrant Responsibility Act were made retroactive by Congress, including, most broadly, the definition of "aggravated felony," which now applies "regardless of whether the conviction was entered before, on, or after the date of enactment." INA §101(a)(43).

114. *St. Cyr* 121 S. Ct. at 2292, 2293 n. 55.

115. *Landgraf,* 511 U.S. at 266.

116. See, e.g., Robert Pauw, "A New Look at Deportation as Punishment: Why at Least Some of the Constitution's Criminal Procedure Protections Must Apply," 52 *Admin. L. Rev.* 305, 340–343 (2000); Kanstroom, "Deportation, Social Control, and Punishment."

117. 3 U.S. (3 Dall.) 386 (1798). See generally Oliver P. Field, Ex Post Facto in the Constitution," 20 *Mich. L. Rev.* 315 (1922); 1 William Winslow Crosskey, *Politics and the Constitution in the History of the United States* 324–351 (1953) (arguing that the ex post facto clauses apply to both civil and criminal statutes); see also 2 Joseph Story, *Commentaries on the Constitution of the United States* 1345, at 219–220 (Melville M. Bigelow ed., 5th ed. 1994) (1833).

118. Nancy Morawetz, "Rethinking Retroactive Deportation Laws and the Due Process Clause," 73 *N.Y.U. L. Rev.* 97, 98 (1998).

119. See Debra Lynn Bassett, "In the Wake of Schooner Peggy: Deconstructing Legislative Retroactivity Analysis," 69 *U. Cin. L. Rev.* 453, 502 (2001).

120. See *A (and others) v. Secretary of State for the Home Department, Opinions of the Lords of Appeal for Judgment in the Cause,* UKHL 56 (2004)(applying expansive view of proportionality requirement to challenge to executive detention of noncitizens).

121. See, e.g., *In re L-G-*, Int. Dec. 3254 (B.I.A. 1995) (state drug offense can qualify as an "aggravated felony"); *United States v. Graham*, 169 F.3d 787, 791–793 (3d Cir.) (misdemeanor petty theft was an "aggravated felony"), cert. denied, 120 S. Ct. 116 (1999).

122. See, e.g., *Riggs v. California*, 525 U.S. 1114, 1114 (1999) (denying certiorari in California "three strikes" challenge); *Harmelin v. Michigan*, 501 U.S. 957, 1001–1009 (1991) (mandatory sentence of life without parole for drug possession did not violate Eighth Amendment); cf. *United States v. Bajakajian*, 524 U.S. 321, 334–344 (1998) (applying proportionality analysis under excessive fines clause). But see *Solem v. Helm*, 463 U.S. 277, 290 (1983) (Eighth Amendment prohibits grossly disproportionate sentences); *Furman v. Georgia*, 408 U.S. 238, 279–280 (1972) (Brennan, J., concurring), quoting *O'Neil v. Vermont*, 144 U.S. 323, 339–340 (1892) (Field, J., dissenting) (punishment is excessive if length or severity is disproportionate to offense); *Trop v. Dulles*, 356 U.S. 86, 99 (1958) (reasoning implicitly that proportionality analysis required under Eighth Amendment).

123. See *Galvan v. Press*, 347 U.S. 522, 531–532 (1954).

124. See Pauw, "New Look" at 330–31.

125. See *In re Gault* 387 U.S. 1, 34–38 (1967); Kanstroom, "Deportation, Social Control, and Punishment" at 1927–1933; Morawetz, "Rethinking"; Pauw, "New Look."

126. See John Hart Ely, *Democracy and Distrust: A Theory of Judicial Review* 161–162 (1980); Harold J. Krent, "The Puzzling Boundary between Criminal and Civil Retroactive Lawmaking," 84 *Geo. L.J.* 2143, 2167 (1996).

127. See *Boyd v. United States*, 116 U.S. 616, 633–635 (1886); *Kennedy v. Mendoza-Martinez*, 372 U.S. 144, 164–167, 186 (1963); *United States v. Halper*, 490 U.S. 435, 447–449 (1989).

128. See Daniel Kanstroom, "Criminalizing the Undocumented: Ironic Boundaries of the Post-September 11th 'Pale of Law.'" 29 *N.C.J. Int'l L. & Com. Reg.* 639 (2004).

129. The legitimacy of the border remains a valid concern, too. See Joseph H. Carens, "Aliens and Citizens: The Case for Open Borders," 49 *Rev. Pol.* 251 (1987); see also Kevin R. Johnson, "Symposium: Law and the Border; Open Borders," 51 *UCLA L. Rev.* 193 (2003).

130. David Cole, "Damage Control? A Comment on Professor Neuman's Reading of Reno v. AADC," 14 *Geo. Immigr. L. J.* 347, 348 (2000).

131. *Reno v. AADC, supra.* It is hard to imagine such a case, however, if "the general rule certainly applies here."

132. Neuman "Terrorism" at 340.

133. See David Cole, "The New McCarthyism: Repeating History in the War on Terrorism," 38 *Harv. C.R.-C.L. L. Rev.* 1, 2 (2003).

134. Guthrie reportedly composed the poem in 1948 after reading that a plane deporting migrant farm workers back to Mexico had crashed. The song was

written "virtually without music—Woody chanted the words—and wasn't performed publicly until a decade later when a schoolteacher named Martin Hoffman added a beautiful melody and Pete Seeger began singing it in concerts." Klein, *Woody Guthrie* at 349–350.

135. Lyrics as reprinted in Pete Seeger, ed., *The Nearly Complete Collection of Woody Guthrie Folk Songs* 24–25 (1973). © 1961 Ludlow Music, Inc.

136.   "Scattered like dust and leaves, when the mighty blasts of October
               Seize them, and whirl them aloft, and sprinkle them far o'er the ocean.
               Naught but tradition remains of the beautiful village of Grand-Pre.

                              —"Evangeline," Henry Wadsworth Longfellow
                                      (Boston: Ticknor & Company, 1847)

137. *Bridges v. Wixon*, 326 U.S. 135, 165 (1945) (Murphy, J. concurring).

Index